T0261923

Computer Science and Engineering: An Integrated Approach

Computer Science and Engineering: An Integrated Approach

Edited by
Bella Cunningham

WILLFORD PRESS
www.willfordpress.com

Published by Willford Press,
118-35 Queens Blvd., Suite 400,
Forest Hills, NY 11375, USA

ISBN: 978-1-68285-771-7

Cataloging-in-Publication Data

Computer science and engineering : an integrated approach / edited by Bella Cunningham.
    p. cm.
Includes bibliographical references and index.
ISBN 978-1-68285-771-7
1. Computer science. 2. Computer engineering. 3. Computer systems. 4. Engineering. I. Cunningham, Bella.
QA76 .C66 2020
004--dc23

For information on all Willford Press publications
visit our website at www.willfordpress.com

Contents

Preface

This book has been an outcome of determined endeavour from a group of educationists in the field. The primary objective was to involve a broad spectrum of professionals from diverse cultural background involved in the field for developing new researches. The book not only targets students but also scholars pursuing higher research for further enhancement of the theoretical and practical applications of the subject.

Computer science is a field that is concerned with the study of the theory of computation and the design of software systems. It encompasses the use of algorithms for storing, manipulating and communicating digital information. Computer science is a broad field that spans diverse theoretical studies such as the study of algorithms and the limits of computation, as well as practical aspects of implementing computing systems in software and hardware. An integration of computer science and electronic engineering is required for developing computer hardware and software which is under the scope of computer engineering. This field encompasses the design of personal computers, supercomputers, individual microcontrollers and circuit design. Designing software, analog sensors, VLSI chips and operating systems, as well as using digital systems for the control and monitoring of electrical systems and robotics are some areas of focus in computer engineering. The ever-growing need of advanced technology is the reason that has fueled the research in the fields of computer science and engineering in recent times. The objective of this book is to give a general view of the different areas of these fields and their applications. Students, researchers, experts and all associated with computer science and engineering will benefit alike from this book.

It was an honour to edit such a profound book and also a challenging task to compile and examine all the relevant data for accuracy and originality. I wish to acknowledge the efforts of the contributors for submitting such brilliant and diverse chapters in the field and for endlessly working for the completion of the book. Last, but not the least; I thank my family for being a constant source of support in all my research endeavours.

Editor

Investigating a Mobility-Aware QoS Model for Multimedia Streaming Rate Adaptation

Fragkiskos Sardis,[1] **Glenford Mapp,**[2] **Jonathan Loo,**[2] **Mahdi Aiash,**[2] **and Alexey Vinel**[3]

[1]*Department of Informatics, King's College London, London WC2R 2LS, UK*
[2]*School of Science and Technology, Middlesex University, London NW44BT, UK*
[3]*Halmstad University, 301 18 Halmstad, Sweden*

Correspondence should be addressed to Fragkiskos Sardis; fragkiskos.sardis@kcl.ac.uk

Academic Editor: Peppino Fazio

Supporting high quality multimedia streaming on wireless devices poses several challenges compared to wired networks due to the high variance in network performance encountered in the mobile environment. Although rate adaptation is commonly used in multimedia applications to compensate for fluctuations in network performance, it is a reactive mechanism which is not aware of the frequently changing connectivity that may occur on mobile devices. This paper proposed a performance evaluation model for multimedia streaming applications that is aware of user mobility and network performance. We presented an example of mathematical solution to the model and demonstrated the functionality using common mobility and connectivity examples that may be found in an urban environment. The proposed model is evaluated based on this functionality and how it may be used to enhance application performance.

1. Introduction

Multimedia content on the Internet has evolved from simple audio and images to high definition video and highly interactive video games. In recent years, this content has made its way to mobile devices such as smartphones and tablets. The capabilities of these devices have tremendously increased over the years in terms of processing power; however, in a mobile environment where network connectivity may be changing frequently, it is very difficult to achieve a high Quality of Experience (QoE) when it comes to streaming multimedia content. Although modern mobile devices are capable of streaming multimedia content at very high bit-rates, it is often the network's Quality of Service (QoS) that cannot deliver such content in a consistent and timely fashion. While this is also true for wired networks, wireless networks are more susceptible to performance degradation due to congestion at the access point or weak signaling, especially when dealing with mobile networks or other open-access wireless networks.

Multimedia streaming applications make up for varying QoS conditions by caching parts of the content opportunistically when possible or scaling the bit-rate and hence the quality of the audiovisual content in response to network conditions. These mechanisms provide a dampening effect on the varying QoS in wired networks; however, in wireless networks where the user may be moving and the device may be switching between heterogeneous networks, the QoS variance can be far greater than that found in wired networks even when not considering packet losses and jitter caused by handover events.

In this paper we present a new approach at modeling the performance of multimedia applications based on the anticipated network connections caused by mobility and the rate of movement of the user. A mathematical solution to the multidimensional Markov model is presented along with examples given to demonstrate the functionality of the model. The novelty of this approach lies in the modeling of a multimedia application in a mobile environment from the perspective of the client rather than the perspective of each individual network and therefore provides an overview of an applications performance over multiple networks.

The rest of the paper is outlined as follows: Section 2 includes background information in the field of scalable multimedia content, mobile service delivery, and mobile network technology. Section 3 presents the model under investigation and Section 4 provides an example solution for a two-dimensional model. Section 5 illustrates the functionality of the model with examples. Section 6 provides critical evaluation of the model and concludes this paper.

2. Background

In this section we present some background information in the fields of wireless network performance and multimedia content delivery mechanisms.

2.1. Mobile Service Delivery. In the context of mobile services, network performance is typically evaluated from the perspective of the network by means of queueing analysis [1–3]. Although the study of wireless network performance from the perspective of the network can help in optimizing their performance and as a result the delivery of Internet services to mobile clients, there is currently no focus on evaluating the performance of networks from the perspective of an application or a service. To this end, a mobile service delivery framework has been proposed [4, 5] in the context of 5th generation networks such as Y-Comm [6] where reliable and constant connectivity is achieved at all times by means of seamless horizontal and vertical handovers. The proposed framework uses network mechanisms to constantly probe networks adjacent to the user and select the best possible connection that satisfies the requirements of the user's applications. Thus far, only the traffic management aspects of the framework have been investigated through the use of Cloud technology for dynamic localization of services by means of Wide-Area-Network (WAN) migrations. In this paper, we explore the QoS aspects of the framework and therefore everything described in the following sections should be considered in the context of [4–6].

For the traffic management aspects of this framework, the network dwell time is considered based on user mobility patterns. However, in order to study the performance of an application over a series of networks, we need to express mobility as a rate of movement in terms of exiting the coverage of a network and entering another.

The cell outgoing rate μ_{dwell} is defined as the average exit rate of uniformly distributed users equally likely to move in any direction with arbitrary distribution of moving speed [3]:

$$M_{cdwell} = \frac{E(v)L}{\pi A},\qquad(1)$$

where $E(v)$ is the average velocity of the users, L is the length of the cell's perimeter, and A is the area of the cell.

Using this expression, we can determine the average exit rate for a given velocity and cell size and thus we can estimate the rate at which a user will be switching between cells. However, it should be noted that this is not an accurate representation for each possible scenario of mobility and cell size but it is a good approximation of the rate without knowing in detail and with great accuracy where the user entered the cell, which direction they are going, and at what speed they are moving.

2.2. Scalable Content Delivery. Scalable multimedia content delivery encompasses mechanisms that dynamically adjust the quality of multimedia streams in such way that it adapts to varying network conditions. The main goal of the technology is to deliver content without interruptions at the cost of decreasing the audiovisual quality when necessary. Such mechanisms have been proposed for more than a decade [7] and are now widely used by online multimedia services such as YouTube [8].

As Rejaie et al. argue [7], multimedia streaming applications are subject to two conflicting requirements. The first requirement is that these applications are delay-sensitive and rate-based, and thus they require isochronous processing and end-to-end QoS guarantees. This stems from the fact that stored video has a predefined bit-rate which needs to be transmitted at a fixed rate and therefore requires constant bandwidth. On the other hand, the second requirement is that the Internet is a shared environment and therefore end systems are expected to cooperate by reacting to congestion properly and promptly by deploying congestion control mechanisms. Thus, the available bandwidth may vary in an unpredictable manner and more importantly large amounts of data streaming over the network may be the cause for triggering congestion control mechanisms. Rejaie et al. demonstrate that, by exploiting the flexibility of layered encoding, it is possible to maintain stable streaming by switching between the different encoding layers according to network performance. With layered encoding, each layer holds incrementally more fine details of the content. When sufficient bandwidth is available, the service streams the information from all the layers. When network QoS degrades and TCP congestion control is activated, the service drops some of the layers and maintains streaming of the more coarse layers which require less throughput.

Raghuveer et al. [9] enhance the layered quality adaptation mechanisms by considering not only the status of the network but also the status of the buffer at the client. When near a buffer underflow, the proposed system increases the sending rate from the service. Conversely when near a buffer overflow, the system decreases the transmission rate even when there is no congestion on the network.

What becomes apparent from the above approaches is that, in order to provide scalable adaptation of content, there must be a strategy which defines how content quality is scaled according to network conditions. Typically, network condition is derived by monitoring the arrival rate of packets and comparing it to the consumption rate at the client which means that by definition, quality adaptation is reactive.

One attempt to probe the network in advance and subsequently at frequent intervals in order to determine the rate adaptation is presented by Li et al. in [10]. They propose a Probe and Adapt (PANDA) mechanism which compares the TCP throughput to the expected throughput for uninterrupted streaming. By probing at frequent intervals they can dynamically adjust subsequent service requests and adapt the quality of the content so that the desired rate is met. This method of probing is quicker at responding to network changes and with sufficient buffering, helping to smooth out aggressive rate adaptation.

The main disadvantage of the state-of-art solutions is that they lack any form of QoS prediction in a mobile environment where even short-term probing may provide completely inaccurate information when network handover occurs. To this end, the optimal solution would be to monitor user mobility, predict future network configurations, probe each network in the user's path, and adjust the rate accordingly in a preemptive manner.

3. Mobile Service Performance Model

The structural complexity of the Internet along with factors such as distance and user demands leads to greatly varying levels of performance between different networks and locations. Latency, throughput, and response time are some of the determining factors to the performance of online multimedia applications and consequently to the perceived QoE. As discussed previously, there are various mechanisms on the network and on the service side that dynamically adapt the behavior of applications to mitigate this performance variance. However, these mechanisms often work independently of each other often resulting in duplicate functionality on the network and service side. For example, networks prioritize packets based on the application while at the same time multimedia applications attempt to adjust the quality of the content to adapt to network conditions.

In this section, we present a novel approach to modeling application performance based on user mobility, application requirements, and network service rates. The distinctive characteristic of the proposed model is that it evaluates the performance of a persistent connection from the perspective of the application rather than from the perspective of the network. As such, it offers insights as to how an application will behave over multiple networks across a user's path without considering the intrinsic details of network mechanisms. In other words, this model can be used to provide an overview of the performance of an application so that the application itself may decide how to best optimize the delivery of multimedia content according to the performance of anticipated network connections resulting from user mobility patterns.

Figure 1 shows a simple Markov chain representing a connection between a service and a client over the network. In this case a queue depth of two requests is depicted; however, this may be scaled to any buffer size desired. In order to introduce mobility and network handover as a factor of the performance, we will need to represent networks as individual chains and the user mobility as a rate of switching between those chains as illustrated in Figure 2.

The service request rate of the application is defined as λ and it is constant across all the networks if we assume a single application used constantly by the client. The service rate (μ_n) of each network is defined individually to represent the varying levels of QoS that each point of attachment

FIGURE 1: Markov chain with a buffer length of two requests.

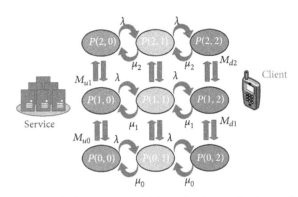

FIGURE 2: Multidimension model for evaluating application performance over a series of networks.

may deliver. The mobility rate of the user is defined as M_{un} and M_{dn} individually for each chain in order to accurately represent different coverage areas of networks and therefore different handover rates from one network to another. Mobility between chains is represented as upwards (M_u) and downwards (M_d) in order to address scenarios where a user may be switching between networks of the same provider or simply to address mobility cases where a user may be moving in such a pattern that causes an oscillating behavior between networks.

Being able to model the performance of an application in this manner presents new possibilities for the delivery of multimedia services over mobile networks. For example, using this model can help predetermine how an application will behave along a user's path provided that we know that the path and velocity are constant and which networks are present along that path. Consequently, we could instruct a multimedia service to preemptively adjust the quality of a stream by means of precaching some sections at lower quality so that they will be ready when needed. Alternatively, in the context of content-centric networks, we could instruct different parts of a multimedia file to be delivered by different locations that may provide better performance on networks that have insufficient service rate for a particular service instance. The same may be applied on service-centric networks where alternate component services may be used for networks where the performance is insufficient for the existing composite service.

To achieve the above, the model assumes that probe connections are used to gather performance metrics for each network along the path. Furthermore, mechanisms that identify where the performance degradation comes from are also needed in order to identify cases where congestion at the access point is causing the problem and therefore there is nothing that can be done on the network or the service side that will improve the performance. Therefore, in this

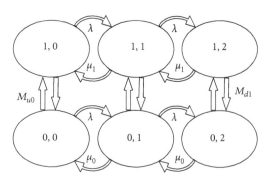

FIGURE 3: 2×3 mobile network QoS model.

paper we explore this model at a theoretical level and assume that performance degradation occurs within the network's backbone infrastructure rather than the client access points.

The next section shows how this model can be solved mathematically followed by some examples of how this model can be used.

4. Example Solution

In this section we present an example solution for a 2×3 model which represents how service requests are being queued in two networks along a user's path and how the user's mobility pattern affects the overall service rate received at the client. The model is illustrated in Figure 3 where λ is the service rate requested by the client, μ_n is the perceived service rate of each network at the client, M_{u0} is the mobility rate at which the client leaves the network represented by the bottom chain and enters the one above, and finally M_{d1} is the mobility rate at which the client leaves the network represented by the top chain and enters the one below.

To solve this model, we start by expressing each state as a function of its inbound and outgoing rates from and to other states. Thus, we have

$$
\begin{aligned}
(M_{u0} + \lambda) P_{0,0} &= \mu_0 P_{0,1} + M_{d1} P_{1,0}, \\
(M_{u0} + \lambda + \mu_0) P_{0,1} &= M_{d1} P_{1,1} + \mu_0 P_{0,2} + \lambda P_{0,0}, \\
(M_{u0} + \mu_0) P_{0,2} &= M_{d1} P_{1,2} + \lambda P_{0,1}, \\
(M_{d1} + \lambda) P_{1,0} &= M_{u0} P_{0,0} + \mu_1 P_{1,1}, \\
(M_{d1} + \lambda + \mu_1) P_{1,1} &= M_{u0} P_{0,1} + \mu_1 P_{1,2} + \lambda P_{1,0}, \\
(M_{d1} + \mu_1) P_{1,2} &= M_{u0} P_{0,2} + \lambda P_{1,1}.
\end{aligned}
\tag{2}
$$

We then proceed to unzip the model by expressing each state as a function of its adjacent states. We have

$$
P_{1,2} = a_{1,2} P_{0,2} + b_{1,2} P_{1,1},
\tag{3}
$$

where

$$
\begin{aligned}
\frac{M_{u0}}{(M_{d1} + \mu_1)} &= a_{1,2}, \\
\frac{\lambda}{(M_{d1} + \mu_1)} &= b_{1,2}.
\end{aligned}
\tag{4}
$$

Now we can express $\mathbf{P}_{1,1}$ by substituting $\mathbf{P}_{1,2}$:

$$
P_{1,1} = a_{1,1} P_{0,1} + b_{1,1} P_{0,2} + c_{1,1} P_{1,0},
\tag{5}
$$

where

$$
\begin{aligned}
a_{1,1} &= \frac{M_{u0}}{(M_{d1} + \lambda + \mu_1 - \mu_1 b_{1,2})}, \\
b_{1,1} &= \frac{\mu_1 a_{1,2}}{(M_{d1} + \lambda + \mu_1 - \mu_1 b_{1,2})}, \\
c_{1,1} &= \frac{\lambda}{(M_{d1} + \lambda + \mu_1 - \mu_1 b_{1,2})}.
\end{aligned}
\tag{6}
$$

We proceed using the same methodology for all the states, at each step substituting the solved state in each equation as an expression of rates. In this example, we derive a final expression for each state as a function of $\mathbf{P}_{0,0}$ and from there we proceed by defining the sum of all the state probabilities to be equal to 1:

$$
1 = P_{0,0} + P_{0,1} + P_{0,2} + P_{1,0} + P_{1,1} + P_{1,2}.
\tag{7}
$$

Thus, we can solve

$$
\begin{aligned}
1 &= \mathbf{P}_{0,0} + f_{0,1}(\mathbf{P}_{0,0}) + f_{0,2}(\mathbf{P}_{0,0}) + f_{1,0}(\mathbf{P}_{0,0}) \\
&\quad + f_{1,1}(\mathbf{P}_{0,0}) + f_{1,2}(\mathbf{P}_{0,0}), \\
P_{0,0} &= \frac{1}{f_{0,1} + f_{0,2} + f_{1,0} + f_{1,1} + f_{1,2}}.
\end{aligned}
\tag{8}
$$

At this point, we have defined every state probability in the model as a function of $\mathbf{P}_{0,0}$ and $\mathbf{P}_{0,0}$ itself as a function of the rates. We can now input values for the different rates that we wish to solve for and examine how the model behaves under different performance and mobility scenarios.

It should be noted that the model may be solved for any $N \times M$; however, as the number of chains increases, the number of variables also increases thus making a closed-form solution very difficult to derive. It would be easier to consider equal mobility rates between chains; however, it would also provide a less accurate model. The following section presents some common mobility scenarios that may be encountered in daily usage and how the model may be used to determine the overall performance of a persistent connection over multiple networks.

5. Common Scenario Results

This section includes some examples of user mobility and network coverage that may be commonly encountered in the real world. The results of these examples can assist in understanding how the model works and what insights it may offer in the context of network performance and multimedia content quality adaptation. Furthermore, these results prove analytically that the model is functioning as expected.

5.1. Fixed-Path Mobility with Overlapping Networks. The first scenario to look at covers a mobile node moving on a fixed

TABLE 1: Fixed-path mobility with overlapping networks.

λ	μ_0	μ_1	μ_2	M_{u0}	M_{d1}	M_{u1}	M_{d2}
60	80	40	20	0.0088	0.0001	0.0088	0.0001

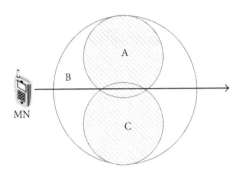

FIGURE 4: Linear mobility example with overlapping networks.

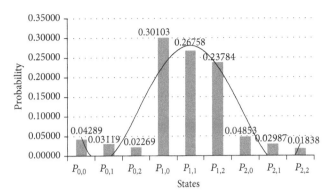

FIGURE 5: Fixed-path example with overlapping networks.

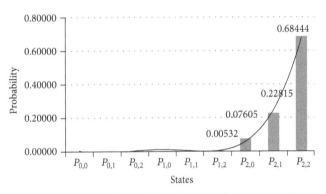

FIGURE 6: Fixed-path example with nonoverlapping networks.

path while being connected to network B as shown in Figure 4. Along the path and within the coverage of network B, there are two smaller networks A and C. The node will enter a small area that is covered by all three networks and subsequently will exit the coverage of A and C and return to network A. This scenario expresses a case where a user may be connected to a large coverage area network such as LTE and reaches an area where smaller Wi-Fi networks are available. Assuming a constant velocity, the user will eventually leave the area of Wi-Fi coverage and fall back to LTE.

In this case, we shall consider a user moving at 5 km/h as a representation of average walking speed. The LTE radius is 500 meters and the Wi-Fi radius is 50 meters. Because in this scenario there are three networks involved, we consider a 3×3 queueing model. The starting position of the user is in the middle chain of the model while networks A and C represent the top and bottom chains.

Table 1 shows the values considered in this scenario. The service rate of the LTE network (μ_1) is lower than the service rates of the other two networks. Additionally, due to the sizes of the coverage areas in the configuration presented in Figure 4, the $\mathbf{Mu_0}$ and $\mathbf{Md_2}$ rates are equal since we are dealing with equally sized networks. Furthermore, $\mathbf{Md_1}$ and $\mathbf{Mu_1}$ are also equal since they represent the exit rate from the LTE network towards two equally sized smaller networks. The service request rate and service rates are arbitrary but they could represent packets, frames, or any other metric significant to the application's performance.

As we see in Figure 5 most of the user's requests will be carried over the LTE network in the middle chain ($P_{1,0}$, $P_{1,1}$, and $P_{1,2}$) based on this mobility pattern and network configuration. Additionally, we see from the state probabilities in each network that all networks can provide sufficient service to support the application, while the Wi-Fi networks can provide better performance. Based on these results we can determine that the device may connect to either of the Wi-Fi networks temporarily to improve the performance of the application. If we consider a multimedia application such as video streaming, based on this model we can determine at which points we may enhance the quality

of the video without having to wait for feedback from the device. This can help multimedia service providers cache the appropriate segments of the video at different bitrates or even preconfigure dynamically the sources of the video segments in a content-centric context.

5.2. Fixed-Path Mobility with Nonoverlapping Networks. For this scenario, we consider a fast-moving user passing through a series of networks that do not have overlapping coverage areas. Such a scenario may be envisioned by considering a car driving by an area with multiple LTE networks. To further demonstrate how this model behaves in different scenarios, we study a case where the LTE networks have different service rates. Once again, we are using a 3×3 model for this example. Table 2 shows the values used for a user speed of 50 km/h and uniform coverage areas with a radius of 1 km.

As we see from Figure 6, below, in this scenario the user is moving very rapidly across the three networks and therefore very few of the service requests are covered by each network. Because this model only represents three networks, in this example we see that the requests converge on the third chain. Since the network represented by the third chain does not have adequate service rate for the user's application, the requests are being queued in $P_{2,2}$ which tells us that as the user is moving quickly, the final network along their path is the one that will have to service any pending requests from other networks and hence the performance of the final network is an important factor to the overall QoS.

TABLE 2: Fixed-path mobility with nonoverlapping networks.

λ	μ_0	μ_1	μ_2	M_{u0}	M_{d1}	M_{u1}	M_{d2}
40	55	45	65	0.015	0.0018	0.0018	0.015

TABLE 3: Random mobility example.

λ	μ_0	μ_1	M_{u0}	M_{d1}
60	30	60	0.0177	0.0177

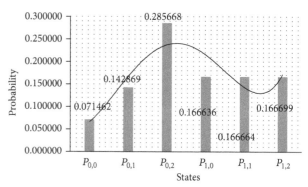

FIGURE 7: Random mobility example using a 2×3 model.

5.3. Random Mobility Examples. The final scenario to look at represents a case of random mobility such as when a user does not exhibit any kind of linear or predictable movement. For this scenario we set a walking speed of 5 km/h and a cell radius of 50 m. We are using a 2×3 model in this case. Table 3 summarizes the values used.

The model shows (Figure 7) that, based on the user mobility, the two networks will have equal probability of receiving service requests as the sum of probabilities for each chain is equal to 0.5. However, we see that the first chain does not have adequate service rate to support the application and hence there is a higher probability of queueing requests for that network. Based on this example it would be difficult to determine exactly the level of QoS delivered to the client at each point and therefore it would be difficult to adjust the quality of multimedia applications accordingly. Nevertheless, this result may also be used as an indication of which networks should be avoided in a particular area so that the user experience will not degrade as the user is moving.

6. Evaluation and Conclusion

The proposed model offers a new approach at evaluating the performance of streaming applications in different mobility and network coverage scenarios; however, there are some limitations that must be highlighted in the interest of further improving the model and understanding its applications.

The mobility rate equation is not accurate for every scenario as it only represents an average approximation. For greater accuracy, we can consider the exact coordinates for the user and cell location and derive the outgoing rate based on the user's direction and speed.

The model relies on knowing in advance and with high confidence the exact route that the user will take and therefore the exact sequence of network handover that will occur. This may be impossible to achieve in real life scenarios but at a theoretical level, it can help analyze the performance of an application under certain network conditions and mobility patterns.

Furthermore, the model relies on knowing in advance and with high confidence the service rate of each network that will carry application traffic. This may be achieved with network mechanisms that report the achievable QoS between a content source and an access point but once more, in a real life environment, it would add to the infrastructure and application complexity. The model also assumes a constant service request rate by the streaming application which may also be unrealistic in real-world scenarios; however, the average

rate may be considered for the purposes of the model in order to provide an approximation of the performance.

The current version of the model has the disadvantage of not taking into account the performance cost of a handover between heterogeneous networks. However, this disadvantage is eliminated in the context of seamless handover technologies such as proposed by Y-Comm.

Despite these restrictions, the model presents a theoretical approach at evaluating the overall performance of a connection in a mobile environment with handover rate awareness and therefore provides a fine-grained analysis of the impact of mobility and network performance on multimedia streaming applications. As this model is still at its early stages conceptually, the authors will appreciate feedback and are open to collaboration.

Conflict of Interests

The authors declare that there is no conflict of interests regarding the publication of this paper.

References

[1] X. Chen and M. R. Lyu, "Message queueing analysis in wireless networks with mobile station failures and handoffs," in *Proceedings of the IEEE Aerospace Conference Proceedings*, vol. 2, pp. 1296–1303, IEEE, March 2004.

[2] A. Rico-Páez, C. B. Rodríguez-Estrello, F. A. Cruz-Pérez, and G. Hernández-Valdez, "Queueing analysis of mobile cellular networks considering wireless channel unreliability and resource insufficiency," in *Managing Traffic Performance in Converged Networks*, pp. 938–949, Springer, Berlin, Germany, 2007.

[3] J. Wang, Q.-A. Zeng, and D. P. Agrawal, "Performance analysis of integrated wireless mobile networks with queueing handoff scheme," in *Proceedings of the IEEE Radio and Wireless Conference (RAWCON '01)*, pp. 69–72, IEEE, Waltham, Mass, USA, August 2001.

[4] F. Sardis, G. Mapp, J. Loo, M. Aiash, and A. Vinel, "On the investigation of cloud-based mobile media environments with service-populating and QoS-aware mechanisms," *IEEE Transactions on Multimedia*, vol. 15, no. 4, pp. 769–777, 2013.

[5] F. Sardis, G. Mapp, J. Loo, and M. Aiash, "Dynamic edge-caching for mobile users: minimising inter-as traffic by moving cloud services and VMs," in *Proceedings of the 28th IEEE International Conference on Advanced Information Networking and Applications Workshops (WAINA '14)*, pp. 144–149, May 2014.

[6] G. Mapp, D. N. Cottingham, F. Shaikh et al., "An architectural framework for heterogeneous networking," in *Proceedings of the International Conference on Wireless Information Networks and Systems (WINSYS '06)*, pp. 5–12, August 2006.

[7] R. Rejaie, M. Handley, and D. Estrin, "Layered quality adaptation for Internet video streaming," *IEEE Journal on Selected Areas in Communications*, vol. 18, no. 12, pp. 2530–2543, 2000.

[8] Computerphile, "How YouTube Works," 2014, https://www.youtube.com/watch?v=OqQk7kLuaK4.

[9] A. Raghuveer, E. Kusmierek, and D. H. C. Du, "Network-aware rate adaptation for video streaming," in *Proceedings of the IEEE International Conference on Multimedia and Expo (ICME '04)*, vol. 2, pp. 1039–1042, IEEE, June 2004.

[10] Z. Li, X. Zhu, J. Gahm et al., "Probe and adapt: rate adaptation for HTTP video streaming at scale," *IEEE Journal on Selected Areas in Communications*, vol. 32, no. 4, pp. 719–733, 2014.

2

A Security Monitoring Method based on Autonomic Computing for the Cloud Platform

Jingjie Zhang, Qingtao Wu ⓘ, Ruijuan Zheng ⓘ, Junlong Zhu ⓘ, Mingchuan Zhang ⓘ, and Ruoshui Liu

Information Engineering College, Henan University of Science and Technology, Luoyang 471023, China

Correspondence should be addressed to Qingtao Wu; wqt8921@haust.edu.cn

Academic Editor: Vincent C. Emeakaroha

With the continuous development of cloud computing, cloud security has become one of the most important issues in cloud computing. For example, data stored in the cloud platform may be attacked, and its security is difficult to be guaranteed. Therefore, we must attach weight to the issue of how to protect the data stored in the cloud. To protect data, data monitoring is a necessary process. Based on autonomic computing, we develop a cloud data monitoring system on the cloud platform, monitoring whether the data is abnormal in the cycle and analyzing the security of the data according to the monitored results. In this paper, the feasibility of the scheme can be verified through simulation. The results show that the proposed method can adapt to the dynamic change of cloud platform load, and it can also accurately evaluate the degree of abnormal data. Meanwhile, by adjusting monitoring frequency automatically, it improves the accuracy and timeliness of monitoring. Furthermore, it can reduce the monitoring cost of the system in normal operation process.

1. Introduction

Resource monitoring in cloud computing environment is an important part of resource management of cloud computing platform. It provides the basis for resource allocation, task scheduling, and load balancing. With the extensive use of cloud computing services, users have made increasing demands on the security of cloud computing. Since the cloud computing environment has the characteristics of transparent virtualization and resource flexibility, it is infeasible for a traditional security program to protect the data security in the cloud platform, which hinders further development and application of cloud computing [1]. Therefore, it is of critical importance to develop new tools suitable for monitoring cloud platform data. However, the collection, transmission, storage, and analysis of a large number of monitored data will bring huge resource overhead, directly affecting system performance, timely detection of anomalies, and pinpoint accuracy of problem. In addition, because cloud computing is essentially developed on the basis of current technology, the existing security vulnerabilities will be inherited directly to the cloud computing platform, which may even bring

greater security threat. It can be seen that, in the cloud computing environment, users basically lost the control of private information and data, which triggered a series of security challenges, such as cloud data storage location, data encryption mechanism, data recovery mechanism, integrity protection, third-party supervision and auditing, virtual machine security, and memory security. At present, there is not enough research on cloud computing resource monitoring, but there are a lot of researches on distributed computing and grid computing, for instance, DRMonitor [2], Ganglia [3], and MDS (Monitoring and Discovery System) [4]. They play important roles in distributed systems or grid systems. However, if the above methods are applied directly in the cloud computing environment, there will be some shortcomings. On the one hand, the resource in the cloud computing environment is highly virtualized and flexible. Moreover, cloud computing provides services such as IaaS, PaaS, and SaaS, in addition to monitoring the resources of the physical server [5]. Users need to monitor the virtual machine running on it. On the other hand, cloud computing is a business model, and the cloud service provider will charge the user for usage accordingly. Monitoring information in existing resource monitoring system is not fine granularity, so it is unable to get to the process level of information and track consumption of CPU, memory, storage and other resources in real time during the user task execution process. Cloud computing environment is dynamic, random, complex, and open. Cloud providers need to collect user-related fees based on resource usage; as a result, original resource monitoring methods cannot fully meet the requirements of the cloud computing environment. Therefore, according to the characteristics of cloud computing itself, some resource monitoring methods for current distributed computing, and grid computing, cannot fully adapt to the cloud computing environment.

In order to adapt to the cloud computing environment, combining with abnormal data mining algorithm, we propose a data monitoring method under cloud environment based on autonomic computing model. In order to address the security challenges for data on the cloud platform, the model uses autonomic computing mechanism and the abnormal data mining idea to transmit the monitoring information to each other. The model is mainly composed of five modules: network monitoring module, data analysis module, response strategy module, system implementation module, and knowledge base. In the network monitoring module, the system gathers the data by collecting the data stream and generates the original data. In addition, through the data preprocessing mechanism, the original data are formatted. The data analysis module evaluates these processed data, extracts useful data from it to determine whether they are abnormal, and then feeds the analysis result back to the response strategy module to adjust the monitoring period. The data collection and analysis of storage are the core parts of this model, which provide users with essential data monitoring information. In the local computer deployment monitoring framework, the cloud is connected to data monitoring. Our contributions are as follows:

(i) We propose a safe and effective model that enables the data on the cloud platform to be monitored in time, and the system adjusts the monitoring cycle to autonomously protect the data.

(ii) We design a data mining algorithm, in which, based on an improved chaotic algorithm, data mining method was proposed for the frequently appearing abnormal data in the cloud computing environment. We also design and implement abnormal behavior detection based on the Poisson process to obtain accurate test results.

(iii) We formally analyze the capability of abnormal behavior monitoring and implement all of these data security monitoring models based on autonomic computing. A large number of experiments are carried out in the simulation environment using prepared dataset, and the results show that our system achieves the desired goals.

This paper is organized as follows. Section 2 states the origin of autonomic computing theory, and its related work. Section 3 analyzes how to establish a security monitoring

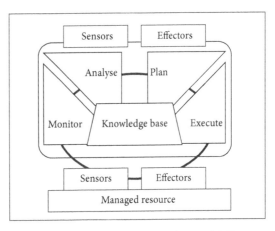

FIGURE 1: MAPE autonomic computing model diagram.

model based on autonomic computing for the cloud platform. Then we analyze the existing security model and safety monitoring method of autonomic computing to the cloud platform oriented metrics and the calculation method. Section 4 analyzes method of simulation and experiment and presents a security monitoring model based on autonomic computing analysis for the cloud platform. Section 5 gives the summary and points out the future research directions.

2. Related Work

The concept of autonomic computing was proposed by IBM's Paul Horn in 2001, which has self-configuring, self-optimization, self-healing, self- protection, and other good features that have been accepted by the computer scientists [6, 7]. Autonomous computing refers to the computing environment with self-management capabilities, dynamically adapting to the increasingly complex environment, and self-discipline since calculation unit (Autonomic Computing Element) is an essential part of the autonomic computing system [8]. At present, the research on autonomic computing is based on a model of control loop proposed by IBM in 2003. It is called the MAPE-K (Monitor, Analyze, Plan, Execute, and Knowledge) cycle. Based on this model, a strategy module has been added to allow IT managers to facilitate the management of autonomic computing units. Its structure is shown in Figure 1. The monitor assembly means collecting information from the managed resource, that is, from the external environment. The analyze assembly is used to analyze the complexity of the internal environment of the system, so that the self-regulatory manager can understand the running state of the system in real time so as to predict the future situation and take right strategy for the future condition. The plan generates a sequence of actions that can be achieved based on the monitoring component and the analysis component's data information from the external and internal environments, as well as previous policies. The execute is given to the effector to adjust the state of the managed resource. The actions generated by the above four components are all based on the knowledge in the knowledge base.

An event classification method used in the fault monitoring of autonomic computing system was introduced by Liu and Zhou in 2010 [9]. In this scheme, the system monitors the status of heterogeneous resources failure. With the self-management system communicating internally, an appropriate strategy is activated to repair the fault for self-repair system. However, there is a lack of research in the field of self-discipline for system performance failures. On the basis of studying the self-monitoring of self-discipline, the team proposed a multipoint detection method in 2011 [10]. Detecting the threshold cross-border and recovery to determine the system performance failure ensures the effectiveness of detection for the system, providing a useful strategy for the repairment failure. On the basis of studying the existing autonomic computing model, they proposed a self-discipline model which is suitable for distributed environment and formalizes the model elements of management resources, resource operation, state and action, and so on, to enhance the application of self-discipline model and practical value [11].

Among these advances of distributed computing, one must take into account the emergence of new paradigms such as cloud computing. In 2012, Yolanda et al. proposed a monitoring tool [12]. The goal of their work is to evaluate existing monitoring tools that can be used in cloud environments and are subsequently included in the monitoring component of the projects.

In order to improve the efficiency of resource management in the cloud environment, Liu and Li proposed a self-regulatory model for the cloud environment [13], which uses the multi-autonomous manager's hierarchical management model to solve the traditional autonomic computing model in dealing with a large number of requests when there is a bottleneck. Moreover, they proposed a hybrid strategy management model to tackle different fault repair requests.

Monitoring is an important factor in improving the quality of service provided in cloud computing. With the increase of cloud system architecture, the workload of data center is also increasing, leading to node failure and performance problems. Suciu et al. proposed a solution for monitoring and service providing cloud computing systems that allows users and providers to optimize the usage of the computational resources according to the constantly changing business requirements inside an organization [14]. The main contribution of their paper consists of the integration of the monitoring system, which is based on Nagios and NConf with test cloud architecture.

Liu and Guo proposed a hardware monitoring system based on cloud platform for data acquisition, storage, and analysis based on cloud computing [15]. Computer hardware monitoring system stores and accesses data based on the cloud platform. Storage hardware in the cloud platform unifies modeling analysis parameters for a large number of data in order to provide users with complete hardware maintenance information.

In 2015, Masmoudi et al. [16] proposed a multitenant monitoring approach based services that keep monitoring service execution at runtime and detecting privacy violations.

In 2016, Peng et al. [17] proposed a sampling method in the compressed sensing theory to implement feature compression for network data flow so that we can gain refined sparse representation. After that SVM (Support Vector Machine) is used to classify the compression results. This method can realize detection of network anomaly behavior quickly without reducing the classification accuracy.

3. Security Monitoring Model Based on Autonomic Computing for the Cloud Platform

With the widespread use of cloud computing services, users have made increasing demands regarding the security of cloud computing systems. The dynamicity, randomness, complexity, and openness of the cloud computing environment make it difficult to apply the conventional security scheme, which also hinders the further development and application of cloud computing [18]. The security requirements of cloud computing include terminal, platform, communication, and information security and confidentiality of the whole cycle. The cycle involves the cloud computing infrastructure layer, platform layer, application layer, and other layers.

Autonomic computing provides an effective way to reduce the complexity of the system management, but what early autonomic computing system mostly considered is physical resource management of distributed heterogeneous environment. It did not include the cloud environment under various restricting factors, such as large-scale virtualized applications, service level agreements, diverse application, and dynamic changes in the deployment environment. The original framework of autonomic computing application cannot be applied directly in the cloud environment [19]. For example, in the virtual layer, monitoring tools usually require on-demand configuration to distinguish the surveillance applications and resources. As a result, the traditional MAPE cycle also needs to be redesigned to fit the cloud. Cloud services have the characteristics of virtualization, liquidity, and boundary ambiguity, so the evaluation of their safety is one of the most important issues. According to the data security problem of the cloud platform, the working mechanism of autonomic computing system model uses the abnormal data mining idea for reference. It contains four self-regulatory elements, which can transmit the monitoring information to one another. The model framework is shown in Figure 2. The model consists of five modules: network monitoring module, data analysis module, response strategy module, system implementation module, knowledge base, and virtual machine (VM).

3.1. Model of the Cloud Security Monitoring. In order to solve the problem of cloud system security, we designed an independent monitoring model based on autonomic computing idea. The model is mainly composed of five modules: network monitoring module, data analysis module, response strategy module, system implementation module, and knowledge base.

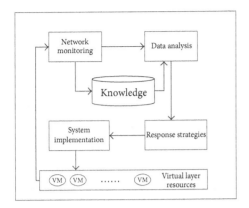

FIGURE 2: The cloud security monitoring model based on autonomic computing.

In the cloud computing environment, the traditional resource monitoring can be in two modes. (1) Active mode; there is the resource monitoring component in the work node and the virtual machine monitor collecting status information of the virtual machine running on it. The monitor activates the master node by sending its own monitoring information. (2) Passive mode: the master node sends request to the work node; then the work node returns their monitoring data back to the main node.

Network monitoring module is the monitoring agent deployed on the physical host, virtual machine, or other containers. It is used to collect monitored data of system at all levels and its persistent storage. Based on the historical monitored data, the data analysis module establishes the correlation of the data to form the metric correlation graph for evaluating the importance degree. It uses the PCA (Principal Component Analysis) to calculate the eigenvector of the monitored data and computes the linear regression equation of the data source in the cloud computing environment to quantitatively evaluate system anomalies. The response strategy module selects the object to be monitored in the next stage according to the importance of the monitored object. The Poisson process is used to establish the software system reliability model, and the probability of the system failure is predicted based on the abnormality degree to adjust the monitoring period. System implementation module is to use the monitoring agent to perform the dynamic adjustment of monitoring objects and monitoring cycle. Knowledge base is the record of operation in the process of learning load patterns and corresponding eigenvectors, so that the system normal operation can be depicted.

The resources of the cloud computing environment monitoring with real-time information need to adopt the strategy of polling-cyclical or event-driven way. Periodic mode refers to two cases. In the first case, the work nodes periodically send their own monitored information to the master node. In the second case, the node that is the main resource monitoring component will send a periodic request to work nodes; then these work nodes will collect and feed back information about themselves to the master node. The event-driven way refers to the fact that the old work nodes will

produce a series of events, and the generation of each event is triggered by monitoring of the corresponding terminal resource state for a check and compared with the last check of the data. If the change between the two events is greater than the threshold set, then the job is in either active or passive mode.

3.2. Monitored Data Collection. In the cloud computing environment, the data collection work is a comprehensive and coordinated process and needs to coordinate with the data storage and analysis work. Then it establishes a data acquisition and analysis model, including data collection, data preprocessing, data analysis, storage, and other components.

After the data collection process, the original data stream is classified and the original data are generated. Then the data preprocessing mechanism is used to format these original data. Finally, through the data analysis and storage parts, the useful data are extracted from the massive data. By these procedures and software, users can use the data directly. This data acquisition and analysis model achieves an integrated data processing process. In this model, the data collection and analysis of storage are two core parts, giving customers meaningful information.

Data Collection. In the cloud computing environment, the data collection consists of three steps, namely, data capture, data filtering, and data classification. Through these three steps, original data flow deals with customer meaningful data [20]. After capturing the data, it needs to filter and remove some useless information and categorize the rest. Then the classification of the data is sent to the preprocessing part.

Data Preprocessing. Data preprocessing includes several methods, that is, data cleaning, data integration, data transformation, and data reduction [21]. After selecting appropriate attributes as the data mining attributes from the original data, the principle of selection process should refer to giving attribute names and attribute values as clear meaning as possible, unifying multiple data source attribute code, and removing the unique attribute. So it can select the appropriate monitoring data for analysis.

Data Analysis. Data collection model must be established with relevant functions and appropriate conditions. Firstly, the data acquisition model needs to understand the expected results. Measuring and verifying the initial model are also required. According to the validation results, the model will be effectively adjusted. Secondly, the data acquisition model needs to be practical. At last, the causal relationship between the data will be revealed in order to make the collected data statistically significant. The establishment of the data model also needs to be improved continuously.

(1) The length of the sliding window is n; multiple measures for monitored data are collected as $x = (x_1, x_2, \ldots, x_m)$, among which each collected monitoring data includes m metrics. The operation and

maintenance personnel can set m value according to their needs. Here, m is a positive integer; x_i is the value of the ith metric. The monitored data slides into the sliding window in the order of time. Monitored data in the sliding window form the matrix A_{nm} (n rows and m columns).

(2) Each column of A_{nm} is standardized with a mean of 0 and the variance of 1. $Z_i = (x_i - u_i)/\sigma_i$, u_i is the mean of the ith column data set, and σ_i is the standard deviation of the ith column data set.

(3) The covariance matrix is obtained:

$$C = \begin{bmatrix} \sigma_{11}^2 & \cdots & \sigma_{1m}^2 \\ \vdots & \ddots & \vdots \\ \sigma_{m1}^2 & \cdots & \sigma_{mm}^2 \end{bmatrix}. \tag{1}$$

(4) Calculate the eigenvector of C, the main direction of the data distribution $\vec{u}$.

(5) When new monitored data arrives, in order to enlarge the influence of outliers on the main direction of change, the sample will be copied nr times, $r \in [0, 1]$, which is a copy of the current samples with the current sample size. The proportion of the updated matrices are shown as follows:

$$A = A \cup \{x_t, x_t, \ldots, x_t\}. \tag{2}$$

(6) Update matrix mean and covariance matrix:

$u = (u + rx_t)/(1 + r)$. Update the eigenvector in the main direction:

$$u_t = \frac{\sum_A u}{\left\| \sum_A u \right\|}. \tag{3}$$

(7) Evaluate abnormality of newly collected monitored data by using cosine similarity. The lower the similarity between the two main eigenvectors, the larger the deviation and the higher the abnormality. This paper describes the degree of anomaly:

$$\text{AutoCos} = \frac{u_t \cdot u}{\left\| u_t \right\| \times \left\| u \right\|}. \tag{4}$$

In this formula, "·" represents the dot product.

Data Storage. Data storage is the most important security issue, which needs to be addressed to ensure the integrity of the data. The access to data can only be granted to those with right authority.

3.3. Monitored Data Analysis. When the traditional mining algorithm is used to excavate the frequent abnormal data, it cannot identify the abnormal data of frequent abnormalities, and there is a big problem of frequent anomaly of data mining. Based on the historical monitored data, the data analysis module establishes the correlation between the metrics to form the metric graph, so that the degree of importance of the metric can be evaluated. A mining method for anomaly data based on the improved chaos algorithm is proposed. The eigenvector of the monitored data is calculated to quantify the system anomalies. Firstly, the data source in the observed cloud computing environment is fused to the partial least squares method to be cleaned and dimensionless processed, and a normalized data matrix, as well as a normalized dimension vector, is obtained. The matrix and the vector are defined respectively. The anomalous data predicting variables and the determinants are observed, and the principal component analysis is extracted to establish the linear regression equation of the data source in the cloud computing environment. The concrete steps are as follows:

(1) We will fuse the observed data to partial least squares, so that the original data can be the cleaned with nondimension. The formula is as follows:

$$x_{ij}^* = \frac{x_{ij} - \bar{x}_j}{\sqrt{S_j S(D)}},$$

$$y_i^* = \frac{y_i - \bar{y}}{\sqrt{S_y}} \times x_{ij}^*. \tag{5}$$

Here, x_{ij} is state space of data source in the cloud computing environment with intrinsic mode function, S_j represents weight vector of each data in the cloud computing environment, S_y represents the steady-state probability of the global data in the cloud computing environment, y_i represents a multivariable time series of given exception data, $\bar{y}$ represents the local thinning ratio, x_{ij}^* represents the source data after cleaning in the cloud computing environment, and y_i^* represents dimensionless processing of data source in cloud computing environment.

(2) We calculate the standardized data matrix and the normalized dimensional vector and provide the data basis for the main component analysis in the next step. We obtain a normalized matrix of $m \times n$ order represented by X_0 and the m-dimensional vector represented by Y_0, as follows:

$$Y_0 = y_i^* \times \begin{bmatrix} y_1^* \\ y_2^* \\ \vdots \\ y_m^* \end{bmatrix},$$

$$X_0 = \begin{pmatrix} x_{11}^* & \cdots & x_{1n}^* \\ \vdots & \ddots & \vdots \\ x_{m1}^* & \cdots & x_{mn}^* \end{pmatrix} \times Y_0. \tag{6}$$

y_1^*, y_2^*, and y_m^* represent the main elements of Y_0, and x_{11}^*, x_{1n}^*, x_{m1}^*, and x_{mn}^* represent the main elements of X_0.

(3) X_0 and Y_0 are defined, respectively, as the results of observation value standardization for prediction variables and the determinant of frequent abnormal data in cloud computing environment. The principal component analysis and extraction will be carried on. The following two formulas are used, respectively, to extract principal components Y_0 and X_0 of Y_1 and X_1, making X_1 maximally reflect Y_1, implementing principal component extraction. The calculation formulas are as follows:

$$
\begin{aligned}
Y_1 &= \frac{t_1 \left(X_0 \omega_1 \right)}{Y_0}, \\
X_1 &= \frac{P_1 \otimes X_0^T t_1}{Y_1},
\end{aligned}
\tag{7}
$$

where P_1 is the frequent abnormal data on behalf of the cloud computing environment, X_0^T represents the eigenvalue vector data of frequent abnormalities in cloud computing environment, ω_1 is the similarity of characteristic value for frequent abnormal data, and t_1 represents the time complexity of the decomposition of matrix X_0.

(4) After extracting the principal components, we need to establish the regression equation of the source data in cloud computing environment. The expression is as follows:

$$
\left(x^*, y^* \right) = X_1 \times \frac{\alpha_1 x_1 + \alpha_2 + x_2{}^* + \alpha_p + x_p{}^*}{\omega_1}.
\tag{8}
$$

$\left(x^*, y^* \right)$ is the linear regression coefficient of data in cloud computing environment, α_1, α_2, and α_p represent relevance between dependent variable and each variable of frequent abnormal data, and $x_2{}^*$ and $x_p{}^*$ represent the correlation between the frequent abnormal data variables.

3.4. Policy Response Method. The nature of the services provided by the cloud computing platform is the Internet access service. Most of the existing methods use the stochastic process model of typical telecommunication access-Poisson process as the basis of system resource scheduling optimization. Poisson process is a class of the most basic independent process in describing random events, in which the time interval of events is considered to be independent random variables, equivalent to an update process [22]. The typical Poisson process is expressed as

$$
\begin{aligned}
&P \left(N(t) - N(t-s) = n \right) \\
&= \frac{e^{-\lambda [(t-(t-s))]} \left[\lambda t - \lambda (t-s) \right]^n}{n!}.
\end{aligned}
\tag{9}
$$

In (9), $N(t)$ is the number of events occurring between 0 and t, and λ is the intensity of the event. In the Internet access services, they can be seen as the number and access strength of Internet services access at time t; $N(t) - N(t-s)$ is the increment of the number of Internet access services in the time $[t-s, t)$.

When the data module is abnormal, it will be sent to the corresponding module of the strategy. The Poisson distribution process is the classical fault prediction model of the reliability engineering. Conventionally, the historical fault data is used to predict the time of the next failure. However, this paper improves the model and introduces the anomaly evaluation to replace the historical fault data and predict the next system failure time. In this way, by assessing the degree of system anomalies, the instantaneous error can be responded to in a timely manner; the monitoring cycle is immediately adjusted to the minimum. The cumulative error can be adjusted according to the degree of abnormal monitoring cycle. We set the probability of a system failure as $F(t) = w$. Then you can calculate the time interval of next failure:

$t = -\ln(1 - w)/\lambda$, so the current monitoring period can be adjusted to

$$
T = \begin{cases}
T_\beta, & 0 \le s_t < \beta \\
-\dfrac{\ln \left(1 - s_t \right)}{\lambda} + e, & \beta \le s_t \le \alpha \\
T_\alpha, & \alpha < s_t \le 1.
\end{cases}
\tag{10}
$$

In (10), T_β is the minimum monitoring period, T_α is the maximum monitoring period, and λ and e are the adjustment parameters. According to the analysis of the function, we find that, if the monitoring cycle is set between the maximum and the minimum monitoring cycle, abnormal monitoring cycle shortens with the increase in the degree of abnormal system, and the shortness degree increases with the range of increase degree of abnormal monitoring cycle. That is to say, the more serious the abnormality is, the shorter the monitoring period is, which the desired result is.

4. Experiments and Simulation

In order to further verify the feasibility and rationality of the autonomous monitoring model based on autonomic computing, a simulation experiment is carried out. MATLAB software is used to build the frequent abnormal data simulation platform in the cloud computing environment. The computer simulation platform configuration includes Intel (R) Core (TM) i3-2130 3.4 GHz CPU, 4.00 GB memory, windows 10 professional 64-bit operating system, MATLAB 2014b. The cloud platform is built on four different operating system application servers. The experimental environment includes Huawei S9303 multilayer routing switch and MySQL database server to provide data operation.

4.1. Experiment Procedure. In the monitoring of data collection, we monitor three kinds of resource types, shown in Table 1. In this paper, we use sliding window technology to temporarily store the monitoring data, mainly to achieve two functions. The first function is to calculate the current sliding window in the vector set of eigenvectors, compared with the reference feature vector to detect the fault. The second one is to learn the new load mode according to current sliding window in the load vector set, so that the exception

TABLE 1: Critical monitoring metrics.

Resource type	Interpretation	Metric
CPU	The system calls the CPU time slice	system_cpu_usage
Internet	Number of packets received	r_packets
	Number of packets sent	s_packets
Data content	Integrity	inf_com

TABLE 2: Frequent abnormal data mining performance.

Number of experiments (times)	Accuracy rate (%)	Error rate (%)	Reliability rate (%)
20	98.2	0.2	98.6
30	97.7	0.1	97.0
40	98.1	0.1	98.3
50	98.2	0.1	98.6
60	98.2	0.1	98.6

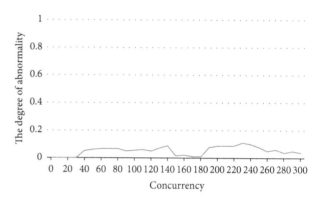

FIGURE 3: Abnormal degree change with concurrency.

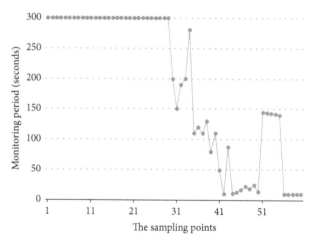

FIGURE 4: Monitoring period adjustment.

in the specific load mode can be detected. When the new monitored data arrives at the end of the sliding window, the larger the length of the first window of the monitoring data to delete is, the more obvious the abnormal performance will be and the better the timeliness of abnormal detection will be. This results in a higher false negative rate. On the contrary, the smaller the window length is, the more obvious the failure performance will be and the greater the impact of noise monitored data will be. The results are in a higher false alarm rate. The experimental results show that when the window length is 17–23, the detection effect is ideal with little difference. So we will set the sliding window size to 20 in this experiment.

In this experiment, the number of concurrent steps between 0 and 2 can be gradually increased to 300. When the number of concurrent steps is set to 5 minutes, and the experiment lasts 500 minutes, then 100 sets of data can be acquired. In the experiment, set the sliding window length to 20. The first 20 data sets in the main direction of the PCA (Principal Component Analysis) feature vector are the benchmark training data, and then the data can be used as an online fault detection.

Based on the improved chaos algorithm, the anomaly data mining method is used to simulate the frequent abnormal data in the cloud environment. The mining accuracy and the mining error rate are compared with different sets of experimental times so as to measure the effectiveness, referring to Table 2.

4.2. Results Analysis. When data analysis is carried out under unchanged condition of load model, the experimental results are shown in Figure 3. It shows that the abscissa is concurrent number and the coordinate is the abnormal degree (1 − |correlation|) with values between 0 and 1. The maximum of abnormal degree is 1, which means that there is a problem in cloud data. The minimum value is 0, implying that cloud

data is normal. In the constant load model, when there is a concurrent number, there is no phenomenon of normal monitoring data to detect anomalies mistakenly. Therefore, the number of concurrent dynamic change situations has good adaptability.

According to the experimental results in this paper, the maximum and minimum monitoring cycles are, respectively, set to 300 seconds and 10 seconds. Initial system abnormal value is 0, and the biggest monitoring cycle is 300 seconds. When the cloud data situation changes, then the monitoring period is adjusted accordingly. When the cycle of sample point is short and the monitoring cost is larger, for example, when the sample point is no more than 20, Figure 4 shows that no matter how the situation changes, monitoring time and the basic monitoring price remain unchanged.

Repeated experiments show that when the degree of network anomaly is low, the method of dynamically adjusting the monitoring period makes the monitoring system adopt a large monitoring period, reduce the number of data collection, reduce the unnecessary overhead, and dynamically adjust the monitoring period to send the network traffic below fixed detection cycle method. Therefore, the model can be adjusted according to the amount of data in cloud platform monitoring cycle, to reduce the monitoring cost.

5. Conclusion and Further Work

Data security in cloud platform is an ongoing challenging issue. We draw lessons from the working mechanism of autonomic computing system and the idea of abnormal data mining. Then we propose a data security monitoring method based on autonomic computing. This method monitors changes of data in the cloud platforms, to ensure the security of these. Simulation results show that the cost can be reduced with the architecture of integrated modules of data collection, analysis, monitoring service, and data volume based monitoring cycle adjustment. However, the ability of repairing the attacked data is not taken into account in the proposed method yet. Therefore, the research on data recovery and related implementation will be considered in the future work.

Conflicts of Interest

The authors declare that they have no conflicts of interest.

Acknowledgments

This work was supported in part by the National Natural Science Foundation of China (NSFC) under Grants no. 61602155, no. U1604155, no. 61370221, and no. U1404611, in part by the Program for Science & Technology Innovation Talents in the University of Henan Province under Grant no. 16HASTIT035, in part by Henan Science and Technology Innovation Project under Grants no. 164200510007 and no. 174100510010, in part by the Industry university research project of Henan Province under Grant no. 172107000005, and in part by the support program for young backbone teachers in Henan Province under Grant no. 2015GGJS-047.

References

[1] G. Komal and G. Parul, *Cloud computing security issues: An analysis*, Institute of Electrical and Electronics Engineers Inc., 2016.

[2] J. J. Jiang and Z. F. Ding, "The design and implementation of cloud computing model and platform," *Applied Mechanics and Materials*, vol. 631-632, pp. 210–217, 2014.

[3] J. Kar and M. R. Mishra, "Mitigating threats and security metrics in cloud computing," *Journal of Information Processing Systems*, vol. 12, no. 2, pp. 226–233, 2016.

[4] I. Diaz, G. Fernandez, M. Martin, P. Gonzalez, and J. Tourino, "Integrating the common information model with MDS4," in *Proceedings of the 2008 9th IEEE/ACM International Conference on Grid Computing (GRID)*, pp. 298–303, Tsukuba, September 2008.

[5] Y. Q. Zhang, X. F. Wang, X. F. Liu, and L. Liu, "Survey on cloud computing security," *Journal of Software. Ruanjian Xuebao*, vol. 27, no. 6, pp. 1328–1348, 2016.

[6] T. B. Mathias and P. J. Callaghan, "Autonomic computing and IBM System z10 active resource monitoring," *IBM Journal of Research and Development*, vol. 53, no. 1, pp. 13:1–13:11, 2009.

[7] Z. Wang, H. Wang, G. Feng, and et al., "Research on Autonomic Computing System and its Key Technologies," *Computer Science*, vol. 40, no. 7, pp. 15–18, 2013.

[8] K. Ahuja and H. Dangey, "Autonomic Computing: An emerging perspective and issues," in *Proceedings of the 2014 International Conference on Issues and Challenges in Intelligent Computing Techniques, ICICT 2014*, pp. 471–475, India, February 2014.

[9] W. Liu and Y. Zhou, "Research and Design of Fault Monitoring Mechanism Based Oil Autonomic Computing," *Computer Science*, vol. 37, no. 8, pp. 175–177, 2010.

[10] W. Liu and Z. Li, "Multiplied Data Threshold Detecting Method Based on Autonomic Computing," *Computer Science*, vol. 38, no. 5, pp. 132–134, 2011.

[11] W. Liu and K. Ren, "Research and Design of an Autonomic Computing System Model Based on Distributed Environment," *Journal of Northwestern Polytechnic University*, vol. 29, no. 2, pp. 160–164, 2011.

[12] S. Yolanda, G. Georgina, and C. Mariela, "Evaluation of monitoring tools for cloud computing environments," *IEEE Computer Society*, pp. 569–578, 2012.

[13] W. Liu and Z. Li, "Autonomic Computing Model Based on Hierarchical Management in Cloud Environment," *Computer Science*, vol. 41, no. 3, pp. 189–192, 2014.

[14] G. Suciu, S. Halunga, A. Ochian, and V. Suciu, "Network management and monitoring for cloud systems," in *Proceedings of the 6th International Conference on Electronics, Computers and Artificial Intelligence, ECAI 2014*, pp. 1–4, Romania, October 2014.

[15] M. Liu and P. Guo, "Design and Implementation of Computer Hardware Monitoring System Based on Cloud Computing," in *Proceedings of the 2016 International Conference on Electronic, Information and Computer Engineering, ICEICE 2016*, Hong Kong, April 2016.

[16] F. Masmoudi, M. Loulou, and A. H. Kacem, "Multi-tenant services monitoring for accountability in cloud computing," *IEEE Computer Society*, pp. 620–625, 2015.

[17] M. Peng, H. Xiong, and X. Yu, "SVM intrusion detection model based on compressed sampling," *Journal of Electrical & Computer Engineering*, pp. 1–7, December 2016.

[18] Z. ZEng and C. Li, "Study on frequent Abnormal Data Mining Method in Cloud Computing Environment," *Computer Simulation*, vol. 33, no. 3, pp. 339–342, 2016.

[19] J. Ge, B. Zhang, and Y. Fang, "Study on Resource Monitoring Model in Cloud Computing Environment," *Computer Enginering*, vol. 37, no. 11, pp. 31–33, 2014.

[20] D. Li, L. Li, L. Jin, G. Huang, and Q. Wu, "Research of load forecasting and elastic resources scheduling of Openstack platform based on time series," *Journal of Chongqing University of Posts and Telecommunications (Natural Science Edition)*, vol. 28, no. 4, pp. 560–566, 2016.

[21] H. Chen, X. Fu, Z. Tang, and X. Zhu, "Resource monitoring and prediction in cloud computing environments," in *Proceedings of the 3rd International Conference on Applied Computing and Information Technology and 2nd International Conference on Computational Science and Intelligence, ACIT-CSI 2015*, pp. 288–292, Japan, July 2015.

[22] Z. Luo, H. Qian, and Z. Jun, "Abnormal Behavior Detection Based on Poisson Equation," *Science Technology and Enginering*, vol. 14, no. 2, pp. 50–54, 2014.

3

Statistical Similarity based Change Detection for Multitemporal Remote Sensing Images

Mumu Aktar, Md. Al Mamun, and Md. Ali Hossain

Computer Science & Engineering Department, Rajshahi University of Engineering & Technology, Rajshahi 6204, Bangladesh

Correspondence should be addressed to Mumu Aktar; mumu.ruet@gmail.com

Academic Editor: Huan Xie

Change detection (CD) of any surface using multitemporal remote sensing images is an important research topic since up-to-date information about earth surface is of great value. Abrupt changes are occurring in different earth surfaces due to natural disasters or man-made activities which cause damage to that place. Therefore, it is necessary to observe the changes for taking necessary steps to recover the subsequent damage. This paper is concerned with this issue and analyzes statistical similarity measure to perform CD using remote sensing images of the same scene taken at two different dates. A variation of normalized mutual information (NMI) as a similarity measure has been developed here using sliding window of different sizes. In sliding window approach, pixels' local neighborhood plays a significant role in computing the similarity compared to the whole image. Thus the insignificant global characteristics containing noise and sparse samples can be avoided when evaluating the probability density function. Therefore, NMI with different window sizes is proposed here to identify changes using multitemporal data. Experiments have been carried out using two separate multitemporal remote sensing images captured one year apart and one month apart, respectively. Experimental analysis reveals that the proposed technique can detect up to 97.71% of changes which outperforms the traditional approaches.

1. Introduction

Change detection (CD) plays an important role in earth observation since a lot of changes occurring on different areas of earth surface cause severe damage to that area. So, it is very important to identify changes occurring on that area to take steps for subsequent recovery from damage. Most of the damage is caused due to natural disasters like flooding, rainfall, and droughts and also by man-made activities and thus it is necessary to observe the areas on regular intervals for detecting that change. Multitemporal remote sensing images taken at different times provide the periodic repeated look of an area which is very necessary for regular observation of earth surface.

The spatial, radiometric, spectral, and temporal resolution of an image has been improved due to recent advances in satellite imaging that has made earth observations much easier [1]. Multispectral remote sensing image is a valuable source of satellite data providing necessary information by each band, that is why in this research two separate multispectral datasets of two different dates have been chosen to identify changes. CD is applied to different tasks including land cover change detection [2, 3], building change detection [4, 5], vegetation change detection [6], wetland monitoring [7], and so on. Generally, CD detection can be categorized in two ways: binary change detection and multiclass change detection. Binary change detection focuses on change versus no change whereas multiclass change detection uses some supervised or unsupervised approaches for classifying multiple classes and further identifies changes of each class separately. This paper is concerned with binary change detection. A number of different techniques are used for binary change detection such as image differencing [8, 9], log-ratio operator [10], Kullback Leibler divergence [11], regression analysis [12], vegetation index differencing [13, 14], and principal component analysis [1, 15].

Ground truth data is needed for supervised approach being used for change detection. When this ground truth or prior knowledge is unavailable then threshold selection is very important to take decision about change/no change. An adaptive threshold can be used for generating a binary change detection map. Change detection of multisensor images at pixel level is verified using manual threshold which faced false alarms because only the mean value is considered for threshold selection [3]. Here in this research a difference image is generated using image differencing method which requires a threshold to take decision about changes. OTSU method for threshold selection [16, 17] has been used here since it maximizes variance between changed and unchanged pixels for generating a binary change detection map.

Since threshold used in image differencing method depends on radiometric differences of pixel values, singly it is not always enough to determine changes between two times' images since they can provide false detection due to registration errors, that is why a new approach is proposed here based on statistical similarity to determine the percentage of changes along with image differencing. In [3] a number of similarity measure techniques such as distance to independence, normalized standard deviation or Woods criterion, correlation ratio, mutual information (MI), and cluster reward algorithm (CRA) have been applied on land cover change detection for multisensor remotely sensed images and the performances have been compared in case of two separate fixed window sizes. Mean value of similarity image has been used there as a threshold for decision about change/no change of any pixel. Although result of the statistical measures has been normalized, optimal dimension of the estimated windows has not been investigated. Land cover change detection has been performed in [2] considering sliding window by transforming spectral values into local spectrum trend using curve fitting and raster encoding techniques. This approach is time consuming and even difficult when calculating the local trend spectrum for different window sizes. Multisensor remote sensing image change detection using mutual information, maximal information coefficient, and distance correlation measure based similarity measures has been developed in [18] using sliding window approach with fixed window size of 21 × 21. This approach used manual threshold for interpreting change and no change regions and generated false positives. Selection of threshold is a difficult task there as it is justified manually.

Among a number of similarity measures, MI has been chosen here for change detection purpose because of its many advantages. MI is a nonparametric approach that does not require any assumption about the shape of the distribution of input variables and able to measure both the linear and nonlinear relationships among input variables [19]. A lot of papers considered MI as a similarity measure for change detection task including multivariate statistical model [20] which concentrated on homogeneous and heterogeneous sensors, SAR image change detection [21] which considered different kind of changes, canonical information analysis [22] for image change detection, multicontextual mutual information data as an improved form of image spatial mutual information [23] for SAR image change detection, and temporal behavior of multichannel scene characterization for change detection [24].

But the value of MI is affected by the entropies of the input variables and the calculated MI without being normalized cannot measure similarity effectively, so the MI measure can be improved by normalizing it to a specified range such as [0, 1] [19], that is why MI being normalized (NMI) has been analyzed here in this research work as a similarity measure to detect changes. But when just traditional NMI is applied on the whole image then a pixels' marginal and joint probability density functions (PDFs) are affected with the globally spread information that can be noisy and has less significance on them. But if sliding window with varying window sizes is considered then pixels' local neighborhood is used for calculating PDF which is the most significant one. The window which is too small or too large affects the CD results [2]. So different window sizes have been considered here in this research to find out which one is more efficient for better change detection result. Thus to significantly perform change detection on multitemporal remote sensing images sliding window based normalized mutual information (SWB-NMI) with varying window sizes has been considered here to statistically detect changes using 1-Imagesimilarity($\mathbf{X}$, $\mathbf{Y}$) concept. Experimental analysis has been performed using remotely sensed multispectral imagery of Canberra region of Australia with multitemporal datasets of two separate dates.

The rest of the paper is organized as follows. Section 2 provides a clear concept of proposed change detection method. The proposed methodology for multispectral images' change detection is presented in Section 3. In Section 4 experimental analysis and performance evaluation of the proposed method have been performed. Finally, a conclusion is given in Section 5.

2. Proposed Change Detection Method

2.1. OTSU Threshold Selection Method. Threshold selection is a key concept used in unsupervised approaches for generating a binary change detection map. OTSU's method is a popular approach which maximizes variance between changed and unchanged pixels to get an optimal threshold [17]. The OTSU algorithm assumes the image containing two classes of pixels as foreground pixels and background pixels; it then calculates the optimum threshold separating the two classes to minimize their combined spread (intraclass variance), $V1$, or equivalently (because the sum of pairwise squared distances is constant), to maximize their interclass variance, V [16]. The optimal threshold, V, can be obtained by maximizing the following criteria with respect to $V1$ [17]:

$$\eta = \theta_0 \times \theta_1 \times (\mu_0 - \mu_1)^2, \tag{1}$$

where θ_0 and μ_0 are the count and mean value of elements in difference image, D which are less than $V1$, and θ_1 and μ_1 are the count and mean value of elements in difference image, D which are no less than $V1$.

Finally the decision about change/no change can be defined as [17]

$$\text{decision function}, d(k) = \begin{cases} \text{change} & \text{if } d(k) \geq v \\ \text{no change} & \text{if } d(k) < v. \end{cases} \tag{2}$$

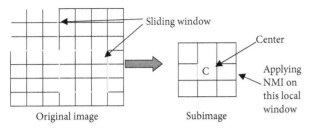

FIGURE 1: Basic concept of sliding window approach.

2.2. NMI as a Statistical Similarity Measure. MI of two discrete random variables **X** and **Y** can be defined as [19] using Shannon entropy theorem [25]:

$$I(\mathbf{X}, \mathbf{Y}) = \sum_{x \in \mathbf{X}} \sum_{y \in \mathbf{Y}} p(x, y) \log\left(\frac{p(x, y)}{p(x)\,p(y)}\right), \quad (3)$$

where $p(x, y)$, $p(x)$, and $p(y)$ are the joint and marginal probability distribution functions of **X** and **Y**, respectively. MI between these two variables is zero if they are independent of each other and will be higher if they are similar to some degree. If the MI value is normalized to the range between 0-1 then the effect of input variables' entropy can be removed and thus MI can be used as an improved similarity measure. Therefore, NMI has been applied here to identify percentage of changes between two images **X** and **Y** in which one is the reference and the other is the target image. The NMI is defined as [19]

$$\dot{I}(\mathbf{X}, \mathbf{Y}) = \frac{I(\mathbf{X}, \mathbf{Y})}{\sqrt{H(\mathbf{X})}\sqrt{H(\mathbf{Y})}}, \quad (4)$$

where $H(\mathbf{X})$ is the entropy of the variable **X** which represents the amount of information held in **X** and the same representation in case of $H(\mathbf{Y})$.

2.3. SWB-NMI as a Statistical Similarity Measure. Figure 1 is an example showing the basic concept of how sliding window can be moved over an image to apply NMI on each local window. An efficient way for remote sensing image change detection is to analyze the image's local geographical layout for its similarity measure. For this purpose the sliding window approach can be considered where a change indicator is applied separately on each window. Thus the statistical properties such as joint and marginal probabilities of the pixels can be calculated from the local neighborhood information which are most significant ones. Different window sizes are considered here to achieve the relevant information. Window sizes such as 3×3, 5×5, 9×9, 13×13, 15×15, 23×23, and 27×27 are used instead of full image to avoid the global statistics of pixels which may contain irrelevant information. Thus SWB-NMI has been chosen in this research with an expectation of detecting changes locally and the initial results are promising. Since a large window results noise and small window do not contain enough spatial contextual information [2], varying sized windows have been applied to the experiment here to find an optimal window size and the performances have been compared with traditional approaches stated in [2, 3].

3. Proposed Methodology

The objective of this research is to identify changes between the same scenes taken at different times to find out the places of any area which may be damaged due to unintended occurrences. For this work two separate multitemporal datasets of two different dates have been chosen. Landsat 7 ETM+ multispectral images have been chosen for this experiment which consists of eight spectral bands with a spatial resolution of 30 meters for bands 1 to 7 and 15 meters for the panchromatic band 8. Among them six bands from 1 to 5 and 7 (band 6 collects both high and low gain for all scenes whereas all other bands collect one of two gains and band 8 has different resolution compared to the others and that is why bands 6 and 8 are ignored here) have been chosen here.

In 1st multispectral dataset, two Landsat ETM+ images of 256 * 256 pixels have been taken one year apart of 2000 and 2001 from Canberra region of Australia.

The 2nd dataset is from another part of Canberra region captured around one month apart at 20.11.2016 and 22.12.2016. These images consist of 512 * 512 pixels. The overall working methodology is stated in Figure 2 as a flowchart.

Let us consider individually the multispectral images of 2000 and 20.11.2016 as the reference image, **X**, and images of 2001 as well as 22.12.2016 as the target image **Y**. Simply the difference between these multitemporal scenes is obtained by the following [26]:

$$\text{Difference Image}, \mathbf{I_D} = \mathbf{X} - \mathbf{Y} \quad (5)$$

Equation (5) subtracts each pixel of target images from each pixel of the reference ones. Since pixel-to-pixel differencing is performed here, so it is very necessary for the reference and target images to be coregistered. Using the concept of (1) a binary change map has been generated by automatic threshold selected using OTSU algorithm. The image differencing has been performed here band by band and the binary change detection map is shown only for band 1 for both multitemporal datasets.

The reference and the target images and the corresponding binary change maps based on the selected threshold value for both datasets are shown in Figure 3.

It can be seen from Figure 3(j) that the binary change map of 2nd dataset contains very little amount of changes, since it is the multitemporal data of one month interval. The red points are defined as changed areas. In one month perhaps some buildings, parks can be changed which can be some pixels in change map image. Since they are very small points, so for better visual interpretation the points are modified as large. It is found in Figures 3(d) and 3(i) that the tail portion of each of the histograms represent the change portion as it is expected that intensity differences due to land cover change reside at the tails of the difference distribution of any image [27].

From this binary change map of Figure 3(e), it can be obtained that around 35% area in the reference image has been changed within one year which has been calculated by subtracting the total number of changed pixels from the total

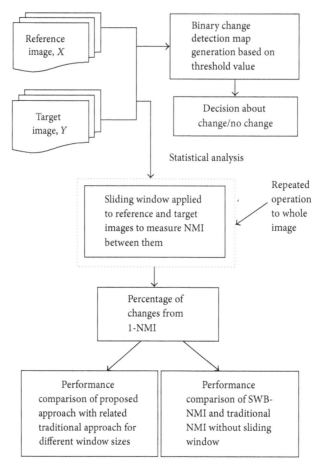

FIGURE 2: Methodology of proposed change detection system.

number of pixels contained on the reference image, dividing the resulting value by the total number of reference image's pixels, and then taking the percentage value of the result obtained. The same method has been applied for 2nd dataset and here around 4% of area has been changed which can be observed from Figure 3(j).

After obtaining the binary change map, statistical similarity has been measured between target and reference images for calculating percentage of changes in both datasets. In both cases, same window for both the reference and target ones is selected for applying NMI on them to measure similarity and find CD by 1-Imagesimilarity($\mathbf{X}$, $\mathbf{Y}$). The sliding window has been iteratively applied to the whole image area starting at location $(1, 1)$. And the process has been repeated for different window sizes and the performances have been compared with [2]. Finally the performance of CD of the proposed SWB-NMI method has been compared with the traditional MI in [3].

4. Experimental Analysis and Performance Evaluation

Change detection operation has been performed using two separate multitemporal multispectral datasets of separate portions of Canberra region, Australia. Percentage of correct

change detection from these multitemporal images has been calculated as (6):

Percentage of correct change detection

$$= 1$$

$$- \text{abs} \left(\frac{\text{original change} - \text{experimental change}}{\text{original change}} \right) \quad (6)$$

$$\times 100\%.$$

It has been obtained from the binary change maps generated by considering threshold values is that the original changes which occurred in the reference images are around 35% and 4% for two datasets, respectively. Therefore, using these values and the percentage of experimental changes, Tables 1–5 show the experimental results on the amount of changes in percentage for different window sizes using the proposed SWB-NMI technique for both datasets. The results of both datasets for different window sizes have been compared with [2].

From Table 1 it can be seen that up to 97.71% of changes can be correctly detected using SWB-NMI approach for window size of 17 and it varies a little for window size of 15. Figure 4 represents the performance of varying window sizes

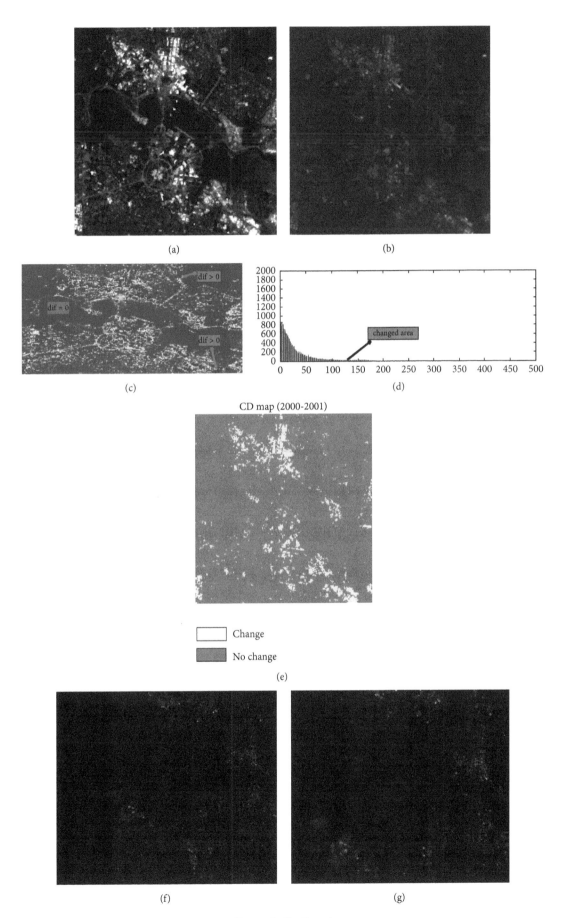

FIGURE 3: Continued.

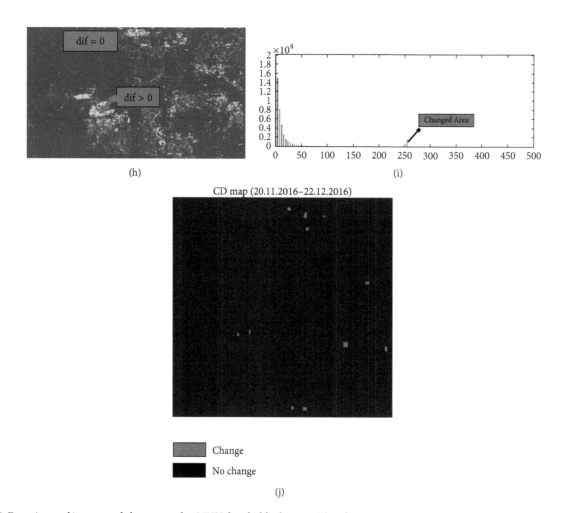

FIGURE 3: Experimental images and change map by OTSU threshold selection. (a) Reference image: 2000. (b) Target image: 2001. (c) Difference image. (d) Histogram of difference image. (e) Corresponding binary change map. (f) Reference image: 20.11.2016. (g) Target image: 22.12.2016. (h) Difference image. (i) Histogram of difference image. (j) Corresponding change map.

TABLE 1: Percentage of changes using SWB-NMI for different window sizes (1st dataset).

Window size	% of similarities	% of changes	% of correct change detection	% of wrong change detection
5	70.0	30.0	85.71	14.28
9	68.0	32.0	91.43	8.57
13	63.5	36.5	95.71	4.29
15	64.0	36.0	97.14	2.86
17	**64.2**	**35.8**	**97.71**	**2.29**
23	61.0	39.0	88.57	11.43
27	59.5	40.5	84.29	15.71

TABLE 2: Performance comparison in percentage between SWB-NMI and approach in [2] with different window sizes for 1st dataset.

Method	Window size, 5×5	Window size, 9×9
SWB-NMI	85.71	91.43
Approach in [2]	84.3	85.3

Experiment has been performed for 2nd dataset using the same window sizes as used in [2] for better performance comparison.

In Table 3 the proposed approach has obtained up to 95% of correct changes with window size of 11 for 2nd dataset.

Now the performance of the proposed approach has been compared with the approach of [2] in Table 4.

Here it is observed that the proposed approach has shown better performance than the related one in [2]. It can also be seen that although the proposed approach has shown highest performance for window size 17 in dataset-1, it has shown highest performance in case of dataset-2 for window size 11. It can be concluded from this scenario that performance depends partially on the dataset also. Also the result has varied a lot when the proposed SWB_NMI approach being

in case of 1st dataset using SWB-NMI for change detection application.

Table 2 compares the performance of proposed approach with the related model given in [2] where 3×3, 5×5, 7×7, and 9×9 window sizes were considered.

Although performance has been compared between these two methods for only 5×5 and 9×9 window sizes, from Table 1 it is seen that window size 17×17 shows the best performance.

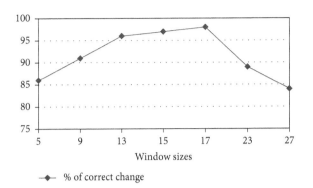

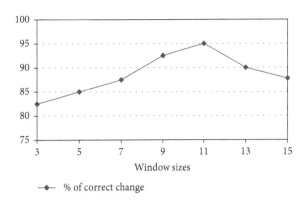

FIGURE 4: Relationship between window sizes and (%) of correct changes.

FIGURE 5: Relationship between window sizes and (%) of correct changes.

TABLE 3: Percentage of changes using SWB-NMI for different window sizes (2nd dataset).

Window size	% of similarities	% of changes	% of correct change detection	% of wrong change detection
3	96.7	3.3	82.5	17.5
5	96.6	3.4	85	15
7	96.5	3.5	87.5	12.5
9	96.3	3.7	92.5	7.5
11	**96.2**	**3.8**	**95**	**5**
13	95.6	4.4	90	10
15	95.5	4.49	87.75	12.25

TABLE 4: Performance comparison in percentage between SWB-NMI and approach in [2] with different window sizes for 2nd dataset.

Method	Window size, 3×3	Window size, 5×5	Window size, 7×7	Window size, 9×9
SWB-NMI	82.5	85	87.5	92.5
Approach in [2]	82.1	84.3	84.8	85.3

TABLE 5: Change detection result based on SWB-NMI and traditional MI used in [3].

Methods	SWB-NMI dataset-1	SWB-NMI dataset-2	MI in [3]
% of correct change detection	97.71	95	86.1

used as a similarity measure has been compared to the related local trend similarity approach and the proposed method has shown better result.

Figure 5 represents the performance of varying window sizes in case of 2nd dataset using SWB-NMI for change detection application.

It can be noticed from Figures 4 and 5 that the smaller as well as larger window size does not mean to have better detection ability. For instance, in case of dataset-1 the lowest value of 84.29% of correct changes is found for the largest 27×27 window size and the same case for the smallest 5×5 window with 85.71% of correct changes. The same case happens for dataset-2 with window sizes 3×3 and 15×15.

It can be observed from the above results that the CD result is affected with varying window sizes and both the smallest and the largest ones lead to the decrease in detection performance and detect the unchanged ones as the changed and vice versa. It is because when a local window is too small then it will not contain enough spatial contextual information and when it is too large then it will contain a lot of noisy as well as irrelevant information. Thus it can be concluded that window size should be an optimal one which is not very large not very small. 17 and 11 are the better and optimal ones for this experiment although it depends on dataset.

Finally, Table 5 shows the performance of proposed SWB-NMI being compared with traditional MI in [3].

From Table 5 it can be observed that the SWB-NMI (for 17×17 window size) can detect 97.71% of changes in case of dataset-1. Although the percentage is less in case of dataset-2, both outperforms the related method used in [3].

5. Conclusion

An efficient change detection approach has been proposed here in this research to identify changes of any geographical area after some natural disasters or artificial changes made by human being. At first a binary change map has been generated using OTSU threshold selection method to show the change/no change area and further statistical similarity has been measured between reference and target images to find percentage of changes. This approach results better change detection by statistical analysis of similarity measure and by considering the local neighborhood characteristics which are insignificant most of the time rather than the global ones. An important finding is also from this research that window size is an important factor when using local window for statistical analysis of similarity. Thus the SWB-NMI approach outperforms the traditional MI method in case of change detection. Image differencing is performed here on pixel-by-pixel basis for generating change detection map, which may often face the registration error and the final performance may be affected greatly. So further interest is to investigate some developed methods which do not directly depend on radiometric values. This research focuses on binary change detection whereas the multiclass change detection is more challenging task which is also a future research interest.

Conflicts of Interest

The authors declare that there are no conflicts of interest regarding the publication of this paper.

References

[1] M. Al Mamun, M. N. I. Mondal, and B. Ahmed, "Change detection-aided single linear prediction of multi-temporal satellite images," in *Proceedings of the 17th International Conference on Computer and Information Technology, ICCIT '14*, pp. 332–335, IEEE, Dhaka, Bangladesh, December 2014.

[2] P. Zhang, Z. Lv, and W. Shi, "Local spectrum-trend similarity approach for detecting land-cover change by using SPOT-5 satellite images," *IEEE Geoscience and Remote Sensing Letters*, vol. 11, no. 4, pp. 738–742, 2014.

[3] V. Alberga, "Similarity measures of remotely sensed multi-sensor images for change detection applications," *Remote Sensing*, vol. 1, no. 3, pp. 122–143, 2009.

[4] J. Tian, S. Cui, and P. Reinartz, "Building change detection based on satellite stereo imagery and digital surface models," *IEEE Transactions on Geoscience and Remote Sensing*, vol. 52, no. 1, pp. 406–417, 2014.

[5] D.-J. Kim, S. Hensley, S.-H. Yun, and M. Neumann, "Detection of durable and permanent changes in urban areas using multitemporal polarimetric UAVSAR data," *IEEE Geoscience and Remote Sensing Letters*, vol. 13, no. 2, pp. 267–271, 2016.

[6] S. Liu, L. Bruzzone, F. Bovolo, and P. Du, "Unsupervised hierarchical spectral analysis for change detection in hyperspectral images," in *Proceedings of the 2012 4th Workshop on Hyperspectral Image and Signal Processing, WHISPERS '12*, IEEE, Shanghai, China, June 2012.

[7] L. Moser, S. Voigt, E. Schoepfer, and S. Palmer, "Multitemporal wetland monitoring in sub-Saharan West-Africa using medium resolution optical satellite data," *IEEE Journal of Selected Topics in Applied Earth Observations and Remote Sensing*, vol. 7, no. 8, pp. 3402–3415, 2014.

[8] P. R. Coppin and M. E. Bauer, "Digital change detection in forest ecosystems with remote sensing imagery," *Remote Sensing Reviews*, vol. 13, no. 3-4, pp. 207–234, 1996.

[9] N. A. Quarmby and J. L. Cushnie, "Monitoring urban land cover changes at the urban fringe from SPOT HRV imagery in southeast England," *International Journal of Remote Sensing*, vol. 10, no. 6, pp. 953–963, 1989.

[10] Y. Bazi, L. Bruzzone, and F. Melgani, "An unsupervised approach based on the generalized Gaussian model to automatic change detection in multitemporal SAR images," *IEEE Transactions on Geoscience and Remote Sensing*, vol. 43, no. 4, pp. 874–886, 2005.

[11] J. Inglacla and G. Mercier, "A new statistical similarity measure for change detection in multitemporal SAR images and its extension to multiscale change analysis," *IEEE Transactions on Geoscience and Remote Sensing*, vol. 45, no. 5, pp. 1432–1445, 2007.

[12] A. K. Ludeke, R. C. Maggio, and L. M. Reid, "An analysis of anthropogenic deforestation using logistic regression and GIS," *Journal of Environmental Management*, vol. 31, no. 3, pp. 247–259, 1990.

[13] E. H. Wilson and S. A. Sader, "Detection of forest harvest type using multiple dates of landsat TM imagery," *Remote Sensing of Environment*, vol. 80, no. 3, pp. 385–396, 2002.

[14] M.-L. Nordberg and J. Evertson, "Vegetation index differencing and linear regression for change detection in a Swedish mountain range using Landsat TM and ETM+imagery," *Land Degradation and Development*, vol. 16, no. 2, pp. 139–149, 2005.

[15] J. S. Deng, K. Wang, Y. H. Deng, and G. J. Qi, "PCA-based land-use change detection and analysis using multitemporal and multisensor satellite data," *International Journal of Remote Sensing*, vol. 29, no. 16, pp. 4823–4838, 2008.

[16] N. Otsu, "A threshold selection method from gray-level histograms," *Automatica*, vol. 11, pp. 23–27, 1975.

[17] L. Li, X. Li, Y. Zhang, L. Wang, and G. Ying, "Change detection for high-resolution remote sensing imagery using object-oriented change vector analysis method," in *Proceedings of the 36th International Geoscience and Remote Sensing Symposium, IGARSS '16*, pp. 2873–2876, IEEE, Beijing, China, July 2016.

[18] K. G. Pillai and R. R. Vatsavai, "Multi-sensor remote sensing image change detection: an evaluation of similarity measures," in *Proceedings of the 2013 13th International Conference on Data Mining Workshops, ICDMW '13*, pp. 1053–1060, IEEE, Dallas, Tex, USA, December 2013.

[19] M. A. Hossain, X. Jia, and M. Pickering, "Subspace detection using a mutual information measure for hyperspectral image classification," *IEEE Geoscience and Remote Sensing Letters*, vol. 11, no. 2, pp. 424–428, 2014.

[20] J. Prendes, M. Chabert, F. Pascal, A. Giros, and J.-Y. Tourneret, "A new multivariate statistical model for change detection in images acquired by homogeneous and heterogeneous sensors," *IEEE Transactions on Image Processing*, vol. 24, no. 3, pp. 799–812, 2015.

[21] S. Cui, G. Schwarz, and M. Datcu, "A benchmark evaluation of similarity measures for multitemporal SAR image change detection," *IEEE Journal of Selected Topics in Applied Earth Observations and Remote Sensing*, vol. 9, no. 3, pp. 1101–1118, 2016.

[22] A. A. Nielsen and J. S. Vestergaard, "Change detection in bi-temporal data by canonical information analysis," in *Proceedings of the 8th International Workshop on the Analysis of Multitemporal Remote Sensing Images, Multi-Temp '15*, IEEE, Annecy, France, July 2015.

[23] L. An, M. Li, P. Zhang, Y. Wu, L. Jia, and W. Song, "Multicontextual mutual information data for SAR image change detection," *IEEE Geoscience and Remote Sensing Letters*, vol. 12, no. 9, 2015.

[24] E. Erten, A. Reigber, L. Ferro-Famil, and O. Hellwich, "A new coherent similarity measure for temporal multichannel scene characterization," *IEEE Transactions on Geoscience and Remote Sensing*, vol. 50, no. 7, pp. 2839–2851, 2012.

[25] T. M. Cover and J. A. Thomas, *Elements of Information Theory*, John Wiley & Sons, Hoboken, NJ, USA, 2nd edition, 2012.

[26] S. Liu, L. Bruzzone, F. Bovolo, and P. Du, "Hierarchical unsupervised change detection in multitemporal hyperspectral images," *IEEE Transactions on Geoscience and Remote Sensing*, vol. 53, no. 1, pp. 244–260, 2015.

[27] M. İlsever and C. Ünsalan, *Two-Dimensional Change Detection Methods*, Springer Briefs in Computer Science, 2012.

4

A Complete Subspace Analysis of Linear Discriminant Analysis and its Robust Implementation

Zhicheng Lu and Zhizheng Liang

School of Computer Science and Technology, China University of Mining and Technology, Xuzhou 221116, China

Correspondence should be addressed to Zhizheng Liang; liang@cumt.edu.cn

Academic Editor: Ping Feng Pai

Linear discriminant analysis has been widely studied in data mining and pattern recognition. However, when performing the eigen-decomposition on the matrix pair (within-class scatter matrix and between-class scatter matrix) in some cases, one can find that there exist some degenerated eigenvalues, thereby resulting in indistinguishability of information from the eigen-subspace corresponding to some degenerated eigenvalue. In order to address this problem, we revisit linear discriminant analysis in this paper and propose a stable and effective algorithm for linear discriminant analysis in terms of an optimization criterion. By discussing the properties of the optimization criterion, we find that the eigenvectors in some eigen-subspaces may be indistinguishable if the degenerated eigenvalue occurs. Inspired from the idea of the maximum margin criterion (MMC), we embed MMC into the eigen-subspace corresponding to the degenerated eigenvalue to exploit discriminability of the eigenvectors in the eigen-subspace. Since the proposed algorithm can deal with the degenerated case of eigenvalues, it not only handles the small-sample-size problem but also enables us to select projection vectors from the null space of the between-class scatter matrix. Extensive experiments on several face images and microarray data sets are conducted to evaluate the proposed algorithm in terms of the classification performance, and experimental results show that our method has smaller standard deviations than other methods in most cases.

1. Introduction

Linear discriminant analysis (LDA) [1–4] plays an important role in data analysis and has been widely used in many fields such as data mining and pattern recognition [5]. The main aim of LDA is to find optimal projection vectors by simultaneously minimizing the within-class distance and maximizing the between-class distance in the projection space and optimal projection vectors can be achieved by solving a generalized eigenvalue problem. In solving classical LDA, the within-class scatter matrix is required to be nonsingular in the general case. However, in many applications such as text classification and face recognition [6], the within-class scatter matrix is often singular since the dimension of data we deal with is much bigger than the number of data points. This is known as the small-sample-size (SSS) problem.

In the past several decades, various variants of LDA [7–10] have been proposed to address the problems of high-dimensional data and the SSS problem. It is noted that most of LDA-based methods are divided into four categories in terms of the combination of spaces of the within-class scatter and between-class scatter matrices [11].

The first category of these methods is to consider the range space of the within-class scatter matrix and the range space of the between-class scatter matrix. The typical algorithm of this category is the Fisherface [1] method where PCA is first employed to reduce the dimension of features to make the within-class scatter matrix be full-rank and then the standard LDA is performed. In the direct LDA method [12], the null space of the between-class scatter matrix is first removed and then the projection vectors are obtained by minimizing the within-class scatter distance in the range space of the between-class scatter matrix. Li et al. [13] proposed an efficient and stable algorithm to extract the discriminant vectors by defining the maximum margin criterion (MMC). The main difference between Fisher's criterion and MMC is that the former is to maximize the Fisher quotient while the latter is to maximize the average distance.

The second category mainly depends on exploiting the null space of within-class scatter matrix and the range space of the between-class scatter matrix. In terms of the null space-based LDA, Chen et al. [14] proposed to maximize the between-class scatter in the null space of the within-class scatter matrix and their method is referred to as the NLDA method. In order to reduce the computational cost of calculating the null space of the within-class scatter matrix, several effective methods have been proposed. Instead of directly obtaining the null space of the within-class scatter matrix, Çevikalp et al. [15] first obtained the range space of the within-class scatter matrix and then defined the scatter matrix of common vectors. Based on this, the projection vectors were obtained from the scatter matrix they defined. They also adopted difference subspaces and the Gram-Schmidt orthogonalization procedure to obtain discriminative common vectors. Chu and Thye [16] adopted the QR factorization on several matrices to exploit a new algorithm for the null space-based LDA method. Sharma and Paliwal [17] proposed an alternative null LDA method and discussed its fast implementation. Paliwal and Sharma [18] also developed a variant of pseudoinverse linear discriminant analysis and this method yields better classification performance.

The third category consists of those methods that make use of the null space of within-class scatter matrix, the range space of between-class scatter matrix, and the range space of within-class scatter matrix. Sharma et al. [19] applied improved RLDA to devise a feature selection method to extract important genes. In order to address the problem of the regularization parameter in RLDA, Sharma and Paliwal [20] applied a deterministic method to estimate the parameter by maximizing modified Fisher's criterion.

The fourth category is made up of those methods that explore all the spaces of the within-class scatter matrix and the between-class scatter matrix. Sharma and Paliwal [11] applied a two-stage technique to regularize both the between-class scatter and within-class scatter matrices to achieve the discriminant information.

In addition, there are other variants of LDA that do not belong to four categories mentioned above. Uncorrelated local Fisher discriminant analysis in terms of manifold learning is devised for ear recognition [21]. An exponential locality preserving projection (ELPP) is presented by introducing the matrix exponential to address the SSS problem. A double shrinking model [22] is constructed for manifold learning and feature selection. Li et al. [23] analyzed linear discriminant analysis in the worst case and reduced this problem to a scalable semidefinite feasibility problem. Zollanvari and Dougherty [24] discussed asymptotic generalization bound of linear discriminant analysis. Lu and Renals [25] used probabilistic linear discriminant analysis to model acoustic data.

In this paper, we revisit the optimization criterion for linear discriminant analysis. We find that there exists the degenerated case for some generalized eigenvalues. In order to deal with the degeneration of eigenvalues, we develop a robust implementation for this criterion in this paper. To be specific, the null space of the total scatter matrix is first removed to remedy the singularity problem. Then the eigen-subspace corresponding to each specific eigenvalue is achieved. Finally, in each eigen-subspace, the discriminability

of eigenvectors is measured by the maximum margin criterion and the projection vectors can be achieved by optimizing this criterion. We also conduct extensive experiments to evaluate the proposed method on various well-known data sets such as face images and microarray data sets. Experimental results show that our method is more stable than other methods in most cases.

2. Related Works

Assume that there are a set of n-dimensional data points, denoted by $\{x_1, \ldots, x_N\}$, where $x_i \in R^n$ $(i = 1, \ldots, N)$. When the labels of data points are available, each data point belongs to exactly one of c object classes $\{l_1, \ldots, l_c\}$ and the number of samples in class l_i is n_i. Thus, $N = \sum_{i=1}^{c} n_i$ is the number of all data points. In classical linear discriminant analysis, the between-class scatter matrix, the within-class scatter matrix, and the total scatter matrix are defined as follows:

$$S_b = \sum_{i=1}^{c} n_i (m_i - m)(m_i - m)^T = H_b H_b^T,$$

$$S_w = \sum_{i=1}^{c} \sum_{x \in l_i} (x - m_i)(x - m_i)^T = H_w H_w^T, \qquad (1)$$

$$S_t = \sum_{i=1}^{N} (x_i - m)(x_i - m)^T = H_t H_t^T,$$

where m_i is the centroid of the ith class and m is the global centroid of the data set. The precursor matrices are defined as

$$H_b = \left[\sqrt{n_1}(m_1 - m), \ldots, \sqrt{n_c}(m_c - m) \right],$$

$$H_w = \left[X_1 - m_1 e_1^T, \ldots, X_c - m_c e_c^T \right], \qquad (2)$$

$$H_t = \left[x_1 - m, \ldots, x_N - m \right],$$

where $e_i = (1, \ldots, 1)^T \in \mathfrak{R}^{n_i}$ and X_i is the data matrix that consists of data points from class l_i.

Classical LDA is to find the projection direction by making data points from different classes far from each other and data points from the same class close to each other. To be specific, LDA is to obtain the optimal projection vector by optimizing the following objective function:

$$\max \quad J_1(w) = \max \left(\frac{w^T S_b w}{w^T S_w w} \right). \qquad (3)$$

The optimal projection direction w can be achieved by solving the generalized eigenproblem: $S_b w = \lambda S_w w$. In general, there are at most $c - 1$ eigenvectors corresponding to nonzero generalized eigenvalues since the rank of the matrix S_b is not bigger than $c - 1$. When S_w is singular, some methods including PCA plus LDA [1], LDA/GSVD [7], and LDA/QR [26] can be used to deal with this problem.

3. Optimization Criterion and Its Robust Implementation

In this section, we revisit an optimization criterion for linear discriminant analysis and its properties are analyzed in detail. Finally, we discuss its robust implementation.

Note that if the matrix S_w is singular, the optimal function value of (3) will take the positive infinity. There are several variants of the model in (3) that can be found [27]. In fact, when the matrix S_w is nonsingular, it is not difficult to verify that these variants of (3) are equivalent [27]. For convenience, we adopt the following optimization criterion to give a stable and efficient algorithm for linear discriminant analysis, denoted by

$$\min \quad J_2(w) = \min \left(\frac{w^T S_w w}{w^T S_t w} \right). \tag{4}$$

The main aim for adopting (4) is based on the following reasons. First, the objective function is a bounded function in the general case, which avoids the case that the objective function takes the infinity. Second, since the null space of S_w plays an important role in some cases, especially in the small-sample-size problem, the optimization criterion of (4) also provides convenience for analyzing the null space of S_w. In fact, it is straightforward to verify that (4) and (3) are equivalent under some conditions. Most importantly, (4) can produce more generalized eigenvalues than (3) since the rank of S_t is not smaller than the rank of S_w. In addition, from the viewpoint of optimization, the objective function we optimize is usually bounded. Thus, (4) is more preferred than (3) in some cases.

It is obvious that the optimal projection w of (4) can be achieved by solving the generalized eigenproblem: $S_w w = \lambda S_t w$ when the matrix S_t is nonsingular. Later we will note that the generalized eigenvalue λ will take values in the interval of 0 and 1. Different from classical LDA, we extract the discriminant vectors which are composed of the first q eigenvectors of $S_t^{-1} S_w$ corresponding to the first q smallest eigenvalues if S_t is nonsingular. In such a case, we can avoid the singularity problem of the matrix S_w. Before giving an explicit implementation of the optimization criterion of (4), we start by giving the definitions of some subspaces [28].

Definition 1. Let A be an $n \times n$ positive semidefinite matrix and λ be an eigenvalue of A. The set of all eigenvectors of A corresponding to the eigenvalue λ, together with the zero vector, forms a subspace. This subspace is referred to as the eigen-subspace of A with λ.

Definition 2. The null space of the matrix A is the set of all eigenvectors of A with $\lambda = 0$.

Definition 3. The range space of the matrix is the set of all eigenvectors of A corresponding to nonzero eigenvalues.

In the case of the positive semidefinite matrix, the number of repeated roots of the characteristic equation det $|\lambda I - A| = 0$ determines the dimension of the eigen-subspace of A with λ. If the dimension of the eigen-subspace of A with λ is bigger than 1, the eigenvalue λ is degenerative since the number of repeated roots of the characteristic equation is bigger than 1. It is observed from (1) that the matrices S_b, S_w, and S_t are positive semidefinite. According to the above definitions, we can obtain the following four subspaces from S_b and S_w [20]:

(a) The null space of S_b is denoted by null (S_b).

(b) The null space of S_w is denoted by null (S_w).

(c) The range space of S_b is denoted by span (S_b).

(d) The range space of S_w is denoted by span (S_w).

Based on these four subspaces, we can construct another four subspaces.

(e) Subspace A is defined as the intersection of span (S_b) and null (S_w).

(f) Subspace B is defined as the intersection of span (S_b) and span (S_w).

(g) Subspace C is defined as the intersection of null (S_b) and span (S_w).

(h) Subspace D is defined as the intersection of null (S_b) and null (S_w).

From Subspaces A, B, C, and D, we find that the objective function $J_2(w)$ of (4) satisfies the following equation:

$$J_2(w) = \begin{cases} 0 & w \in \text{Subspace } A \\ (0,1) & w \in \text{Subspace } B \\ 1 & w \in \text{Subspace } C \\ \dfrac{0}{0} & w \in \text{Subspace } D. \end{cases} \tag{5}$$

From (5), one can see that if w is taken from Subspace A, Subspace B, or Subspace C, the objective function $J_2(w)$ is bounded. If w belongs to Subspace D, the objective function $J_2(w)$ takes the indefinite value. It is of interest to note that the null space of S_t is the intersection of the null space of S_b and the null space of S_w. It has been proved that the null space of S_t does not contain any discriminant information [29]. Thus, Subspace D does not contain any discriminant information and this also shows that part of the null space of S_w does not contain discriminant information. Therefore, Subspace D can be removed without losing any information and this can be done by removing the null space of S_t. An effective method to remove the null space of S_t is to perform the singular value decomposition (SVD) [28] on H_t, denoted by $H_t = U_t \Sigma_t V_t^T$, where U_t consists of the left singular vectors corresponding to the nonzero singular values of H_t. In such a case, we do not lose any information of data. By doing so, we also remove part of the null space of S_w that does not contain discriminant information. Since we focus on (4), the range space of S_t must be considered. If the null space of S_t is removed, it is necessary to consider three subspaces in the case of (4): the null space of S_w, the range space of S_w, and the range space of S_t. For these three subspaces, we also give their relations with Subspace A, Subspace B, and Subspace C. It is not difficult to verify that the intersection of the null space of S_w and the range space of S_t is equivalent to Subspace A, and the intersection of the range space of S_w and the range space of S_t contains Subspaces B and C. This shows that we do not lose any discriminant information from Subspace A, Subspace B, and Subspace C if we solve (4). In such a case, we first remove the null space of S_t. That is, we consider the following optimization function in the case of the range space of S_t,

$$\min \quad J_3(a) = \min \left(\frac{a^T \bar{S}_w a}{a^T \bar{S}_t a} \right), \quad (6)$$

where $\bar{S}_t = U_t^T S_t U_t$, $\bar{S}_w = U_t^T S_w U_t$.

It is evident that $\bar{S}_t$ in (6) is nonsingular when the null space of S_t is removed. In such a case, we obtain the projection vectors which are composed of t eigenvectors of $\bar{S}_t^{-1} \bar{S}_w$ corresponding to t eigenvalues. From (6), we can see that $J_3(a)$ takes values in the interval of 0 and 1. In fact, the value $J_3(a)$ gives an indicator of choosing the effective subspace. According to the definition of the optimization criterion, we have the following conclusions: the subspace corresponding to $J_3(a) = 0$ is the most important; the subspace corresponding to $J_3(a) \in (0, 1)$ is the second important; the subspace corresponding to $J_3(a) = 1$ is the least important.

By solving the generalized eigenproblem, $\bar{S}_w a = \lambda \bar{S}_t a$, we can obtain $t (= \text{rank}(H_t))$ eigenvalues, which produces t eigenvectors. In some cases some of these t eigenvalues may be equal. In other words, some eigenvalues degenerate into the same eigenvalue, which may affect the performance of some algorithms. Assume that these t eigenvalues consist of d ($d \leq t = \text{rank}(S_t)$) different values λ_i ($i = 1, \ldots, d$) in an increasing order and have multiplicities s_i ($i = 1, \ldots, d$), where s_i denotes the algebraic multiplicities of the eigenvalue λ_i and $\sum_{i=1}^d s_i = t$. In some situations, it is useful to work with the set of all eigenvectors associated with a specific value λ_i. Let us define the following set:

$$S(\lambda_i) = \left\{ a : a \in R^t \text{ and } \bar{S}_w a = \lambda_i \bar{S}_t a \right\}. \quad (7)$$

The dimension of $S(\lambda_i)$ is in general equal to the algebraic multiplicities of λ_i since $\bar{S}_w$ and $\bar{S}_t$ are symmetric real matrices. The set $S(\lambda_i)$ forms the eigen-subspace of the matrix pairs $(\bar{S}_w, \bar{S}_t)$ corresponding to the generalized eigenvalue λ_i. When the dimension of $S(\lambda_i)$ is equal to 1, it is not necessary to deal with this subspace since it only contains an eigenvector. However, when the dimension of $S(\lambda_i)$ is bigger than 1, it is impossible to determine which eigenvector in this eigen-subspace is the most important since all the eigenvectors correspond to the same eigenvalue. The case often occurs in the small-sample-size problem where the dimension of the eigen-subspace of $S(\lambda_i = 0)$ is relatively high. In such a case, it is infeasible to determine which projection vector in the eigen-subspace of $S(\lambda_i = 0)$ is the most important if we only use (7). For some nonzero generalized eigenvalues from the matrix pair $(\bar{S}_w, \bar{S}_t)$, the dimension of $S(\lambda_i \neq 0)$ may be bigger than 1. For example,

$S(\lambda_i = 1)$ shows that the eigenvector is taken from the null space of $\bar{S}_b = \bar{S}_t - \bar{S}_w$. Generally speaking, the dimension of the null space $\bar{S}_b$ is bigger than 1 and this makes the dimension of $S(\lambda_i = 1)$ be bigger than 1. So it is necessary to use an additional strategy to determine the importance of eigenvectors if the dimension of $S(\lambda_i)$ is bigger than 1. For the subspace $S(\lambda_i)$, we can obtain a matrix whose columns consist of the eigenvectors of the generalized eigenvalue λ_i, denoted by P_{λ_i}. Obviously the dimension of $S(\lambda_i)$ is equal to the number of the columns of P_{λ_i}. If this matrix is provided, it is straightforward to obtain an orthogonal basis by performing the QR decomposition on P_{λ_i} and the orthogonal basis can be expressed in the matrix form: Q_{λ_i}. Note that the space spanned by the column vectors of P_{λ_i} is equivalent to the space spanned by the column vectors of Q_{λ_i}. Thus, in the space spanned by the column vectors of Q_{λ_i}, we formulate the following objective function based on the maximum margin criterion.

$$\max \quad J_4(g) = \max \left(g^T \hat{S}_b g - g^T \hat{S}_w g \right),$$
$$g^T g = 1, \quad (8)$$

where $\hat{S}_b = Q_{\lambda_i}^T U_t^T S_b U_t Q_{\lambda_i}$, $\hat{S}_w = Q_{\lambda_i}^T U_t^T S_w U_t Q_{\lambda_i}$.

When the dimension of the set $S(\lambda_i)$ is 1, it is easy to prove that $g = \pm 1$. When the dimension of the set $S(\lambda_i)$ is bigger than 1, it is necessary to obtain s_i eigenvectors of $\hat{S}_b - \hat{S}_w$ corresponding to s_i eigenvalues in a decreasing order. These s_i eigenvectors form the matrix $G_{\lambda_i} (= [g_1, \ldots, g_{s_i}])$. Thus, the discriminability of eigenvectors in the eigen-subspace of $S(\lambda_i)$ can be measured by the eigenvalues of $\hat{S}_b - \hat{S}_w$. This gives suggestions on how to choose effective discriminant vectors in the eigen-subspace $S(\lambda_i)$, which solves the degenerated case of eigenvalues. In classical LDA, the discriminability of eigenvectors in the eigen-subspace is sometimes neglected.

Note that, in the small-sample-size problem, the dimension of the eigen-subspace of $S(\lambda_i = 0)$ is relatively high. In such a case, we need to obtain this eigen-subspace. In fact, it is noted that the eigen-subspace $S(\lambda_i = 0)$ is the null space of $\bar{S}_w$ and obtaining the null space $\bar{S}_w$ may be time consuming when the dimension of the null space of $\bar{S}_w$ is high. Fortunately, several effective methods have been proposed to obtain the null space of $\bar{S}_w$. Çevikalp et al. [15] have proposed an effective algorithm to avoid computing the null space of $\bar{S}_w$ by finding the range space of $\bar{S}_w$. Note that the dimension of the range space of $\bar{S}_w$ is equal to the rank of the matrix $\bar{S}_w$. Based on the range space of $\bar{S}_w$, we can obtain common vectors for each class and construct the scatter matrix of the common vectors as done in [15]. Finally, the projection vectors can be obtained by performing eigen-decomposition on the scatter matrix of the common vectors.

As a summary of the above discussion, we list the detailed steps for solving linear discriminant analysis in Algorithm 4.

Algorithm 4. It is a stable and efficient algorithm for solving linear discriminant analysis.

Step 1. Construct H_w, H_b, and H_t, and compute the left singular matrix U_t of H_t by performing the SVD on $H_t = U_t \Sigma_t V_t^T$, where U_t consists of singular vectors corresponding to the nonzero singular values of H_t; obtain $\overline{H}_w = (U_t \Sigma_t^{-1})^T H_w$.

Step 2. Obtain the range space of $\overline{H}_w$, denoted by $\overline{U}_w$ whose column vectors are orthogonal; perform the SVD on $(\overline{U}_w)^T \overline{H}_w = U_w \Sigma_w V_w^T$ and assign σ_i in an increasing order from the diagonal elements of Σ_w.

Step 3. Let $Y = I_{t \times t} - \overline{U}_w \overline{U}_w^T$. If Y is not a zero matrix, perform Step 4; otherwise, go to Step 5.

Step 4. Based on Y, obtain the common vectors of each class, compute the scatter matrix of common vectors, and perform the eigen-decomposition on the scatter matrix of common vectors to obtain projection vectors, denoted by Q_0.

Step 5. For each nonzero σ_i, do the following.

Step 5(a). Obtain the singular submatrix U_{σ_i} by searching the column vectors of U_w corresponding to the singular value σ_i; let $P_{\sigma_i} = U_t \Sigma_t^{-1} U_{\sigma_i}$; apply the QR decomposition on P_{σ_i} to obtain the matrix Q_{σ_i} whose column vectors are orthogonal.

Step 5(b). Let $\widehat{S}_b = ((Q_{\sigma_i})^T H_b)(H_b^T Q_{\sigma_i})$ and $\widehat{S}_w = ((Q_{\sigma_i})^T H_w)(H_w^T Q_{\sigma_i})$; compute all discriminant vectors which are the eigenvectors of $\widehat{S}_b - \widehat{S}_w$; sort the eigenvectors according to the eigenvalues of $\widehat{S}_b - \widehat{S}_w$ in a decreasing order and form the matrix G_{σ_i}.

Step 6. Obtain the transformation matrix $T = [U_t Q_0, Q_{\sigma_1} G_{\sigma_1}, \ldots, Q_{\sigma_d} G_{\sigma_d}]$.

Note that, in Step 2 of Algorithm 4, we only need to obtain the range space of $\overline{H}_w$, that is, an orthonormal basis of $\overline{H}_w$. There are some effective methods for obtaining the range space of $\overline{H}_w$. For example, the range space of $\overline{H}_w$ can be achieved by finding the left singular matrix U_t of $\overline{H}_w$ corresponding to nonzero singular values. It is pointed out in [28] that computing left singular vectors of $\overline{H}_w$ corresponding to nonzero singular values is more efficient than finding left singular vectors of $\overline{H}_w$ corresponding to all singular values including zeros. In addition, one may resort to difference subspaces and the Gram-Schmidt orthogonalization procedure [15] to obtain the range space of $\overline{H}_w$. Note that, in Step 3 of Algorithm 4, we use a criterion to judge whether the null space of $\overline{H}_w \overline{H}_w^T$ exists. If $Y = I_{t \times t} - \overline{U}_w \overline{U}_w^T$ is not a zero matrix, this shows that there exists the null space of $\overline{H}_w \overline{H}_w^T$. In such a case, one may use the method (Step 4 of Algorithm 4) proposed in [15] to further deal with the null space of $\overline{H}_w \overline{H}_w^T$. It is observed from Algorithm 4 that we need to perform Step 5 of Algorithm 4 regardless of the existence of the null space of $\overline{H}_w \overline{H}_w^T$. In such a case, we can see that

TABLE 1: Statistics of the data sets we use.

Datasets	Number of samples	Number of dimensions	Number of classes
ORL	400	112 * 92	40
Yale	165	112 * 92	15
ALLAML	72	7129	2
Duke-Breast	42	7129	2
Colon	62	2000	2
Prostate	102	5966	2
Leukemia	72	7129	2
MLL	72	5848	3

$t (= s_1 + \cdots + s_d)$ eigenvectors can be ordered in terms of their importance. By performing Algorithm 4, we can evaluate the projection vectors from Subspace C which is often neglected in the previous literature. It is obvious that the above method can provide t discriminant vectors because the rank of H_t is t which is much bigger than $c - 1$. As a result, this method may be helpful when the number of classes is relatively small. Note that we use the eigenvalue λ_i in (7) and it is not difficult to verify that $\lambda_i = (\sigma_i)^2$. If the singular value σ_i occurs only once in the diagonal elements of Σ_w, we do not need to perform Step 5(b) in real applications.

4. Experiments Results

In our experiments, we use the ORL face database, the Yale face database, and microarray data sets to evaluate the performance of Algorithm 4. The ORL face database consists of 40 distinct persons, with each containing 10 different images with variations in poses, illumination, facial expressions, and facial details. The original face images are resized to 112×92 pixels with 256-level gray scales. The Yale face database contains 165 gray-scale images of 15 individuals. The images demonstrate variations in lighting condition and facial expressions. All of these face images are aligned based on eye coordinates and are resized to 112×92 pixels. Six microarray data sets including ALLMLL [30], Duke-Breast [31], Colon [32], Prostate [32], Leukemia [32], and MLL [32] are used to test the proposed method. Table 1 lists the statistics of the data sets we use. It is observed that the dimensions of features of samples on these data sets are much higher than the number of samples. The experiments are performed on a PC with the operating system of Windows 8.1, an i3 CPU (3.30 GHz) and an 8 G memory. The programming environment is MATLAB 2014a.

4.1. Face Recognition. In this set of experiments, the number of each individual in the training set varies from 2 to $\min\{n_1, \ldots, n_c\} - 1$, and the remaining images in the data set are used to form the testing set. To reduce the variations of the accuracies from randomness, the classification performance we report in the experiments is achieved over twenty runs. That is, there are twenty different training and testing sets used for evaluating the classification performance. We compare the proposed method with some

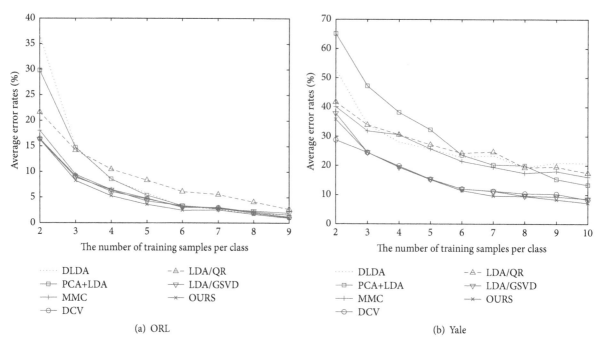

FIGURE 1: The error rates of each algorithm on two face databases.

TABLE 2: Performance comparisons (%) of some methods on face databases.

Databases	TS	DLDA	PCA+LDA	MMC	DCV	LDA/QR	LDA/GSVD	Ours
ORL	2	36.73 (4.05)	29.82 (3.08)	18.04 (2.35)	16.43 (1.95)	21.62 (3.08)	19.92 (2.08)	**16.32** (1.91)
	4	8.45 (1.45)	8.60 (1.83)	6.52 (1.60)	6.12 (1.95)	8.45 (1.45)	10.45 (1.72)	**5.31** (1.70)
	6	3.21 (1.31)	3.37 (1.62)	2.96 (1.31)	3.26 (1.14)	3.21 (1.31)	7.09 (1.34)	**2.50** (1.11)
	8	**1.75** (2.99)	2.00 (1.68)	2.18 (2.29)	2.00 (2.20)	**1.75** (2.29)	4.12 (1.76)	**1.75** (1.33)
Yale	2	52.88 (4.68)	65.14 (8.70)	40.07 (4.35)	**28.77** (15.25)	41.66 (5.23)	37.81 (4.45)	35.81 (3.85)
	4	28.09 (4.51)	38.23 (3.68)	30.61 (4.80)	19.85 (4.18)	30.61 (4.80)	**19.47** (4.02)	**19.47** (3.06)
	6	22.86 (4.07)	23.60 (5.24)	21.53 (4.56)	12.06 (3.76)	24.26 (6.08)	12.06 (3.87)	**11.53** (3.27)
	8	19.33 (4.45)	20.00 (5.67)	17.44 (6.29)	10.44 (3.80)	19.33 (4.45)	9.66 (3.61)	**9.55** (3.25)

previous methods including LDA/GSVD [7], LDA/QR [26], DLDA [12], PCA+LDA [1], MMC [13], and the discriminant common vector (DCV) approach [15] which is an effective approach for solving NLDA [14]. Note that these methods are designed to solve the small-sample-size problem when linear discriminant analysis is used. Subspace A or Subspace B are considered in LDA/QR, DLDA, PCA+LDA, and DCV. Although LDA/GSVD makes use of three subspaces (Subspace A, Subspace B, and Subspace C), the importance of projection vectors in some eigen-subspaces is not effectively measured in some cases. In this paper we do not compare other discriminant methods since the main objective of paper is to provide a stable and efficient algorithm for solving the degenerated eigenvalue of LDA. Note that we do not give the running time of algorithms we test since some methods only make use of part of subspaces in (5). Generally speaking, the performance of each algorithm varies with the change of the dimension of features. For comparisons, we try to search for the performance on all the feature dimensions and list the best one.

Figure 1 shows the error rate of each method we test with different training images in each class on the ORL and Yale face databases. For clarity, we also show the mean and standard deviation in the parentheses of the error rates of each method in Table 2. Note that the best performance of each method in each line is highlighted in bold and we show the results of 2, 4, 6, and 8 training images per class.

From Figure 1 and Table 2, one can see that the error rate of each algorithm decreases as the number of the training samples in each class increases in most cases. It is observed from Table 2 that the standard deviation of our method is smaller than that of the other methods in most cases. On the ORL face database, the error rate of our method decreases from 16.32% with 2 training samples per class to 1% with 9 training samples per class, while the error rates of DLDA, PCA+LDA, MMC, DCV, LDA/QR, and LDA/GSVD decrease from 36.73%, 29.82%, 18.04%, 16.43%, 21.62%, and 19.92% with 2 training samples per class to 1.75%, 1.25%, 1.625%, 1.125%, 2.75%, and 3% with 9 training samples per class, respectively. The results show that our method outperforms

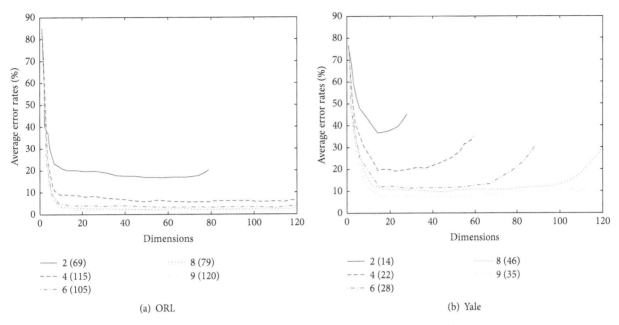

(a) ORL

(b) Yale

FIGURE 2: The error rate of the proposed method with the change of features.

other methods in most cases. On the Yale face database, although the DCV method gives the best result in the case of 2 training samples per class, it obtains the biggest standard deviation. It is also observed that our method is superior to other methods in terms of the classification performance with the increase of training samples.

Since the number of the extracted features of samples by using the proposed method is not limited by the number of classes and only limited by the rank of S_t, we can project the samples onto the space whose dimension is greater than the number of classes. Figure 2 shows a plot of the error rate versus dimensionality. The numbers in the parentheses denote the optimal dimension corresponding to the best classification performance. As can be seen from Figure 2, the error rate of the proposed method decreases with the increase of training samples per class. It is also found from Figure 2 that the classification performance may be improved when the dimension of the reduced space is bigger than the number of classes. On the Yale face database, it is observed that the error rate of the proposed method first decreases and then rises with the increase of dimensions, which shows that choosing too many features yields the overfitting phenomenon in the classification task. On the ORL face database, the error rate of the proposed method first decreases drastically and then becomes flat when the number of training samples is bigger than 2. It is found that the best performance of our method is achieved when the number of extracted features is much bigger than the number of classes. In short, these experimental results show that Subspace C which is often neglected in classical LDA in (5) may play a role in face recognition in some cases.

Now let us explain the reason why our method can achieve the good classification performance. The DLDA and LDA/QR methods first remove the null space of S_b. However, removing the null space of S_b will also lose part of the

null space of S_w and may result in the loss of important information in the null space of S_w. The PCA+LDA method does not consider the null space of S_w. It has been proved that the null space of S_w will play an important role in the SSS problem [14]. The DCV method does not make use of subspace B in (5) and this subspace may be helpful in obtaining discriminant vectors in the SSS problem. Although the LDA/GSVD method considers three subspaces, the discriminability of each eigen-subspace is not analyzed. In the MMC method, the discriminant vectors in Subspace A and Subspace B in (5) may have the same objective function. This results in the difficulty in determining which discriminant vector is the most important. In fact, Subspace C in (5) is often neglected in LDA-based methods in the previous literature. We give a strategy to measure the importance of each discriminant vector in all subspaces including Subspace C for the first time. As can be seen from Figure 2, Subspace C also plays a role in face recognition. As a result, the proposed method can achieve better classification performance than other methods in the general case.

In the following experiments, we study the effect of image sizes on the classification performance in terms of two face databases. Since the number of face images on these two face databases is relatively small, the leave-one-out method is performed where it takes one image for testing and the remaining images for training. By reducing the image resolution of $112 * 92$ pixels, we can obtain $56 * 46$ pixels where each pixel value is the average value of a $2 * 2$ subimage of the original images. Similarly, we can achieve the images with $28 * 23$ pixels. In such cases, there exists the null space of the within-class scatter matrix. Table 3 shows the experimental results of each method in three resolutions on two face databases.

As can be seen from Table 3, the error rate of each method does not always increase with the reduction of image

TABLE 3: Comparisons of misclassification rates (%) of several methods on face databases.

Databases	Training size	DLDA	PCA+LDA	MMC	DCV	LDA/QR	LDA/GSVD	Ours
ORL	112 * 92	2.25 (1.68)	2.50 (2.68)	2.50 (1.66)	**1.50** (1.74)	3.25 (2.68)	2.50 (2.04)	2.25 (1.84)
	56 * 46	2.00 (2.58)	2.00 (2.83)	2.50 (2.83)	2.00 (2.58)	3.00 (2.35)	2.75 (3.40)	**1.25** (1.31)
	28 * 23	**2.00** (2.29)	4.75 (2.94)	**2.00** (2.58)	5.25 (4.31)	3.75 (2.58)	6.25 (4.75)	**2.00** (2.37)
Yale	112 * 92	21.00 (10.24)	16.36 (8.62)	11.51 (6.72)	12.12 (8.33)	20.60 (9.16)	12.12 (9.34)	**9.09** (6.22)
	56 * 46	20.00 (6.66)	15.15 (7.93)	27.27 (10.21)	10.90 (8.85)	21.21 (8.85)	10.90 (5.39)	**7.87** (5.19)
	28 * 23	19.39 (10.93)	12.72 (8.66)	14.54 (9.34)	9.09 (9.07)	20.00 (11.15)	9.09 (9.07)	**8.48** (9.02)

TABLE 4: Error rates (%) of each method on microarray data sets.

Datasets	DLDA	PCA+LDA	MMC	DCV	LDA/QR	LDA/GSVD	Ours
ALLMLL	4.27 (3.50)	5.00 (4.27)	4.11 (4.32)	3.99 (4.01)	4.32 (5.05)	4.01 (4.72)	**3.78 (3.23)**
Duke-Breast	14.32 (9.15)	12.67 (8.96)	11.98 (7.69)	12.05 (8.99)	13.03 (9.45)	11.88 (8.22)	**11.56 (8.03)**
Colon	31.11 (18.28)	22.78 (19.24)	23.33 (19.56)	23.33 (19.56)	31.11 (18.92)	23.33 (19.56)	**20.00 (17.21)**
Prostate	6.88 (6.32)	6.94 (7.51)	6.74 (8.02)	6.63 (7.03)	7.88 (6.23)	6.55 (6.21)	**6.32 (5.99)**
Leukemia	12.85 (17.10)	16.28 (17.10)	2.85 (6.02)	2.85 (6.02)	12.95 (6.02)	2.85 (6.20)	**1.42 (4.51)**
MLL	9.88 (5.52)	13.93 (6.02)	9.52 (5.09)	9.34 (5.85)	10.93 (5.42)	9.62 (5.45)	**9.01 (5.01)**

resolutions. On the ORL face database, the DCV method obtains the best classification result on the resolution of 112 * 92 pixels. With the reduction of image resolutions, the performance of NLDA becomes worse since the dimension of the null space of S_w becomes smaller. On the ORL face database, the proposed method is better than LDA/GSVD and has a smaller standard deviation than other methods in most cases. The main reason is that we consider the degenerated case of the eigenvalue. It is noted that our method achieves the best classification result when the resolution of images is 56 * 46 pixels. On the Yale face database, the proposed method outperforms other methods in terms of the classification performance. It is also observed that the best recognition rate among all methods is 92.13% and is achieved by the proposed method when the images are 56 * 46 pixels on the Yale face database. From these experiments, we can also notice that it is not necessary to use the large-size images to obtain good classification performance in the classification task.

4.2. Applications to Microarray Data Sets. In this set of experiments, we further validate the proposed method on microarray data sets. In order to evaluate the classification performance of various LDA methods, we adopt the tenfold cross validation on these data sets. In other words, we divide each data set into ten subsets of approximately equal sizes. Then we perform training and testing ten times, each time leaving out one of the subsets for training and the discarded subset for testing. The classification performance is averaged over ten runs. Table 4 shows the mean and the standard deviation of the error rate of each method.

As can be seen from Table 4, the classification performance of the proposed method is consistently superior to that of other methods on all the data sets we tested. It is found that our method is more stable than other methods since the standard deviation of our method is smaller than that of other methods on all of data sets we tested. It is noted that PCA+LDA performs poorly on Leukemia and

MLL data sets. This may come from the fact that the null space of the within-class scatter matrix is removed and it plays an important role in obtaining discriminant feature vectors. It is also found that DLDA does not give satisfactory results on Duke-Breast and Colon data sets since DLDA may remove the part of the null space of the within-class scatter matrix. One can see from Table 4 that the NLDA method achieves good classification accuracies on these data sets since these data sets are the small-sample-size sets. One can also observe that the LDA/QR method does not perform well on some data sets. This may be explained by the fact that the LDA/QR method may remove part of the range space of S_w and part of the null space of S_b. It is found that LDA/GSVD is not better than our method although LDA/GSVD considers three subspaces. This is possibly because in LDA/GSVD the discriminability of each eigen-subspace is not given. Because the discriminant vectors in Subspace A and Subspace B in the MMC method may correspond to the same objective function, this may lead to the degradation in MMC. Overall, the proposed method is very stable on these data sets due to the fact that we consider the degenerated eigenvalues of scatter matrices, especially for Subspace C which is neglected in previous literature.

5. Conclusions

In this paper, we revisit linear discriminant analysis based on an optimization criterion. Different from the existing LDA-based algorithms, the new algorithm adopts the spirit of the maximum margin criterion (MMC) and applies MMC to the eigen-subspace when the eigenvalue is degenerative. The new implementation avoids the singularity problem in the SSS problem and provides more than $c - 1$ discriminant vectors. We also conduct a series of comparative studies on face images and microarray data sets to evaluate the proposed method. Our experiments on face images and microarray data sets demonstrate that the classification performance achieved by our method is better than that of other LDA-based algorithms in most cases and the proposed method is an effective and stable linear discriminant method for dealing with high-dimensional data.

Competing Interests

The authors declare that they have no competing interests.

Acknowledgments

This work was partially supported by the Fundamental Research Funds for the Central Universities (2015XKMS084).

References

[1] P. N. Belhumeur, J. P. Hespanha, and D. J. Kriegman, "Eigenfaces vs. fisherfaces: recognition using class specific linear projection," *IEEE Transactions on Pattern Analysis and Machine Intelligence*, vol. 19, no. 7, pp. 711–720, 1997.

[2] X. Jin, M. Zhao, T. W. S. Chow, and M. Pecht, "Motor bearing fault diagnosis using trace ratio linear discriminant analysis," *IEEE Transactions on Industrial Electronics*, vol. 61, no. 5, pp. 2441–2451, 2014.

[3] M. Kolar and H. Liu, "Optimal feature selection in high-dimensional discriminant analysis," *IEEE Transactions on Information Theory*, vol. 61, no. 2, pp. 1063–1083, 2015.

[4] J.-H. Xue and P. Hall, "Why does rebalancing class-unbalanced data improve AUC for linear discriminant analysis?" *IEEE Transactions on Pattern Analysis and Machine Intelligence*, vol. 37, no. 5, pp. 1109–1112, 2015.

[5] C. Hou, C. Zhang, Y. Wu, and Y. Jiao, "Stable local dimensionality reduction approaches," *Pattern Recognition*, vol. 42, no. 9, pp. 2054–2066, 2009.

[6] Y. Zhang and D.-Y. Yeung, "Semisupervised generalized discriminant analysis," *IEEE Transactions on Neural Networks*, vol. 22, no. 8, pp. 1207–1217, 2011.

[7] P. Howland and H. Park, "Generalizing discriminant analysis using the generalized singular value decomposition," *IEEE Transactions on Pattern Analysis and Machine Intelligence*, vol. 26, no. 8, pp. 995–1006, 2004.

[8] W. Bian and D. Tao, "Asymptotic generalization bound of fisher's linear discriminant analysis," *IEEE Transactions on Pattern Analysis and Machine Intelligence*, vol. 36, no. 12, pp. 2325–2337, 2014.

[9] D. Chu, L.-Z. Liao, M. K. Ng, and X. Wang, "Incremental linear discriminant analysis: a fast algorithm and comparisons," *IEEE Transactions on Neural Networks and Learning Systems*, vol. 26, no. 11, pp. 2716–2735, 2015.

[10] J. Zhao, L. Shi, and J. Zhu, "Two-stage regularized linear discriminant analysis for 2-D data," *IEEE Transactions on Neural Networks and Learning Systems*, vol. 26, no. 8, pp. 1669–1681, 2015.

[11] A. Sharma and K. K. Paliwal, "Linear discriminant analysis for the small sample size problem: an overview," *International Journal of Machine Learning and Cybernetics*, vol. 6, no. 3, pp. 443–454, 2015.

[12] H. Yu and J. Yang, "A direct LDA algorithm for high-dimensional data—with application to face recognition," *Pattern Recognition*, vol. 34, no. 10, pp. 2067–2070, 2001.

[13] H. Li, T. Jiang, and K. Zhang, "Efficient and robust feature extraction by maximum margin criterion," *IEEE Transactions on Neural Networks*, vol. 17, no. 1, pp. 157–165, 2006.

[14] L.-F. Chen, H.-Y. M. Liao, M.-T. Ko, J.-C. Lin, and G.-J. Yu, "New LDA-based face recognition system which can solve the small sample size problem," *Pattern Recognition*, vol. 33, no. 10, pp. 1713–1726, 2000.

[15] H. Çevikalp, M. Neamtu, M. Wilkes, and A. Barkana, "Discriminative common vectors for face recognition," *IEEE Transactions on Pattern Analysis and Machine Intelligence*, vol. 27, no. 1, pp. 4–13, 2005.

[16] D. Chu and G. S. Thye, "A new and fast implementation for null space based linear discriminant analysis," *Pattern Recognition*, vol. 43, no. 4, pp. 1373–1379, 2010.

[17] A. Sharma and K. K. Paliwal, "A new perspective to null linear discriminant analysis method and its fast implementation using random matrix multiplication with scatter matrices," *Pattern Recognition*, vol. 45, no. 6, pp. 2205–2213, 2012.

[18] K. K. Paliwal and A. Sharma, "Improved pseudoinverse linear discriminant analysis method for dimensionality reduction," *International Journal of Pattern Recognition and Artificial Intelligence*, vol. 26, no. 1, Article ID 1250002, 9 pages, 2012.

[19] A. Sharma, K. K. Paliwal, S. Imoto, and S. Miyano, "A feature selection method using improved regularized linear discriminant analysis," *Machine Vision and Applications*, vol. 25, no. 3, pp. 775–786, 2014.

[20] A. Sharma and K. K. Paliwal, "A deterministic approach to regularized linear discriminant analysis," *Neurocomputing*, vol. 151, no. 1, pp. 207–214, 2015.

[21] H. Huang, J. Liu, H. Feng, and T. He, "Ear recognition based on uncorrelated local Fisher discriminant analysis," *Neurocomputing*, vol. 74, no. 17, pp. 3103–3113, 2011.

[22] T. Zhou and D. Tao, "Double shrinking sparse dimension reduction," *IEEE Transactions on Image Processing*, vol. 22, no. 1, pp. 244–257, 2013.

[23] H. Li, C. Shen, A. van den Hengel, and Q. Shi, "Worst case linear discriminant analysis as scalable semidefinite feasibility problems," *IEEE Transactions on Image Processing*, vol. 24, no. 8, pp. 2382–2392, 2015.

[24] A. Zollanvari and E. R. Dougherty, "Generalized consistent error estimator of linear discriminant analysis," *IEEE Transactions on Signal Processing*, vol. 63, no. 11, pp. 2804–2814, 2015.

[25] L. Lu and S. Renals, "Probabilistic linear discriminant analysis for acoustic modeling," *IEEE Signal Processing Letters*, vol. 21, no. 6, pp. 702–706, 2014.

[26] J. Ye and Q. Li, "A two-stage linear discriminant analysis via QR-decomposition," *IEEE Transactions on Pattern Analysis and Machine Intelligence*, vol. 27, no. 6, pp. 929–941, 2005.

[27] K. Fukunaga, *Introduction to Statistical Pattern Recognition*, Academic Press, New York, NY, USA, 2nd edition, 1990.

[28] G. H. Folub and C. F. Van Loan, *Matrix Computation*, The Johns Hopkins University Press, Baltimore, Md, USA, 1996.

[29] R. Huang, Q. Liu, H. Lu et al., "Solving the small sample size problem of LDA," in *Proceedings of the 16th International Conference on Pattern Recognition (ICPR '02)*, IEEE Computer Society, August 2002.

[30] S. A. Armstorng, J. E. Staunton, L. B. Silverman et al., "MLL translocation specify a district gene expression profile at distinguishes a unique leukemia," *Nature Genetics*, vol. 30, no. 1, pp. 41–47, 2002.

5

User Adaptive and Context-Aware Smart Home using Pervasive and Semantic Technologies

Aggeliki Vlachostergiou,[1] Georgios Stratogiannis,[1] George Caridakis,[1,2]
George Siolas,[1] and Phivos Mylonas[1,3]

[1] *Intelligent Systems Content and Interaction Laboratory, National Technical University of Athens, Iroon Polytexneiou 9,*
15780 Zografou, Greece
[2] *Department of Cultural Technology and Communication, University of the Aegean, Mytilene, Lesvos, Greece*
[3] *Department of Informatics, Ionian University, Corfu, Greece*

Correspondence should be addressed to Aggeliki Vlachostergiou; aggelikivl@image.ntua.gr

Academic Editor: John N. Sahalos

Ubiquitous Computing is moving the interaction away from the human-computer paradigm and towards the creation of smart environments that users and things, from the IoT perspective, interact with. User modeling and adaptation is consistently present having the human user as a constant but pervasive interaction introduces the need for context incorporation towards context-aware smart environments. The current article discusses both aspects of the user modeling and adaptation as well as context awareness and incorporation into the smart home domain. Users are modeled as fuzzy personas and these models are semantically related. Context information is collected via sensors and corresponds to various aspects of the pervasive interaction such as temperature and humidity, but also smart city sensors and services. This context information enhances the smart home environment via the incorporation of user defined home rules. Semantic Web technologies support the knowledge representation of this ecosystem while the overall architecture has been experimentally verified using input from the SmartSantander smart city and applying it to the SandS smart home within FIRE and FIWARE frameworks.

1. Introduction

Although in their initial definition and development stages pervasive computing practices did not necessarily rely on the use of the Internet, current trends show the emergence of many convergence points with the Internet of Things (IoT) paradigm, where objects are identified as Internet resources and can be accessed and utilized as such. In the same time, the Human-Computer Interaction (HCI) paradigm in the domain of domotics has widened its scope considerably, placing the human inhabitant in a pervasive environment and in a continuous interaction with smart objects and appliances. Smart homes that additionally adhere to the IoT approach consider that this data continuously produced by appliances, sensors, and humans can be processed and assessed collaboratively, remotely, and even socially. In the present paper, we try to build a new knowledge representation framework where we first place the human user in the center

of this interaction. We then propose to break down the multitude of possible user behaviors to a few prototypical user models and then to resynthesize them using fuzzy reasoning. Then, we discuss the ubiquity of context information in relation to the user and the difficulty of proposing a universal formalization framework for the open world. We show that, by restricting user-related context to the smart home environment, we can reliably define simple rule structures that correlate specific sensor input data and user actions that can be used to trigger arbitrary smart home events. This rationale is then evolved to a higher level semantic representation of the domotic ecosystem in which complex home rules can be defined using Semantic Web technologies.

It is thus observed that a smart home using pervasive and semantic technologies in which the human user is in the center of the interaction has to be adaptive (its behavior can change in response to a person's actions and environment) and personalized (its behavior can be tailored to the user's needs and expressed using more advanced and complex home rules). In the case of smart homes, the user's acceptance has become one of the key factors to determine the success of the system. If the home system aims to be universally usable, it will have to accommodate a diverse set of users [1] and adjust to fulfill their needs in case they change. With the aim of helping practitioners to improve their user modeling techniques, some researchers have established rules to follow, for example, the set of user modeling guidelines for adaptive interfaces created by [2]. A context-sensitive smart home should reckon dynamically to accommodate the needs of users, taking into account a wide range of users and context or behavior situations. This user-centric functioning of smart home systems has to be supported by an adequate user model. The intelligence and interface of the system have to be aware of the user abilities and limitations to interact with the person properly. The user model must include information about the person's cognitive level and sensorial and physical disabilities.

To be more precise, a user model [3] is a computational representation of the information existent in a user's cognitive system, along with the processes acting on this information to produce an observable behavior. User stereotype or persona is a quite common approach in UM due to its correlation with the actors and roles used in software engineering systems and its flexibility, extensibility, reusability, and applicability [4]. The "personas" concept was originally introduced by Cooper in [5], where, according to his definition, "personas are not real people, but they represent them throughout the design process. They are hypothetical archetypes of actual users." There are two different types of personas: primary personas, which represent the main target group, and secondary personas, which can use the primary personas' interfaces but have specific additional requirements [6, 7]. Even though personas are fictional characters, they need to be created with rigor and precision; they tell stories about potential users in ways that allow designers to understand them and what they really want. Characteristics like name, age, profession, or any other relevant information are given to each persona in order to make them look more realistic or "alive." The most accurate way of creating personas, also known as "cast of characters," is to go through a phase of observation of real users within the environment in which the system will exist and eventually interview them with the intention of finding a common set of motivations, behaviors, and goals among the end-users. However, this method is expensive and time-consuming. A low-cost approach is to create them based on Norman's assumption personas [8] where designers use their own experience to identify the different user groups. Thus, in the same way, in our work, the personas technique fulfills the need of mapping and grouping a huge number of users based on the profile data, aims, and behavior which can be collected during both design time and run time and users and usage design, respectively.

Recently, the emergence of ubiquitous or pervasive computing technologies that offer "anytime, anywhere, anyone" computing by decoupling users from devices has introduced the challenge of context-aware user modeling. So far, most of the context-aware systems focus on the external context known as physical context which refers to context data collected by physical sensors. Thus, they involve context data of physical environment, distance, temperature, sound, air pressure, lighting levels, and so forth. The external context is important and very useful for context-aware systems, as context-aware systems provide recommended services. However, from a broader scope, context may be considered as information used to characterize the situation of an entity [9]. An entity is a person, place, or object that is considered relevant to the interaction between a user and an application, including location, time, activities, and the preferences of each entity. A user model is context-aware if it can express aspects of the user's contextual information and subsequently help the system adapt its functionality to the context of use. Many aspects of contextual information used in modeling are discussed in [10, 11]. Nevertheless, to provide personalized services to user models according to user preferences, task, and emotional state of user, the cognitive domains such as situational monitoring are needed; so far, a few authors have addressed utilizing the cognitive elements of a user's context and the semantics of the relations between the user and the system's entities. Several researchers have proposed models to capture the internal elements of context. Our proposed model differs from many of the previous approaches, as it focuses on extracting a user's cognitive activities, rather than extracting the user's movement based on physical environment. Cognitive context information given through a semantic formalization idea is key information to satisfy users by providing personalized context-aware computing services.

The semantic formalization idea is to provide a functional ontological and reasoning platform that offers unified data access, processing, and services on top of the existing IoT-A ubiquitous services and to integrate heterogeneous home sensors and actuators in a uniform way. From an application perspective, a set of basic services encapsulates sensor and actuators network infrastructures hiding the underlying layers with the network communication details and heterogeneous sensor hardware and lower-level protocols. A heterogeneous networking environment indeed calls for means to hide the complexity from the end-user as well as applications by providing intelligent and adaptable connectivity services, thus providing an efficient application development framework. Thus, to face the coexistence of many heterogeneous sets of things and home appliances, a common trend in IoT applications is the adoption of an abstraction layer capable of harmonizing the access to the different devices with a common language and procedure [12]. Our approach is to further encapsulate this abstraction layer into "if then that" rule sets and then to OWL ontologies that combined with home rules defined in Semantic Web Rule Language (SWRL) form the domotic intelligence that continuously adapts home environment conditions to the user's actions and preferences.

The scope of most of the applications or services with respect to smart homes so far has focused on the concept of small regions like laboratory, school, hospital, smart room, and so forth. Furthermore, algorithmic and strategic models for gaining the revenue by using context-aware systems are very few. Additionally, technologies related to context-aware systems are merely standardized. The architecture, the context modeling method, the algorithm, and the network implementation as well as the devices of users in each project are different. Moreover, middleware, applications, and services make use of different level of contexts and adapt the way they behave based on the current context. Therefore, according to the level and type of contexts along with the goal of context-aware systems, the context modeling process, the inference algorithm, and interaction method of personas (humans known as personas for computational representation purposes) are changed. Although the interaction between personas and cooperation between components of the same architecture have been investigated, standard interaction, cooperation, and operation in the different context-aware systems have not been studied. Thus, the novelty of our proposed approach is to provide a common context-aware architecture system in which the user ("eahouker" in SandS) is able to control his household appliances in a collective way via the SNS (Social Network Service) and in an intelligent way via the adaptive social network intelligence. As our system is human-centered, the UM (user modeling) is related to the user's activity inside the ESN (Eahoukers Social Network), while the context-aware environment refers to the contextual information that characterizes the situation and conditions of the system's entities.

Finally, the modeling of the contextual information is completed through the capture of the semantics of the relationships between the user and the various entities of the ecosystem (other users, appliances, and recipes) to further improve the overall user experience. The semantic description framework of our proposed approach is based on a number of home rules that are defined for a specific household and eahouker. Since the SandS architecture consists of two layers, high and low, respectively, we have on the one hand recipes for common household tasks produced and exchanged in the SandS Social Network that are described in near-natural language. Additionally, on the other hand, we have every user's context which consists of the actual appliances that the user has in house with their particular characteristics (type, model, brand, etc.). Finally, to ensure the executability and compatibility of a recipe and to deal as well with any uncertainty and vagueness in modeling the contextual information, a number of some axioms, to enforce constraints to all objects (things in IoT paradigm) of the ecosystem, have been introduced in the proposed Web Ontology Language (OWL) that was adopted. To conclude, the experimental results for the above framework are presented which have been conducted inside the "Social & Smart" (SandS) [13] FP7 European Project which aims to highlight the potential of IoT technologies in a concrete user-centric domestic pervasive environment. Large-scale experiments are planned at SmartSantander [14], a city-scale experimental research facility in support of typical applications and services for a smart city, comprising a very large number of online ambient sensors inside a real-life human environment.

2. User Modeling

2.1. Related Work. As correctly stated in [15], user modeling is the process through which systems gather information and knowledge about users and their individual characteristics. Therefore, a user model is considered a source of information about the user of the system which contains several assumptions about several relevant behavior or adaptation data. Approaching user modeling from the HCI perspective, there is the potential that user modeling techniques will improve the collaborative nature of human-computer systems. During the last 20 years, there has been a lot of work done in this area. Authors attempted to cover all possible scenarios through the development of different definition for users and user modeling approaches, respectively.

Reviewing how "user models" term has been approached, within the HCI literature, it is indicated that users are part of an enlarged communication group in which users change through time and according to the environmental conditions and the experience they gain. Thus, in the end, there are three types of users: "novel," "intermediate," and "expert" [15]. Another more oriented work is that of [16], as it focuses on the specific group of elderly people with none, one, or more than one disability, whose needs and capabilities change as they grow older, underlying the need for having more diverse and dynamic computing systems for modeling users. A few years later, in terms of maintaining rich and adaptive output information, ontology-based approaches have been used for the design of the Ec(h)o audio reality system for museums to further support experience design and functionality related to museum visits, through user models. This work has been later extended [17] by incorporating rich contextual information such as social, cultural, historical, and psychological factors related to the user experience.

Within the area of multimedia content, the work presented in [18] is the first to introduce a triple layered sensation-perception-emotion user model to evaluate the experience in a video scenario. In this work, low-level characteristics such as light variation are combined with the knowing and learning cognition process and emotions for entertainment product designs. In a similar way, in [19], the authors consider four crucial parameters for the interaction between people and technology: the user, the product, the contextual environment, and the tasks to specify the interaction process.

Based on ontology approaches to characterize users capabilities within adaptive environments, in 2007, the GUMO ontology has been proposed [20] which takes into account the emotional state, the personality, the physiological state of the user, and particularly stress. Five years later, Evers and his colleagues [21] implemented an automatic and self-sufficient adaptation interface to measure the user's stress levels. Finally, in 2004, the research in user modeling has started to shift from focusing not on users capabilities but on users' needs. This work has incorporated the "persona" concept [22], which has been introduced to distinguish between different user groups within an adaptive user interface domain. These "persona" concepts have been proved really useful as a wide range of potential users could be covered by assigning random values to characteristics like age, education, profession, family conditions, and so forth. It is thus observed that, from product design to multimedia and user interfaces adaptation, the approaches described above, even though the collected personal data characteristics to improve the system and user's satisfaction and product or service usability differ a lot, share the same goal. For a more extended review, the reader is directed to [23].

Typically, a user model represents a collection of personal data associated with a specific user of a system. Following a similar definition, a user model [3] is a computational representation of the information existent in a user's cognitive system, along with the processes acting on this information to produce an observable behavior. Thus, the act of user modeling identifies the users of the application and their goals for interacting with the application. As a result, a user model is considered to be the foundation of any adaptive changes to the system's behavior. The main question to answer when dealing with this kind of information is which data is included in the model; as it is expected, the type of data used depends on the purpose of each application and the domain where the latter is applied. A user model can in principle include personal information, such as users' names and ages, their interests, their skills and knowledge, their goals and plans, their preferences, and their dislikes or data about their behavior and their interactions with the system.

As one may expect, there are also different design patterns for user models, though often a mixture of them is used [24]. In an attempt to describe a system's users in the most relevant way, one may start from the humble "actor," which provides a common name for a user type. In use case modeling, actors are people who interact with the system and they are often described using job titles or a common name for the type of user. On the other hand, a "role" names a relationship between a user type and a process or a software tool. A user role generally refers to a user's responsibility when using an application or participating in a business process. To help us understand the characteristics of our users that might have bearing on our design, we may then construct a "profile," containing information about the type of user relevant to the application being created. Still, user profiles contain general characteristics about the groups of users. User stereotype or "persona" is a quite common approach in UM due to its correlation with the actors and roles used in software engineering systems and its flexibility, extensibility, reusability, and applicability [4].

A persona is an archetypal user that is derived from specific profile data to create a representative user containing general characteristics about the users and user groups and is used as a powerful complement to other usability methods, whereas it is more tangible, less ambiguous, easier to envision, and easier to empathize with. The use of personas is an increasingly popular way to customize, incorporate, and share the research about users [25]. The personas technique fulfills the need of mapping and grouping a huge number of users based on the profile data, aims, and behavior which can be collected during both design and run time and users and usage design, respectively.

Personas development supports the design process by identifying and prioritizing the roles and user characteristics of a system's key audience. In the general case, personas development is initiated by introducing assumptions about user profiles, based on data from initial research steps conducted. Through interviews and observation, researchers expand and validate the profiles by identifying goals, motivations, contextual influences, and typical user stories for each profile. Having such a fictional person (persona) representing a profile grounds the design effort in so-called "real users." For each persona, the user modeling description typically includes key attributes and user characteristics, such as name, age, and information that distinguishes each persona from others.

2.2. Basic Characteristics. The herein proposed approach for modeling user information following a personas-based inspiration is discussed within this subsection. More specifically, according to the notation followed within our system, the so-called "eahouker profile" (E_p) is a set of properties of the system's users ("eahoukers," e) that can be exploited for determining eahoukers with similar characteristics. These properties are stored in a database, that is, the Eahoukers Social Network's Database (EDB), and are continuously updated. The profile contents are rather static in the sense that the information is present in the database when the eahouker joins the SandS system and seldom changes in everyday activities. The interested reader should at this point note that a quasistatic approach would have been more accurate, since a number of user attributes, like, for instance, a user's marital status and the number of children she/he may have, can change over time. Basic information about the user is also included in the profile and consists of gender, age, number of children, social status, and his/her house appliances and geographical position.

In a more formal manner, the profile of an eahouker e, denoted by E_p, contains the following information about the user: $E_p \in$ {gender, age, children, city, houseRole, socialStatus}, where gender $\in$ {male, female} is the gender of e, age $\in N$ is the age of e, children $\in N$ denote the number of children of e, city is a string describing the city of e, houseRole $\in$ {owner, junior, senior} is the house role of e, and socialStatus $\in$ {single, married, young} corresponds to the marital status of e. Considering the above user profile definition at hand, the semantic description framework of the eahoukers can be directly interfaced and queried, but more importantly it enables us to define a personas-based user similarity measure. The latter is considered to outperform a traditional rating-based user similarity measure and is described in the following.

As a last point to consider and in order to further illustrate the herein proposed approach, we provide an example of a typical eahouker persona: the Papadopoulos family composed of four family members, namely, the parents, John and Maria, and their children, Nikos and Ioanna. Their household is located in Athens, Greece, and it contains five smart household appliances:

(1) A Samsung 55″ TV set, model UN55F6300

(2) An AEG washing machine, model AEG L60260

(3) A Nescafe coffee machine, model KP1006

(4) An LG refrigerator, model LFX31995ST

(5) A GE bread maker, model GE106732

Potential users are of course {John, Maria, Nikos, Ioanna}; however, as rather obvious, Nikos and Ioanna are not allowed to interact directly with the above devices apart from the TV. Following the above notation, their profiles are modeled as follows:

(i) $John_p$ = ⟨male, 37, 2, athens, owner, married, UN55F6300, AEGL60260, KP1006, LFX31995ST, GE106732⟩

(ii) $Maria_p$ = ⟨female, 36, 2, athens, owner, married, UN55F6300, AEGL60260, KP1006, LFX31995ST, GE106732⟩

(iii) $Nikos_p$ = ⟨male, 4, 0, athens, young, single, UN55F6300⟩

(iv) $Ioanna_p$ = ⟨female, 1, 0, athens, young, single, UN55F6300⟩

2.3. Fuzzification. Let us consider a set of eahoukers $\mathscr{E}$ that interact with information objects and a set M of *meanings* that can be found or referred to in items. Within our approach, M is described as a set of semantic entities that the eahouker has interest in to varying degrees. This interpretation provides fairly precise, expressive, and unified representational grounding, in which both user interests and content meaning are represented in the same space, in which they can be conveniently compared [26].

In addition, the use of ontologies for capturing knowledge from a domain of interest has grown significantly lately; thus, we also consider a domain ontology $\mathcal{O}$ herein. According to one of the core ideas of the Semantic Web, that is, that of sharing, linking, and reusing data from multiple sources, the availability of semantically described data sources and thus the uptake of Semantic Web technologies is important to applications in which rich domain descriptions can play a significant role. Still, considering the inherent complexity of a decent knowledge representation formalism (e.g., Web Ontology Language (OWL) [27]), convincing domain experts and thus potential ontology authors of the usefulness and benefits of using ontologies is one of the major barriers to broader ontology adoption [28].

Efficient user model representation formalism using ontologies [29, 30] presents a number of advantages. In the context of this work, ontologies are suitable for expressing user modeling semantics in a formal, machine-processable representation. As an ontology is considered to be "a formal specification of a shared understanding of a domain," this formal specification is usually carried out using a subclass hierarchy with relationships among classes, where one can define complex class descriptions (e.g., in Description Logics (DLs) [29] or OWL).

As far as a relevant mathematical notation is concerned, given a universe $\mathscr{X}$ of eahoukers $\mathscr{E}$, one may identify two distinct sets of concepts, namely, a crisp (i.e., nonfuzzy) set and a fuzzy set. The crisp set of concepts on $\mathscr{X}$ may be described by a membership function $\mu_C : \mathscr{X} \rightarrow \{0, 1\}$, whereas the actual crisp set C may be defined as $C = \{c_i\}$, $i = 1, \dots, N$. Quite similarly, a *fuzzy* set F on C may be described by a membership function $\mu_F : C \rightarrow [0, 1]$. We may describe the

fuzzy set F using the well-known sum notation for fuzzy sets introduced by Miyamoto [31] as

$$F = \sum_i \frac{c_i}{w_i} = \left\{ \frac{c_1}{w_1}, \frac{c_2}{w_2}, \dots, \frac{c_n}{w_n} \right\}, \quad (1)$$

where $i \in N_n$, $n = |C|$, is the well-known cardinality of the crisp set C and $w_i = \mu_F(c_i)$, or more simply $w_i = F(c_i)$, is the membership degree of concept $c_i \in C$. Consequently, (1) for a concept $c \in C$ can be written equivalently as

$$F = \sum_{c \in C} \frac{c}{\mu_F(c)} = \sum_{c \in C} \frac{c}{F(c)}. \quad (2)$$

Apart from the above described set of concepts, we need to introduce and illustrate a set depicting potential relations between the aforementioned concepts. Thus, we introduce R to be the crisp set of fuzzy relations defined as

$$R = \{R_i\},$$
$$R_i : C \times C \longrightarrow [0, 1], \quad (3)$$
$$i = 1, \dots, M,$$

and discussed within Section 2.4.

2.4. Fuzzy Personas Similarity. In order to define, extract, and use a set of concepts, we rely on the semantics of their fuzzy semantic relations. As discussed in Section 2.3, a *fuzzy binary relation* on C is defined as a function $R_i : C \times C \rightarrow [0, 1]$, $i = 1, \dots, M$. The inverse relation of relation $R_i(x, y)$, $x, y \in C$, is defined as $R_i^{-1}(x, y) = R_i(y, x)$, following the prefix notation $R_i(x, y)$ for fuzzy relations. The definitions of the *intersection*, *union*, and *sup-t composition* of any two fuzzy relations R_1 and R_2 on the same set of concepts C are given by equations

$$(R_1 \cap R_2)(x, y) = t(R_1(x, y), R_2(x, y)),$$
$$(R_1 \cup R_2)(x, y) = u(R_1(x, y), R_2(x, y)), \quad (4)$$
$$(R_1 \circ R_2)(x, y) = \sup_{w \in S} t(R_1(x, w), R_2(w, y)),$$

where t and u are a fuzzy t-norm and a fuzzy t-conorm, respectively. The standard t-norm and t-conorm are the min and max functions, respectively, but others may be used if considered more appropriate. The operation of the union of fuzzy relations can be generalized to N relations. If $R_1, R_2, \dots, R_N$ are fuzzy relations in $C \times C$, then their union R^u is a relation defined in $C \times C$ such that, for all $(x, y) \in C \times C$, $R^u(x, y) = u(R_i(x, y))$. A transitive closure of a relation R_i is the smallest transitive relation that contains the original relation and has the fewest possible members. In general, the closure of a relation is the smallest extension of the relation that has a certain specific property such as the reflexivity, symmetry, or transitivity, as the latter are defined in [32]. The sup-t transitive closure $\text{Tr}^t(R_i)$ of a fuzzy relation R_i is formally given by equation

$$\text{Tr}^t(R_i) = \bigcup_{j=1}^{\infty} R_i^{(j)}, \quad (5)$$

where $R_i^{(j)} = R_i \circ R_i^{(j-1)}$ and $R_i^{(1)} = R_i$.

TABLE 1: Semantic relations used for generation of combined relation R_C.

Name	Inverse	Symbol	Meaning	Example a	b
Belongs	Owns	Bel(a,b)	b belongs to a	House	Device
Manufactured by	Constructs	Made(a,b)	b is manufactured by a	Siemens	Fridge
Friend	NotRelated	Fr(a,b)	b is a friend of a	George	Bruno
Execute	ExecutedBy	Exec(a,b)	b executes a or a undergoes the action of b	Recipe	User
Triggers	TriggeredBy	Trig(a,b)	b triggers a	Recipe	Rule

Based on the relations R_i, we construct a combined relation R_C:

$$R_C = \mathrm{Tr}^t \left(\bigcup_i R_i^{p_i} \right), \quad p_i \in \{-1, 0, 1\}, \ i = 1, \ldots, N, \quad (6)$$

where the value of p_i is determined by the semantics of each relation R_i used in the construction of R_C. The latter may take one of three values, namely, $p_i = 1$, if the semantics of R_i imply it should be considered as is; $p_i = -1$, if the semantics of R_i imply its inverse should be considered; and $p_i = 0$, if the semantics of R_i do not allow its participation in the construction of the combined relation R_C. The transitive closure in (6) is required in order for R_C to be taxonomic, as the union of transitive relations is not necessarily transitive, independently of the fuzzy t-conorm used. In the above context, a fuzzy semantic relation defines, for each element $c \in C$, the fuzzy set of its ancestors and its descendants. For instance, if our knowledge states that "LG refrigerator" is produced before "Samsung TV" and "Nescafe coffee machine" is produced before "Samsung TV," it is not certain that it also states that "LG refrigerator" is produced before "Nescafe coffee machine." A transitive closure would correct this inconsistency.

Last but not least, thing to consider in our approach is the actual selection of meaningful relations to consider for the production of combined relation R_C. R_C has been generated with the help of fuzzy taxonomic relations, whose semantics are derived primarily from both the MPEG-7 standard and the specific user requirements. The utilized relations are summarized within Table 1. This approach is ideal for the user modeling interpretation followed herein because when dealing with generic user information, focus is given to the semantics of high-level abstract concepts.

It is worth noticing that all relations depicted within Table 1 are traditionally defined as crisp relations. However, in this work, we consider them to be fuzzy, where fuzziness has the following meaning: high values of Bel(a,b), for instance, imply that the meaning of b approaches the meaning of a, while as Bel(a,b) decreases, the meaning of b becomes narrower than the meaning of a. A similar meaning is given to fuzziness of the rest of the semantic relations of Table 1 as well. Based on the fuzzy roles and semantic interpretations of R_i, it is easy to see that relation 8 combines them in a straightforward and meaningful way, utilizing inverse functionality where it is semantically appropriate.

More specifically, in our implementation relation R_C utilizes the following subset of relations:

$$R_C = \mathrm{Tr}^t \left(\mathrm{Bel} \cup \mathrm{Made}^{-1} \cup \mathrm{Fr} \cup \mathrm{Exec} \cup \mathrm{Trig}^{-1} \right). \quad (7)$$

Relation R_C is of great importance, as it allows us to define, extract, and use contextual aspects of a set of concepts. All relations used for its generation are partial taxonomic relations, thus abandoning properties like synonymity. Still, this does not entail that their union is also antisymmetric. Quite the contrary, R_C may vary from being a partial taxonomic to being an equivalence relation. This is an important observation, as true semantic relations also fit in this range (total symmetricity as well as total antisymmetricity often has to be abandoned when modeling real-life relationships). Still, the taxonomic assumption and the semantics of the used individual relations, as well as our experiments, indicate that R_C is "almost" antisymmetric and we may refer to it as ("almost") taxonomic. Considering the semantics of the R_C relation, it is easy to realize that when the concepts in a set are highly related to a common meaning, the context will have high degrees of membership for the concepts that represent this common meaning. Understanding the great importance of the latter observation, we plan to integrate such contextual aspects of user models in our future work.

As observed in Figure 1, concepts *household appliance* and *eahouker* are the antecedents of concepts *household* and *appliance manufacturer* in relation R_C, whereas concept *eahouker* is the only antecedent of concept *recipe*.

So far and in compliance with the notion introduced in [33], the herein introduced fuzzy ontology will contain both concepts and relations and may be formalized using the crisp set of concepts C described by the ontology and the crisp set of fuzzy semantic relations amongst these concepts, R, as

$$\mathcal{O} = \{C, R\}. \quad (8)$$

In order for us to provide a measure for the evaluation of similarity between two eahoukers' profiles, we first need to establish an evaluation of similarity for each profile component. In the following, we define a set of functions $\{CS_i | \leq i \leq \mathrm{size}(E_p)\}$, one for each attribute of the eahouker' profile.

User Profile Similarity Functions

$$CS_{1/4/5/6}(x, y) = \begin{cases} 1 & \text{if } x = y \\ 0 & \text{otherwise,} \end{cases}$$

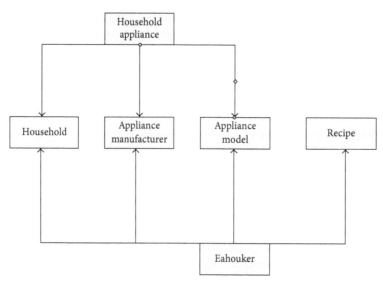

FIGURE 1: Concepts and relations example.

$$CS_2(x, y) = \begin{cases} 1 & \text{if } |x - y| \leq 5 \\ 0 & \text{otherwise,} \end{cases}$$

$$CS_3(x, y) = \begin{cases} 1 & \text{if } |x - y| \leq 1 \\ 0 & \text{otherwise.} \end{cases} \tag{9}$$

(i) Two eahoukers are considered identical if their gender, city, role in the house, and marital status are the same. This property is expressed through functions CS_1, C_4, CS_5, and CS_6 that are collectively represented in user profile similarity functions as $CS_{1/4/5/6}$.

(ii) Two eahoukers are considered identical if their difference of age is less than 5 years. Indeed, their behavior and habits inside the house can be considered the same even if they have a slight difference of age. For example, two people, one at the age of 30 and one at the age of 32, probably would have the same behaviors, according to their age. On the other hand, a person at the age of 30 would have quite different behaviors from a person at the age of 50 or 60. This property is expressed by the function CS_2.

(iii) Finally, two eahoukers are considered identical if they have more or less the same number of children. For example, a parent with 3 children would have similar behaviors and demands to a parent of 4 children. This property is expressed by the function CS_3 in user profile similarity functions.

Having introduced the functions for the evaluation of profile similarity, we can define a function that uses these evaluations to provide the level of similarity of two eahoukers. Let E_{p_i} denote the ith attribute of E_p. In addition, let E_{p_u}

and E_{p_z} be the profiles of eahoukers u and z, respectively. The eahouker profile similarity function $\mathcal{S}$ is then defined as follows:

$$\mathcal{S}(u, z) = \frac{\sum_1^n CS_i\left(E_{p_{ui}}, E_{p_{zi}}\right)}{n}, \tag{10}$$

where n is actually the cardinality of E_p (which equals six in the herein presented use case example).

3. Context

3.1. Related Work. Filling a home with sensors and controlling devices by a computer are nowadays not only possible, but also common. Sensors are available off the shelf which localize movement in the home, provide readings for light and temperature levels, and monitor usage of doors, phones, and appliances. Small inexpensive sensors are attached to objects not only to register their presence but also to record histories of recent social interactions [34].

As social interaction is an aspect of our daily life; social signals have long been recognized as important for establishing relationships, but only with the introduction of sensed environments where researchers have become able to monitor these signals. Hence, it is possible to look at socialization within the smart home and cities (such as entertaining guests, interacting with residents, or making phone calls) and examine the correlation between the socialization parameters and productivity, behavioral patterns, or even health. These results will help researchers not just to understand social interactions but also to design products and behavioral interventions that will promote more social interactions.

Proliferation of sensors in the home results in large amounts of raw data that must be analyzed to extract relevant information. Most smart home data from environmental sensors can be processed with a small computer. Once data is gathered from wearable sensors and smartphones (largely accelerometers and gyroscopes, sometimes adding camera, microphone, and physiological data), the amount of data may get too large to handle on a single computer, and cloud computing might be more appropriate. Cloud computing is also useful if data are collected for an entire community of smart homes to analyze community-wide trends and behaviors.

Collecting and handling with concurrently enormous ubiquitous data, information, and knowledge that have different formats within the SmartSantander [14] are a hard task. According to the level of abstraction of context-aware systems in HCI, context is divided into low-level context and high-level context, respectively. The raw data of low-level context are usually gathered from different physical sensors. Data type, formats, and abstraction level from different physical sensors are different. Devices and physical sensors of context-aware systems use various scales and units, and low-level context has different elements. Context-aware systems store data, information, and knowledge that have different relationship, format, and abstraction level in the context base. Furthermore, context-aware systems collect context history storing sensor data over time to offer proactive service. Context history stores huge amount of data on location, temperature, lighting level, task, utilized devices, selected services, and so forth. To quickly provide suitable services to users, context-aware systems should manage variety, diversity, and numerous amounts of context. However, previous research suggested only a concept to control this problem. Therefore, our methodology ensures semantic interoperability by bridging the gap between the expressively rich natural language vocabulary used in the recipes and the low-level machine-readable instructions with very precise and restricted semantic content.

3.2. Context-Aware HCI. In everyday social contextual situations, humans are able to, in real time, perceive, combine, process, respond to, and evaluate a multitude of information including semantics meaning of the content of an interaction, nonverbal information such as facial and body gestures, subtle vocal cues, and context, that is, events happening in the environment. Multimodal cues unfold, sometimes asynchronously, and continuously express the interlocutors' underlying affective and cognitive states, which evolve through time and are often influenced by environmental and social contextual parameters that entail ambiguities. These ambiguities with respect to contextual aspect range from the multimodal nature of emotional expressions in different situational interactional patterns [35], the ongoing task [36], the natural expressiveness of the individual, and his/her personality [37] to the intra- and interpersonal relational context [38, 39]. Additionally, in human communication, the literature indicates that people evaluate situations based on contextual information such as past visual information [40], general situational understanding, past verbal information [41], cultural background [42], gender of the participants, knowledge of the phenomenon that is taking place [36], discourse and social situations [43], and personality traits under varied situational context [44]. Without context, even humans may misinterpret the observed affective cues such as facial, vocal, or gestural behavior.

Understanding that the human behavior in terms of decision-making process is inherently a multidisciplinary problem involving different research fields, such as psychology, linguistics, computer vision, and machine learning, there is no doubt that the progress in machine understanding of human interactive behavior and personality is contingent on the progress in the research in each of those fields.

Attempting to provide a formal definition for context-aware applications and Human-Computer Interaction (HCI) systems, a starting point would be to investigate how the term context has been defined. The word "context" has a multitude of meanings even within the field of Computer Science (CS). To illustrate this, we group the different definitions of the term context in the area of artificial intelligence, natural language processing, image analysis, and mobile computing, where every discipline has its very own understanding of what context is.

According to the first work which introduced the term context awareness in CS [45], the important aspects of context are as follows: who you are with, when, where you are, and what resources are nearby. Thus, context-aware applications look at the who, where, when, and what (the user is doing) entities and use this information to determine why the situation is occurring. In a similar definition, Brown et al. [36] define context as location, identities of the people around the user, the time of day, season, temperature, and so forth. Other approaches such as that of Ryan et al. [46] include context as the user's location, environment, identity, and time while others have simply provided synonyms for context, for example, referring to context as the environment [47] or situation [48]. However, to characterize a situation, the categories provided by [45] have been extended to include activity and timing of the HCI. Reference [49] views context as the state of the application's surroundings and [50] defines it to be the application's setting. Reference [51] included the entire environment by defining context as the aspects of the current situation. However, even though there has been a development in the area, both definitions by example and those which use synonyms for context are extremely difficult to apply in practice. For a more extended overview on context awareness, the reader is referred to [52].

Based on context's broader approach [52], context can be formalized as a combination of four contextual types, identity, time, location, and activity, which are the primary context types for characterizing the situation of a particular entity and also act as indices to other sources of contextual information.

With an entity's location, we can determine what other objects or people are near the entity and what activity is occurring near the entity. From these examples, it should be evident that the primary pieces of context for one entity can be used as indices to find secondary context (e.g., geolocalization) for that same entity as well as primary context for other related entities (e.g., proximity to other homes). This context model was later enlarged [9] to include an additional context type called Relations, to define dependencies between different entities (information specific to the social network itself). Relations describe whether the entity is a part of a greater whole (multiparty interactions within Brown's family) and how it can be used in the functionality of some other entities.

Recently, the term Relations has been used to refer to the relation between the individual and the social context in terms of perceived involvement [35] and to the changes detected in a group's involvement in a multiparty interaction [43].

Identity specifies personal user information like gender, age, children, social and marital status, and so forth. Time, in addition to its intuitive meaning, can utilize overlay models to depict events like working hours, holidays, days of week, and so on. Location refers either to geographical location or to symbolic location (e.g., at home, in the shop, or at work). Activity relates to what is occurring in the situation. It concerns both the activity of the entity itself and the activities in the surroundings of the entity.

For real-world context-aware HCI computing frameworks, context is defined as any information that can be used to characterize the situation that is relevant to the interaction between the users and the system [45]. Thus, this definition approaches better the understanding of human affect signals. An even more suitable definition is the one that summarizes the key aspects of context with respect to the human interaction behavior (who is involved (e.g., dyadic/triadic interactions among persons), what is communicated (e.g., "recipes" to perform a specific task), how the information is communicated (the person's cues), why, that is, in which context, the information is passed on, where the proactive user is, what his current task is, and which (re)action should be taken to participate actively in content creation [53]).

All these context-aware systems that model the relevant context parameters of the environment depend on the application domain and hence face difficulties in modeling context in an independent way and also lack of models to be compared. Setting aside the fact that sometimes the domains such as context-aware computing, pervasive environments, and Ubiquitous Computing entail similarities with respect to the necessity of managing context knowledge, the concrete applications and approaches domains are different. In the area of pervasive computing, the work of [54] refers to context in environments taking into account the user's activity, the devices being used, the available resources, the relationships between people, and the available communication channels. To allow developers to consider richer information as activities and abstract knowledge about the current global context and to model specific knowledge of the current subdomain, an ontology-based approach has been proposed [55] in which context information is modeled into two separate layers (high and low level, resp.). Modeling high-level information allows performing deeper computations taking into account behavioral characteristics, trends information, and so forth. On the other hand, modeling low-level information, such as location, time, and environmental conditions, is used to achieve the system's final goal which is the adaptation to the user interface. Besides, several approaches consider user-related characteristics to fulfill their purposes. For example, Schmidt and his colleagues [56] also remark social environments as relevant for context modeling. Another interesting point highlighted in this work is the user's tasks. This topic has been studied also in the past [52, 54, 57] where the aspect of activities has been used to enrich contextual information about the user. Nevertheless, as it occurs with

user information, sometimes the collected data might lead to misunderstandings. In [58], ambiguity and uncertainty of user data are attempted to be solved through an ontology-based process which allows modeling them within a smart environment. A related work that deals with the uncertainty of context data in intelligent applications [59] extends the OWL web ontology language, with fuzzy set theory, to further capture, represent, and reason with such type of information. For a more extended review on representing and reasoning with uncertainty and vagueness in ontologies for the Semantic Web, the reader is referred to [60].

Unfortunately, such ambiguities with respect to the human behavior data understanding are usually context independent due to the fact that the human behavioral signals are easily misinterpreted if the information about the situation in which the shown behavioral cues have been displayed is not taken into account. Thus, to date, the proposed methodology has approached one or more of the above presented contextual aspects either separately or in groups of two or three using the information extracted from multimodal input streams [37]. Overall, further research is needed in approaching this contextual information in a continuous way.

3.3. Ubiquitous Contextual Information. An issue related to the use of data collected continuously [61] is that both psychologists and engineers tend to acquire their data in laboratories and artificial settings [62], to elicit explicitly the specific phenomena they want to observe. However, this is likely to simplify excessively the situation and to improve artificially the performance of the automatic approaches. For the last 20 years, well-established datasets and benchmarks have been developed for automatic affect analysis. Nevertheless, there are some important problems with respect to the analysis of facial behavior, such as (a) estimation of affect in continuous dimensional space (e.g., valence and arousal) in videos displaying spontaneous facial behavior and (b) detection of the activated facial muscle. That is, the majority of the publicly available corpora for the above tasks contain samples that have been captured in controlled recording conditions and/or captured under a specific social contextual environment. Arguably, in order to make further progress in automatic analysis of affect behavior, datasets that have been captured in the wild and in various contextual social environments have to be developed.

Recently, many face analysis research works have gradually shifted to facial images captured in the wild with the introduction of Labelled Faces in the Wild (LFW) [63], FDDB for face detection [64], and 300-W series of databases for facial tracking [65, 66]. To a great extent, the progress we are currently witnessing in the above face analysis problem is largely attributed to the collection and annotation of "in-the-wild" datasets. The contributions of the already developed datasets and benchmarks for analysis of facial expression in the wild have been demonstrated during the challenges in Representation Learning (ICML 2013) [67], in the series of Emotion Recognition in the wild challenges (EmotiW 2013, 2014, 2015 [61, 68–70], and 2016 (https://sites.google.com/site/emotiw2016/)) and in the recently organized workshop on context-based affect recognition (CBAR 2016 (http://cbar2016.blogspot.gr/)). For a more extended overview on datasets collected in the wild, the reader is referred to [71].

Aligned with the aforementioned trend of collecting contextual data in nonstandard situations (in the wild), there also has been much work in creating large-scale semantic ontologies and datasets. Typically, such vocabularies are defined according to utility for retrieval, coverage, diversity, availability, and reusability. Moreover, semantic concepts such as objects, locations, and activities in visual data can be easily automatically detected [72]. Recent approaches have also turned towards semantic concept-level analysis approaches.

Nevertheless, not all of them are full of rich meta information such as the entities involved, the situational context, the demographic aspects, their social status, their cultural background, and their dialect and, thus, it is not certain whether tasks such as these can be used to make reliable generalizations about natural conversation [73]. For these reasons, researchers have started to record smart homes or work situations to further achieve even higher levels of social naturalistic data. Representative examples are the collection of natural telephonic data that have been gathered by recording large numbers of real phone conversations, as in the Switchboard corpus [74] or audio corpora of nontelephonic spoken interaction or even collections of everyday interactions by having subjects wear a microphone during their daily lives for extended periods due to the great level of advancements in the area of pervasive computing [75–77].

However, the main criticism of that type of data is that they do not address all aspects of social interactions. Consequently, the existing resources should be revisited and repurposed every time new research questions arise. The above presented reasons justify the quality of data that we have so far, where the context is relatively stable (meetings, radio programs, laboratory sessions, etc.) and the variability related to such a factor is limited. Thus, there is a need for having mechanisms to collect feedback from users in the wild (such as software systems upon smartphones that ran continuously in the background to monitor user's mood and emotional states), to further establish large-scale spontaneous affect databases efficiently with very low cost [77]. This need has been fulfilled by the great level of advancement with respect to such a situation as follows: the diffusion of mobile devices equipped with multiple sensors [78] and the advent of Big Data [79].

Mobile devices can collect a large amount of contextual information (geographic position, proximity to other people, audio environment, etc.) for extended periods of time. Big Data analytics can make sense of that data and provide information about context and its effect on behavior. Thus, it is possible to overcome limitations such as the collection of affect-related data in a large population as well as having involved participants in the experiment for too long. With the advent of powerful smart devices with built-in microphones [80], Bluetooth patterns, cameras, usage log, and so on, it is possible for researchers to identify new ways for capturing spontaneous face expression databases. Unfortunately, these studies have been carried out mainly in a social context (person-person communication) and only through acted scenarios. Further studies are needed in a variety of contexts to establish a better understanding of this relationship and identify whether and how these models could be generalized over different types of tactile behavior, activity, context, and personality traits. However, most of the approaches concentrate on offline analysis and no results that take context into account that could clarify any ambiguities in the interpretation of social cues have been presented so far.

Due to the huge growth of collecting wearable data in the wild and access to more contextual information, respectively, affect analysis has recently started to move into the realm of Big Data. For example, in terms of physiological data, having enough participants being able to own and wear sensors at all times and being willing to allow contextual data to be collected from their phones, it might allow a large collection of physiological signals with high-confidence affect labels. Data could then be labelled with both self-report and contextual information such as time of day, weather, activity, and who the subject was with so as to make an assessment of affective state. Consequently, with sufficiently ground truth datasets, it will likely be able to develop better contextually aware algorithms for individuals and like groups even if the sensor data are noisier. These algorithms will enable HCI in a private, personal, and continuous way and allow our sensors to both know us better and be able to communicate more effectively on our behalf with the world around us. Taking into account the fact that personalization is desirable, that is, the system adapts itself to the user by regarding this behavior, emotions, and intentions, specifically this leads to technologies with companion-like characteristics [81–83] that can interact with a certain user in a more efficient way independent of the contextual social situation and the environment.

Another important issue is the interplay among the personality, the situational context, and the contextualized behavior. The problem of context has been controversial in the HCI community [37, 84–86]. The ultimate goal is to have context-aware technology that is capable of working and interacting differently depending on the context (e.g., a phone should not ring during a meeting). The key issue is how to encode and represent context, even in the case of identifying a set of features of the surrounding environment, location, identities of the people around the user, and so forth [36]. Furthermore, of equal importance is the understanding of how people achieve and maintain a mutual understanding of the context according to their dependency [9] or how the social relations are structured in small [87] and large groups (friends, colleagues, families, students, etc.) and finally how the changes in individuals' behaviors [43, 88] and attitudes occur due to their membership in social and situational settings.

So far, the issue is still open for technologies dealing with social and psychological phenomena like personality [89]. Besides the difficulties in representing context, current approaches for human behavior understanding (facial expression analysis, speaker diarization, action recognition, etc.) are still sensitive to factors like illumination changes, environmental noise, or sensor placement. It is not clear whether personality should be considered as a stable construct or as a process that involves changes and evolution over time, as this decision depends on how it is measured and aggregated [90]. In this view, personality ranges from highly stable and trait-like to highly variable and adaptive to context.

Particularly, data from smart wearable devices can indicate personality traits using machine learning approaches to extract useful features, providing fruitful pathways to study relationships between users and personalities, by building social networks with the rich contextual information available in applications usage, call, and SMS logs. "Designing" smart homes in terms of enhancing the comfort is also challenging for mobile emotion detection. The friendly design of an intelligent ecosystem responsive to our needs that can make users feel more comfortable for affective feedback collection and may change user's social behavior is very promising to boost the affect detection performance and explore the possibility of further HCI techniques.

Moreover, it is necessary to discover new emotional features, which may exist in application logs, smart device usage patterns, locations, order histories, and so forth. There is a great need to thoroughly monitor and investigate the new personality and behavioral features. In other words, establishing new HCI databases in terms of new social features could be a very significant research topic and could bring "ambient intelligence" in the home closer to reality.

Gradually, the new multidisciplinary area that lies at the crossroads between Human-Computer Interaction (HCI), social sciences, linguistics, psychology, and context awareness is distinguishing itself as a separate field. It is thus possible to better recognize, interpret, and process "recipes," to incorporate contextual information, and finally to understand the related ethical issues about the creation of homes that can enhance shelter. For applications in fields such as real-time HCI and big social data analysis [91], deep natural language understanding is not strictly required; a sense of the semantics associated with text and some extra information such as social parameters associated with such semantics are often sufficient to quickly perform tasks such as capturing and modeling social behavior.

Semantic context concept-based approaches [92–95] aim to grasp the conceptual and affective information associated with natural language semantic rules. Additionally, concept-based approaches can analyze multiword expressions that do not explicitly convey emotion but are related to concepts that do. Rather than gathering isolated rules about a whole item (e.g., iPhone 5), users are generally more interested in comparing different products according to their specific features (e.g., iPhone 5's versus Galaxy S3's touchscreen), or even subfeatures (e.g., fragility of iPhone 5's versus Galaxy S3's touchscreen). This taken-for-granted information referring to obvious things people normally know and usually leave unstated/uncommented, in particular, is necessary to properly deconstruct natural language text into rules, for example, to appraise the concept small room as negative for a hotel review and small queue as positive for a post office or the concept "go read the book" as positive for a book review but negative for a movie review.

Context-level analysis also ensures that all gathered rules are relevant for the specific user. In the era of social context (where intelligent systems have access to a great deal of personal identities and social dependencies), such rules will

be tailored to each user's preferences and intent. Irrelevant opinions will be accordingly filtered with respect to their source (e.g., a relevant circle of friends or users with similar interests) and intent.

3.4. Pervasive Context Awareness Environments

3.4.1. Context Sources. Context data in a smart pervasive environment such as a smart home can come from various sources as follows:

(i) In-place sensors such as temperature, humidity, luminosity, noise, or human presence sensors located in the various rooms or outside, in the vicinity of the house

(ii) Power and water consumption meters of the house

(iii) Smart city sensors providing additional information such as pollution levels, temperature, and total electrical power consumption of the city, optionally with geospatial information

3.4.2. Home Rules. Users sometimes need their appliances to perform a specific action in their house taking into account the context information. For example, they may not want to wash clothes when it is raining or the temperature in the city is quite low. For this reason, there are defined actions for the smart home system. These actions are called home rules. These home rules are handling whether the appliances should be switched on or off.

In a more high-level approach, the structure of the home rules can be customized as "if it is valid, do/do not do that." Figure 2 illustrates an example of that.

The "if it is valid, do/do not do that" structure consists of three parts:

(i) "If it is valid," a trigger that consists of the following:

　(a) An input type and the value of the input that is defined by pervasive and context information such as the ones described in Section 3.4

　(b) An operator $<, \leq, =, \neq, \geq, >$

　(c) A reference value, which is input by the user (e.g., 20 degrees Celsius)

(ii) "Do/do not," what to do when the rule is triggered, where any smart home system action/reaction can be inserted

(iii) "That," which consists of an optional parameter (e.g., lower the house blinds by using that percentage)

Moreover, more complex rules such as the temperature in specific interval of values are expressed with multiple rules that are logically joined together.

4. Semantic Representation

In this section, semantic technologies are used in order to represent the knowledge of an ecosystem. In general terms, an

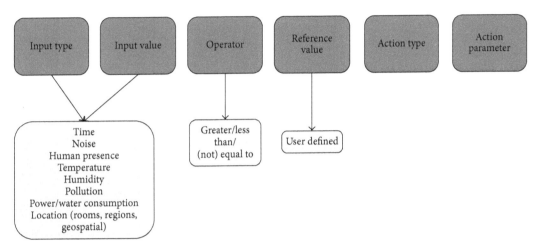

FIGURE 2: Home rules structure.

ecosystem with respect to the Internet of Things (IoT) which is often considered as the next step in Ubiquitous Computing [96] is particular IoT implementation (a smart grid, a smart home, a smart city, or personalized wearables) focusing on standards, protocols, or abilities from the technical perspective while at the same time analyzing the social relationships of the users from a social point perspective. According to the formal definition given in [97], an ecosystem consists of a set of solutions that enable, support, and automate the activities and transactions by the actors in the associated social environment. Furthermore, it enables relationships among the sensors, the actuators (complex devices), and their users. The relationships are based on a common platform and operate through the exchange of information, resources, and artifacts [98]. In our work, we merge the two areas of IoT ecosystems implementation: home automation systems (smart homes) and IoT based solutions for smart cities. Particularly, our ecosystem consists of cities, comprising a number of houses. Additionally, in every city and in every house, a number of sensors are located which give data for the environmental context, for example, humidity and temperature. They are also able to give more specific information such as noise and pollution levels or information about the human presence inside the house. All these data are received from the sensors and are stored in a database.

In this ecosystem, we can define a number of rules, which we will call home rules, for example, defining under which conditions house appliances should be switched on or off. Another more concrete example would be "do not operate the air-condition when the outside temperature is high."

The OWL 2 Web Ontology Language (OWL 2) [99], an ontology language for the Semantic Web with formally defined meaning, was adopted for the semantic representation of our ecosystem. OWL 2 ontologies provide classes, properties, individuals, and data values and they are stored as Semantic Web entities. The following sections (from Section 4.1 to Section 4.4) explain in more detail how the ecosystem is represented by our ontology. The ontology was created using the open-source Protégé 4.2 platform [100].

4.1. Ontology Hierarchy. Figure 3(c) illustrates the ontology's hierarchy. The ontology's classes describe different aspects of the ecosystem which may be as follows:

(i) The Appliances which contain all the different types of the ecosystem's appliances, such as (a) the refrigerator, (b) the washing machine, (c) the air-condition, and (d) the television

(ii) The Location, which contains both the house and the city

(iii) The Sensor, which is a class that contains the individuals of all the existing sensors

(iv) The Person, which contains all the individuals

(v) The Gender, the HouseRole, and the SocialStatus which for the different types of gender, house roles, and social status implement the user model

4.2. Properties. The ontology also comprises a series of properties. These properties are both object properties and data properties. Object properties provide ways to relate two objects (also called predicates). Object properties relate two objects (classes), of which one is the domain and the other is the range. The object properties of the ontology of this ecosystem are mainly used to relate the sensors with a specific location and the inhabitants of the house and the appliances. Some of the ontology's object properties are described below:

(i) hasGender, which relates a Person class with a Gender class according to Section 4.1

(ii) hasSensor, which relates a Sensor class with a specific location

(iii) hasHouseRole, which relates a Person class with a house role

(iv) isLocatedIn, which relates a house with a city

(v) livesIn, which relates a person with a house

(vi) builtIn, which relates a house with a city

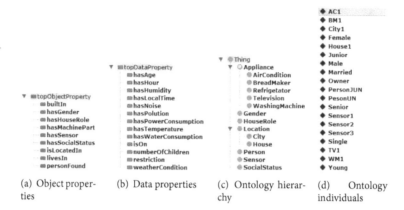

(a) Object proper- (b) Data properties (c) Ontology hierar- (d) Ontology
ties   chy   individuals

FIGURE 3: An example of the ontology properties, the hierarchical structure, and the individuals used for our experiments.

On the other hand, data properties are similar to object properties with the sole difference that their domains are typed words. In our ontology, they relate the actual sensor values with a sensor, power on or off status of the appliances, and the user properties with numerical features. Some of them are described below:

(i) hasNoise, which relates a sensor with the actual captured noise value, for example, 40 dB

(ii) hasTemperature, which relates a sensor with the actual captured temperature value, for example, 25°C

(iii) isOn, which has a true value if the appliance is turned on and is false otherwise

(iv) numberOfChildren, which relates a person with the number of his/her children, which must be a nonnegative integer

The object's and the data's properties of the ontology appear in Figure 3.

4.3. Individuals. The ecosystem in all contains a large number of appliances, sensors, and people. Every single appliance, sensor, and person is represented in the ontology as an individual of the Appliances, Sensor, or Person class, respectively. Figure 3(d) illustrates a small set of individuals contained in the ontology.

4.4. Rules and Consistency Check. In the current section, we provide a novel semantic representation of the home rules of the ecosystem. These home rules are expressed using the Semantic Web Rule Language (SWRL) [101]. SWRL has the full power of OWL DL, only at the price of decidability and practical implementations. However, decidability can be regained by restricting the form of admissible rules, typically by imposing a suitable safety condition. Rules have the form of an implication between an antecedent (body) and a consequent (head). This meaning can be read as follows: "whenever the conditions that are specified in the antecedent may hold, the conditions that are specified in the consequent must also hold." A critical property of our ontology is that the ontology should always be consistent, a condition that

is verified with the use of a Pellet reasoner [102]. Thereat, whenever a home rule is violated, an inconsistency must be detected. Taking this into account, whenever the conditions that are specified in the antecedent hold, the conditions specified in the consequent must also hold; hence, the home rule's violation is transformed to the respective antecedent of the SWRL.

For this reason, a data restriction has to be created in the Appliances class. A data property called "restriction" is created. Its domain is an appliance and its range is boolean, but it is also restricted to create an appliance with the restriction property. Then, every home rule is transformed to a SWRL, and if the left side of the rule is satisfied, it leads to the creation of the "restriction" property for an appliance. This makes our ontolgy inconsistent; in other words, the appliance is restricted to start working. So every time a database record changes or a new one is added, the ontology individuals are populated with the new values querying the database. Then, using the Pellet reasoner, the system checks for possible existence of any inconsistency. Finally, the inconsistency is being handled by forcing the appliance to switch off or switch on. Using the Semantic Web technologies, the restriction is added to every appliance in order not to create any restriction data property for any individual of the class after the reasoning. In this subsection, some indicative home rules transformed to SWRLs are presented.

(1) Do not operate any washing machine when the external temperature is greater than 26°C:

```
City(?city) ^ House(?house) ^
Sensor(?sensor) ^
WashingMachine(?wm) ^
builtIn(?house, ?city) ^
hasSensor(?city, ?sensor) ^
isLocatedIn(?wm, ?house) ^
hasTemperature(?sensor,
?temperature) ^ isOn(?wm, true) ^
greaterThan(?temperature, 26) =>
restriction(?wm, true)
```

(2) The washing machine must not be operating if a person is in the house and there exists too much noise:

```
House(?house) ^ Person(?per) ^
Sensor (?sensor) ^
WashingMachine(?wm) ^
hasSensor(?house, ?sensor) ^
isLocatedIn(?wm, ?house) ^
personFound(?sensor, ?per) ^
hasNoise(?sensor, ?noise) ^
isOn(?wm, true) ^
greaterThan(?noise, 40) =>
restriction(?wm, true)
```

(3) If the local time is between 10 p.m. and 8 a.m., the television must not be switched on:

```
Television(?tv) ^ House(?house) ^
Sensor(?sensor) ^
isOn(?tv,true) ^
isLocatedIn(?tv,?house) ^
hasSensor(?house,?sensor) ^
hasHour(?sensor,?hour) ^
greaterThan(?hour, 22) =>
restriction(?tv, true)
Television(?tv) ^ House(?house) ^
Sensor(?sensor) ^ isOn(?tv,true) ^
isLocatedIn(?tv,?house) ^
hasSensor(?house,?sensor) ^
hasHour(?sensor,?hour) ^
lessThan(?hour, 8) =>
restriction(?tv, true)
```

As it is clear, the built-ins for SWRLs, such as "equal," "lessThan," "greaterThan," "lessThanOrEqual," and "lessThanOrEqual," are used for comparisons. By using these built-ins, it is possible to create home rules in which a value comparison of environmental values is needed such as the temperature, the humidity, and the noise level, or more elaborated boolean values such as the human presence detection in a house. Additionally, rules can be used in conjunction between each other in order to express more elaborated rules, such as the third home rule.

5. Experiments

In this section, we present the rudiments of what constitutes SandS, our smart home environment, which we define as a city in which information and communication technologies are merged with traditional infrastructures, coordinated, and integrated using the IoT technologies. These technologies establish the functions of the city and also provide ways in which citizen groups can interact in augmenting their understanding of the city and also provide essential engagement in the design and planning process. We first sketch our vision defining three goals which concern us: feeding the home rules with the signals provided by the smart city system, to represent a simple interoperability test; introducing limitations on the use of the appliances related to environment conditions, like the power or water consumption reckoned by the city environment sensors, the short-term weather forecasting, and so forth, which represents a logical test on the

FIGURE 4: SandS user registration form.

DI scheduler and consistency checker; and managing alarm messages sent by the municipality. We begin by presenting how our data have been collected within a social network in order to create and exchange content in the form of so-called recipes and to develop collective intelligence which adapts its operation through appropriate feedback provided by the user. Additionally, we approach SandS from the user's perspective and illustrate how users and their relationships can be modeled through a number of fuzzy stereotypical profiles (user-centered experimental validation). Furthermore, the context modeling in our smart home paradigm is examined through appropriate representation of context cues in the overall interaction (pervasive experimental validation).

5.1. Data Collection. In this subsection, we present our approach towards the vision of smart home that supports inhabitants' high-level goals, emphasizing collecting our data in the wild in terms of having been captured in real-world and unconstrained conditions. Thus, our smart home technologies deal with interference with IoT technologies and react to nonstandard situations. More precisely, data was collected by the SandS consortium and partners during a small-scale mockup according to the "in-house" and "out-house" sensors such as mobility sensors, traffic and parking sensors, environmental sensors, and park and garden irrigation sensors, respectively. Finally, this context data information collected through the sensors is sent periodically to the ecosystem. These values are stored in a specific table of a database overwriting the previous record that was stored.

5.1.1. User Models. Regarding the experimental dataset to validate the formation of personas, data was collected by the SandS consortium and partners during a small-scale mockup. SandS also opened up its user base towards the FIRE and related communities such as the Open Living Labs. The dissemination call for user participation pointed to a user registration form, illustrated in Figure 4.

This registration form comprised several user-related fields: first name, last name, date of birth, senior/junior, gender, single/married, and city.

5.1.2. Smart City Sensors. In large-scale tests of the unified user in a smart home in a smart city, SandS will use context

FIGURE 5: SmartSantander sensors locations.

sensor data gathered at SmartSantander. SmartSantander [14], born as a European project, is turning into a living experimental laboratory as part of the EU's Future Internet initiative. Major companies involved in the project include Telefonica Digital, the company's R&D wing, along with other smaller suppliers as well as utility and service companies. In terms of application areas, five main areas have initially been targeted in the trials so far: traffic management and parking, street lighting, waste disposal management, pollution monitoring, and parks and garden management. To this aim, the city of Santander, Spain, has been equipped with a large number of sensors (Figure 5) used to collect a huge amount of information. We can divide the sensors into several categories based on the data they should collect.

(i) Mobility sensors: they are placed on buses, taxis, and police cars. They are in charge of measuring main parameters associated with the vehicle (GPS position, altitude, speed, course, and odometer)

(ii) Traffic and parking sensors: they are buried under the asphalt. They are accountable for sensing the corresponding traffic parameters (traffic volumes, road occupancy, vehicle speed, queue length, and free parking availability)

(iii) Environmental sensors: the task is to collect data concerning temperature, noise, light, humidity, wind speed, and detection of specific gases like CO, PM10, O_3, and NO_2

(iv) Park and garden irrigation sensors: in order to control and make the irrigation in certain parks and gardens more efficient, these sensors register information about wind's speed, quantity of rain, soil temperature, soil humidity, atmospheric pressure, solar radiation, air humidity, and temperature, as well as water consumption

At the moment, the data collected by these sensors are stored in the USN/IDAS SmartSantander cloud storage platform. This platform stores in its databases all the observations and measurements gathered by the sensors. It contains live and historical data. These databases are migrating on the Fi-lab platform as an instance of the FIWARE [103] ecosystem.

In very minimal terms, our experiments will manage the integration of the two systems only in one direction: by exploiting SmartSantander data in favor of SandS with special regard to the empowerment of the home rules used by the domestic infrastructure (DI), which is the core of the proposed system and handles the home rules and the appliances, manages the users, and updates the database with any new value gathered from a sensor. Hence, the contact between the two systems will happen via the home rules which may be fed by the smart city sensor data either in their current version or in an enlarged one to be capable of profiting from the data. Available sensor data, related to the SandS domain, include the following: temperature, noise, light, humidity, and quantity of rain. Other data, for instance, those concerning traffic, could be considered in a more long-term planning and scheduling approach.

Finally, our goal would be to stress the following case studies:

(1) Feeding the home rules with the signals provided by the smart city system. It represents a simple inter-operability test

(2) Introducing limitations on the use of the appliances related to environment conditions, such as the power or water consumption reckoned by the city environment sensors and the short-term weather forecasting. It represents a logical test on the DI scheduler and consistency checker

(3) Managing alarm messages sent by the municipality. It will represent a stress test for the entire system

5.1.3. Sensor Integration. In the ecosystem, there are sensors both in every house and for the whole city. These sensors send periodically information about the temperature, the luminosity, and the humidity. Both the in-house and the city sensors send the values of the sensors periodically to the ecosystem. These values are stored in a specific table of a database overwriting the previous record that was stored. The in-house sensors send information about the humidity in the house, the inside house temperature, the human presence in it, the power consumption and the water consumption of all the appliances inside it, the location where the sensor is installed (e.g., the kitchen, the bathroom, or the bedroom), the noise, and the local timestamp. Moreover, the city sensor values are collected at a specific moment using the FIWARE Ops tools (https://data.lab.fiware.org/dataset?tags=sensor&_organization_limit=0&organization=santander) [104]. The data of the sensors are periodically sent to the system in a JSON format using an HTTP connection. Then, the JSONs are parsed and the information is stored to the database. The city sensors, like SmartSantander [14], are sending information of the noise inside the city, the temperature, and the exact location where they are installed. Adding all these pieces of information of the sensors to a database, it is every time feasible for the system to identify the exact condition inside and outside the house, where the sensors are installed, just by doing a simple query in the database. Due to the structure of the home rules, it is possible in a very short time for the ecosystem to know if a home rule is triggered and if an appliance in a house should be switched on or off.

5.2. User-Centered Experimental Validation. A user can get the best recipe for him by comparing his request for a recipe with other users' requests of using the fuzzy similarity method presented in Section 2.4. The fuzzy similarity method

FIGURE 6: SandS recipe request similarity form.

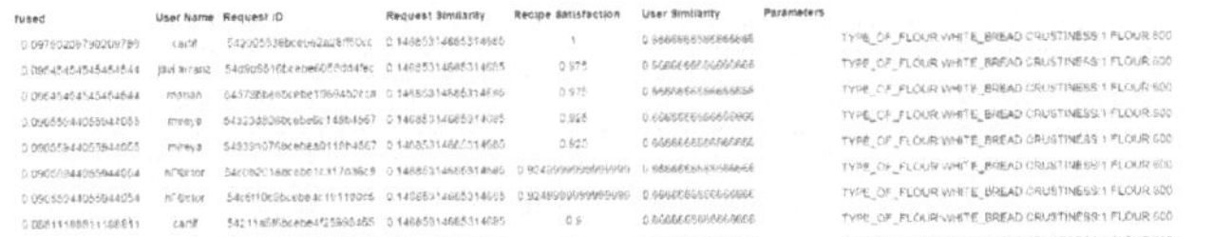

FIGURE 7: SandS recipe request similarity resulting table.

is taking into account both the similarity of the users (e.g., their gender, age, house role) and the similarity between the request parameters. A request parameter for a request of a recipe in order to bake bread might be the crustness, the amount of the water that should be used for the dough, or the flour's type that is going to be used. Figure 6 illustrates a form where a user can insert his database ID and some request parameters in order to get the similarity with other requests. Then, clicking the submit button, a table with all the requests of other users, ranked by their total similarity, is returned, as the one illustrated in Figure 7. The first column shows the total similarity taking into account both the user similarity and the similarity of request parameters. The sixth column shows only the user similarity and the fourth only the request parameters similarity. The fifth column shows the satisfaction of the users that have used this recipe in the past. One means "fully satisfied" and, on the other hand, zero means "not satisfied at all."

5.3. Pervasive Experimental Validation. The system is periodically querying the database and, more specifically, the collection where the sensor values are stored. Then, using the home rules, which have been added in the ecosystem, it checks whether the consistency of the ontology still holds for the new sensor values. If any of the home rules is triggered, it denotes that an inconsistency has been detected from the system for a specific appliance. This specific appliance is switched off, until none of the home rules related to this appliance are inconsistent. As it has been mentioned previously, a home rule could be triggered by both the in-house sensor value changes and the value changes detected by

the SmartSantander sensors. In order to be clear, an example is presented. Figure 8(a) illustrates the noise levels in the house, which follow the Gaussian function. These values are received by the in-house noise detection sensors and they are stored in the database. In addition, Figure 8(b) presents the human presence in the house at the same period of time. In case the value is equal to one, this means that there exists a human in the house this specific period of time. In case there is not anyone in the house, the value is equal to zero. Considering that the house is a part of the ecosystem where the home rules presented in Section 4.4 are defined, the second home rule is triggered. At the beginning, the washing machine is switched on, executing the clothes' washing program, until the noise volume tides over 40 dB at 10:00. Then, the appliance is switched off until 18:00, when the noise levels fall below 40 dB. In case a washing program for the clothes was interrupted during its execution, the program starts its execution from the beginning or continues from the step it was stopped, depending on the users' choices. If an inconsistency is detected but the washing machine is not executing any laundry program or it is scheduled to start it immediately, then, the washing machine is switched off, without affecting any scheduled process.

Moreover, in case the system receives from a city sensor, such as the SmartSantander sensors, temperature values equal to or greater than 26°C, then the first home rule would be triggered because an inconsistency would have been detected. As a result, the house's washing machine would be switched off. The temperature values of such an occasion are presented in Figure 9. Between 11:00 and 15:00, a city sensor receives temperature values higher than 26°C. Consequently, an inconsistency is detected, which forces the house's washing machine to switch off. Finally, later than 15:00, when the temperature is again lower than 26°C, the washing machine is switched on again.

6. Conclusions and Future Work

In this paper, we illustrated how the emerging semantics of the smart home environments can be captured through a novel formalism and how expert knowledge can be used to ensure semantic interoperability. User stereotypes or personas on the one hand provide flexibility, extensibility, reusability, and applicability and on the other hand knowledge management is incorporated as an efficient user and context model representation formalism. In addition, this formal, machine-processable representation is used in order to define, extract, and use a set of concepts and their fuzzy semantic relations. This user modeling approach is put into a rich smart home context representation which abstracts raw sensor data to a high-level semantic representation language in which complex home rules can be defined.

Future work includes further incorporation of user, usage, and context information, through a unified semantic representation, driving an adaptation mechanism aiming to provide a personalized service and optimizing the user experience. Among the aspects of the architecture that will be stressed through experimental validation is the computational cost and the scaling of SandS to a wider user group.

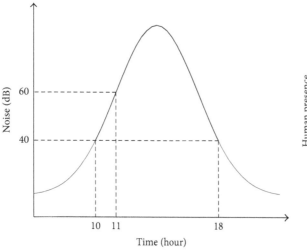

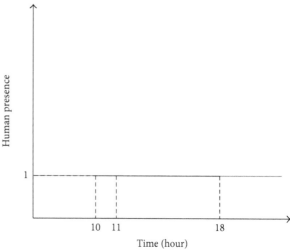

(a) Plot of the noise levels per second of a day window

(b) Plot of the human presence in the house, per second of a day window. "1" means that there is a human in the house and "0" means that none is in the house

FIGURE 8: In-house sensor values of the noise and the human presence.

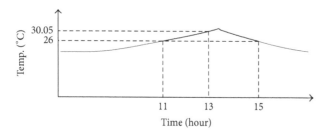

FIGURE 9: SmartSantander sensor values of the temperature for a specific period in a day.

Based on the SandS architecture, the cloud infrastructure ensures the optimal handling of the computational load since the intermediate processes are not computationally demanding. On the other hand, issues that may arise from the scaling of the platform application are part of the experimental validation since the load is directly correlated with the user activity. The large-scale validation at SmartSantander will provide us with useful insights about the latter.

Competing Interests

The authors declare that they have no competing interests.

Acknowledgments

This work was supported by the European Commission under Contract FP7-317947, FIRE project, "Social & Smart."

References

[1] B. Shneiderman, *Universal Usability: Pushing Human-Computer Interaction Research to Empower Every Citizen*, 1999.

[2] B. Kules, "User modeling for adaptive and adaptable software systems," in *Proceedings of the ACM Conference on Universal Usability (CUU '00)*, pp. 16–17, November 2000.

[3] A. Kobsa, "Generic user modeling systems," *User Modeling and User-Adapted Interaction*, vol. 11, no. 12, pp. 49–63, 2001.

[4] L. Nielsen, *Personas. The Encyclopedia of Human-Computer Interaction*, The Interaction Design Foundation, Aarhus, Denmark, 2nd edition, 2013.

[5] A. Cooper, *The Inmates Are Running the Asylum: Why High Tech Products Drive Us Crazy and How to Restore the Sanity*, 2004.

[6] D. Saffer, *Designing for Interaction: Creating Smart Applications and Clever Devices*, New Riders Press, 2007, http://www.designingforinteraction.com.

[7] J. Pruitt and T. Adlin, *The Persona Lifecycle: Keeping People in Mind Throughout the Design Process*, 2006.

[8] D. Norman, "Ad-hoc personas empathetic focus," 2004, http://jnd.org/.

[9] A. Zimmermann, A. Lorenz, and R. Oppermann, "An operational definition of context," in *Modeling and Using Context*, B. Kokinov, D. C. Richardson, T. R. Roth-Berghofer, and L. Vieu, Eds., vol. 4635 of *Lecture Notes in Computer Science*, pp. 558–571, Springer, Berlin, Germany, 2007.

[10] M. Baldauf, S. Dustdar, and F. Rosenberg, "A survey on context-aware systems," *International Journal of Ad Hoc and Ubiquitous Computing*, vol. 2, no. 4, pp. 263–277, 2007.

[11] C. Bettini, O. Brdiczka, K. Henricksen et al., "A survey of context modelling and reasoning techniques," *Pervasive and Mobile Computing*, vol. 6, no. 2, pp. 161–180, 2010.

[12] M. Eisenhauer, P. Rosengren, and P. Antolin, "A development platform for integrating wireless devices and sensors into ambient intelligence systems," in *Proceedings of the 6th Annual IEEE Communications Society Conference on Sensor, Mesh and Ad Hoc Communications and Networks Workshops*, pp. 1–3, IEEE, Rome, Italy, June 2009.

[13] SandS, "Sands-project," 2015, http://www.sands-project.eu/.

[14] SmartSantander, 2015, https://www.fi-xifi.eu/fiware-ops/service-offer-management.html.

[15] G. Fischer, "User modeling in human-computer interaction," *User Modeling and User-Adapted Interaction*, vol. 11, no. 1-2, pp. 65–86, 2001.

[16] P. Gregor, A. F. Newell, and M. Zajicek, "Designing for dynamic diversity: interfaces for older people," in *Proceedings of the 5th International Conference on Assistive Technologies (ASSETS '02)*, pp. 151–156, ACM, Edinburgh, UK, July 2002.

[17] M. Hatala and R. Wakkary, "Ontology-based user modeling in an augmented audio reality system for museums," *User Modelling and User-Adapted Interaction*, vol. 15, no. 3-4, pp. 339–380, 2005.

[18] F. Pereira, "A triple user characterization model for video adaptation and quality of experience evaluation," in *Proceedings of the IEEE 7th Workshop on Multimedia Signal Processing (MMSP '05)*, pp. 1–4, IEEE, Shanghai, China, November 2005.

[19] U. Persad, P. Langdon, and J. Clarkson, "Characterising user capabilities to support inclusive design evaluation," *Universal Access in the Information Society*, vol. 6, no. 2, pp. 119–135, 2007.

[20] D. Heckmann, E. Schwarzkopf, J. Mori, D. Dengler, and A. Kroner, "The user model and context ontology GUMO revisited for future web 2.0 extensions," in *Contexts and Ontologies Representation and Reasoning*, p. 42, 2007.

[21] C. Evers, R. Kniewel, K. Geihs, and L. Schmidt, "Achieving user participation for adaptive applications," in *Ubiquitous Computing and Ambient Intelligence*, pp. 200–207, Springer, Berlin, Germany, 2012.

[22] R. Casas, R. Blasco Marín, A. Robinet et al., "User modelling in ambient intelligence for elderly and disabled people," in *Computers Helping People with Special Needs: 11th International Conference, ICCHP 2008, Linz, Austria, July 9–11, 2008. Proceedings*, vol. 5105 of *Lecture Notes in Computer Science*, pp. 114–122, Springer, Berlin, Germany, 2008.

[23] E. Castillejo, A. Almeida, D. López-De-Ipiña, and L. Chen, "Modeling users, context and devices for ambient assisted living environments," *Sensors*, vol. 14, no. 3, pp. 5354–5391, 2014.

[24] A. Johnson and N. Taatgen, *User Modeling, Handbook of Human Factors in Web Design*, Lawrence Erlbaum Associates, 2005.

[25] P. T. Aquino Jr. and L. V. L. Filgueiras, "User modeling with personas," in *Proceedings of the Latin American Conference on Human-Computer Interaction (CLIHC '05)*, pp. 277–282, October 2005.

[26] P. Castells, M. Fernández, D. Vallet, P. Mylonas, and Y. Avrithis, "Self-tuning personalized information retrieval in an ontology-based framework," in *On the Move to Meaningful Internet Systems 2005: OTM 2005 Workshops*, pp. 977–986, Springer, Berlin, Germany, 2005.

[27] D. L. McGuinness and F. Van Harmelen, "Owl web ontology language overview," W3C Recommendation, 2004.

[28] M. Hepp, "Possible ontologies: how reality constrains the development of relevant ontologies," *IEEE Internet Computing*, vol. 11, no. 1, pp. 90–96, 2007.

[29] F. Baader, *The Description Logic Handbook: Theory, Implementation, and Applications*, Cambridge University Press, Cambridge, UK, 2003.

[30] T. R. Gruber, "A translation approach to portable ontology specifications," *Knowledge Acquisition*, vol. 5, no. 2, pp. 199–220, 1993.

[31] S. Miyamoto, *Fuzzy Sets in Information Retrieval and Cluster Analysis*, vol. 4 of *Theory and Decision Library, Series D: System Theory, Knowledge Engineering and Problem Solving*, Kluwer Academic Publishers, Dordrecht, The Netherlands, 1990.

[32] G. J. Klir and B. Yuan, *Fuzzy Sets and Fuzzy Logic*, Prentice Hall, New Jersey, NJ, USA, 1995.

[33] S. Calegari and D. Ciucci, "Fuzzy ontology, fuzzy description logics and fuzzy-owl," in *Applications of Fuzzy Sets Theory*, pp. 118–126, Springer, Berlin, Germany, 2007.

[34] E. Y. Song and K. B. Lee, "Service-oriented sensor data interoperability for IEEE 1451 smart transducers," in *Proceedings of the IEEE Intrumentation and Measurement Technology Conference (I2MTC '09)*, pp. 1043–1048, IEEE, Singapore, May 2009.

[35] F. Bonin, R. Bock, and N. Campbell, "How do we react to context? Annotation of individual and group engagement in a video corpus," in *Proceedings of the International Conference on Privacy, Security, Risk and Trust (PASSAT '12) and International Confernece on Social Computing (SocialCom '12)*, pp. 899–903, IEEE, Amsterdam, The Netherlands, September 2012.

[36] P. J. Brown, J. D. Bovey, and X. Chen, "Context-aware applications: from the laboratory to the marketplace," *IEEE Personal Communications*, vol. 4, no. 5, pp. 58–64, 1997.

[37] Z. Zeng, M. Pantic, G. I. Roisman, and T. S. Huang, "A survey of affect recognition methods: audio, visual, and spontaneous expressions," *IEEE Transactions on Pattern Analysis and Machine Intelligence*, vol. 31, no. 1, pp. 39–58, 2009.

[38] R. Böck, S. Glüge, A. Wendemuth et al., "Intraindividual and interindividual multimodal emotion analyses in human-machine-interaction," in *Proceedings of the IEEE International Multi-Disciplinary Conference on Cognitive Methods in Situation Awareness and Decision Support (CogSIMA '12)*, pp. 59–64, IEEE, New Orleans, La, USA, March 2012.

[39] Z. Hammal and J. F. Cohn, "Intra-and interpersonal functions of head motion in emotion communication," in *Proceedings of the 2014 Workshop on Roadmapping the Future of Multimodal Interaction Research including Business Opportunities and Challenges (RFMIR '14)*, pp. 19–22, ACM, Istanbul, Turkey, 2014.

[40] R. El Kaliouby, P. Robinson, and S. Keates, "Temporal context and the recognition of emotion from facial expression," in *Proceedings of the HCI International Conference*, pp. 631–635, American Psychological Association, 2003.

[41] H. R. Knudsen and L. H. Muzekari, "The effects of verbal statements of context on facial expressions of emotion," *Journal of Nonverbal Behavior*, vol. 7, no. 4, pp. 202–212, 1983.

[42] T. Masuda, P. C. Ellsworth, B. Mesquita, J. Leu, S. Tanida, and E. Van de Veerdonk, "Placing the face in context: cultural differences in the perception of facial emotion," *Journal of Personality and Social Psychology*, vol. 94, no. 3, pp. 365–381, 2008.

[43] R. Böck, S. Glüge, I. Siegert, A. Wendemuth, and S. Glüge, "Annotation and classification of changes of involvement in group conversation," in *Proceedings of the Humaine Association Conference on Affective Computing and Intelligent Interaction (ACII '13)*, pp. 803–808, Geneva, Switzerland, September 2013.

[44] J. Joshi, H. Gunes, and R. Goecke, "Automatic prediction of perceived traits using visual cues under varied situational context," in *Proceedings of the 22nd International Conference*

on Pattern Recognition (ICPR '14), pp. 2855–2860, IEEE, Stockholm, Sweden, August 2014.

[45] B. Schilit, N. Adams, and R. Want, "Context-aware computing applications," in *Proceedings of the Workshop on Mobile Computing Systems and Applications*, pp. 85–90, December 1994.

[46] N. S. Ryan, J. Pascoe, and D. R. Morse, "Enhanced reality fieldwork: the context-aware archaeological assistant," in *Computer Applications in Archaeology, British Archaeological Reports*, V. Gaffney, M. van Leusen, and S. Exxon, Eds., pp. 182–196, Tempus Reparatum, 1998.

[47] P. J. Brown, "The stick-e document: a framework for creating context-aware applications," *j-EPODD*, vol. 8, no. 2-3, pp. 259–272, 1995.

[48] D. Franklin and J. Flaschbart, "All gadget and no representation makes jack a dull environment," in *Proceedings of the AAAI Spring Symposium on Intelligent Environments*, pp. 155–160, Menlo Park, Calif, USA, 1998.

[49] A. Ward, A. Jones, and A. Hopper, "A new location technique for the active office," *IEEE Personal Communications*, vol. 4, no. 5, pp. 42–47, 1997.

[50] T. Rodden, K. Cheverst, K. Davies, and A. Dix, "Exploiting context in HCI design for mobile systems," in *Proceedings of the Workshop on Human Computer Interaction with Mobile Devices*, pp. 21–22, Citeseer, Glasgow, UK, May 1998.

[51] R. Hull, P. Neaves, and J. Bedford-Roberts, "Towards situated computing," in *Proceedings of the 1st International Symposium on Wearable Computers*, pp. 146–153, October 1997.

[52] G. D. Abowd, A. K. Dey, P. J. Brown, N. Davies, M. Smith, and P. Steggles, "Towards a better understanding of context and context-awareness," in *Handheld and Ubiquitous Computing*, H.-W. Gellersen, Ed., vol. 1707 of *Lecture Notes in Computer Science*, pp. 304–307, Springer, Berlin, Germany, 1999.

[53] Z. Duric, W. D. Gray, R. Heishman et al., "Integrating perceptual and cognitive modeling for adaptive and intelligent human-computer interaction," *Proceedings of the IEEE*, vol. 90, no. 7, pp. 1272–1289, 2002.

[54] K. Henricksen, J. Indulska, and A. Rakotonirainy, "Modeling context information in pervasive computing systems," in *Pervasive Computing*, pp. 167–180, Springer, Berlin, Germany, 2002.

[55] T. Gu, X. H. Wang, H. K. Pung, and D. Q. Zhang, "An ontology-based context model in intelligent environments," in *Proceedings of the Communication Networks and Distributed Systems Modeling and Simulation Conference*, pp. 270–275, 2004.

[56] A. Schmidt, M. Beigl, and H.-W. Gellersen, "There is more to context than location," *Computers & Graphics*, vol. 23, no. 6, pp. 893–901, 1999.

[57] T. Gu, H. K. Pung, and D. Q. Zhang, "Toward an OSGi-based infrastructure for context-aware applications," *IEEE Pervasive Computing*, vol. 3, no. 4, pp. 66–74, 2004.

[58] A. Almeida and D. López-de-Ipiña, "Assessing ambiguity of context data in intelligent environments: towards a more reliable context managing system," *Sensors*, vol. 12, no. 4, pp. 4934–4951, 2012.

[59] G. Stoilos, G. Stamou, V. Tzouvaras, J. Pan, and I. Horrocks, "Fuzzy owl: uncertainty and the semantic web," in *Proceedings of the International Workshop of OWL: Experiences and Directions*, Galway, Ireland, November 2005.

[60] T. Lukasiewicz and U. Straccia, "Managing uncertainty and vagueness in description logics for the semantic web," *Web Semantics: Science, Services and Agents on the World Wide Web*, vol. 6, no. 4, pp. 291–308, 2008.

[61] A. Dhall, R. Goecke, S. Lucey, and T. Gedeon, "Collecting large, richly annotated facial-expression databases from movies," *IEEE MultiMedia*, vol. 19, no. 3, pp. 34–41, 2012.

[62] J. R. Curhan and A. Pentland, "Thin slices of negotiation: predicting outcomes from conversational dynamics within the first 5 minutes," *Journal of Applied Psychology*, vol. 92, no. 3, pp. 802–811, 2007.

[63] G. B. Huang, M. Ramesh, T. Berg, and E. Learned-Miller, "Labeled faces in the wild: a database for studying face recognition in unconstrained environments," Tech. Rep. 07-49, University of Massachusetts, Amherst, Mass, USA, 2007.

[64] V. Jain and E. G. Learned-Miller, "FDDB: a benchmark for face detection in unconstrained settings," UMass Amherst Technical Report, 2010.

[65] C. Sagonas, G. Tzimiropoulos, S. Zafeiriou, and M. Pantic, "300 Faces in-the-wild challenge: the first facial landmark localization challenge," in *Proceedings of the 14th IEEE International Conference on Computer Vision Workshops (ICCVW '13)*, pp. 397–403, Sydney, Australia, December 2013.

[66] J. Shen, S. Zafeiriou, G. G. Chrysos, J. Kossaifi, G. Tzimiropoulos, and M. Pantic, "The first facial landmark tracking in-the-wild challenge: benchmark and results," in *Proceedings of the IEEE International Conference on Computer Vision Workshop (ICCVW '15)*, pp. 1003–1011, Santiago, Chile, December 2015.

[67] I. J. Goodfellow, D. Erhan, P. Luc Carrier et al., "Challenges in representation learning: a report on three machine learning contests," *Neural Networks*, vol. 64, pp. 59–63, 2015.

[68] A. Dhall, R. Goecke, J. Joshi, M. Wagner, and T. Gedeon, "Emotion recognition in the wild challenge 2013," in *Proceedings of the 15th ACM International Conference on Multimodal Interaction (ICMI '13)*, pp. 509–516, ACM, Sydney, Australia, December 2013.

[69] A. Dhall, R. Goecke, J. Joshi, K. Sikka, and T. Gedeon, "Emotion recognition in the wild challenge 2014: baseline, data and protocol," in *Proceedings of the 16th ACM International Conference on Multimodal Interaction (ICMI '14)*, pp. 461–466, ACM, Istanbul, Turkey, November 2014.

[70] A. Dhall, O. Ramana Murthy, R. Goecke, J. Joshi, and T. Gedeon, "Video and image based emotion recognition challenges in the wild: Emotiw 2015," in *Proceedings of the 2015 ACM on International Conference on Multimodal Interaction (ICMI '15)*, pp. 423–426, ACM, Seattle, Wash, USA, 2015.

[71] S. Zafeiriou, A. Papaioannou, I. Kotsia, M. A. Nicolaou, and G. Zhao, "Facial affect 'in-the-wild': a survey and a new database," in *Proceedings of the International Conference on Computer Vision and Pattern Recognition (CVPR '16) Workshops, Affect "In-the-Wild" Workshop*, June 2016.

[72] P. Over, G. M. Awad, J. Fiscus et al., *TRECVID 2010—An Overview of the Goals, Tasks, Data, Evaluation Mechanisms, and Metrics*, 2011.

[73] J. L. Lemke, "Analyzing verbal data: principles, methods, and problems," in *Second International Handbook of Science Education*, vol. 24, pp. 1471–1484, Springer, Dordrecht, Netherlands, 2012.

[74] J. J. Godfrey, E. C. Holliman, and J. McDaniel, "Switchboard, telephone speech corpus for research and development," in *Proceedings of the IEEE International Conference on Acoustics, Speech, and Signal Processing (ICASP '92)*, vol. 1, pp. 517–520, San Francisco, Calif, USA, March 1992.

[75] D. O. Olguin, P. A. Gloor, and A. S. Pentland, "Capturing individual and group behavior with wearable sensors," in *Proceedings of the AAAI Spring Symposium on Human Behavior Modeling, SSS*, vol. 9, Stanford, Calif, USA, March 2009.

[76] J. Staiano, B. Lepri, N. Aharony, F. Pianesi, N. Sebe, and A. Pentland, "Friends don't Lie— Inferring personality traits from social network structure," in *Proceedings of the 14th International Conference on Ubiquitous Computing (UbiComp '12)*, pp. 321–330, Pittsburgh, Pa, USA, September 2012.

[77] A. Vinciarelli and A. S. Pentland, "New social signals in a new interaction world: the next frontier for social signal processing," *IEEE Systems, Man, and Cybernetics Magazine*, vol. 1, no. 2, pp. 10–17, 2015.

[78] M. Raento, A. Oulasvirta, and N. Eagle, "Smartphones: an emerging tool for social scientists," *Sociological Methods & Research*, vol. 37, no. 3, pp. 426–454, 2009.

[79] M. Minelli, M. Chambers, and A. Dhiraj, *Big Data, Big Analytics: Emerging Business Intelligence and Analytic Trends for Today's Businesses*, John Wiley & Sons, New York, NY, USA, 2012.

[80] K.-H. Chang, D. Fisher, J. Canny, and B. Hartmann, "How's my mood and stress?: an efficient speech analysis library for unobtrusive monitoring on mobile phones," in *Proceedings of the 6th International Conference on Body Area Networks (BodyNets '11)*, pp. 71–77, Beijing, China, November 2011.

[81] A. Wendemuth and S. Biundo, "A companion technology for cognitive technical systems," in *Cognitive Behavioural Systems*, A. Esposito, A. M. Esposito, A. Vinciarelli, R. Hoffmann, and V. C. Müller, Eds., vol. 7403 of *Lecture Notes in Computer Science*, pp. 89–103, Springer, Berlin, Germany, 2012.

[82] Y. Wilks, "Artificial companions as a new kind of interface to the future internet," Research Report 13, Oxford Internet Institute, Oxford, UK, 2006.

[83] Y. Wilks, "Artificial companions," in *Proceedings of the International Workshop on Machine Learning for Multimodal Interaction*, pp. 36–45, Springer, 2004.

[84] R. A. Calvo and S. D'Mello, "Affect detection: an interdisciplinary review of models, methods, and their applications," *IEEE Transactions on Affective Computing*, vol. 1, no. 1, pp. 18–37, 2010.

[85] H. Gunes and B. Schuller, "Categorical and dimensional affect analysis in continuous input: current trends and future directions," *Image and Vision Computing*, vol. 31, no. 2, pp. 120–136, 2013.

[86] A. Vlachostergiou, G. Caridakis, and S. Kollias, "Context in affective multiparty and multimodal interaction: why, which, how and where?" in *Proceedings of the ACM Workshop on Understanding and Modeling Multiparty, Multimodal Interactions*, pp. 3–8, Istanbul, Turkey, November 2014.

[87] D. Gatica-Perez, "Automatic nonverbal analysis of social interaction in small groups: a review," *Image and Vision Computing*, vol. 27, no. 12, pp. 1775–1787, 2009.

[88] M. Yang, R. Bock, D. Zhang et al., "do you like a cup of 'coffee?'- the casia coffee house corpus," in *Proceedings of the 11th International Workshop on Multimodal Corpora (MMC '16)*, pp. 13–16, IEEE, Portoroz, Slovenia, May 2016.

[89] A. Vinciarelli, M. Pantic, and H. Bourlard, "Social signal processing: survey of an emerging domain," *Image and Vision Computing*, vol. 27, no. 12, pp. 1743–1759, 2009.

[90] H. C. Traue, F. Ohl, A. Brechmann et al., "A framework for emotions and dispositions in man-companion interaction," in *Chapter in Coverbal Synchrony in Human-Machine Interaction*, M. Rojc and N. Campbell, Eds., pp. 99–140, Science, New Hampshire, NH, USA, 2013.

[91] R. Akerkar, *Big Data Computing*, CRC Press, 2013.

[92] A. C.-R. Tsai, C.-E. Wu, R. T.-H. Tsai, and J. Y.-J. Hsu, "Building a concept-level sentiment dictionary based on commonsense knowledge," *IEEE Intelligent Systems*, vol. 28, no. 2, pp. 22–30, 2013.

[93] S. Poria, A. Gelbukh, A. Hussain, N. Howard, D. Das, and S. Bandyopadhyay, "Enhanced senticnet with affective labels for concept-based opinion mining," *Intelligent Systems*, vol. 28, no. 2, pp. 31–38, 2013.

[94] C. Hung and H.-K. Lin, "Using objective words in sentiwordnet to improve word-of-mouth sentiment classification," *IEEE Intelligent Systems*, vol. 28, no. 2, pp. 47–54, 2013.

[95] C. Bosco, V. Patti, and A. Bolioli, "Developing corpora for sentiment analysis: the case of irony and senti-TUT," *IEEE Intelligent Systems*, vol. 28, no. 2, pp. 55–63, 2013.

[96] A. McEwen and H. Cassimally, *Designing the Internet of Things*, John Wiley & Sons, New York, NY, USA, 2013.

[97] J. Bosch and P. M. Bosch-Sijtsema, "Softwares product lines, global development and ecosystems: collaboration in software engineering," in *Collaborative Software Engineering*, I. Mistrík, J. Grundy, A. Hoek, and J. Whitehead, Eds., pp. 77–92, Springer, Berlin, Germany, 2010.

[98] S. Jansen, A. Finkelstein, and S. Brinkkemper, "A sense of community: a research agenda for software ecosystems," in *Proceedings of the In 31st International Conference on Software Engineering-Companion*, pp. 187–190, IEEE, Vancouver, Canada, May 2009.

[99] W3C OWL Working Group, "OWL 2 web ontology language: document overview," W3C Recommendation, 2009, http://www.w3.org/TR/owl2-overview/.

[100] Stanford University, "Protégé," April 2015, http://protege.stanford.edu/.

[101] I. Horrocks, P. F. Patel-Schneider, H. Boley, S. Tabet, B. Grosof, and M. Dean, "Swrl: a semantic web rule language combining owl and ruleml," *W3C Member Submission*, vol. 21, article 79, 2004.

[102] B. Parsia and E. Sirin, "Pellet: a practical OWL-DL reasoner," in *Proceedings of the 3rd International Semantic Web Conference-Poster*, vol. 18, Citeceer, 2004.

[103] F. LAB, Fiware lab, April 2015, http://www.fi-ware.org/lab/.

[104] F. Ops, Fiware, April 2015, https://www.fi-xifi.eu/fiware-ops/service-offer-management.html.

6

State Fusion of Decentralized Optimal Unbiased FIR Filters

Xuefeng Fan and Fei Liu (iD)

Key Laboratory of Advanced Process Control for Light Industry, Jiangnan University, Wuxi 214122, China

Correspondence should be addressed to Fei Liu; fliu@jiangnan.edu.cn

Academic Editor: Rajesh Khanna

The paper presents a decentralized fusion strategy based on the optimal unbiased finite impulse response (OUFIR) filter for discrete systems with correlated process and measurement noise. We extend OUFIR filter to apply in the model with control inputs. Taking it as local filters, cross covariance between any two is calculated; then it is expressed to the fast iterative form. Finally based on cross covariance, optimal weights are utilized to fuse local estimates and the overall outcome is obtained. The numerical examples show that the proposed filter exhibits better robustness against temporary modeling uncertainties than the fusion Kalman filter used commonly.

1. Introduction

State estimation plays an important role in many applications such as control, moving target tracking, and timekeeping and clock synchronization [1]. The existing filtering methods can be classified by two types: the infinite impulse response (IIR) filter and the finite impulse response (FIR) filter [2]. Specifically, the former uses all the historical measurements, and a special case is the Kalman filter (KF) [3], while the latter utilizes limited memory over the most recent time interval [4]. It is due to the difference of structure that FIR-type filters exhibit some useful engineering features such as bounded input/bounded output (BIBO) stability, round off errors [5], and better robustness against temporary uncertainties [6].

With higher requirements of flexibility and accuracy, information fusion filtering theory for multisensor systems has been studied and widely applied [7, 8]. For example, [9, 10] proposed the weighted fusion estimator according to the maximum likelihood and weight least square respectively with local filtering error cross covariance zero or not. In [11], an optimal decentralized fusion weighted by matrix was proposed to fuse local KF in the linear unbiased minimum variance (LUMV) sense. Furthermore, the situation of correlated multiplicative and additive noise was analyzed in [8], and the decentralized KF fusion problem for cross-correlated measurement noises was investigated in [12] which also discussed the cases with feedback from the fusion center

to local sensors. Reference [13] focused on the decentralized fusion estimation problem for networked systems with random delays and packet losses, while [14] aimed at missing measurements and correlated noises. Reference [15] applied decentralized fusion to the maneuvering target tracking with multirate sampling and uncertainties in wireless sensor networks.

The fusion filtering methods nowadays take the KF as local filters mostly, so that they inherit the properties of KF, optimal but not robust under some uncertainties. Meanwhile there are few results considering decentralized FIR-type filter to deal with multisensor systems. Basically optimal FIR (OFIR) filter was obtained in [16] by minimum mean square error sense. Besides unbiased FIR (UFIR) filter was derived for real-time models and realized iteratively in [17], which can ignore the noise statistics but does not guarantee optimality. In between, [18] represents two forms of optimal unbiased FIR (OUFIR) filter, minimum variance unbiased FIR and embedded unbiasedness (EU) constraint on OFIR, and proved the identity of the two further. Contrary to the KF, the OUFIR filter is more robust and performs lower sensitivity to the initial condition [19]. In addition, there are a few new study and improved solutions on FIR filtering [20–22] developed nowadays. Some practical applications were reported [23, 24] as well.

In this correspondence, we firstly develop OUFIR filter to an extension to handle the system with or without the control inputs universally. Then considering it as local filters, cross covariance between any two is determined by batch and iterative form under the LUMV sense. Finally an optimal decentralized state fusion filter is proposed, which shows better immunity against temporary model uncertainties than traditional KF. The rest of this paper is organized as follows. In Section 2, we describe the preliminaries of system model. Local OUFIR filters are developed in Section 3. Main results about fusion and cross covariance are given in Section 4. The simulation and conclusions are provided in Sections 5 and 6, respectively.

2. System Model and Preliminaries

Consider the following linear discrete time-invariant system with multiple sensors:

$$x_n = Ax_{n-1} + Eu_n + Bw_n, \qquad (1)$$

$$y_n^{[i]} = C^{[i]}x_n + v_n^{[i]}, \qquad (2)$$

where $i = 1, 2, \cdots, r$ denotes the index of sensor, n is the discrete time index, $x_n \in \mathbb{R}^k$ and $y_n^{[i]} \in \mathbb{R}^{m_i}$ denote the state and measurement vectors, respectively, $u_n \in \mathbb{R}^p$ is the known control signal, and the system matrices A, E, B, and $C^{[i]}$ are known with appropriate dimensions. In this paper, the process noise $w_n \in \mathbb{R}^q$ and measurement noise $v_n^{[i]} \in \mathbb{R}^{m_i}$ are assumed to be correlated white noises with zero mean and

$$E\left\{ \begin{bmatrix} w_n \\ v_n^{[i]} \end{bmatrix} \begin{bmatrix} w_m^T & (v_m^{[i]})^T \end{bmatrix} \right\} = \begin{bmatrix} Q & S_i \\ S_i^T & R_i \end{bmatrix} \delta_{nm}, \qquad (3)$$

$$E\left\{ v_n^{[i]} \left(v_m^{[j]} \right)^T \right\} = R_{ij}\delta_{nm}, \quad i \neq j \qquad (4)$$

where δ_{nm} is the Kronecker delta function, i.e., if $n = m$, $\delta_{nm} = 1$, otherwise, $\delta_{nm} = 0$. For notational convenience, we assign $R_{ii} = R_i$, $Q_{ii} = Q_i$ when $i = j$. That is, the process noise w_n is correlated with each sensor noise $v_n^{[i]}$ which is also correlated with each other.

Firstly the original state-space model (1) and (2) needs to be transformed to be a form with uncorrelated noise. In this way, we add the right-hand side of (1) with a zero term $y_n^{[i]} - C^{[i]}x_n - v_n^{[i]}$ as

$$
\begin{aligned}
x_n &= Ax_{n-1} + Eu_n + Bw_n + J_i \left[y_n^{[i]} - C^{[i]}x_n - v_n^{[i]} \right] \\
&= Ax_{n-1} + Eu_n + Bw_n \\
&\quad + J_i \left[y_n^{[i]} - C^{[i]}\left(Ax_{n-1} + Eu_n + Bw_n \right) - v_n^{[i]} \right] \\
&= \overline{A}^{[i]}x_{n-1} + \overline{u}_n^{[i]} + \overline{w}_n^{[i]},
\end{aligned} \qquad (5)
$$

where $\overline{A}^{[i]} \triangleq (I - J_iC^{[i]})A$, $\overline{u}_n^{[i]} \triangleq (I - J_iC^{[i]})Eu_n + J_iy_n^{[i]}$, $\overline{w}_n^{[i]} \triangleq (I - J_iC^{[i]})Bw_n - J_iv_n^{[i]}$, and J_i is a coefficient matrix. To remove the relevance between $\overline{w}_n^{[i]}$ and $v_n^{[i]}$, the expectation

term $\mathbb{E}\{\overline{w}_n^{[i]}(v_n^{[i]})^T\}$ should be zero by definition. That is,

$$0 = \mathbb{E}\left\{ \overline{w}_n^{[i]} \left(v_m^{[i]} \right)^T \right\} = \left[\left(I - J_iC^{[i]} \right) BS_i - J_iR_i \right] \delta_{nm}, \qquad (6)$$

which further gives us $J_i = BS_i(C^{[i]}BS_i + R_i)^{-1}$. It is not difficult to find that $\mathbb{E}\{\overline{w}_n^{[i]}\} = \mathbb{E}\{(I - J_iC^{[i]})Bw_n - J_iv_n^{[i]}\} = 0$, which means that the new-defined noise term $\overline{w}_n^{[i]}$ is zero mean also. Accordingly, the cross state noise variance can be computed as

$$
\begin{aligned}
Q_{ij} &= \mathbb{E}\left\{ \overline{w}_n^{[i]} \left(\overline{w}_m^{[j]} \right)^T \right\} \\
&= \mathbb{E}\left\{ \left[\left(I - J_iC^{[i]} \right) Bw_n - J_iv_n^{[i]} \right] [\cdots]^T \right\} \\
&= \left\{ \left(I - J_iC^{[i]} \right) BQ \left[\left(I - J_iC^{[i]} \right) B \right]^T - \left(I - J_iC^{[i]} \right) \right. \\
&\quad \left. \times BS_jJ_j^T - J_iS_i^T \left[\left(I - J_jC^{[j]} \right) B \right]^T + J_iR_{ij}J_j^T \right\} \delta_{nm}.
\end{aligned} \qquad (7)
$$

As can be seen, with an auxiliary matrix J_i, there is no correlation between $\overline{w}_m^{[i]}$ and $v_n^{[i]}$, and we consider the state transition equation (5) and measurement equation (2) subsequently.

By defining an estimation horizon as $[m, n]$, where $m \triangleq n - N + 1$ is the initial time step and N is the horizon length, models (5) and (2) within the estimation horizon can be extended as [16] similarly,

$$X_{n,m} = A_{n,m}^{[i]}x_m + E_{n,m}^{[i]}U_{n,m}^{[i]} + B_{n,m}^{[i]}W_{n,m}^{[i]}, \qquad (8)$$

$$Y_{n,m}^{[i]} = C_{n,m}^{[i]}x_m + G_{n,m}^{[i]}U_{n,m}^{[i]} + F_{n,m}^{[i]}W_{n,m}^{[i]} + V_{n,m}^{[i]}, \qquad (9)$$

where the initial state x_m is assumed to be known, and the extended vectors are specified as

$$
\begin{aligned}
X_{n,m} &= \begin{bmatrix} x_n^T & x_{n-1}^T & \cdots & x_m^T \end{bmatrix}_{kN\times 1}^T, \\
U_{n,m}^{[i]} &= \begin{bmatrix} \left(\overline{u}_n^{[i]} \right)^T & \left(\overline{u}_{n-1}^{[i]} \right)^T & \cdots & \left(\overline{u}_m^{[i]} \right)^T \end{bmatrix}_{pN\times 1}^T, \\
Y_{n,m}^{[i]} &= \begin{bmatrix} \left(y_n^{[i]} \right)^T & \left(y_{n-1}^{[i]} \right)^T & \cdots & \left(y_m^{[i]} \right)^T \end{bmatrix}_{m_iN\times 1}^T, \\
W_{n,m}^{[i]} &= \begin{bmatrix} \left(\overline{w}_n^{[i]} \right)^T & \left(\overline{w}_{n-1}^{[i]} \right)^T & \cdots & \left(\overline{w}_m^{[i]} \right)^T \end{bmatrix}_{qN\times 1}^T, \\
V_{n,m}^{[i]} &= \begin{bmatrix} \left(v_n^{[i]} \right)^T & \left(v_{n-1}^{[i]} \right)^T & \cdots & \left(v_m^{[i]} \right)^T \end{bmatrix}_{m_iN\times 1}^T.
\end{aligned} \qquad (10)
$$

The involved extended matrices $A_{n,m}^{[i]} \in \mathbb{R}^{kN\times k}$, $E_{n,m}^{[i]} \in \mathbb{R}^{kN\times kN}$, $B_{n,m}^{[i]} \in \mathbb{R}^{kN\times kN}$, $C_{n,m}^{[i]} \in \mathbb{R}^{m_iN\times k}$, $G_{n,m}^{[i]} \in \mathbb{R}^{m_iN\times kN}$, and $F_{n,m}^{[i]} \in \mathbb{R}^{m_iN\times kN}$ are all N-dependent, which have the forms of

$$A_{n,m}^{[i]} = \left[\left(\overline{A}^{[i]^T} \right)^{N-1} \left(\overline{A}^{[i]^T} \right)^{N-2} \cdots \overline{A}^{[i]^T} \quad I \right]^T, \qquad (11)$$

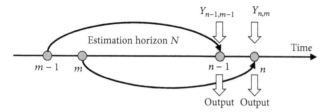

FIGURE 1: Operation time diagrams of the FIR structures.

$$B_{n,m}^{[i]} = \begin{bmatrix} I & \overline{A}^{[i]} & \cdots & \left(\overline{A}^{[i]}\right)^{N-2} & \left(\overline{A}^{[i]}\right)^{N-1} \\ 0 & I & \cdots & \left(\overline{A}^{[i]}\right)^{N-3} & \left(\overline{A}^{[i]}\right)^{N-2} \\ 0 & 0 & \ddots & \vdots & \vdots \\ 0 & 0 & \cdots & I & \overline{A}^{[i]} \\ 0 & 0 & \cdots & 0 & I \end{bmatrix}, \quad (12)$$

$$C_{n,m}^{[i]} = \overline{C}_{n,m}^{[i]} A_{n,m}^{[i]}, \quad (13)$$

$$G_{n,m}^{[i]} = \overline{C}_{n,m}^{[i]} E_{n,m}^{[i]}, \quad (14)$$

$$F_{n,m}^{[i]} = \overline{C}_{n,m}^{[i]} B_{n,m}^{[i]}, \quad (15)$$

where we assign

$$\overline{C}_{n,m}^{[i]} = \mathrm{diag}\underbrace{\left(C^{[i]} \quad C^{[i]} \quad \cdots \quad C^{[i]}\right)}_{N}, \quad (16)$$

and $E_{n,m}^{[i]} = B_{n,m}^{[i]}$.

Once the extended state-space models (8) and (9) are available, the problem considered in this paper can be formulated as follows. Given the state-space model (1) and (2), we would like to design local OUFIR filter for each sensor.

3. Local Optimal Unbiased FIR Filter

A demonstration of the FIR filter structure is provided in Figure 1. From the figure, FIR estimators explicitly employ N most recent measurements unlike KF. It is in this way that some nice properties like better robustness are achieved. Based on it, for i^{th} subsystem represented as (8) and (9), we design a local OUFIR filter in this section.

3.1. Batch Form. The linear FIR filter for each sensor can be expressed as the following batch form [25] generally:

$$\hat{x}_n^{[i]} = H_n^{[i]} Y_{n,m}^{[i]} + L_n^{[i]} U_{n,m}^{[i]} \quad (17)$$

for gain matrices $H_n^{[i]}$ and $L_n^{[i]}$. It is noted that the filter defined as (17) handles all the measurements and input values collected within the estimation horizon at one time.

Introduce unbiasedness constraint (or deadbeat constraint) [26]:

$$\mathbb{E}\left\{\hat{x}_n^{[i]}\right\} = \mathbb{E}\left\{x_n\right\} \quad (18)$$

in the estimation (17) where x_n can be specified as

$$x_n = \left(\overline{A}^{[i]}\right)^{n-m} x_m + \overline{E}_{n,m}^{[i]} U_{n,m}^{[i]} + \overline{B}_{n,m}^{[i]} W_{n,m}^{[i]}, \quad (19)$$

and $\overline{E}_{n,m}^{[i]}, \overline{B}_{n,m}^{[i]}$ are the first vector rows of $E_{n,m}^{[i]}, B_{n,m}^{[i]}$ respectively. By substituting (19) and (17) into (18), replacing the term $Y_{n,m}^{[i]}$ with (9), and providing the averaging, one arrives at two following constraints

$$H_n^{[i]} C_{n,m}^{[i]} = \left(\overline{A}^{[i]}\right)^{n-m}, \quad (20)$$

$$L_n^{[i]} = \overline{E}_{n,m}^{[i]} - H_n^{[i]} G_{n,m}^{[i]}. \quad (21)$$

Substituting (21) into (17) yields

$$\hat{x}_n^{[i]} = H_n^{[i]} \left(Y_{n,m}^{[i]} - G_{n,m}^{[i]} U_{n,m}^{[i]}\right) + \overline{E}_{n,m}^{[i]} U_{n,m}^{[i]}. \quad (22)$$

Provided $\hat{x}_n^{[i]}$, the instantaneous filtering error can be defined as $e_n^{[i]} = x_n - \hat{x}_n^{[i]}$, then the OUFIR filter is derived by solving the following optimization problem

$$H_n^{[i]} = \arg\min_{H_n^{[i]}} \mathbb{E}\left\{\left[e_n^{[i]}\left(e_n^{[i]}\right)^T\right]\right\}, \quad (23)$$

where $H_n^{[i]}$ should satisfy the constrain (20).

By replacing x_n with (19) and $\hat{x}_n^{[i]}$ with (22), and substituting the unbiasedness constrain (20), filtering error is obtained

$$e_n^{[i]} = \left[\left(\overline{A}^{[i]}\right)^{n-m} - H_n^{[i]} C_{n,m}^{[i]}\right] x_m$$
$$+ \left(\overline{B}_{n,m}^{[i]} - H_n^{[i]} F_{n,m}^{[i]}\right) W_{n,m}^{[i]} - H_n^{[i]} V_{n,m}^{[i]} \quad (24)$$
$$= \left(\overline{B}_{n,m}^{[i]} - H_n^{[i]} F_{n,m}^{[i]}\right) W_{n,m}^{[i]} - H_n^{[i]} V_{n,m}^{[i]}.$$

Employing the trace operation and providing the averaging, the optimization problem (23) can be rewritten as

$$H_n^{[i]} = \arg\min_{H_n^{[i]}} \mathrm{tr}\left[\left(\overline{B}_{n,m}^{[i]} - H_n^{[i]} F_{n,m}^{[i]}\right)\right.$$
$$\left. \cdot Q_{n,m}^{[ii]} \left(\overline{B}_{n,m}^{[i]} - H_n^{[i]} F_{n,m}^{[i]}\right)^T - H_n^{[i]} R_{n,m}^{[ii]} \left(H_n^{[i]}\right)^T\right]. \quad (25)$$

It is not difficult to get

$$Q_{n,m}^{[ij]} = \mathrm{diag}\underbrace{\left(Q_{ij} \quad Q_{ij} \quad \cdots \quad Q_{ij}\right)}_{N},$$
$$R_{n,m}^{[ij]} = \mathrm{diag}\underbrace{\left(R_{ij} \quad R_{ij} \quad \cdots \quad R_{ij}\right)}_{N}, \quad (26)$$

where Q_{ij} is given in (7), and R_{ij} is defined in (4). Referring to [19], we can obtain the following gain:

$$H_n^{[i]} = \left(\overline{A}^{[i]}\right)^{n-m} \left[\left(C_{n,m}^{[i]}\right)^T Z_{w+v,n}^{-1} C_{n,m}^{[i]}\right]^{-1} \left(C_{n,m}^{[i]}\right)^T$$
$$\times Z_{w+v,n}^{-1} + \overline{B}_{n,m}^{[i]} Q_{n,m} \left(F_{n,m}^{[i]}\right)^T Z_{w+v,n}^{-1} \left\{I - C_{n,m}^{[i]}\right. \quad (27)$$
$$\times \left[\left(C_{n,m}^{[i]}\right)^T Z_{w+v,n}^{-1} C_{n,m}^{[i]}\right]^{-1} \left(C_{n,m}^{[i]}\right)^T Z_{w+v,n}^{-1}\right\},$$

where $Z_{w+v,n} = Z_{w,n} + R_{n,m}$ and

$$Z_{w,n} = F_{n,m}^{[i]} Q_{n,m}^{[ii]} \left(F_{n,m}^{[i]} \right)^T. \tag{28}$$

At this point, the local OUFIR filter with batch form is specified by (22) with filter gain $H_n^{[i]}$ provided as (26). As mentioned, this structure is not suitable for the subsequent fusion step, as N measurements are operated at one time and there is no error covariance available to quantify the estimation accuracy. To address these issues, an equivalent iterative computational formula is given below.

3.2. Equivalent Iterative Computation. Introducing $\hat{x}_n^{[i]} = \hat{x}_{1,n}^{[i]} + \hat{x}_{2,n}^{[i]}$, (22) can be divided into two parts shown as follows:

$$\hat{x}_{1,n}^{[i]} = \overline{E}_{n,m}^{[i]} U_{n,m}^{[i]}, \tag{29}$$

$$\hat{x}_{2,n}^{[i]} = H_n^{[i]} \left(Y_{n,m}^{[i]} - G_{n,m}^{[i]} U_{n,m}^{[i]} \right), \tag{30}$$

and consider each components separately.

By former transformations, for (29), recursive algorithm is represented easily as

$$\hat{x}_{1,n}^{[i]} = \overline{u}_n^{[i]} + \overline{A}^{[i]} \overline{u}_{n-1}^{[i]} + \left(\overline{A}^{[i]} \right)^2 \overline{u}_{n-2}^{[i]} + \cdots$$

$$+ \left(\overline{A}^{[i]} \right)^{N-1} \overline{u}_m^{[i]} = \overline{u}_n^{[i]} + \overline{A}^{[i]} \overline{E}_{n-1,m}^{[i]} U_{n-1,m}^{[i]} \tag{31}$$

$$= \overline{u}_n^{[i]} + \overline{A}^{[i]} \hat{x}_{1,n-1}^{[i]}$$

Assigning $\widetilde{Y}_{n,m}^{[i]} = Y_{n,m}^{[i]} - G_{n,m}^{[i]} U_{n,m}^{[i]}$, this part becomes $\hat{x}_{2,n}^{[i]} = H_n^{[i]} \widetilde{Y}_{n,m}^{[i]}$. For this estimate, we notice a iterative form proposed in [19], which is represented similarly

$$\hat{x}_{2,n}^{[i]} = A^{[i]} \hat{x}_{2,n-1}^{[i]}$$

$$+ \left(\widetilde{H}_n^{[i]} + \overline{H}_n^{[i]} \right) \left(\widetilde{y}_n^{[i]} - C^{[i]} \times A^{[i]} \hat{x}_{2,n-1}^{[i]} \right) \tag{32}$$

where $\widetilde{H}_n^{[i]}$ and $\overline{H}_n^{[i]}$ are gain matrices. Besides, $\widetilde{y}_n^{[i]}$ is the first vector rows of $\widetilde{Y}_{n,m}^{[i]}$, substituting (31), which is given by

$$\widetilde{y}_n^{[i]} = y_n^{[i]} - C^{[i]} \overline{E}_{n,m}^{[i]} U_{n,m}^{[i]} \tag{33}$$

$$= y_n^{[i]} - C^{[i]} \left(u_n^{[i]} + \overline{A}^{[i]} \hat{x}_{1,n-1}^{[i]} \right) \tag{34}$$

Then putting (33) into (32), iterative form is

$$\hat{x}_{2,n}^{[i]} = \overline{A}^{[i]} \hat{x}_{2,n-1}^{[i]} + \left(\widetilde{H}_n^{[i]} + \overline{H}_n^{[i]} \right)$$

$$\cdot \left[y_n^{[i]} - C^{[i]} \left(u_n^{[i]} + \overline{A}^{[i]} \hat{x}_{1,n-1}^{[i]} \right) - C^{[i]} \overline{A}^{[i]} \hat{x}_{2,n-1}^{[i]} \right]. \tag{35}$$

TABLE 1: Computation of the initial state.

1: $m = n - N + 1$, $s = m + k$
2: $M_{s-2} = \overline{B}_{s-2,m}^{[i]} Q_{s-2,m}(F_{s-2,m}^{[i]})^T$
3: $M_{s-1} = \overline{B}_{s-1,m}^{[i]} Q_{s-1,m}(F_{s-1,m}^{[i]})^T$
4: $U_{s-1} = \overline{B}_{s-1,m}^{[i]} Q_{s-1,m}(\overline{B}_{s-1,m}^{[i]})^T$
5: $P_{s-1} = U_{s-1} - \overline{A}^{[i]} M_{s-2} Z_{w+v,s-2}^{-1} (M_{s-2})^T (\overline{A}^{[i]})^T$
6: $N_{s-1} = [(C_{s-1,m}^{[i]})^T Z_{w+v,s-1}^{-1} C_{s-1,m}^{[i]}]^{-1}$
7: $G_{s-1} = A_{s-1,m}^{[i]} - \overline{A}^{[i]} M_{s-2} Z_{w+v,s-2}^{-1} C_{s-1,m}^{[i]}$
8: $\hat{x}_{s-1}^{[i]} = [(\overline{A}^{[i]})^{s-m-1} N_{s-1} (C_{s-1,m}^{[i]})^T + M_{s-1} - M_{s-1}$
$\times Z_{w+v,s-1}^{-1} C_{s-1,m}^{[i]} N_{s-1} (C_{s-1,m}^{[i]})^T] Z_{w+v,s-1}^{-1}$
$\times (Y_{s-1,m}^{[i]} - G_{s-1,m}^{[i]} U_{s-1,m}^{[i]}) + \overline{E}_{s-1,m}^{[i]} U_{s-1,m}^{[i]}$

Combining (31) and (35), we arrive at

$$\hat{x}_n^{[i]} = \hat{x}_{1,n}^{[i]} + \hat{x}_{2,n}^{[i]} = u_n^{[i]} + \overline{A}^{[i]} \hat{x}_{1,n-1}^{[i]} + \overline{A}^{[i]} \hat{x}_{2,n-1}^{[i]}$$

$$+ \left(\widetilde{H}_n^{[i]} + \overline{H}_n^{[i]} \right)$$

$$\cdot \left[y_n^{[i]} - C^{[i]} \times \left(u_n^{[i]} + \overline{A}^{[i]} \hat{x}_{1,n-1}^{[i]} \right) - C^{[i]} \overline{A}^{[i]} \hat{x}_{2,n-1}^{[i]} \right] \tag{36}$$

$$= \hat{x}_n^{[i]*} + \left(\widetilde{H}_n^{[i]} + \overline{H}_n^{[i]} \right) \left(y_n^{[i]} - C^{[i]} \hat{x}_n^{[i]*} \right).$$

which suggests easily that the prior estimate is $\hat{x}_n^{[i]*} = \overline{A}^{[i]} \hat{x}_{n-1}^{[i]} + u_n^{[i]}$. Referring to [27], we finally come up with a general iterative OUFIR filtering algorithm similarly whose pseudocode is summarized as Algorithm 1 in which l is an auxiliary variable replaced with n. Unlike the OFIR or KF, it is because of unbiasedness condition that the filter does not require initial information. Instead that can be defined at $s = m + k$ using a short batch form given in Table 1; k is the number of system states. In the Algorithm 1, variable l ranges from s to n. The true filtering result corresponds to $l = n$.

Once the local estimates $\hat{x}_n^{[i]}$ are corrected, $i = 1, 2, \ldots, r$, an optimal fusion strategy based on cross covariance is employed to get the overall estimates, which is introduced below.

4. Decentralized Fusion Filter

In this section, we will investigate the decentralized fusion filters and first deduce the corresponding filtering error cross covariance between any two local subsystems with FIR structure. Due to inefficient computation, then we find its fast iterative form. Based on these, a multisensor decentralized fusion OUFIR filtering algorithm is finally presented.

4.1. Cross Covariance Matrices and Iterative Computation. For the ith sensor subsystem, filtering error $e_n^{[i]}$ is written as (24) where filtering gain $H_n^{[i]}$ is specified as (27). So the cross covariance matrix between the ith and the jth subsystem can be showed as

$$P_n^{[ij]} = E \left\{ e_n^{[i]} \left(e_n^{[j]} \right)^T \right\}$$

$$= E \left\{ \left[\left(\overline{B}_{n,m}^{[i]} - H_n^{[i]} F_{n,m}^{[i]} \right) W_{n,m}^{[i]} - H_n^{[i]} V_{n,m}^{[i]} \right] [\cdots]^T \right\}$$

```
1:  for n = N − 1, N, . . . do
2:      m = n − N + 1, s = m + k
        Table 1: Computation of the initial state
3:      for l = s : n do
```
$$4: \quad P_l^{[i]} = \overline{A}^{[i]} P_{l-1}^{[i]} (\overline{A}^{[i]})^T + Q_{ii} - \overline{A}^{[i]} P_{l-1}^{[i]} \times (C^{[i]})^T \Upsilon_{l-1}^{[i]} C^{[i]} P_{l-1}^{[i]} (\overline{A}^{[i]})^T$$
$$5: \quad G_l^{[i]} = \overline{A}^{[i]} [I - P_{l-1}^{[i]} (C^{[i]})^T \Upsilon_{l-1}^{[i]} C^{[i]}] G_{l-1}^{[i]}$$
$$6: \quad \Upsilon_l^{[i]} = [C^{[i]} P_l^{[i]} (C^{[i]})^T + R_{ij}]^{-1}$$
$$7: \quad N_l^{[i]} = [N_{l-1}^{[i]} + (G_l^{[i]})^T (C^{[i]})^T \Upsilon_l^{[i]} C^{[i]} G_l^{[i]}]^{-1}$$
$$8: \quad \widetilde{H}_l^{[i]} = P_l^{[i]} (C^{[i]})^T \Upsilon_l^{[i]}$$
$$9: \quad \overline{H}_l^{[i]} = (I - \widetilde{H}_l^{[i]} C^{[i]}) G_l^{[i]} N_l^{[i]} (G_l^{[i]})^T (C^{[i]})^T \Upsilon_l^{[i]}$$
$$10: \quad \widehat{x}_l^{[i]*} = \overline{A}^{[i]} \widehat{x}_{l-1}^{[i]} + u_l^{[i]}$$
$$11: \quad \widehat{x}_l^{[i]} = \widehat{x}_l^{[i]*} + (\widetilde{H}_l^{[i]} + \overline{H}_l^{[i]})(y_l^{[i]} - C^{[i]} \widehat{x}_l^{[i]*})$$
```
12:     end for
13:     x̂_n^[i] = x̂_l^[i]
14: end for
```

ALGORITHM 1: General iterative OUFIR filtering algorithm.

$$= \left(\overline{B}_{n,m}^{[i]} - H_n^{[i]} F_{n,m}^{[i]}\right) Q_{n,m}^{[ij]} \left(\overline{B}_{n,m}^{[j]} - H_n^{[j]} F_{n,m}^{[j]}\right)^T$$
$$+ H_n^{[i]} R_{n,m}^{[ij]} \left(H_n^{[j]}\right)^T \tag{37}$$

where $Q_{n,m}^{[ij]}, R_{n,m}^{[ij]}$ are defined in (26).

The batch cross covariance given by (37) is exact but takes a large amount of computation. To find a recursive formula, one may combine $\widehat{x}_l^{[i]}$ given in Algorithm 1 and (5) with respect to an auxiliary variable l, so $e_l^{[i]}$ can be rewritten as

$$e_l^{[i]} = \overline{A}^{[i]} x_{l-1} + \overline{u}_l^{[i]} + \overline{w}_l^{[i]} - \widehat{x}_l^{[i]*} - \left(\widetilde{H}_l^{[i]} + \overline{H}_l^{[i]}\right) \tag{38}$$
$$\times \left(y_l^{[i]} - C^{[i]} \widehat{x}_l^{[i]*}\right).$$

Substitute x_l given by (5) and (2) into (38), then transform it into

$$e_l^{[i]} = \overline{A}^{[i]} x_{l-1} + \overline{u}_l^{[i]} + \overline{w}_l^{[i]} - \overline{A}^{[i]} \widehat{x}_{l-1}^{[i]} - u_l^{[i]} - \left(\widetilde{H}_l^{[i]}\right.$$
$$\left. + \overline{H}_l^{[i]}\right) \left(C^{[i]} \overline{A}^{[i]} x_{l-1} + C^{[i]} \overline{u}_l^{[i]} + C^{[i]} \overline{w}_l^{[i]} + v_l^{[i]}\right.$$
$$\left. - C^{[i]} \overline{A}^{[i]} \widehat{x}_{l-1}^{[i]} - C^{[i]} u_l^{[i]}\right) = \left[\overline{A}^{[i]}\right. \tag{39}$$
$$\left. - \left(\widetilde{H}_l^{[i]} + \overline{H}_l^{[i]}\right) C^{[i]} \overline{A}^{[i]}\right] e_{l-1}^{[i]} - \left[I\right.$$
$$\left. - \left(\widetilde{H}_l^{[i]} + \overline{H}_l^{[i]}\right) C^{[i]}\right] \overline{w}_l^{[i]} - \left(\widetilde{H}_l^{[i]} + \overline{H}_l^{[i]}\right) v_l^{[i]}.$$

So $P_l^{[ij]}$ can now be computed iteratively over the recursive form of

$$P_l^{[ij]} = E \left\{ \left(\left[\overline{A}^{[i]} - \left(\widetilde{H}_l^{[i]} + \overline{H}_l^{[i]}\right) C^{[i]} \overline{A}^{[i]}\right] e_{l-1}^{[i]}\right.\right.$$
$$\left. - \left[I - \left(\widetilde{H}_l^{[i]} + \overline{H}_l^{[i]}\right) C^{[i]}\right] \overline{w}_l^{[i]}\right.$$

$$\left. - \left(\widetilde{H}_l^{[i]} + \overline{H}_l^{[i]}\right) v_l^{[i]}\right) (\cdots)^T \right\} = \left[\overline{A}^{[i]} - \left(\widetilde{H}_l^{[i]}\right.\right.$$
$$\left. + \overline{H}_l^{[i]}\right) C^{[i]} \overline{A}^{[i]}\right] P_{l-1}^{[ij]} (\cdots)^T + \left[I - \left(\widetilde{H}_l^{[i]} + \overline{H}_l^{[i]}\right)\right.$$
$$\left. \cdot C^{[i]}\right] Q_{ij} (\cdots)^T + \left(\widetilde{H}_l^{[i]} + \overline{H}_l^{[i]}\right) R_{ij} (\cdots)^T \tag{40}$$

where l ranges from s to n, and the output is taken when $l = n$ similarly. The initial value $P_{s-1}^{[ij]}$ is given in a short batch form by (37) as

$$P_{s-1}^{[ij]} = E \left\{ e_{s-1}^{[i]} \left(e_{s-1}^{[i]}\right)^T \right\} = \left(\overline{B}_{s-1,m}^{[i]} - H_{s-1}^{[i]} F_{s-1,m}^{[i]}\right)$$
$$\cdot Q_{n,m}^{[ij]} \left(\overline{B}_{s-1,m}^{[j]} - H_{s-1}^{[j]} F_{s-1,m}^{[j]}\right)^T \tag{41}$$
$$+ H_{s-1}^{[j]} R_{n,m}^{[ij]} \left(H_{s-1}^{[j]}\right)^T.$$

Clearly the pseudocode is shown in Algorithm 2.

4.2. Decentralized OUFIR Filtering Algorithm. Based on the local filters $\widehat{x}_n^{[i]}$ in Algorithm 1 and the filtering error cross covariance matrices between any two local filters in Algorithm 2, we can get the decentralized fusion filter weighted by matrices in the LUMV sense [7]. Introduce the synthetically unbiased estimator

$$\widehat{x}_n^o = \alpha_1 \widehat{x}_n^{[1]} + \alpha_2 \widehat{x}_n^{[2]} + \cdots + \alpha_r \widehat{x}_n^{[r]}, \tag{42}$$

where α_i are arbitrary matrices. From the unbiasedness assumption, we have $E\{\widehat{x}_n\} = E\{x_n\}$ and $E\{\widehat{x}_n^{[i]}\} = E\{x_n\}$. Taking the expectation in (42) yields

$$\alpha_1 + \alpha_2 + \cdots + \alpha_r = \overline{I} \tag{43}$$

```
 1: for n = N - 1, N, ... do
 2:     m = n - N + 1, s = m + k
 3:     for i = 1 : r do
 4:         for j = 1 : r do
 5:             P_{s-1}^{[ij]} = (\overline{B}_{s-1,m}^{[i]} - H_{s-1}^{[i]} F_{s-1,m}^{[i]}) Q_{s-1,m}^{[ij]} (\overline{B}_{s-1,m}^{[j]} - H_{s-1}^{[j]} F_{s-1,m}^{[j]})^T + H_{s-1}^{[i]} R_{s-1,m}^{[ij]} (H_{s-1}^{[j]})^T
 6:             for l = s : n do
 7:                 P_l^{[ij]} = [\overline{A}^{[i]} - (\widetilde{H}_l^{[i]} + \overline{H}_l^{[i]}) C^{[i]} \overline{A}^{[i]}] P_{l-1}^{[ij]} (\cdots)^T + [I - (\widetilde{H}_l^{[i]} + \overline{H}_l^{[i]}) C^{[i]}] Q_{ij}(\cdots)^T + (\widetilde{H}_l^{[i]} + \overline{H}_l^{[i]}) R_{ij}(\cdots)^T
 8:             end for
 9:             P_n^{[ij]} = P_l^{[ij]}
10:         end for
11:     end for
12: end for
```

ALGORITHM 2: Iterative form for $P_n^{[ij]}$.

```
1: J_i = BS_i(C^{[i]} BS_i + R_i)^{-1}
2: \overline{A}^{[i]} = (I - J_i C^{[i]})A
3: \overline{u}_n^{[i]} = (I - J_i C^{[i]})Eu_n + J_i y_n^{[i]}
4: \overline{w}_n^{[i]} = (I - J_i C^{[i]})Bw_n - J_i v_n^{[i]}
5: Algorithm 1: General Iterative OUFIR Filtering Algorithm
6: Algorithm 2: Iterative Form for P_n^{[ij]}
7: \Sigma = [P_n^{[ij]}], i = 1, 2 \cdots r
8: \overline{\Lambda} = (\overline{I}^T \Sigma^{-1} \overline{I})^{-1} \overline{I}^T \Sigma^{-1}
9: \widehat{x}_n^o = \overline{\alpha}_1 \widehat{x}_n^{[1]} + \overline{\alpha}_2 \widehat{x}_n^{[2]} + \cdots + \overline{\alpha}_r \widehat{x}_n^{[r]}
```

ALGORITHM 3: Optimal decentralized fusion OUFIR filter.

where $\overline{I} = \begin{bmatrix} I_k & I_k & \cdots & I_k \end{bmatrix}^T_{kr \times k}$ and I_k denotes $k \times k$ identity matrix. Then fusion estimation error is $e_n = x_n - \widehat{x}_n^o = \sum_{i=1}^r \alpha_i e_n^{[i]}$. Let $\Lambda = \begin{bmatrix} \alpha_1 & \alpha_2 & \cdots & \alpha_r \end{bmatrix}_{kr \times k}$; the error variance matrix of the fusion estimator is

$$P = E\left\{e_n e_n^T\right\} = \Lambda \Sigma \Lambda^T \tag{44}$$

where $\Sigma \triangleq [P_n^{[ij]}]_{i,j=1,2,\cdots,r}$ is an $kr \times kr$ symmetric positive definite matrix where $P_n^{[ij]} \triangleq \{(x_n - \widehat{x}_n^{[i]})(x_n - \widehat{x}_n^{[j]})^T\}$ is from (40).

To find the optimal weights Λ under the constrain (43), applying the Lagrange multiplier approach, the target function is defined as

$$J = \text{tr}\left(\Lambda \Sigma \Lambda^T\right) + 2\Gamma\left(\Lambda \overline{I} - I_k\right) \tag{45}$$

where $\Gamma = (\lambda_{ij})_{k \times k}$. Set $\partial J/\partial \Lambda = 0$ and note that $\Sigma^T = \Sigma$; we have

$$2\Lambda\Sigma + 2\Gamma\overline{I}^T = 0 \tag{46}$$

Combining (43) and (46) yields the matrix equation as

$$\begin{bmatrix} \Lambda & \Gamma \end{bmatrix} = \begin{bmatrix} 0 & I_k \end{bmatrix} \begin{bmatrix} \Sigma & \overline{I} \\ \overline{I}^T & 0 \end{bmatrix}^{-1}. \tag{47}$$

Noted Σ is a symmetric positive definite matrix and using the formula of the inverse matrix [28] we have

$$\Lambda = \left(\overline{I}^T \Sigma^{-1} \overline{I}\right)^{-1} \overline{I}^T \Sigma^{-1} \tag{48}$$

Pseudocode is summarized by Algorithm 3, and the corresponding structure is shown in Figure 2. As can be seen, each sensor subsystem estimates the state independently at time n. Next fusion layer determines optimal matrix weights. As a basic requirement, the proposed decentralized fusion filter will have better accuracy than any local one. Different from fusion KF, the proposed method does not relay on the initial information about $\widehat{x}_0$, P_0, and $P_0^{[ij]}$, and it performs better robustness.

5. Simulation

In this section, we consider two basic models of moving target tracking system and 1 degree of freedom (1-DOF) torsion system. Fusion OUFIR filter is applied to above models under various conditions such as temporary modeling uncertainties and unknown noise statistics. Compared to fusion Kalman filter (conveniently FOUF and FKF denote as fusion OUFIR filter and fusion KF filter respectively next), it demonstrates better performance.

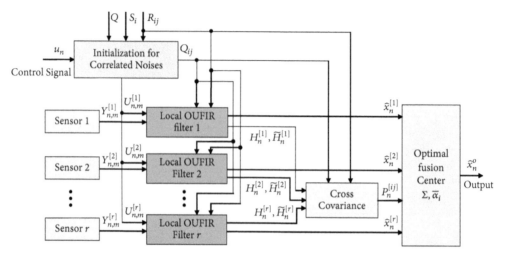

FIGURE 2: The structure of decentralized OUFIR filter.

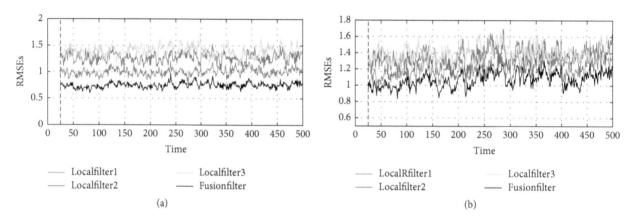

FIGURE 3: RMSEs produced by local and fusion filters: (a) the first state and (b) the second state.

5.1. Moving Target Tracking System. With three sensors, a simplified model can be specified by (1) and (2) with $E = [1 \ 1]^T$, $B = [0.1 \ 1]^T$, and

$$A = \begin{bmatrix} 1 & \tau \\ 0 & 1 \end{bmatrix} \quad (49)$$

where $i = 1, 2, 3$, $\tau = 0.1$, control signal $u_n = 0.1$, and $C_1 = C_2 = C_3 = [1 \ 0]$. And the measurement noise $v_n^{[i]}$ is represented as $v_n^{[i]} = b_i w_n + \xi_n^{[i]}$, which are correlated with the white process noise $\sigma_w^2 = 0.1$. The correlation coefficients are $b_1 = 0.5$, $b_2 = 0.8$, and $b_3 = 0.4$. $\xi_n^{[i]}$ are white Gaussian noise with zero mean and variances $R_{\xi[1]} = 5$, $R_{\xi[2]} = 8$, and $R_{\xi[3]} = 10$, respectively, and are independent of w_n. Easily we can get R_{ij} and S_i as

$$R_{ij} = b_i Q b_j^T + R_{\xi[i]} \delta_{ij} \quad (50)$$

$$S_i = E\left\{w_n \left(v_n^{[i]}\right)^T\right\} = Q b_i^T \quad (51)$$

5.1.1. Estimation Accuracy with Correct Noise Variances. In this section, we assume that all the modeling parameters are known accurately and show that FOUF outperforms any local filter. The process was simulated over 500 points, and the estimation horizon length used is $N = 20$. The average root mean square error (RMSE) based on 100 Monte-Carlo (MC) runs is shown in Figure 3. The result proves that the proposed approach has better accuracy exactly.

5.1.2. Sensitivity to Incorrect Noise Variance. The knowledge of noise is typically not known exactly in practice, which does not guarantee optimality. To figure out the effect of noise variances, we give an idea about the FKF and FOUF immunity to noise statistics' errors in the worst case. Introducing error coefficient β, designed covariances are substituted here with $Q^* = \beta Q$.

$\sqrt{\text{tr}(J_n)}$ of FKF and FOUF over 100 MC runs for $\beta = 0.01, 0.1, 1, 10, 100$ are shown in Figure 4 and also listed in Table 2. As can be seen, errors in the FKF grow rapidly with β and even become unacceptable, while the proposed FOUF has much higher immunity against noise error when $\beta \le 1$. Otherwise, performance of FOUF exhibits closely to FKFs.

TABLE 2: Performance of FOUF and FKF with respect to different β.

β	0.01	0.1	1	10	100
FKF	4.42	1.86	1.24	1.28	2.53
FOUF	1.58	1.47	1.28	1.29	2.58

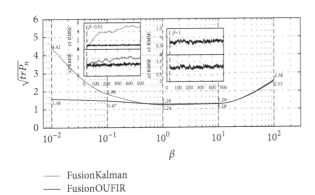

—— FusionKalman
—— FusionOUFIR

FIGURE 4: Average $\sqrt{\mathrm{tr}(J_n)}$ against system noises uncertainties $\beta = 0.01, 0.1, 1, 10, 100$ between FKF and FOUF.

5.1.3. Immunity to Errors in the Noise Statistics. To investigate the effect of temporary inaccurate statistics, the state noise variance is set to vary as follows: $\sigma_w^2 = 0.5$ when $100 \le n \le 200$ and $\sigma_w^2 = 0.1$ otherwise. And invariable value $\sigma_w^2 = 0.1$ is used in all the algorithms. The average RMSEs based on 100 MC runs are provides by Figure 5. One can see that FOUF has much higher immunity against errors of noise statistic than FKF. Besides it is noted that the first state is more obvious about robustness performance.

5.1.4. Robustness against Model Uncertainties. To identify the robustness of each tracker against temporary model uncertainties, we set

$$A = \begin{bmatrix} 1 & \tau + d \\ 0 & 1 \end{bmatrix} \tag{52}$$

where $d = 0.1$ when $100 \le n \le 300$ and $d = 0$ otherwise. The process is simulated over 500 subsequent points with correct noise statistics. Comparing the FKF as a benchmark, Figures 6(a) and 6(b) illustrate the typical response under the model mismatch introduced. From figures, one infers that the FOUF's peak value is smaller and recovers to normal faster than the FKF's, particularly with the first state.

5.2. 1-DOF Torsion System. We consider 1-DOF torsion system [29] as the object whose schematic and parameters are provided by Figure 7 and Table 3. Referring from [29] of the equations of motion, the continuous-time model can be described by

$$\frac{\partial x}{\partial t} = Ax + Bu, \tag{53}$$

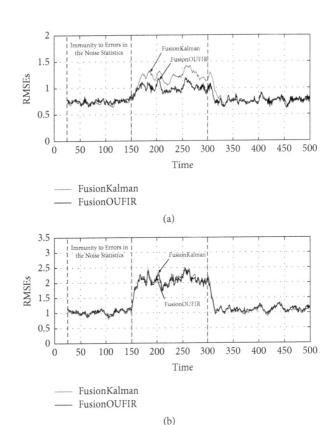

—— FusionKalman
—— FusionOUFIR

(a)

—— FusionKalman
—— FusionOUFIR

(b)

FIGURE 5: RMSEs produced by FKF and FUF with imprecisely defined noise statistics: (a) the first state and (b) the second state.

where $x = \begin{bmatrix} \theta_1 & \theta_2 & \dot{\theta}_1 & \dot{\theta}_2 \end{bmatrix}^T$ and

$$A = \begin{bmatrix} 0 & 0 & 1 & 0 \\ 0 & 0 & 0 & 1 \\ -\dfrac{K_s}{J_1} & \dfrac{K_s}{J_1} & -\dfrac{B_1}{J_1} & 0 \\ \dfrac{K_s}{J_2} & -\dfrac{K_s}{J_2} & 0 & -\dfrac{B_2}{J_2} \end{bmatrix},$$

$$B = \begin{bmatrix} 0 \\ 0 \\ \dfrac{1}{J_1} \\ 0 \end{bmatrix}. \tag{54}$$

Discretize this process with sampling time $T_s = 0.01s$, and the discrete state-space model is achieved as

$$x_{n+1} = Gx_n + Fu_n + w_n, \tag{55}$$

where w_n is introduced to describe the stochastic properties of states, u_n is input signal, $G = e^{AT_s}$, and $F = \int_0^{T_s} e^{A\tau} d\tau B$. The angular positions of two loads are measured using three groups of sensors, and the observation equation is given by $y_n^{[i]} = C^{[i]} x_n + v_n^{[i]}$, where $i = 1, 2, 3$,

$$C^{[1]} = C^{[2]} = C^{[3]} = \begin{bmatrix} 1 & 0 & 0 & 0 \\ 0 & 1 & 0 & 0 \end{bmatrix}. \tag{56}$$

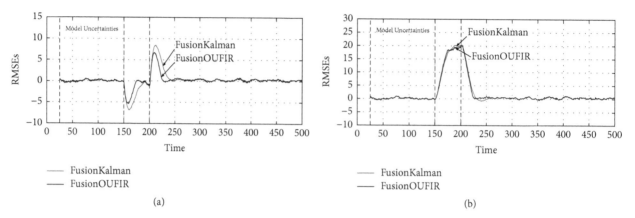

(a)   (b)

FIGURE 6: Estimation errors by FKF and FOUF filter against temporary model uncertainty in a gap of $100 \leq n \leq 150$: (a) the first state and (b) the second state.

TABLE 3: Physical parameters of 1-DOF torsion system, where EMI is equal to equivalent moment of inertia, and EVD is equivalent viscous damping.

Constant	Value	Unit	Description
K_s	1.0	N.m/rad	Stiffness of flexible coupling
J_1	2.2e-4	Kg.m^2	EMI at the rigid load shaft
J_2	5.45e-4	Kg.m^2	EMI at the torsion load shaft
B_1	0.015	N.m.s/rad^2	EVD of rigid load
B_2	0.015	N.m.s/rad	EVD of torsion load
θ_1	–	rad	angular positions of rigid load
θ_1	–	rad	angular positions of torsion load

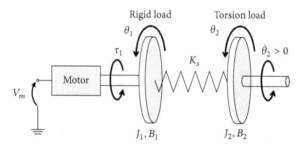

FIGURE 7: Schematic of 1-DOF Torsion system.

The correlation between state and measurement noises is described as $v_n^{[i]} = b^{[i]} w_n + \xi_n^{[i]}$, where the coefficients are

$$b^{[1]} = \begin{bmatrix} 0.5 & 0 & 0 & 0 \\ 0 & 0.5 & 0 & 0 \end{bmatrix},$$

$$b^{[2]} = \begin{bmatrix} 0.8 & 0 & 0 & 0 \\ 0 & 0.8 & 0 & 0 \end{bmatrix}, \quad (57)$$

$$b^{[3]} = \begin{bmatrix} 0.4 & 0 & 0 & 0 \\ 0 & 0.4 & 0 & 0 \end{bmatrix}.$$

The measurement noises variances are assigned as $\sigma_{\xi_1^{[1]}}^2 = \sigma_{\xi_2^{[1]}}^2 = 5$, $\sigma_{\xi_1^{[2]}}^2 = \sigma_{\xi_2^{[2]}}^2 = 8$, and $\sigma_{\xi_1^{[3]}}^2 = \sigma_{\xi_2^{[3]}}^2 = 3$.

5.2.1. Imprecisely Defined Noise Statistics. With inaccurateness, the state noise variance is set to vary as follows: $\sigma_{w_j}^2 = 0.05$ when $150 \leq n \leq 300$ and $\sigma_{w_j}^2 = 0.01$ otherwise. Meanwhile invariable value $\sigma_{w_j}^2 = 0.01$, $j = 1, 2, 3, 4$, is used in the filter. The average RMSEs based on 100 MC runs are provided by Figure 8. It suggests again that FOUF performs closely to the FKF under the correct noise, but it has better robustness against noise errors than FKF.

5.2.2. Temporary Model Uncertainty. Similarly, we assume that B_2 changes unpredictably as $B_2 = 0.5$ when $150 \leq n \leq 300$ and $B_2 = 0.015$ otherwise, which makes A vary simultaneously. Average RMSEs produced by FKF and FOUF over 100 Monte-Carlo simulations are shown Figure 9.

Clearly the result obtained in this case coincides with that in the previous model. At this point, one can conclude that proposed FOUF is less influenced by noise and more robust against temporary model mismatch.

6. Conclusion

Based on optimal fusion weighted by matrices in the LUMV sense, this paper presents a decentralized fusion OUFIR filter for discrete-invariant control system. Fundamentally the FOUF has higher accuracy than each local filter. The simulation results show that the proposed algorithm maintains the advantages of OUFIR filter and suggests lowlier

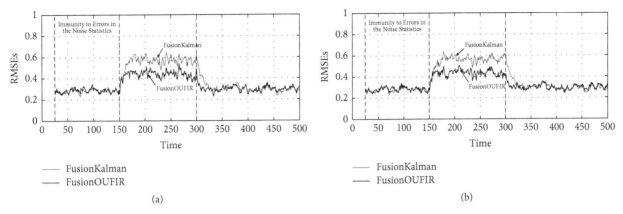

FIGURE 8: RMSEs produced by FKF and FOUF with imprecisely defined noise statistics: (a) the first state and (b) the second state.

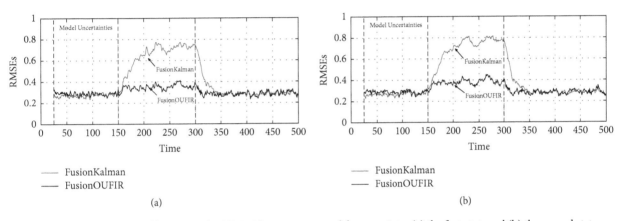

FIGURE 9: RMSEs produced by FKF and FOUF with temporary model uncertainty: (a) the first state and (b) the second state.

sensitive to noise statistics and more robust against modeling uncertainties.

Conflicts of Interest

The authors declare that there are no conflicts of interest regarding the publication of this paper.

Acknowledgments

This paper is supported by the National Natural Science Foundation of China (NSFC 61773183).

References

[1] D. Simon, *Optimal State Estimation: Kalman, H∞, and Nonlinear Approaches*, Wiley-Interscience, 2006.

[2] V. R. Algazi, M. Suk, and C.-S. Rim, "Design of almost minimax FIR filters in one and two dimensions by WLS techniques," *IEEE Transactions on Circuits and Systems II: Express Briefs*, vol. 33, no. 6, pp. 590–596, 1986.

[3] R. E. Kalman, "A new approach to linear filtering and prediction problems," *Journal of Basic Engineering*, vol. 82, no. 1, pp. 34–45, 1960.

[4] S. Zhao, Y. S. Shmaliy, B. Huang, and F. Liu, "Minimum variance unbiased FIR filter for discrete time-variant systems," *Automatica*, vol. 53, pp. 355–361, 2015.

[5] W. H. Kwon, P. S. Kim, and S. H. Han, "A receding horizon unbiased FIR filter for discrete-time state space models," *Automatica*, vol. 38, no. 3, pp. 545–551, 2002.

[6] A. H. Jazwinski, *Stochastic Process and Filtering Theory*, Academic Press, New York, NY, USA, 1970.

[7] S.-L. Sun and Z.-L. Deng, "Multi-sensor optimal information fusion Kalman filter," *Automatica*, vol. 40, no. 6, pp. 1017–1023 (2005), 2004.

[8] T. Tian, S. Sun, and N. Li, "Multi-sensor information fusion estimators for stochastic uncertain systems with correlated noises," *Information Fusion*, vol. 27, pp. 126–137, 2016.

[9] N. A. Carlson, "Federated square root filter for decentralized parallel processes," *IEEE Transactions on Aerospace and Electronic Systems*, vol. 26, no. 3, pp. 517–525, 1990.

[10] K. C. Chang, R. K. Saha, and Y. Bar-Shalom, "On optimal track-to-track fusion," *IEEE Transactions on Aerospace and Electronic Systems*, vol. 33, no. 4, pp. 1271–1276, 1997.

[11] S.-L. Sun, "Multi-sensor optimal information fusion Kalman filters with applications," *Aerospace Science and Technology*, vol. 8, no. 1, pp. 57–62, 2004.

[12] E. Song, Y. Zhu, J. Zhou, and Z. You, "Optimal Kalman filtering fusion with cross-correlated sensor noises," *Automatica*, vol. 43, no. 8, pp. 1450–1456, 2007.

[13] N. Li, S. Sun, and J. Ma, "Multi-sensor distributed fusion filtering for networked systems with different delay and loss rates," *Digital Signal Processing*, vol. 34, pp. 29–38, 2014.

[14] R. Caballero-Águila, I. García-Garrido, and J. Linares-Pérez, "Optimal fusion filtering in multisensor stochastic systems with missing measurements and correlated noises," *Mathematical Problems in Engineering*, vol. 2013, Article ID 418678, 14 pages, 2013.

[15] X. Yang, W.-A. Zhang, L. Yu, and K. Xing, "Multi-rate distributed fusion estimation for sensor network-based target tracking," *IEEE Sensors Journal*, vol. 16, no. 5, pp. 1233–1242, 2016.

[16] Y. S. Shmaliy, "Linear optimal FIR estimation of discrete time-invariant state-space models," *IEEE Transactions on Signal Processing*, vol. 58, no. 6, pp. 3086–3096, 2010.

[17] Y. S. Shmaliy, "An iterative Kalman-like algorithm ignoring noise and initial conditions," *IEEE Transactions on Signal Processing*, vol. 59, no. 6, pp. 2465–2473, 2011.

[18] S. Zhao, Y. S. Shmaliy, F. Liu, O. Ibarra-Manzano, and S. H. Khan, "Effect of embedded unbiasedness on discrete-time optimal FIR filtering estimates," *EURASIP Journal on Advances in Signal Processing*, vol. 2015, no. 1, Article ID 83, 2015.

[19] S. Zhao, Y. S. Shmaliy, and F. Liu, "Fast Kalman-like optimal unbiased FIR filtering with applications," *IEEE Transactions on Signal Processing*, vol. 64, no. 9, pp. 2284–2297, 2016.

[20] C. K. Ahn, S. Zhao, Y. S. Shmaliy, and H. Li, "On the l_2-l∞ and H∞ performances of continuous-time deadbeat H_2 FIR filter," *IEEE Transactions on Circuits and Systems II: Express Briefs*, vol. PP, no. 99, pp. 1-1, 2017.

[21] C. K. Ahn, Y. S. Shmaliy, P. Shi, and Y. Zhao, "Receding-Horizon l2-l∞ FIR filter with embedded deadbeat property," *IEEE Transactions on Circuits and Systems II: Express Briefs*, vol. 64, no. 2, pp. 211–215, 2017.

[22] C. K. Ahn and Y. S. Shmaliy, "New receding horizon fir estimator for blind smart sensing of velocity via position measurements," *IEEE Transactions on Circuits and Systems II: Express Briefs*, vol. 65, no. 1, pp. 135–139, 2018.

[23] Y. Xu, Y. S. Shmaliy, Y. Li, and X. Chen, "UWB-based indoor human localization with time-delayed data using EFIR filtering," *IEEE Access*, vol. 5, pp. 16676–16683, 2017.

[24] R. Rasoulzadeh and A. M. Shahri, "Accuracy improvement of a multi-MEMS inertial measurement unit by using an iterative UFIR filter," in *Proceedings of the 25th European Navigation Conference, ENC 2017*, pp. 279–286, che, May 2017.

[25] S. H. Han, W. H. Kwon, and P. S. Kim, "Quasi-deadbeat minimax filters for deterministic state-space models," *Institute of Electrical and Electronics Engineers Transactions on Automatic Control*, vol. 47, no. 11, pp. 1904–1908, 2002.

[26] W. H. Kwon and S. H. Han, *Receding Horizon Control: Model Predictive Control for State Models*, Springer Science & Business Media, 2006.

[27] Y. S. Shmaliy, S. H. Khan, S. Zhao, and O. Ibarra-Manzano, "General unbiased FIR filter with applications to GPS-based steering of oscillator frequency," *IEEE Transactions on Control Systems Technology*, vol. 25, no. 3, pp. 1141–1148, 2017.

[28] N. Xu, *Stochastic Signal Estimation and System Control*, Beijing Industry University Press, Beijing, China, 2001.

[29] G. Fuchs, V. Šátek, V. Vopěnka, J. Kunovský, and M. Kozek, "Application of the Modern Taylor Series Method to a multi-torsion chain," *Simulation Modelling Practice and Theory*, vol. 33, pp. 89–101, 2013.

7

A Fusion Face Recognition Approach based on 7-Layer Deep Learning Neural Network

Jianzheng Liu, Chunlin Fang, and Chao Wu

College of Computer Science and Information Engineering, Tianjin University of Science & Technology, No. 1038, DaGu Road, HeXi District, Tianjin 300222, China

Correspondence should be addressed to Jianzheng Liu; jz_leo@tust.edu.cn

Academic Editor: Sook Yoon

This paper presents a method for recognizing human faces with facial expression. In the proposed approach, a motion history image (MHI) is employed to get the features in an expressive face. The face can be seen as a kind of physiological characteristic of a human and the expressions are behavioral characteristics. We fused the 2D images of a face and MHIs which were generated from the same face's image sequences with expression. Then the fusion features were used to feed a 7-layer deep learning neural network. The previous 6 layers of the whole network can be seen as an autoencoder network which can reduce the dimension of the fusion features. The last layer of the network can be seen as a softmax regression; we used it to get the identification decision. Experimental results demonstrated that our proposed method performs favorably against several state-of-the-art methods.

1. Introduction

Face recognition has been one of the hot topics in the biometrics in the past several years. There have been many approaches proposed for this topic. In general, the research of face recognition is focused on verifying or identifying a face from its image.

In 1991, Turk and Pentland present a near-real-time system which tracks a subject's head and recognizes the person by comparing characteristics of the face to those of known individuals [1]. He projected face images onto a feature space which was named face space. The face space was defined by the "eigenfaces," which were the eigenvectors of the set faces. This framework provided the ability to learn to recognize new faces in an unsupervised manner. Hence, most researchers' work was focused on facial feature extraction.

Furthermore, there were some other approaches worthy of attention. In [2] Belhumeur et al. presented an approach based on linear discriminant analysis (LDA). Zhao et al. proposed an approach in [3] which was based on PCA and LDA; they projected the face image to a face subspace via PCA and then LDA is used to obtain a linear classifier. There are also some representative approaches such as locality preserving projections (LPP) which were proposed by He et al. [4] in 2005, as well as marginal fisher analysis (MFA) presented by Yan et al. [5] in 2007.

Some new methods were presented recently. Lu et al. presented an approach in 2013 [6]. Most face recognition methods usually use multiple samples for each subject, but the approach proposed by Lu et al. can work on the condition of only a single sample per person. Yang et al. focused on the speed and scalability of face recognition algorithms [7]. They investigated a new solution based on a classical convex optimization framework, known as Augmented Lagrangian Methods (ALM). Their method provided a viable solution to real-world, time-critical applications. Liao et al.'s study addresses partial faces recognition [8]. They propose a general partial face recognition approach that does not require face alignment by eye coordinates or any other fiducial points. Wagner et al. proposed a conceptually simple face recognition system [9] that achieved a high degree of robustness and stability to illumination variation, image misalignment, and partial occlusion.

These algorithms mentioned above can be summarized into two categories on how to extract facial features: holistic template matching based systems and geometrical local feature based systems [10]. However, these algorithms utilized only one sort of features in their approach. In [11], a novel multimodal biometrics recognition method was proposed by Yang et al.. To overcome the shortcomings of these traditional methods, the proposed method integrated a variety of biological characteristics to identify a subject.

Most classical methods were based on the 2D or 3D images of the face; it could be seen as a kind of physiological characteristic. Human facial expressions are the movements of his facial muscle and can be seen as a kind of behavioral characteristics. All of the characteristics can be used to identify the subject. The research on expression recognition is developing rapidly in recent years, such as the proposed studies in [12–14]. In 2006, Chang et al. proposed a method for 3D face recognition in the presence of varied facial expressions [15]. But in their research, the facial expressions were not used as a kind of characteristics. So in this paper, we propose a face recognition approach based on the fusion of 2D face image and expression. We fuse the physiological and behavioral characteristics in order to improve the performance of our face recognition system. In this paper, we only discuss how to fuse the 2D face images and the expression of "surprise" into a vector to identify the subject. The rest of the paper is organized as follows: in Section 2, we present the relevant theories of our method. Our method is elaborated in Section 3. In Section 4, we report on the experimental setup and results. Section 5 discusses the results of the several experiments, concludes the paper, and outlines directions for future work.

2. Methodology

2.1. Motion Templates. In 1996, motion templates were invented in the MIT Media Lab by Bobick and Davis [16, 17] and were further developed jointly with one of the authors [18, 19]. Initially, motion templates were used to identify the movements of human body by research video or image sequences. For example, Figure 1 shows a schematic representation for a person doing shaking head movement. The algorithm depends on generating silhouettes of the object of interest. There are many ways to get the silhouettes, but it is not the focus of this paper.

Assume that we have an object silhouette. A floating point MHI (motion history image) [20] where new silhouette values are copied with a floating point timestamp is updated as follows:

$$\text{MHI}_\delta\,(x, y) = \begin{cases} \tau & \text{if current silhouette at } (x, y) \\ 0 & \text{else if } \text{MHI}_\delta < (\tau - \delta). \end{cases} \quad (1)$$

In the formula, τ is the current timestamp, and δ is the maximum time duration constant associated with the template. This method makes the representation independent of system speed or frame rate so that a given gesture will cover the same MHI area at different capture rates [18]. Assume the movement lasted 0.5 seconds. Regardless of the number of pictures in the sequence between the first image and the last one, the area of the MHI was determined by the movement of the head during the time.

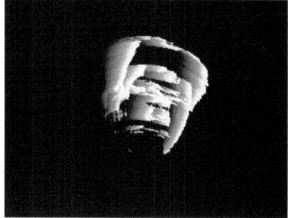

FIGURE 1: Motion history image.

2.2. Deep Learning Neural Network. Depth learning neural network has become the most interesting method in the field of machine learning. Essentially, it is the expanding of the traditional neural network approach. The proposed famous training method makes it receive much attention. In 2006, Hinton and Salakhutdinov published a paper in the journal Science [21]. The paper presented a way which can extract features from the raw data automatically. In the paper, Hinton and Salakhutdinov showed a way to reduce a 784-dimensional data (a picture) to a 30-dimensional feature via a 4-layer deep network which was called a DBN (deep belief network). Because the multiplayer neural network was trained by using unsupervised algorithms and can convert high-dimensional data to low-dimensional codes, it is also called "autoencoder." In general, autoencoder systems were made of more than three layers. The first layer of the network was an input layer, then there were several hidden layers, and the last layer was an output layer.

Each layer of the autoencoder systems is often constituted by RBM (restricted Boltzmann machine). RBMs were invented by Smolensky [22] in 1986. It is a kind of generative stochastic artificial neural network that can learn a probability distribution over its set of inputs. However, the network was growing concern since 2006 until Hinton and Salakhutdinov's paper was published. The reason they have attracted much attention was because they were used as a single layer to build the multilayer learning systems called deep belief networks, and variants and extensions of RBMs have found applications in a wide range of pattern recognition tasks [23].

An RBM can be seen as an MRF (Markov Random Field) associated with a bipartite undirected graph. The architecture

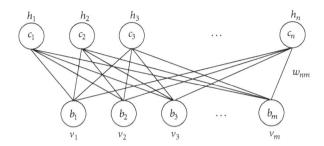

FIGURE 2: Architecture of an RBM.

of an RBM is shown in Figure 2. It is a one-layer network which consists of two kinds of units: m visible units and n hidden units. There is a matrix $W = \{w_{nm}\}$ that is the weight between the visible units and the hidden units. The visible units correspond to the components of an input vector (e.g., one visible unit for each gray pixel's value of an image). The input data were fed to the network via these units. The hidden units model dependencies between the components of vector (e.g., point, line, or corner in the image) and can be viewed as nonlinear feature detectors [24].

Different with the classical neural network, the deep learning neural networks require more huge samples to train the network. Many deep learning algorithms used unsupervised learning algorithms to train the network. That means the training set was unlabeled samples. It is obvious that capturing unlabeled samples is much easier than making labeled samples. So it is a very important benefit of unsupervised algorithms. The network Hinton and Salakhutdinov used in paper [21] was an example of a deep structure that can be trained in an unsupervised manner. Because of the benefit mentioned above, we used a DBN to solve the face recognition problem in this paper.

3. The Proposed Approach

Figure 3 shows the workflow of our proposed approach. Comparing with other algorithms, our method uses a face image and an MHI (generated from a sequence of images) instead of the single face image as a sample. In order to get the region of interest (ROI), we detect the face in image sequences firstly. After being aligned the ROI images were transformed to gray images and used to generate the MHIs. The MHIs and the features extracted from gray images were resized into vectors and normalized and fused together as features. We therefore used this kind of features to feed a DBN (7-layer deep learning neural network) to recognize faces. The count of input units of the whole network was 20000 and the count of output units was 100.

3.1. Preprocessing. Similar to most of face reorganization algorithms, the first phase of our approach is also locating the face region in images. Plenty of methods can be used to locate faces position. For example, the method proposed by Viola and Jones was a very classical algorithm [25]. How to detect faces in complex background is not the focus of this paper;

we used a more smart method via a library proposed by Yu [26], which can detect faces more effectively.

Performance of face recognition systems relies on the accuracy of face alignment and most face alignment methods are based on eye localization algorithm. Hence, we used an eye localization approach proposed by Wang et al. in 2005 [27]. This proposed method had an overall 94.5% eye detection rate and was very close to the manually provided eye positions. Figure 4 is the comparing of the original images and the images after alignment.

3.2. Fusion Features. The aligned face images were resized into a resolution of 100×100 pixels. Then we calculated the MHIs on these images. Figure 5 demonstrates an MHI generated from an image sequence which contains an expression "surprise." In the MHI image, it is clear that most pixels' gray value is zero. The pixels which have a nonzero gray value are concentrated in the region of mouth, eyes, and eyebrows. The MHIs contain the facial muscles' movement, such as the region, direction, and speed of a facial organ's movement. Therefore, all the movement can be seen as behavioral characteristics which can be used to identify a subject.

Then we fuse the image features and motion features together. For example, the pixels' gray values in an image can be seen as a kind of features. We selected the first image in a sequence and the MHI calculated from the sequence as raw features. The gray image and the MHI were resized into 1×10000-dimensional vectors and normalized into $[-1, 1]$ firstly. Then we connected the two vectors to form a new 1×20000-dimensional vector. This vector contains gray image's information and MHI's information.

Most face recognition algorithms use single image as a sample, so features extracted from this kind of samples would only contain contour and texture information of a subject. The extracted features can be seen as physiological characteristics. It is difficult to identify subjects by using the facial expression features directly because of the large within-class distance and the small among-class distance. The fusion features contain more information than a single image and have larger among-class distance than expression features. Actually, many kinds of features such as those mentioned in [2–5] can fuse with the expression features and the fused features will improve the performance of the original algorithms.

Finally, all image sequences were transformed into this set of vectors and were fed into the network. The network was made of 7 layers, the previous 6 layers were constituted by RBM, and the last layer was a softmax regression. After training, the trained network would output the recognition results.

3.3. Training Algorithm. Hinton and Salakhutdinov proposed an efficient method in [21] to train a deep belief network. The training process was divided into two stages. The first stage was pretraining phase. In this phase, a stack of RBMs was trained. Each RBM was having only one layer of feature detectors. The outputs of a trained RBM could be seen as features extracted from its input data and were used as the

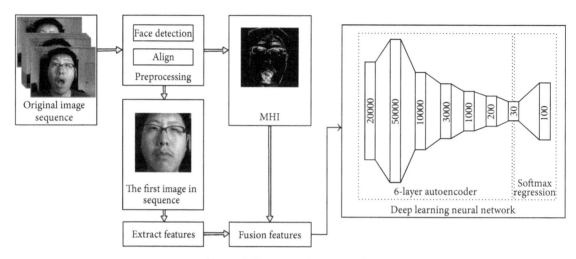

FIGURE 3: Structure of our network.

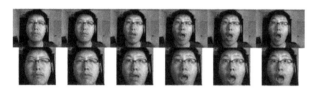

FIGURE 4: Comparing of the original images and the images after alignment.

FIGURE 5: An MHI calculated from image sequence.

"input data" for training the next RBM in the stack. Actually, the pretraining was a kind of unsupervised learning. After pretraining, the RBMs were "unrolled" to create a deep neural network, which is then fine-tuned by using the algorithm of backpropagation.

In this paper, the proposed method used a 7-layer deep learning neural network, the previous 6 layers were constituted by RBM, and the last layer consisted of a softmax regression. So, we used a different way to train the network. The training process can be divided into three stages. Firstly, we pretrained the whole network but not the last layer using

unsupervised learning algorithm, just like the first phase in Hinton's method. Because of the benefit of unsupervised learning, we could train the network by feeding a training set consisting of massive unlabeled data to it. After training, the previous 6-layer network could be seen as a features extractor which could extract the most valuable features from the raw data automatically. Then, the last layer was trained in supervised learning with a part of training set and its labels. Lastly, as the way Hinton and Salakhutdinov [21] proposed, the whole network was fine-tuned.

4. Experimental Results

4.1. Training Set and Test Set. Most popular face recognition databases such as the Extended Yale B database do not contain expression image sequences which are not suitable for testing on our method. We therefore established a database in our laboratory. In this database there are 1000 real-color videos in nearly frontal view from 100 subjects, male and female, between 20 and 70 years old. In each section, the subject was asked to make the expression of "surprise" clearly in one time. We captured ten videos from one subject. Each sequence begins with a neutral expression and proceeds to a peak expression, which is similar to the CK+ Expression Database. Each video's resolution is 640 × 480 pixels, and the width of a face in frame is in the range of 180 pixels to 250 pixels. All the video clips were captured at 30 frames per second (fps), and each video contained 15 frames. There were four frontal illumination videos, two left side light videos, two right side light videos, and two wearing sunglasses video in the ten videos mentioned above. It should be noted that all samples in our database are using the same pair of sunglasses when they were captured. Figure 6 shows the first frames of the videos in our database.

There are four stages in our experiment. In the first stage, three of the four frontal illumination video segments are used as training samples, and the remaining one was used as test sample. In the second stage, the training set consisted of half of the video clips captured from each subject except the

FIGURE 6: The samples of our database.

TABLE 1: Results of the second stage.

Algorithms	Front	Left	Right	Sunglass
PCA	96.5%	95.5%	96%	93.5%
DBN	97.5%	97%	97%	95%

TABLE 2: Results of the third stage.

Algorithms	Left	Right	Sunglass
PCA	92.5%	92%	90.5%
PCA + MHI	95%	95.5%	93%
DCT	93.5%	93%	91%
DCT + MHI	95.5%	95.5%	93.5%

TABLE 3: Results of the fourth stage.

Algorithms	Left	Right	Sunglass
MKD-SRC	93.5%	93%	90%
Our method	95.5%	95.5%	93.5%

sunglasses videos. That means for each subject we selected two frontal illumination videos, one left side light video, and one right side light video from his samples. The rest of the videos were used as test samples. In the third stage, the training set consisted of the four frontal illumination videos; the other six videos were used as test samples. We compared PCA features [1], DCT features [28], and fusion features in this stage. In the last stage, we used the same training set in stage 3 to compare our method with the algorithm presented in [8].

4.2. Results. In our previous work, we presented a method for recognizing faces via the same fusion features mentioned in this paper based on principal component analysis (PCA). To show the advantages of the method proposed in this paper, we compared the results here. In the first stage, the method proposed in this paper was yielding 100% recognition accuracy against frontal illumination and the result based on PCA was 97%. Table 1 shows the recognition rate of the second stage. In the table, "front" means frontal illumination, "left" means left side light, "right" means right side light, and "sunglass" means wearing sunglasses. The first row in Table 1 is the results based on PCA; the second row is the results based on the method proposed in this paper which were output by a deep belief network (DBN).

Since our method cannot work on the popular published face database, thus, we did not compare our method with other approaches. However, the rate of our method's recognition accuracy was a little better than our previous work and some popular methods, such as the reported recognition rate in [29–31].

Table 2 shows the recognition rate of the third stage. The first row in Table 2 is the results based on PCA features, the third row is the results based on DCT features, and the second row and the fourth row are the results based on the fusion features.

Table 3 shows the recognition rate of the fourth stage. The first row in Table 3 is the results based on the method proposed in [8]; the second row is the results based on our method.

4.3. Discussion. Experimental results show that the fusion features proposed in this paper are superior to single features. The MHIs we used to fuse features contain abundant expression characteristics. So there is more information in the fusion features which can be used to identify subjects. In particular, our method has superior performance in the sunglasses tests. The fusion features contain plentiful behavioral characteristics issued by the lower half of human face.

5. Conclusion

In this paper we proposed a novel method for recognizing human faces with facial expression. In order to improve the recognition accuracy rate, we use a kind of fusion features. Normally, the popular methods recognize human face via the image of faces, which can be seen as a kind of physiological characteristic. Facial expressions are the movements of human facial muscles, which also can be used to identify humans faces. It is a kind of behavioral characteristics. Hence, the fusion features contain more information than human face images that can be used for identification and increase the recognition rate especially on illumination variant faces or wearing sunglasses faces.

The approach and experiments presented in this paper are only the preliminary work of our research. In future work we will continuously investigate to try to research the proposed method into two issues. Firstly, we will not only analyze the expression "surprise" emotion in this paper, but also focus on extending our method to all sorts of expression emotions. Actually, we also tested our method with the expression "laugh" in our laboratory. We got a similar recognition accuracy rate which was presented in the paper. But in the condition of wearing scarves, our method did not get a satisfactory result. The reason is that the bottom half of human face contains more expression information than the top half. Secondly, we will study how to combine the popular algorithms into our approach to improve the recognition accuracy rate.

Competing Interests

The authors declare that they have no competing interests.

Acknowledgments

This work was supported by the National Natural Science Foundation of China under Grant no. 61502338, the 2015 key projects of Tianjin Science and Technology Support Program no. 15ZCZDGX00200, and the Open Fund of Guangdong Provincial Key Laboratory of Petrochemical Equipment Fault Diagnosis no. GDUPTKLAB201334.

References

[1] M. A. Turk and A. P. Pentland, "Face recognition using eigenfaces," in *Proceedings of the IEEE Computer Society Conference on Computer Vision and Pattern Recognition (CVPR '91)*, pp. 586–591, June 1991.

[2] P. N. Belhumeur, J. P. Hespanha, and D. J. Kriegman, "Eigenfaces vs. fisherfaces: recognition using class specific linear projection," *IEEE Transactions on Pattern Analysis and Machine Intelligence*, vol. 19, no. 7, pp. 711–720, 1997.

[3] W. Zhao, R. Chellappa, and A. Krishnaswamy, "Discriminant analysis of principal components for face recognition," in *Proceedings of the 3rd IEEE International Conference on Automatic Face and Gesture Recognition (FG '98)*, pp. 336–341, Springer, Nara, Japan, April 1998.

[4] X. He, S. Yan, Y. Hu, P. Niyogi, and H.-J. Zhang, "Face recognition using laplacianfaces," *IEEE Transactions on Pattern Analysis and Machine Intelligence*, vol. 27, no. 3, pp. 328–340, 2005.

[5] S. Yan, D. Xu, B. Zhang, H.-J. Zhang, Q. Yang, and S. Lin, "Graph embedding and extensions: a general framework for dimensionality reduction," *IEEE Transactions on Pattern Analysis and Machine Intelligence*, vol. 29, no. 1, pp. 40–51, 2007.

[6] J. Lu, Y.-P. Tan, and G. Wang, "Discriminative multimanifold analysis for face recognition from a single training sample per person," *IEEE Transactions on Pattern Analysis and Machine Intelligence*, vol. 35, no. 1, pp. 39–51, 2013.

[7] A. Y. Yang, S. S. Sastry, A. Ganesh, and Y. Ma, "Fast 1-minimization algorithms and an application in robust face recognition: a review," in *Proceedings of the 17th IEEE International Conference on in Image Processing (ICIP '10)*, pp. 1849–1852, IEEE, Hong Kong, September 2010.

[8] S. Liao, A. K. Jain, and S. Z. Li, "Partial face recognition: alignment-free approach," *IEEE Transactions on Pattern Analysis and Machine Intelligence*, vol. 35, no. 5, pp. 1193–1205, 2013.

[9] A. Wagner, J. Wright, A. Ganesh, Z. Zhou, H. Mobahi, and Y. Ma, "Toward a practical face recognition system: robust alignment and illumination by sparse representation," *IEEE Transactions on Pattern Analysis and Machine Intelligence*, vol. 34, no. 2, pp. 372–386, 2012.

[10] R. Chellappa, S. Sirohey, and C. L. Wilson, "Human and machine recognition of faces: a survey," *Proceedings of the IEEE*, vol. 83, no. 5, pp. 705–741, 1995.

[11] J. Yang, Y. Jiao, C. Wang, C. Wu, and Y. Chen, "Multimodal biometrics recognition based on image latent semantic analysis and extreme learning machine," in *Biometric Recognition*, pp. 433–440, Springer, 2013.

[12] C. Shan, S. Gong, and P. W. McOwan, "Facial expression recognition based on local binary patterns: a comprehensive study," *Image and Vision Computing*, vol. 27, no. 6, pp. 803–816, 2009.

[13] M. F. Valstar, M. Mehu, B. Jiang, M. Pantic, and K. Scherer, "Metaanalysis of the first facial expression recognition challenge," *IEEE Transactions on Systems, Man, and Cybernetics, Part B: Cybernetics*, vol. 42, no. 4, pp. 966–979, 2012.

[14] W. Gu, C. Xiang, Y. V. Venkatesh, D. Huang, and H. Lin, "Facial expression recognition using radial encoding of local Gabor features and classifier synthesis," *Pattern Recognition*, vol. 45, no. 1, pp. 80–91, 2012.

[15] K. I. Chang, K. W. Bowyer, and P. J. Flynn, "Multiple nose region matching for 3D face recognition under varying facial expression," *IEEE Transactions on Pattern Analysis and Machine Intelligence*, vol. 28, no. 10, pp. 1695–1700, 2006.

[16] A. Bobick and J. Davis, "Real-time recognition of activity using temporal templates," in *Proceedings of the 3rd IEEE Workshop on Applications of Computer Vision (WACV '96)*, pp. 39–42, IEEE, Sarasota, Fla, USA, December 1996.

[17] J. W. Davis and A. F. Bobick, "The representation and recognition of human movement using temporal templates," in *Proceedings of the IEEE Computer Society Conference on Computer Vision and Pattern Recognition (CVPR '97)*, pp. 928–934, June 1997.

[18] G. R. Bradski and J. W. Davis, "Motion segmentation and pose recognition with motion history gradients," *Machine Vision and Applications*, vol. 13, no. 3, pp. 174–1843, 2002.

[19] J. Davis and G. Bradski, "Real-time motion template gradients using intel cvlib," in *Proceedings of the IEEE ICCV Workshop on Framerate Vision*, pp. 1–20, Kerkyra, Greece, September 1999.

[20] J. Davis, "Recognizing movement using motion histograms," Tech. Rep. 487, MIT Media Lab, 1999.

[21] G. E. Hinton and R. R. Salakhutdinov, "Reducing the dimensionality of data with neural networks," *Science*, vol. 313, no. 5786, pp. 504–507, 2006.

[22] P. Smolensky, "Information processing in dynamical systems: foundations of harmony theory," in *Parallel Distributed Processing: Explorations in the Microstructure of Cognition*, MIT Press, 1986.

[23] A. Fischer and C. Igel, "Training restricted Boltzmann machines: an introduction," *Pattern Recognition*, vol. 47, no. 1, pp. 25–39, 2014.

[24] R. Salakhutdinov, A. Mnih, and G. Hinton, "Restricted Boltzmann machines for collaborative filtering," in *Proceedings of the 24th International Conference on Machine Learning (ICML '07)*, pp. 791–798, ACM, Corvallis, Ore, USA, June 2007.

[25] P. Viola and M. J. Jones, "Robust real-time face detection," *International Journal of Computer Vision*, vol. 57, no. 2, pp. 137–154, 2004.

[26] S. Yu, "A binary library for face detection in images," https://github.com/ShiqiYu/libfacedetection.

[27] P. Wang, M. B. Green, Q. Ji, and J. Wayman, "Automatic eye detection and its validation," in *Proceedings of the IEEE Computer Society Conference on Computer Vision and Pattern Recognition Workshops (CVPR Workshops '05)*, p. 164, San Diego, Calif, USA, June 2005.

[28] X.-Y. Jing and D. Zhang, "A face and palmprint recognition approach based on discriminant DCT feature extraction," *IEEE Transactions on Systems, Man, and Cybernetics, Part B: Cybernetics*, vol. 34, no. 6, pp. 2405–2415, 2004.

[29] J. Wright, A. Y. Yang, A. Ganesh, S. S. Sastry, and Y. Ma, "Robust face recognition via sparse representation," *IEEE Transactions on Pattern Analysis and Machine Intelligence*, vol. 31, no. 2, pp. 210–227, 2009.

8

The Comparison of Distributed P2P Trust Models based on Quantitative Parameters in the File Downloading Scenarios

Jingpei Wang and Jie Liu

Information Security Research Center, China CEPREI Laboratory, Guangzhou 510610, China

Correspondence should be addressed to Jingpei Wang; wjpbupt@163.com

Academic Editor: Arash Habibi Lashkari

Varied P2P trust models have been proposed recently; it is necessary to develop an effective method to evaluate these trust models to resolve the commonalities (guiding the newly generated trust models in theory) and individuality (assisting a decision maker in choosing an optimal trust model to implement in specific context) issues. A new method for analyzing and comparing P2P trust models based on hierarchical parameters quantization in the file downloading scenarios is proposed in this paper. Several parameters are extracted from the functional attributes and quality feature of trust relationship, as well as requirements from the specific network context and the evaluators. Several distributed P2P trust models are analyzed quantitatively with extracted parameters modeled into a hierarchical model. The fuzzy inferring method is applied to the hierarchical modeling of parameters to fuse the evaluated values of the candidate trust models, and then the relative optimal one is selected based on the sorted overall quantitative values. Finally, analyses and simulation are performed. The results show that the proposed method is reasonable and effective compared with the previous algorithms.

1. Introduction

Due to the openness of distributed networks, security issue becomes one of the most important challenges when deploying these networks into application. Traditional strategies, such as traditional encryption and access control, because of their poor scalability, are no longer suited for resolving security issues of distributed P2P system. Trust management resolves the security issues in semantic and behavioral levels and filters malicious nodes based on their real-time behaviors between transactions. Trust mechanism can transfer between heterogeneous mixed networks seamlessly, and the researches of trust management are of considerable interest in recent years [1, 2].

The researches of trust in computer network have emerged several years ago. However, there are no uniform definitions of trust related issues. First, we give our definition of trust and trust management in this paper.

Trust. Trust has been interpreted as opinion, reputation, probability, and so forth. In the trust management based on trust degree, trust is defined as subjective expectations that denote the uncertainty in collaboration between the subjects and agents.

Trust Model. Trust model defines the method and procedure of trust modeling and trust evaluation.

Trust Management. Trust management is a service mechanism that self-organizes a set of items based on their trust status to take an informed decision.

The core issue of trust management is constructing reliable trust models, and a wide range of P2P trust models for distributed P2P network is proposed during the last decades [3–14]. One problem is that there are no evaluating criteria for comparing these varied models, making it difficult for an interested party to decide upon an optimal trust model to implement. We give a P2P scenario as follows.

One user (service requester) performs the file download in P2P network, supposing that varied trust models are available for computing the trust values of the target service provider. The user should ask some questions firstly:

(1) Which trust model is the most consistent to compute and guide the trust flows?

(2) Which trust model can assist in providing more qualified service in this application context?

(3) The diverse requirements from decision maker would influence the results of choosing the optimal trust model; what is the degree of this influence?

In order to resolve the above quandaries, it is necessary to develop a quantitative method to analyze some trust models and induce choosing the most proper one according to the application context and multiple requirements of user.

In this paper, a method for comparing trust models based on hierarchical model of parameters is proposed. The evaluated parameters are extracted from the trust related concepts, network context, and the requirements of users. The evaluated values of trust models are obtained by quantitative calculation of the parameters model with the Delphi and fuzzy inference methods. The optimal trust model is selected based on the sorted quantized values. Analysis and simulation results show that the proposed algorithm is reasonable and effective.

The rest of the paper is organized as follows. Section 2 presents the related works. Section 3 outlines the parameters and gives qualitative analysis. In Section 4, hierarchical parameter modeling and formal quantization are proposed. Further, parameter fusion and trust model evaluation are given in Section 5. Section 6 presents analysis and simulation, followed by the conclusions in Section 7.

2. Related Works

Various trust models have been proposed for the P2P in the past decade [3–14]. From the aspect of trust measurement and modeling method, the trust models can be divided into hybrid distributed approach [5], trust model based on weighted average method [6, 7], trust model based on game theory [8], multiple factors trust model [9, 10], Bayesian trust model [11], fuzzy inferring trust model [12, 13], trust model based evidence theory [14], and so forth. However, there are rare sound researches on how to compare trust models. Some researchers focus on the qualitative analysis or guidance of the trust models; some others focus on the quantitative evaluation.

Wojcik et al. introduced a set of criteria to analyze trust models [15]. The criteria consist of four parts: trust establishment, trust initialization, trust updating, and trust evaluation. Each part is followed by some suggestions. It provided a common framework for the development of a sound trust model, though there is no concrete realization. Rodriguez-Perez et al. discussed the main issues that a reputation framework must address and analyzed the most representative reputation systems in fully distributed peer-to-peer systems [16]. They also discussed the main advantages and drawbacks of each proposal in relation to peer-to-peer reputation system requirements. Mármol and Pérez described several trust and reputation models for distributed and heterogeneous networks and compared to provide an evaluation of the most relevant works [17]. They suggested that certain security threats and the specific features of the distributed network where a model is to be deployed should be considered carefully to improve the evaluation accuracy. He and Wu discussed the theory basics, applications, advantages, and disadvantages of some reputation systems [18]. They considered that aggregation overhead, storage efficiency, and reputation accuracy are three key issues in the design of reputation for P2P network. Azzedin proposed a reputation assessment process and used it to classify the existing reputation systems [19]. He focused on the different methods in selecting the recommendation sources and collecting the recommendations. These two phases can contribute significantly to the overall performance owing to precision, recall, and communication cost. All the above methods take the right direction to analyze trust model, but there is no concrete algorithm to compare the investigated trust models to select an optimal one to implement.

Schlosser et al. presented a formal model for describing reputation systems [20]. Based on the formal model, a generic simulation framework was implemented. The defects of this simulation framework are shortage of theoretical analysis for parameter settings and that only reputation systems are taken into account. Yang et al. proposed a method to evaluate the trust model by treating the trust model as a black box and comparing the output with the input [21]. Their work is similar to software testing in software engineering. The evaluated results are compared with two parameters: sensibility and foreseeability. However, it is difficult to model the overall features of trust models using merely two measurable parameters. In a word, the existing methods have some deficiencies, and trust model evaluation remains an open issue.

3. Parameters Extracting and Qualitative Analysis of Trust Models

3.1. Parameters Extracting. From the user perspective, the P2P can be considered as a service supporter and trust management is an integral mechanism of the network system that assists the system in providing qualified service. There are some parameters existing in trust relationship and trust models.

Subjectivity. From the definition of trust we can see that trust is a subjective concept. It is provided by observers based on their subjective judgment. Different observer, different period, different mood, and different scenario may induce different judgments. Notice that reputation is not subjective as it is based on the historical behavior. Also, not all parameters are subjective; there are some QoS parameters that can be perfectly quantified (delay, jitter, etc.)

Fuzziness. Trust is a blurry concept. Three factors induce the fuzziness: uncertainty, inaccuracy, and no clarity. A proper trust model should be able to express these blurry concepts in trust establishing and measurement. However, most trust models proposed are based on numerical computing and the methods of quantization and inference of the fuzzy relationship varied from one to another. How to express, quantize, and infer fuzzy relationship also belongs to the scope of the fuzziness.

Time Decay. Trust should decay as time passes by. For example, trust relationship formed 3 years ago is less credible than that formed 3 days ago. However, the decayed amplitude and range have no unified conclusion in varied trust models. Whether to introduce the decay factor and what decayed range is reasonable need evaluation for the trust models.

Robustness. There are malicious attacks in distributed system, including unintentional attacks, for example, data transmission delay and block induced denial of service, and malicious attacks, for example, false feedback, collusive cheating, and malicious calumniation. An excellent trust model should be able to resist various attacks and avoid the malicious nodes from transactions.

Reward and Punishment. In a trust system, various nodes have different performance according to their ability and wish. Trust models should provide a proper mechanism to reward nodes with high trust values to encourage them to provide better service. Meanwhile, punish nodes with malicious performance by reducing their trust values or forbidding their transaction.

Sensitivity. This feature reflects the evolution speed of the trust relationship with the disturbance of the network behaviors. The evaluated factors of sensitivity include the changing speed of trust value, handing speed of malicious attack, and the speed of searching. Moreover, sensitivity is associated with application scenario; that is, higher sensitivity is suited for high precision network (i.e., military network), while lower sensitivity is popular with tolerant network.

Transitivity. When an entity needs to judge the globe trust value of another entity within the domain or in the distance, the trust transitivity is necessary. Trust or reputation transmitted mainly through recommended mechanism from a series of middle nodes. However, this recommended relationship is not always true; if node A trusts node B and node B trusts node C, we cannot infer that node A always trusts node C. A good trust model should include recommended mechanism as well as the reasonable disposal of asymmetric recommendation.

Scalability. This parameter mainly depicts the relationship between network size and network load in dealing with the trust relationship. The calculation complexity remains low or increases slowly with the increase of network nodes meaning better scalability. Specifically, trust model with lower time complexity, lower space complexity, and more efficient transmission pattern is a better model.

Other parameters could be considered in deciding the performance of a trust model, for example, the assessment or evolution of trust, usability, variable assignments.

3.2. Qualitative Analysis of Trust Models. In this section, we will address the characteristics of some traditional P2P trust models based on the extracted functions.

Rodriguez-Perez et al. [5] proposed a superpeer reputation framework for P2P network. There are single peer and sure-peer. The peers always maintain their own local reputation database; the system is fault tolerant to sure-peer unavailability. Surework introduces incentives in order to promote that nodes with higher capabilities become superpeers and assume more tasks than normal peers. Reciprocity is also promoted by encouraging peers to provide better services to most reputable client peers. Therefore, the robustness and reward-punishment are obvious. Malicious actions can be found by local reputation and clusters' opinion quickly, which reflects some sensibility. Reputation can be calculated and transferred to other sure-peers and clusters. The drawbacks of surework are increasing system complexity and computational cost, the scalability being not very good, and the other parameters being not mentioned.

EigenTrust [6] is a trust and reputation model for P2P networks where each peer is assigned a global trust value based on its transaction history. The trust value changes gradually, and the trust level determines the different transaction chance. The subjectivity, fuzziness, and time decay are not found in this model, as it adopted objective calculation of transaction results and did not consider the time decay factor. An important feature of this model is the presence of some pretrusted peers that help to break up malicious collectives, and peers can avoid transactions with partial malicious peers, so the robustness and punishment mechanism are qualified, whereas the handing speed of malicious attack and the changing speed of trust value are not obvious, which mean lower sensitivity. The transitivity is clearly presented though the asymmetric recommendation is not considered. The pretrusted peers change the convergence and achieve a significant reduction of overhead in the system, so the performance of scalability is acceptable.

PeerTrust [7] is a reputation based trust model, where more factors are introduced to compute trust value for each peer. The feedback-based evaluation, satisfaction of transaction, participating degree, community context, credibility, and so forth are considered in the trust evaluation. The subjectivity is presented with the participation of the peers' judgment of satisfaction and credibility. PeerTrust algorithm also proposed an adaptive time window-based algorithm to reflect the most recent behaviors, so time decay is considered. Good feedback will gain better results and bad feedback will be found, which means the presence of reward-punishment mechanism. The robustness and transitivity are improved compared with EigenTrust, whereas the scalability is decreased as complexity computation.

Harish et al. designed and analyzed a game theoretic model for P2P trust management [8]. The trust framework incorporated self-experience and reputation to calculate trustworthiness of a peer. Various strategies like game tree strategy, dynamic strategy, and auditing strategy were proposed for selecting peers for doing job. The method addressed the problem of the selfish behavior; different entity uses different strategy. The intelligent entity can update the reputation values of other interactive nodes; and reward and punishment are performed directly by the payoff. Therefore, subjectivity, transitivity, and reward-punishment are obvious. It can avoid internal malicious behaviors and the robustness is presented, but the calculation of reputation and strategies and their evolution induce larger overhead. Fuzziness, time decay, and sensitivity are not mentioned.

Li et al. proposed a multidimensional trust model for large scale P2P computing [9]. It involves many factors, that is, assumptions, expectations, behaviors, and risks, to reflect the complexity of trust. Moreover, the weights of these factors are dynamically assigned by series of objective algorithms. The subjectivity, fuzziness, and time decay are not mentioned. This model gave a scene where malicious feedback is changing while the accuracy and the adaptability maintain a proper level, which means good robustness. The reward-punishment of trust value as well as sensitivity is not obvious, the transitivity is mentioned, and finally the scalability is excellent with the mechanism of direct trust tree.

Wang and Vassileva proposed a Bayesian trust model in P2P networks [11], it takes trust as a multifaceted concept, and peers need to develop differentiated trust in different aspects of other peers' capability. Bayesian network provides a flexible method to combine different aspects of trust. The subjectivity is obvious, and the calculation of differentiated trust is rapid, though the final results are measured by the number of transactions meaning low sensitivity. The transitivity is considered and the scalability is excellent as the lower load of computation. However, the fuzziness, time decay, robustness, and reward-punishment mechanism are not mentioned in this model.

There are other trust models proposed by different methods, for example, fuzzy trust model [13] and D-S evidence trust model [14]. The analysis procedure is the same as that of the above trust models and omitted here. The results of qualitative analysis are shown in Table 1. In this table, "√" stands for trust models having responding parameters and "×" means not having related parameters or the merits of related parameters are not obvious. From the analysis we can see that the investigated trust models all have their advantages and disadvantages from the aspect of the parameters. And it can be inferred that the degree for one parameter owned by several trust models differs from one to another; for example, EigenTrust and PeerTrust both have robustness, whereas the intensity of robustness is varied as adopting different mechanism. The subjectivity between Jøsang model and Bayesian model is varied as different number of factors is adopted in each model.

In a word, parameter distribution and parameters degree among trust models are unbalanced, making it difficult for an interested party to decide upon a particular trust model to implement. Nevertheless, we can find the relatively optimal trust model through quantitative comparison in a concrete scene. In the next section, a quantized evaluation is addressed.

4. Hierarchical Parameters Modeling and Formal Quantization

4.1. Hierarchical Modeling of Parameters. On one hand, it is difficult to analyze trust models using more than eight parameters directly and simultaneously. Some parameters are conflicted; for example, complicated algorithms are used to deal with attacks, which increase robustness but deteriorate scalability. Some parameters are correlative; better punishment mechanisms would lead to better robustness. Moreover, different parameters concern different aspects of service, and sometime the same parameters may concern more than one aspect; for example, scalability is involved in network structure, and robustness concerns the service reliability as well as network structure.

On the other hand, there are other decision factors, such as network scene and individual policy of observer. According to previous definition, trust management is a third-party auxiliary mechanism assisting the system in providing qualified service. From the service perspective, we can extract some factors of the quality of service with a trust model: function conformance, reliability, the adaptability for network context, and the specific requirement of a user, each of which is followed by some parameters; for example, function conformance includes transitivity and flexibility which reflect the reasonability of trust modeling. The performance of each factor can be evaluated by some low-level parameters.

A natural method is establishing a hierarchical structure to combine the above two aspects; the parameters and their upper factors (criteria layer) can be considered comprehensively. It can distribute conflicting parameters to different decision criteria layer, and correlative parameters can be laid into one layer for coordinate evaluation. Then, a fusion method is designed to fuse these parameters and criteria layer to obtain the overall performance of trust models. In this paper, the decision factors in criteria layer are described as follows.

Function Conformance. This layer mainly focuses on the reasonability of trust representation, the conformance of trust attributes, and the mechanism of performing the service task properly. The most obvious functions of trust management are measuring the uncertainty of the nodes' behaviors and self-organizing a set of objects to perform the task (e.g., routing or transmitting data). Whether the uncertainty can be measured properly or not will be evaluated in this layer. Subjectivity, fuzziness, time decay, and transitivity will be used to characterize the conformance of trust mechanism and be distributed to this layer.

Service Reliability. This layer estimates whether the service provided by trust mechanism is reliable. Trust management is a third-party auxiliary mechanism. The provided service should be qualified. The robustness describes how the trusted cooperators resist malicious attacks or shield from the malicious node to maintain the stability of service. The reward and punishment (with more reasonable resource distribution) and sensitivity (reflecting the reaction speed of attacks and

TABLE 1: The distribution of parameters of some P2P trust models.

Trust model	Parameters							
	Subjectivity	Fuzziness	Time decay	Robustness	Reward & punishment	Sensibility	Transitivity	Scalability
EigenTrust	×	×	×	√	√	×	√	√
PeerTrust	√	×	√	√	√	×	√	×
Surework	×	×	×	√	√	√	√	×
Harish et al. [8]	√	×	×	√	√	×	√	×
Li et al. [9]	×	√	×	√	×	×	√	√
Wang and Vassileva [11]	√	×	×	×	×	√	√	√
Wang et al. [12]	√	√	√	×	×	√	×	√
Tian and Yang [14]	×	√	√	√	×	×	√	×

the sensitive degree of the changeable trust value) will be evaluated in this layer.

Structure Adaptability. This layer mainly evaluates the dynamic relationship between the trust model and network environment. The structure, size, topology, and the dynamics of the target network all will influence the execution of task. A reasonable model should be able to adjust to the change of network structure. The scalability should maintain excellent state with the expansion of nodes, the transitive path is available with the change of structure, and the reaction is timely when important nodes change or immediate service is needed. Therefore, scalability, transitivity, and sensitivity are related to this layer.

Strategies Differences of Observer. The observer may have different requirement and secure policies and even different interest and preferences, in using the trust model for certain context. In addition, it also includes some performance index, such as the usage of resource (overhead or scalability), disposal speed and quality of service of trust mechanism, the ability of surviving (mainly robustness), and the special need of sensitivity (i.e., higher accurate application).

Other criteria will be populated to add in criteria layers. The detailed hierarchical structure of parameters and factors are shown in Figure 1. Parameters act as basic layer, middle service factors act as criteria layer, and the top layer is goal layer.

The comprehensive assessment of the trust models for performing a specific task in a certain context can be derived from reasonable evaluation of the following criteria layer and basic layer in succession.

4.2. Formal Evaluation of Trust Model.

The extracted parameters characterize the basic functional feature of a trust model, $P = \{p_1, p_2, \ldots, p_n\}$ denote the set of parameters, and n is the number of parameters. In order to perform quantitative analysis, we quantify the parameters and select an algorithm to fuse these parameters; that is $C : \mapsto (TM, P, I)$, where TM is a trust model, I denote an integration algorithm, and C is evaluation result. A direct evaluation can be modeled into a functional form, as shown in

$$C(TM) = f_I(f_1(p_1), f_2(p_2), \ldots, f_n(p_n)), \quad (1)$$

where $f_i(p_i)$, $i \in [1, n]$, denotes the quantization of ith parameter. In order to achieve the overall unified value, the normalization is embedded in the quantization of $f_i(p_i)$; in other words $Q(P) = (f_1(p_1), f_2(p_2), \ldots, f_n(p_n))$ is a dimensionless vector. $f_I(\cdot)$ denote an integrating function. A simple integration is weighted average of $Q(P)$. A more complicate but rational method is fuzzy fusion that will be used in this paper.

4.3. Quantization of Parameters.

There exists a mapping f between the impact factors and the quantified value of each parameter for a given trust model. In our algorithm, the quantitative procedure of a parameter includes extracting the impact factors of each parameter, scoring the impact factors, and performing normalization and fuzzy integration of the impact factors to obtain the quantitative value of single parameter.

For a single parameter p_i, C denotes the factor set: $C = \{c_1, c_2, \ldots, c_m\}$, and m is the number of factors. The factor is extracted based on three considerations: the definition of parameter, evaluated points, range of parameter and some experience of experts. For example, scalability is related to time complexity, space complexity, transmission, and efficient storage of data; the impact factors of sensitivity include the changing speed of trust value and handing speed of malicious attack and the speed of searching and timely reaction when network topology changes.

For a single impact factor c_j, $j \in [1, m]$, we evaluate it with specific measure, range. A simple method is using fuzzy theory to determine the range and level of the evaluated factor according to the experience of observer (i.e., for the rationality, irrational, default, and lowest rationality, medium rationality, favorable rationality, and highest rationality, denoted as five intervals from 0 upper to 1, resp.; quantized step is 0.2 that denotes the uncertainty). Considering that there are some manufactured discrepancies for each factor, Delphi method can be introduced to collect and filter the divergent answers and obtain the quantified value.

The Delphi method is an interactive forecasting method that relies on a group of experts. The experts answer questions in two or more rounds. It is believed that, after several rounds, the range of the answers will decrease and the group will converge towards the "correct" answer. Finally, the process is stopped after a predefined stop criterion (e.g., stability). In

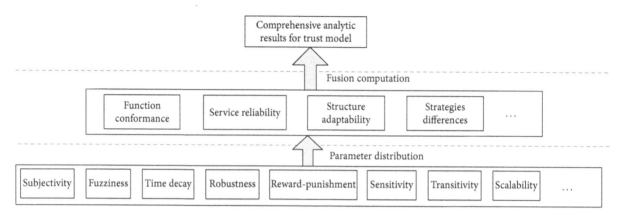

FIGURE 1: Hierarchical structure of parameters for trust models.

this paper, several questions are defined firstly based on the multiple factors of a particular c_j. Each question is followed by certain options that denote the level of possible answers (i.e., rationality, from being irrational to highest rationality). These questionnaires are provided to several experts. After several rounds, the final correct feedback will be determined, and the final quantized value of a factor $Q(c_j)$ can be obtained. Repeat above quantization until all m factors are quantized, denoted as $Q(C) = \{Q(c_1), Q(c_2), \ldots, Q(c_m)\}$.

Notice that m elements in $Q(c_j)$ may be measured in different unit; take the scalability as an example; the units of time complexity and space complexity are time (ms) and capacity (kb). Firstly, we normalize these different units. The popular method of normalization is max–min method:

$$Q_m\left(c_j\right) = \frac{Q\left(c_j\right) - \min\left(Q\left(c_j\right)\right)}{\max\left(Q\left(c_j\right)\right) - \min\left(Q\left(c_j\right)\right)}, \quad j \in [1,m], \quad (2)$$

where $\max\left(Q(c_j)\right)$ and $\min\left(Q(c_j)\right)$ are the maximum quantized value and the minimum value determined by the range of jth factor. $Q_m(c_j)$ is a numeric value between 0 and 1 after normalization. Repeat above disposal until all m factors are normalized, denoted as $Q_m(C) = \{Q_m(c_1), Q_m(c_2), \ldots, Q_m(c_m)\}$.

The final procedure is integrating the impact factors to obtain the overall quantized value of single parameter. As the impact factors are independent of each other, a simple integration is weighted sum of the quantized value of each factor. The integral is defined as follows:

$$
\begin{aligned}
Q\left(p_i\right) &= \sum_{j=1}^{m} w_{c_j} Q_m\left(C_j\right) \\
&= w_{c_1} Q_m\left(C_1\right) + w_{c_2} Q_m\left(C_2\right) + \cdots \\
&\quad + w_{c_m} Q_m\left(C_m\right),
\end{aligned}
\tag{3}
$$

where w_{c_j}, $j \in [1,m]$, denote the weight of $Q_m(c_j)$ and satisfy $w_{c_1} + w_{c_2} + \cdots + w_{c_m} = 1$. The weights are determined by the experience of the experts in consideration of importance degrees of evaluation criteria. The final integration is finished through (3), and the quantized value of parameter p_i is obtained, denoted as $Q\left(p_i\right)$.

Repeat all the above procedures until all n parameters are quantized, denoted as

$$
\begin{aligned}
Q\left(P\right) &= \left(f_1\left(p_1\right), f_2\left(p_2\right), \ldots, f_n\left(p_n\right)\right) \\
&= \left(Q\left(p_1\right), Q\left(p_2\right), \ldots, Q\left(p_n\right)\right),
\end{aligned}
\tag{4}
$$

where $f_i(p_i)$ is a quantification function with all the above procedures and varied for different parameter.

5. Parameter Fusion and Trust Model Evaluation

A fusion algorithm based on fuzzy inference is proposed to combine the parameters in hierarchical structure in Figure 1.

5.1. The Weights of Distributive Parameters. In Figure 1, the middle criteria layer and lower parameters have certain relation. Several parameters are related to one or more factors in criteria layer. As the parameters are dependent on each other, fuzzy integral in (3) is inappropriate. Without loss of generality, we suppose that one factor in criteria layer is related to all the parameters, and the goal layer is related to all the factors in criteria layer. Firstly, the weights of parameters to single factor in criteria layer and the weights of factors in criteria layer to the goal layer are calculated. The entropy-weight coefficient method is a quantitative objective method and will be applied in our paper.

Entropy-weight coefficient method is a quantitative risk evaluation method [22]. The relative importance of a risk factor to an evaluated system can be measured by its entropy, which is calculated by the fusion of probability values denoting the supporting degree of risk factors to indexes of evaluation set for the system. In this paper, the parameters are considered as risk factors; one factor in the criteria layer is considered as evaluated object. Set several statuses for the evaluated object, give the probability of each parameter at each status, and apply entropy-weight coefficient method calculating the relative importance (weight) of each parameter to one upper factor. The statuses can be set based on certain evaluation set (i.e., rationality, from being irrational to highest rationality) used in previous parameter quantitation, and the probabilities that each parameter stay at certain status of the evaluation set can be determined by the same experts that used the Delphi method in Section 4.3. The detailed procedure of entropyweight coefficient method is referred to in related book (i.e., [22]) and omitted here.

Repeat the above calculation until all the weights are obtained. The weight of parameters of kth ($k \in [1, s]$, s being the number of factors in criteria layer) factor in middle criteria layer is denoted as $W_{pk} = \{w_{k1}, w_{k2}, \ldots, w_{kn}\}$, where n is the number of parameters. For the sake of simplicity, discard the weights that equaled 0 (e.g., time decay has no relation with structure adaptability of a trust model; the probability density function of status is always 0), and obtain effective weights, denoted as $W_k = \{w_{k1}, w_{k2}, \ldots, w_{kb}\}$, where $b \in [1, n]$. Repeat the above filtering; the weights of parameters to one factor in criteria layer and the weights of factors in criteria layer to the goal layer are obtained.

5.2. The Fusion of Parameters Based on Fuzzy Inference. The evaluated values of single factor in criteria layer and the evaluated value of goal layer will be fused by fuzzy inference in succession. In fuzzy set theory, a variable $V_T = \{v_1, v_2, \ldots, v_b\}$, v_k ($k = 1, 2, \ldots, b$) denoting the value of object T at the point k (k-level value) according to the defined membership functions in a given discourse domain, and the problem is how to obtain V_T under a given tree (i.e., Figure 1).

We evaluate kth factor in the criteria layer followed by b parameters. Set a discourse domain for the kth factor (e.g., reliability, from the least reliable to the most reliable and 5 levels are divided as the least reliable, little reliable, medium reliable, favorite reliable, and the most reliable and $V_q = \{0, 0.2, 0.4, 0.6, 0.8, 1\}$ stands for quantitative border value). The membership function is a trapezoidal function; the prototype is shown below:

$$\mu_T(x) = \begin{cases} \left(\dfrac{x-t}{1-t}\right)^2, & 0 \le x \le \dfrac{a+1}{2} \\ 1 - \left(\dfrac{x-t}{1-t}\right)^2, & \dfrac{a+1}{2} \le x \le 1, \end{cases} \quad (5)$$

where a is a defined threshold and t ($t \in [0, 1]$) is the offset of positive x and is set to 0.2 to form 5 curves.

The quantitative values of b parameters have been achieved in Section 4.3; each value can be mapped to a membership degree according to membership function, eventually formed into an evaluation matrix $R = (r_{gh})_{b \times l}$. The weighted vector is $W_k = \{w_{k1}, w_{k2}, \ldots, w_{kb}\}$, and then the overall vector of the kth factor is denoted as

$$V_T = \{v_1, v_2, \ldots, v_l\} = (w_{k1}, w_{k2}, \ldots, w_{kb}) \times (r_{gh})_{b \times l}. \quad (6)$$

Define the evaluated value of the kth factor: $V_k = \max(V_T)$, where $\max(V_T)$ is the maximum membership degree of V_T.

Repeat the above procedure until all the evaluated values of the factors in the criteria layer are obtained. Based on the evaluated value of the factors in the criteria layer and the weights of factors in middle layer to the final goal layer, the fuzzy comprehensive judgment is performed with the same

method as that used in calculating the evaluated value of the kth factor V_k to obtain the comprehensive analytic value for a trust model.

Then, the observer can compare the eventual evaluated value with the threshold to judge whether the trust model is qualified. The threshold is set based on some factors, for example, accuracy and fee. We can evaluate a set of trust models, sort the evaluated values, and choose an optimal trust model (usually the model with maximal evaluated value) for implementation.

5.3. The Outline of the Evaluated Procedure. The main steps of the proposed method are summarized:

(1) Based on the structure in Figure 1, apply entropy-weight coefficient method to calculate the weights of parameters to factors in criteria layer and the weights of factors in criteria layer to goal layer. Meanwhile, determine the distributive b parameters for kth factor in criteria layer.

(2) Parameter quantitation: for a trust model, quantize the extracted parameters with a series of procedures described in Section 4.3, and obtain the vector $Q(P) = (f_1(p_1), f_2(p_2), \ldots, f_n(p_n))$.

(3) Parameter fusion: the evaluated value of a trust model is calculated by the fusion of quantitative values and weights of parameters by fuzzy inference described in Section 5.2. And judge whether the given model satisfies the request according to the defined threshold.

(4) Select a set of trust models, repeat step (2) and step (3), calculate and sort the overall evaluated values, and choose an optimal trust model for implementation.

6. Method Analysis and Simulation

In this section, some discussion, a concrete evaluation experiment, and the effectiveness of the proposed method are addressed in Sections 6.1, 6.2, and 6.3, respectively.

6.1. Some Discussion of the Proposed Method. Consider the following:

(1) Notice that the hierarchical model is an open structure that other parameters and decision factors can be integrated into this model, which reflect the flexibility of the proposed method. Moreover, the hierarchical model is a reference model, and more than three layers might exist when subfactors are being linked to the parameters or the factor in criteria layer.

(2) The weights calculated by our method are stable under the condition that distributed scene and individual policy are determined. And the quantized values of parameters varied from one trust model to another.

6.2. A Concrete Evaluation Experiment. A concrete evaluation experiment is performed. Six traditional trust models

TABLE 2: Sorted results of evaluated trust models.

Overall score	0.79	0.78	0.65	0.63	0.62
Sorted models	MdTrust	Bayesian	EigenTrust	GTM	PeerTrust

analyzed in Section 3.2 are selected: EigenTrust, PeerTrust, game theory model (GTM for short) [8], multidimensional trust (MdTrust for short) model [9], and Bayesian model [11]. Some conditions are set as follows:

(1) A concrete scene: one user (service requester) performs the file download in P2P network. And the service requester pays more attention to the speed and quality of file download.

(2) The eight parameters and four factors in the middle layer are all considered.

(3) The number of statuses of the four factors is set to 5 (measured by rationality, I-irrational, L-lowest rationality, M-medium rationality, F-favorable rationality, and H-highest rationality); the probabilities of each status for parameters are determined by the same 7 experts in parameter quantitation with Delphi method; the range of quantized value of parameters is 0-1, with quantized step being 0.2.

According to the procedures in Section 5.3, the evaluated values of the 6 trust models are shown in Table 2.

From Table 2, we can see that multidimensional trust model reaches the highest score, as it has more parameters than others, and the robustness and scalability receive higher score in quantitation. PeerTrust compared to EigenTrust, although with better transitivity; worse scalability eventually leads to a smaller overall evaluated score, as the weight of scalability is larger than that of transitivity under the service requester policy.

We can see that none of the candidate trust models satisfies all the parameters. If the threshold is 0.8, then no trust model is qualified. Nevertheless, we can select the relatively optimal trust model (i.e., one received the highest evaluated value) to implement for a special application.

6.3. The Effectiveness of the Method. In this section, we will analyze the effectiveness of the proposed method.

The efficiency of the proposed method: for a given model, for n parameters, suppose that there are m factors mostly. Seven experts carry out two rounds of consultation, each of which needs time t_1, and the combination of m factors costs $O(m)$. The overall time complexity is $n \times (2t_1 \times m + O(m))$, m being small (around 3–5 for each parameter), so the time complexity is controlled. For the weights of parameters, it is needed to calculate the process of the entropy-weight coefficient, time complexity being $O(n)$. Moreover, the weights can be reutilized for the same scene and task.

We further validate the effectiveness of the proposed method by comparing it with previous methods [15, 20, 21]. For the convenience, [15] is denoted as Wojcik's method and [20, 21] are Schlosser's method and Yang's method.

Firstly, the proposed method adopts multiple parameters to evaluate trust model; it is more comprehensive than other works in characterizing the trust issues. Wojcik introduced a series of factors classified into four aspects in establishing a trust model, but the parameter functions were not considered. Yang's method judged the performance of trust model with two parameters: sensibility and foreseeability. In Schlosser, three parameters were used to reflect trust. These methods had failed to reflect the comprehensive characteristics of a trust model.

Secondly, in terms of accuracy, Yang proposed a black box model and compared a set of trust history sequences in the input with the output and then determined the performance of the trust model with sensibility and foreseeability. Its accuracy depends on the initialization of trust and behavioral characteristic. Wojcik displayed entire process of establishing trust comprehensively, but no specific assessment is performed. Schlosser presented a formal model for describing multiple reputation systems, but only reputation systems are taken into account. In our proposal, objective disposal of parameters as well as fuzzy inference is used to quantify the evaluated value of a trust model, the results are more objective and with higher accuracy.

Thirdly, in terms of efficiency, the overhead for our method is controllable and man-made evaluation in Delphi method and the calculation of weights and the fuzzy inference contribute to the calculation load. Wojcik's method does not involve load, and the overhead varied with varied algorithms. Yang's method searched for the history scorings of trusted entities according to the defined behavior characteristics; the time complexity is about $O(n)$, where n is the number of behaviors collected. Schlosser simulated the reputation system in the performance of resisting attacks with the granularity of single node, and the consumption increases with the increase of nodes. The analysis results are shown in Table 3.

In Table 3, the proposed method is denoted as "new method"; the performance is denoted as three levels: good (high), medium, and bad (low). Table 3 explains the superiority of the proposed method.

Further, we present a quantitative comparison among Schlosser's method and Yang's method with simulation. The accuracy and efficiency are compared among three methods.

Accuracy simulation: reflect the change of deviation (y-axis) of evaluated results with the increasing experiment time (x-axis). The conditions are the same as that set in Section 6.2; the deviation is defined as $d = |d_e - d_t| \times 100\%$, where d_e is current evaluated value of the optimal trust model and d_t is the statistical average of its former values. We perform the experiment 20 times. The number of initial nodes of P2P network is 20, where malicious nodes are 20%. The network nodes increase by 5, where the malicious nodes increase with the same percentage (20%), when the experiment time increases by 1.

Efficiency simulation: reflect the relationship between resource consumption (i.e., time consumption) and the number of experiments. The initial number of evaluated trust models is 1 and increases by 1 when the experiment time increases by 1. The simulation results are shown in Figure 2.

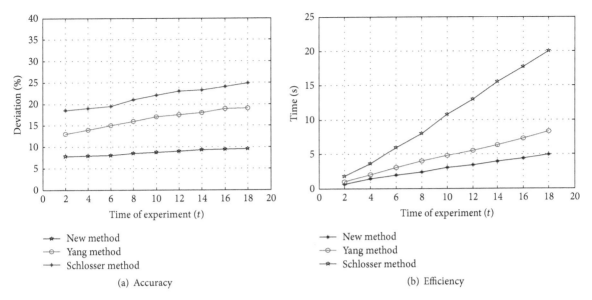

FIGURE 2: Simulation results.

TABLE 3: The comparison of the previous methods.

	Wojcik's method	Yang's method	Schlosser's method	New method
Comprehensiveness	Good	Medium	Medium	Very good
Accuracy	High	Medium	Low	Very high
Efficiency	Uncertain	High	Medium	High

Figure 2(a) describes the accuracy of the three methods. We can find that the deviation of the proposed method is smaller than Yang's method and Schlosser's method; the deviation is controlled within 10%. Therefore, the proposed method is more accurate.

Figure 2(b) describes the efficiency of the three methods; the calculation load increases with the increasing of evaluated models. The proposed method is similar to Yang's method, increasing linearly, but Schlosser's method increases rapidly. The results are in accord with analysis in Table 3.

7. Conclusions

A new method is proposed to compare and evaluate the trust models with quantitative parameters in P2P file downloading scene in this paper. The evaluated parameters are extracted from the trust related concepts and modeled into a hierarchical structure. The Delphi method, entropy-weight coefficient method, and fuzzy inference are applied to obtain a comprehensive evaluated value of a trust model. The optimal trust model is selected according to the sorted overall quantized values of candidate trust models. Analysis and simulation results show that the proposed evaluation algorithm is reasonable and effective. The proposed method resolves the individuality issues, assisting a decision maker in choosing an optimal trust model to implement in specific context. Moreover, the method also can be used to guide the newly generated trust model in theory so that it has better performance in parameter function and adaptability.

Competing Interests

The authors declare that they have no competing interests.

References

[1] Y. Zhong, B. Bhargava, Y. Lu, and P. Angin, "A computational dynamic trust model for user authorization," *IEEE Transactions on Dependable and Secure Computing*, vol. 12, no. 1, pp. 1–15, 2015.

[2] I.-R. Chen, J. Guo, and F. Bao, "Trust management for service composition in SOA-based IoT systems," in *Proceedings of the IEEE Wireless Communications and Networking Conference (WCNC '14)*, pp. 3444–3449, Istanbul, Turkey, April 2014.

[3] E. Damiani, S. De Capitani di Vimercati, S. Paraboschi, and P. Samarati, "Managing and sharing servants' reputations in P2P systems," *IEEE Transactions on Knowledge and Data Engineering*, vol. 15, no. 4, pp. 840–854, 2003.

[4] L. Mekouar, Y. Iraqi, and R. Boutaba, "Detecting malicious peers in a reputation-based peer-to-peer system," in *Proceedings of the 2nd IEEE Consumer Communications and Networking Conference (CCNC '05)*, pp. 37–42, IEEE, Las Vegas, Nev, USA, January 2005.

[5] M. Rodriguez-Perez, O. Esparza, and J. L. Muñoz, "Surework: a super-peer reputation framework for p2p networks," in *Proceedings of the 23rd Annual ACM Symposium on Applied Computing (SAC '08)*, pp. 2019–2023, Fortaleza, Brazil, March 2008.

[6] S. D. Kamvar, M. T. Schlosser, and H. Garcia-Molina, "The eigentrust algorithm for reputation management in P2P networks," in *Proceedings of the 12th International Conference on World Wide Web (WWW '03)*, pp. 640–651, ACM, Budapest, Hungary, May 2003.

[7] L. Xiong and L. Liu, "A reputation-based trust model for peer-to-peer eCommerce communities," in *Proceedings of the ACM Conference on Electronic Commerce (EC '03)*, pp. 275–284, San Diego, Calif, USA, June 2003.

[8] M. Harish, N. Anandavelu, N. Anbalagan, G. S. Mahalakshmi, and T. V. Geetha, "Design and analysis of a game theoretic model for P2P trust management," in *Distributed Computing and Internet Technology: 4th International Conference, ICDCIT 2007, Bangalore, India, December 17–20. Proceedings*, vol. 4882 of *Lecture Notes in Computer Science*, pp. 110–115, Springer, Berlin, Germany, 2007.

[9] X. Li, F. Zhou, and X. Yang, "A multi-dimensional trust evaluation model for large-scale P2P computing," *Journal of Parallel and Distributed Computing*, vol. 71, no. 6, pp. 837–847, 2011.

[10] L. Srour, A. Kayssi, and A. Chehab, "Reputation-based algorithm for managing trust in file sharing networks," in *Proceedings of the Securecomm and Workshops*, pp. 1–10, IEEE, Baltimore, Md, USA, September 2006.

[11] Y. Wang and J. Vassileva, "Bayesian network-based trust model in peer-to-peer networks," in *Proceedings of IEEE/WIC International Conference on Web Intelligence*, pp. 372–378, Halifax, Canada, 2003.

[12] Y. Wang, R. Wang, and Z. Han, "Dynamical trust construction schema with fuzzy decision in P2P systems," *Chinese Journal of Electronics*, vol. 18, no. 3, pp. 417–421, 2009.

[13] S. Song, K. Hwang, R. Zhou, and Y.-K. Kwok, "Trusted P2P transactions with fuzzy reputation aggregation," *IEEE Internet Computing*, vol. 9, no. 6, pp. 24–34, 2005.

[14] C. Tian and B. Yang, "A D-S evidence theory based fuzzy trust model in file-sharing P2P networks," *Peer-to-Peer Networking and Applications*, vol. 7, no. 4, pp. 332–345, 2014.

[15] M. Wojcik, H. S. Venter, and J. H. P. Eloff, "Trust model evaluation criteria: a detailed analysis of trust representation," in *Proceedings of the South African Telecommunications Networks and Applications Conference (SATNAC '06)*, Western Cape, South Africa, September 2006.

[16] M. Rodriguez-Perez, O. Esparza, and J. L. Muñoz, "Analysis of peer-to-peer distributed reputation schemes," in *Proceedings of the IEEE International Conference on Collaborative Computing: Networking, Applications and Worksharing (CollaborateCom '05)*, pp. 1811–1817, San Jose, Calif, USA, December 2005.

[17] F. G. Mármol and G. M. Pérez, "Trust and reputation models comparison," *Internet Research*, vol. 21, no. 2, pp. 138–153, 2011.

[18] C. He and M. Wu, "Comparison and analysis of different reputation systems for peer-to-peer networks," in *Proceedings of the 3rd International Conference on Advanced Computer Theory and Engineering (ICACTE '10)*, vol. 3, pp. V3-20–V3-23, IEEE, Chengdu, China, August 2010.

[19] F. Azzedin, "Taxonomy of reputation assessment in peer-to-peer systems and analysis of their data retrieval," *Knowledge Engineering Review*, vol. 29, no. 4, pp. 463–483, 2014.

[20] A. Schlosser, M. Voss, and L. Brückner, "Comparing and evaluating metrics for reputation systems by simulation," in *Proceedings of the IAT Workshop on Reputation in Agent Societies*, 2004.

[21] M. Yang, L. Wang, and Y. Lei, "Research on evaluation of trust model," in *Proceedings of the International Conference on Computational Intelligence and Security (CIS '08)*, vol. 1, pp. 345–349, Suzhou, China, December 2008.

[22] H. Su and C. Zhu, "Application of entropy weight coefficient method in evaluation of soil fertility," in *Recent Advances in Computer Science and Information Engineering*, vol. 126 of *Lecture Notes in Electrical Engineering*, pp. 697–703, Springer, Berlin, Germany, 2012.

9

Moisture Content Quantization of Masson Pine Seedling Leaf based on Stacked Autoencoder with Near-Infrared Spectroscopy

Chao Ni [ID],[1,2] Yun Zhang,[1] and Dongyi Wang [ID][2]

[1]*School of Mechanical and Electrical Engineering, Nanjing Forestry University, Nanjing 210037, China*
[2]*Bio-Imaging and Machine Vision Lab, Fischell Department of Bioengineering, University of Maryland, College Park 20740, USA*

Correspondence should be addressed to Chao Ni; chaoni@njfu.edu.cn

Academic Editor: Hai Guo

Masson pine is widely planted in southern China, and moisture content of the pine seedling leaves is an important index for evaluating the vigor of seedlings. For precisely predicting leaf moisture content, near-infrared spectroscopy analysis is applied in the experiment, which is a cost-effective, high-speed, and noninvasive material content prediction tool. To further improve the spectroscopy analysis accuracy, in this study, a new analysis model is proposed which integrates a stacked autoencoder for extracting hierarchical output-related features layer by layer and a support vector regression model to leverage these features for precisely predicting moisture contents. Compared with traditional spectroscopy analysis method like partial least squares regression and basic support vector regression, the proposed model shows great superiority for leaf moisture content prediction, with R^2 value 0.9946 and root-mean squared error (RMSE) value 0.1636 in calibration set and R^2 value 0.9621 and RMSE 0.4249 in prediction set.

1. Introduction

Masson pine is an important species for forestation in southern China due to its broad distribution. It has been widely applied in pulp and building materials, petroleum extraction, and forestry chemicals [1] because of its desirable features including fast growth, high yield, variable light tolerance, and drought resistance [2]. To ensure the quality of masson pine seedlings, the moisture content of seedling leaves is an important evaluation index and should be assessed before plantation. Physiologically, leaf moisture content plays an important role in photosynthesis, material transport, and maintaining leaf morphological and physiological functions [3]. Traditional moisture measurements are almost chemical-based methods, which are complex, time-consuming, and laborious [4, 5]. As a result, it is urgent to establish a fast, nondestructive, and accurate measurement method for moisture content prediction.

The near-infrared (NIR) spectroscopy technique has been widely used for material content prediction, such as moisture content [6], nitrogen content [7], and chlorophyll content [8] of plants. To date, many researchers have constructed different NIR spectral calibration models to detect the moisture content of different plants such as sunflower [9], populous tree [10], and eucalyptus tree [11]. Although there are many successful spectroscopy applications, there is no research reported for the moisture content prediction of masson pine seedling leaves.

For spectroscopy data analysis, there are many common used calibration models such as partial least squares regression (PLSR) [12], multiple linear regression (MLR) [13], support vector machines for regression (SVR) [14–16], artificial neural networks (ANNs) [17], and so on. However, the prediction results from these models are hopeful to be improved due to the limitations of the models. PLSR and MLR are widely used methods in the spectroscopy area. Both of them are linear models, which means the model can hardly describe the nonlinear relationship between the input spectroscopy data and output material content value. SVR, a nonlinear model, is suitable for small dataset analysis. It usually has strong generalization ability and self-learning capacity. The performance of SVR model usually depends on the quality input features, and determined representative data features are the premise for training a good SVR model [16]. ANNs offer a simple solution to model complex nonlinear data relationship [18]. The multiple layers in the ANN model can map the data input to the high-level feature representations. With the increasing number of hidden layers, the imbalance between the trainable network parameters and the limited training samples hinders the network training process in practice [19]. Stacked autoencoder (SAE) [20] is a variant of the ANN model, which usually is composed of an encoder and decoder. The encoder can map the input into few high-dimensional data features, and the decoder is expected to reconstruct the raw data. SAE can be trained without supervision, and the high dimensional data features from the encoder have been successfully applied in different tasks [21–24].

In this paper, to combine the advantages of different existing data analysis methods, a new model is proposed for predicting the moisture content in masson pine seedling leaves. In the model, a SAE is pretrained layer by layer without supervision to get the high-level data features. Then, based on the properties of the ANN model, the high-level data can be fine-tuned in a supervised way. Once the high-level data features are determined, the SVR model is established to describe the relationship between the high-level data features and the moisture content. Compared with other traditional spectroscopy analysis methods, the proposed model shows better performance.

2. Materials and Methods

2.1. Materials. A total of 100 annual masson pine seedling samples were obtained from forest farm in Huangping, Guizhou Province, China. Seventy-five of them were used to establish a calibration model, and the remaining 25 were used for prediction. Before measuring the spectra and moisture content, the leaves were cleaned to remove the impurities such as soil and sand, and then the surface of the leaves were naturally dried to prepare for the later experiment.

2.2. Spectra Acquisition and Moisture Quantitative Analysis. All NIR spectra of masson pine seedling leaves were measured using an MPA Fourier-Transform Near-Infrared spectrometer (Bruker Optics, Inc., Germany), equipped with an PbS detector and controlled by OPUS Analyst version 7.0 using a spectral range from 4,000 to 12,493 cm^{-1} in the reflectance mode. Measurements were conducted with the resolution of 4 cm^{-1}, ensuring an adequate signal-to-noise ratio. There are 2203 wavelength variables in the spectrum. The experiment was carried out at approximately 24°C. The spectral reflectance of the top, middle, and bottom areas of the sample were scanned two times each. The final value of the sample spectral reflectance was obtained by calculating the average of the six scans. From each sample, six spectra were collected and averaged for further analysis. Figure 1 shows the raw absorptance spectra of masson pine seedling leaves.

Total moisture content of masson pine seedling leaves was determined using the HB43-S Halogen Moisture

analyzer (Mettler Toledo, Inc., Switzerland). The instrument is working based on the thermogravimetric principle, i.e., the moisture is determined from the weight loss of a sample dried by heating. After putting a sample in the sampling chamber, the temperature was immediately increased and maintained at 125°C. The halogen lamp of the instrument heated the sample until the sample stopped losing mass; then the moisture content of the samples is automatically given by the instrument. Normally, the measurements were completed in a few minutes. The reference moisture content value for the samples was 64.97% ± 2.21%, with a minimum of 59.13% and a maximum of 70.74%.

2.3. Spectra Pretreatment. Two preprocessing transformations were applied as a standard preparation for the masson pine seedling absorbance curves. Firstly, a Savitzky–Golay (S-G) smoothing with a second-degree polynomial was used for denoising, and the first-order numerical derivative was made to correct the baseline drift. The window width of S-G smoothing was set as 17. Secondly, the spectral matrix was converted into the number between 0 and 1 by vector normalization, which was used to reduce the orders of magnitude difference among the data of different dimensions.

2.4. The Proposed Method

2.4.1. Autoencoder. The basic structure of autoencoder is a kind of unsupervised ANN with one hidden layer, and it consists of an input layer, a hidden layer, and an output layer as Figure 2. The aim of autoencoder is to reduce the data dimension and to map the input data into high dimensional data features.

Define the input as $x = [x_{(1)}, x_{(2)}, \ldots, x_{(d)}]'$, where d is the dimension of the inputs. The encoder maps x into the hidden layer $h = [h_1, h_2, \ldots, h_{d_h}]'$ by the function f as follows:

$$h = f(x) = s_f(Wx + b), \qquad (1)$$

where d_h is the dimension of the hidden layer variable vector h, W is a $d_h * d$ weight matrix, b is the bias vector, and s_f is the nonlinear activation function, which can be chosen as the sigmoid function or other functions such as the tanh function and the rectified linear unit function. Then, the hidden representation vector h is mapped to the output layer $\tilde{x}$ by the function $\tilde{f}$.

$$\tilde{x} = \tilde{f}(h) = s_{\tilde{f}}(\widetilde{W}h + \tilde{b}), \qquad (2)$$

where $\widetilde{W}$ is a $d * d_h$ weight matrix, $\tilde{b}$ is the bias vector for the output layer, and $s_{\tilde{f}}$ is the nonlinear activation function of decoder. The aim of autoencoder is to search the parameter set $\theta = \{W, \widetilde{W}, b, \tilde{b}\}$ to satisfy the equation $\tilde{x} = \tilde{f}(h) = \tilde{f}(f(x)) \approx x$. Define the training input as $X = \{x_1, x_2, \ldots, x_N\}$, where N is the number of the training samples and $x_i = [x_{i(1)}, x_{i(2)}, \ldots, x_{i(d)}]$ is the vector data of ith training sample. The loss function is defined as follows:

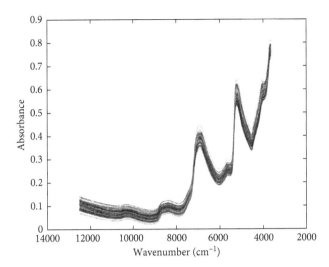

FIGURE 1: Raw absorptance spectra of masson pine seedling leaves.

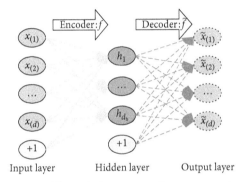

FIGURE 2: The typical structure of an autoencoder.

$$J(W, \widetilde{W}, b, \widetilde{b}) = \frac{1}{2N} \sum_{i=1}^{N} \left\| x_i - \widetilde{x}_i \right\|^2$$

$$= \frac{1}{2N} \sum_{i=1}^{N} \sum_{j=1}^{d} \left(x_{i(j)} - \widetilde{x}_{i(j)} \right)^2. \tag{3}$$

Then, the parameter set $\theta = \left\{ W, \widetilde{W}, b, \widetilde{b} \right\}$ is updated with the gradient descent algorithm.

In practice, multiple basic autoencoder structures are usually stacked together, and a new network structure is constructed, named SAE, for better dimensional reduction and feature extraction performance. The extracted data feature can be further used for different tasks [25, 26].

2.4.2. Support Vector Machine Regression. Support vector machine (SVM) is a powerful and robust method based on the principle of structural risk minimization, which has an advantage of computational efficiency for the data sets that have many more variables than observations. Compared with ANN, SVM can obtain more reliable and better performance under same training conditions. Recently, SVM has been successfully extended to SVR, especially in chemometrics for quantitative analysis due to its excellent ability of dealing with nonlinearity and small sample size.

The purpose of SVR is to find the underlying relationship between input and output, and a regression function $y(x) = f(x) + b = w^T \phi(x) + b$ is used with an ε-insensitive loss function as follows:

$$|\xi|_\varepsilon = \begin{cases} 0 & \text{if} |\xi| \leq \varepsilon, \\ |\xi| \text{-} \varepsilon & \text{otherwise.} \end{cases} \tag{4}$$

Then, the regression problem is equivalent to the following formulations:

$$\min \left(\frac{1}{2} \|w\|^2 + C \sum_{i=1}^{l} (\xi_i + \xi_i^*) \right),$$

$$\text{s.t.} \begin{cases} y_i - w^T \phi(x) - b \leq \varepsilon + \xi_i, \\ -y_i + w^T \phi(x) + b \leq \varepsilon + \xi_i^*, \\ \xi_i, \xi_i^* \geq 0, \end{cases} \tag{5}$$

where ξ_i and ξ_i^* are slack variables, and the regularization parameter $C > 0$ is used to avoid overfitting. Further, the optimization problem can be converted into the new optimization problem as the following:

$$\max \left(\frac{1}{2} \sum_{i,j=1}^{l} (\alpha_i - \alpha_i^*)(\alpha_j - \alpha_j^*) K(x_i, x_j) \right.$$

$$\left. - \varepsilon \sum_{i=1}^{l} (\alpha_i + \alpha_i^*) + \sum_{i=1}^{l} y_i \left(\alpha_i - \alpha_i^* \right) \right),$$

$$\text{s.t.} \begin{cases} \sum_{i=1}^{l} (\alpha_i - \alpha_i^*), \\ \alpha_i, \alpha_i^* \in [0, C], \end{cases} \tag{6}$$

where α_i and α_i^* are Lagrange multipliers and $K(x_i, x_j)$ is a kernel function. The kernel function maps the nonlinear optimization problem to a linear problem in higher dimensional space. There are several commonly used kernel functions such as linear kernel, polynomial kernel, and radical basis function kernel. In this study, radical basis function kernel is selected as follows:

$$K(x_i, x) = \exp \left(\frac{-\|x - x_i\|^2}{\gamma^2} \right), \tag{7}$$

where γ determines width of the kernel function. Once radical basis function kernel is selected, there are only three parameters to be decided. The parameter ε is to control the error. A larger ε can speed up the train process with low accuracy. Whereas, a smaller ε can achieve better accuracy and reduce the training speed. In this paper, the parameter is set fixed as 0.004. Besides the parameter ε, the regularization parameter C and the kernel function parameter γ are both application-based parameters, which can greatly affect accuracy of the regression. In this paper, genetic algorithm is utilized to search optimal parameters for SVR [27].

2.4.3. Regression Model Based on SAE with SVR. To estimate moisture content in masson pine seedling leaves, a novel regression model based on SAE with SVR is proposed as shown in Figure 3. The procedure of the proposed method is described as follows:

Step 1. Several AEs are stacked layer by layer to form deep neural networks. The deep neural networks can convert a complex input data into a series of simple high-level features by reducing the dimensionality of the input data. To train the networks, the first AE is trained in an unsupervised manner. After training is finished, its decoder is abandoned, and the output of the hidden layer is used as the input of the second AE with same fashion. Till all AEs have been trained layer by layer, the weights of these AEs had been assigned to initialize the deep neural networks. The topmost hidden layer outputs the elementary high-level features of the input data.

Step 2. To achieve better feature representation of the input data, the supervision method is used to tune the weights. A two-layer neural network is added after the topmost layer, and the output of this neural network is the target output. Then, the back-propagation algorithm is utilized to update the weights layer by layer. At last, the fine-tuning weights have been obtained, and then the improved high-level features have been achieved.

Step 3. Feed the improved high-level features into SVR as input data, and then build the regression model using GA algorithm to select the optimal parameters.

2.5. Evaluation Criteria. As normal, the root-mean squared error (RMSE) and the coefficient of determination are widely used as the evaluating criteria for the calibration model. RMSE is defined as follows:

$$\text{RMSE} = \sqrt{\sum_{i=1}^{N_T} \frac{(y_i - \hat{y}_i)^2}{(N_T)}}, \tag{8}$$

where y_i and $\hat{y}_i$ are the actual and predicted target output values of the *i*th sample, respectively and N_T is the number of the testing samples. RMSE indicates the accuracy of the model, and a small RMSE value shows better prediction performance than larger RMSE.

The coefficient of determination R^2 represents a squared correlation between the actual and predicted output, and the reliability of model can be reflected as R^2. R^2 is defined as follows:

$$R^2 = 1 - \frac{\sum_{i=1}^{N_T}(y_i - \hat{y}_i)^2}{\sum_{i=1}^{N_T}(y_i - \overline{y})^2}, \tag{9}$$

where $\overline{y}$ is the mean of the actual output in the testing samples. When R^2 is closer to 1, it indicates good prediction performance of the calibration model. In a word, a better calibration model should have small RMSE and large R^2.

3. Results and Discussion

3.1. Result and Settings of the Proposed Model. For the proposed model construction and test, 100 samples were divided into 75 samples for calibration dataset and 25 samples for prediction dataset. The first step is to decide the settings of the model. It is evident that the number of the hidden layers and the number of the neuron in each hidden layer can have major influence on the performance of the model. However, there is still no automatic method that can be utilized to achieve the selection of the parameters. In this paper, trial and error is used to choose these parameters, and RMSE is adopted to access the performance of the model. The weights and bias for each AE is obtained by greedy layerwise pretraining technique, and each AE is trained with gradient descent algorithm. After the SAE is layerwise trained, the two-layer neural network is connected to the output of SAE for weight fine tuning of ANN. After that, SVR is connected to the high-level features to output the predicted value. After experiments, the proposed model structure is composed of three-layer AEs, and the hidden neurons number is 1600, 1100, and 512, respectively. The batch size is set as 40 samples, and each AE is trained 500 iterations iteratively. Figure 4 shows the training loss trends with the iteration number for each AE. As shown in Figure 4, the SAE model can converge quickly in 500 iterations for each AE.

After the weights are pretrained and fine-tuned, the SVR is connected to output the predicted value. The detailed prediction results are shown in Figure 5, and C and γ of SVR are set as 4.79 and 1.97, respectively, using GA algorithm. The RMSE and R^2 of the prediction dataset are 0.4249 and 0.9621, respectively. As can be seen from Figure 5, the predicted output can match well with the real values. The prediction error is mainly caused by the points which are located in the interval with few samples in the calibration dataset.

3.2. Discussion. To verify the effectiveness of the proposed method, there are several methods to be used to build the calibration model. Each method is trained with the same calibration dataset, and the average result of 4-folder cross-validation in each method is adopted in Table 1 and Figure 6. The results of MLR, PLS, and SVR are directly obtained using PLS_Toolbox (Eigenvector Research, Inc., USA) running on MATLAB 2016. The other methods are implemented by the deep learning framework Keras using Python. As can be seen in Table 1, MLR and PLS produce the worst prediction results since they cannot deal with nonlinear correlative data for its linear essence. SVR is inferior to other methods and just outperforms above two methods, because it cannot describe the nonlinear data adequately. The last three methods all adopt the same network structure. The ANN method is composed of five layers of neural networks, and the first three layers have the same network structure as SAE. The last two layers have the same structure with neural networks as being connected to SAE. The same two-layer neural networks with the neuron layer structure

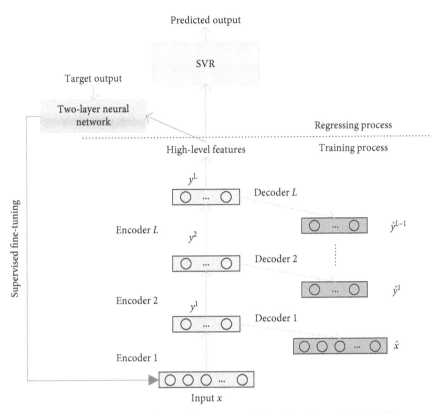

FIGURE 3: The proposed network structure of deep learning with SAE-SVR.

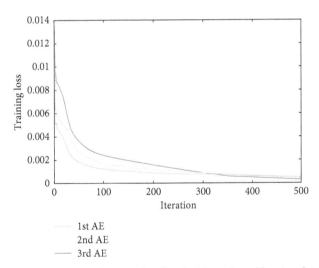

FIGURE 4: The training loss trends of each AE on the calibration dataset.

[512, 128] are connected to SAE for fine tuning the weights. ANN method outperforms above three methods, but it is easily trapped in local optima. By adopting the SAE, high-level abstract features can be extracted layer by layer in SAE. Further, by using the pretrained weights and bias terms in the full connected network, the methods can avoid the inferior local optima and speed up the learning process. Thus, the last two methods can describe the complex data structure more accurately. Besides, a small size of training samples used in this study may also limit the predictive power of the ANN model. Then, SVR with genetic algorithm is connected to SAE to achieve better performance in small training samples. The regression plot between the predicted moisture content and the reference content is shown in Figure 6. It can visualize the regression performance of different models. If the scatter data points are closer to the perfect correlation line (with slope = 1), the prediction model is more accurate (larger R^2 value and smaller RMSE

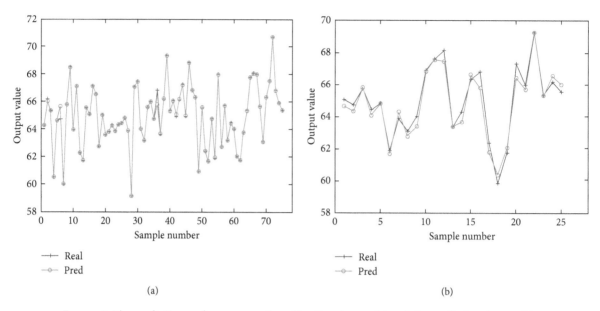

FIGURE 5: The prediction performance on the calibration dataset (a) and the prediction dataset (b).

TABLE 1: Calibration and prediction results of the moisture content in masson pine seedling leaves using different regression models.

Model	Calibration dataset		Prediction dataset	
	R_C^2	RMSEC	R_P^2	RMSEP
MLR	0.9267	0.5619	0.3915	2.879
PLSR	0.9658	0.4079	0.8981	0.6774
SVR	0.9892	0.2285	0.9016	0.7052
ANN	0.9974	0.1123	0.9322	0.5559
SAE-ANN	0.9944	0.1644	0.9421	0.5228
SAE-SVR	0.9946	0.1636	0.9621	0.4249

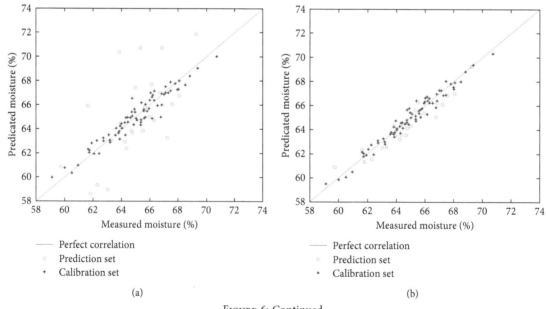

FIGURE 6: Continued.

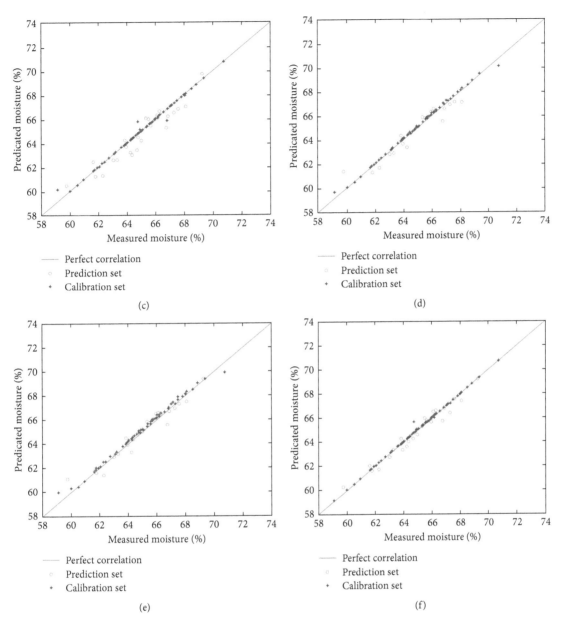

FIGURE 6: Measured vs. predicated moisture content for masson pine seedling leaves by the regression models of MLR (a), PLSR (b), SVR (c), ANN (d), SAE-ANN (e), and SAE-SVR (f).

value). Overall, the proposed method outperforms the other methods for moisture concentration prediction of masson pine seedling leaves.

4. Conclusion

In this study, a new method of stacked autoencoder with SVR is introduced and applied to estimate the moisture content in masson pine seedlings. Compared with MLR, PLSR, SVR, ANN, and SAE-ANN, the SAE-SVR shows superior performances, and gets R^2 value 0.9946 and RMSE 0.1636 in calibration dataset, and R^2 value 0.9621 and RMSE 0.4249 in prediction dataset. The results of this study demonstrate that deep neural networks pretrained by SAE

are feasible to be used as the data analysis method for moisture prediction in masson pine seedling leaves.

Conflicts of Interest

The authors declare that there are no conflicts of interest regarding the publication of this paper.

Acknowledgments

The authors gratefully acknowledge the financial support provided by the National Natural Science Foundation of China (NSFC: 31570714) and Jiangsu Overseas Research & Training Program for University Prominent Young & Middle-Aged Teachers and Presidents Program.

References

[1] Y. Wang, S. Solberg, P. Yu et al., "Assessments of tree crown condition of two Masson pine forests in the acid rain region in south China," *Forest Ecology and Management*, vol. 242, no. 2-3, pp. 530–540, 2007.

[2] Y. You, X. Huang, H. Zhu et al., "Positive interactions between *Pinus massoniana* and *Castanopsis hystrix* species in the uneven-aged mixed plantations can produce more ecosystem carbon in subtropical China," *Forest Ecology and Management*, vol. 410, pp. 193–210, 2017.

[3] V. Suguiyama, R. Sanches, S. Meirelles, D. C. Centeno, E. A. Da Silva, and M. R. Braga, "Physiological responses to water deficit and changes in leaf cell wall composition as modulated by seasonality in the Brazilian resurrection plant *Barbacenia purpurea*," *South African Journal of Botany*, vol. 105, pp. 270–278, 2016.

[4] T. A. Oyehan, I. O. Alade, A. Bagudu, K. O. Sulaiman, S. O. Olatunji, and T. A. Saleh, "Predicting of the refractive index of haemoglobin using the Hybrid GA-SVR approach," *Computers in Biology and Medicine*, vol. 98, pp. 85–92, 2018.

[5] T. A. Saleh, S. O. Adio, M. Asif, and H. Dafalla, "Statistical analysis of phenols adsorption on diethylenetriamine-modified activated carbon," *Journal of Cleaner Production*, vol. 182, pp. 960–968, 2018.

[6] J. Posom and P. Sirisomboon, "Evaluation of the moisture content of Jatropha curcas kernels and the heating value of the oil-extracted residue using near-infrared spectroscopy," *Biosystems Engineering*, vol. 130, pp. 52–59, 2015.

[7] R. Tang, X. Chen, and C. Li, "Detection of nitrogen content in rubber leaves using near-infrared (NIR) spectroscopy with correlation based successive projections algorithm (SPA)," *Applied spectroscopy*, vol. 72, no. 5, pp. 740–749, 2018.

[8] J. Zhang, W. Han, L. Huang, Z. Zhang, Y. Ma, and Y. Hu, "Leaf chlorophyll content estimation of winter wheat based on visible and near-infrared sensors," *Sensors*, vol. 16, no. 4, p. 437, 2016.

[9] A. J. S. Neto, D. De Carvalho Lopes, T. G. F. Da Silva, S. O. Ferreira, and J. A. S. Grossi, "Estimation of leaf water content in sunflower under drought conditions by means of spectral reflectance," *Engineering in Agriculture, Environment and Food*, vol. 10, no. 2, pp. 104–108, 2017.

[10] G. Hans, B. Leblon, P. Cooper, A. La Rocque, and J. Nader, "Determination of moisture content and basic specific gravity of *Populus tremuloides* (Michx.) and *Populus balsamifera* (L.) logs using a portable near-infrared spectrometer," *Wood Material Science & Engineering*, vol. 10, no. 1, pp. 3–16, 2015.

[11] G. Yang, W. Lu, Y. Lin et al., "Monitoring water potential and relative water content in *Eucalyptus camaldulensis* using near infrared spectroscopy," *Journal of Tropical Forest Science*, vol. 29, no. 1, pp. 121–128, 2017.

[12] S. Wold, M. Sjöström, and L. Eriksson, "PLS-regression: a basic tool of chemometrics," *Chemometrics and Intelligent Laboratory Systems*, vol. 58, no. 2, pp. 109–130, 2001.

[13] L. S. Aiken, S. G. West, and S. C. Pitts, "Multiple linear regression," in *Handbook of Psychology*, pp. 481–507, John Wiley & Sons, Inc., Hoboken, NJ, USA, 2003.

[14] O. Devos, C. Ruckebusch, A. Durand, L. Duponchel, and J.-P. Huvenne, "Support vector machines (SVM) in near infrared (NIR) spectroscopy: focus on parameters optimization and model interpretation," *Chemometrics and Intelligent Laboratory Systems*, vol. 96, no. 1, pp. 27–33, 2009.

[15] B. Üstün, W. Melssen, and L. Buydens, "Visualisation and interpretation of support vector regression models," *Analytica Chimica Acta*, vol. 595, no. 1-2, pp. 299–309, 2007.

[16] I. O. Alade, A. Bagudu, T. A. Oyehan, M. A. A. Rahman, T. A. Saleh, and S. O. Olatunji, "Estimating the refractive index of oxygenated and deoxygenated hemoglobin using genetic algorithm-support vector machine approach," *Computer Methods and Programs in Biomedicine*, vol. 163, pp. 135–142, 2018.

[17] R. M. Balabin, E. I. Lomakina, and R. Z. Safieva, "Neural network (ANN) approach to biodiesel analysis: analysis of biodiesel density, kinematic viscosity, methanol and water contents using near infrared (NIR) spectroscopy," *Fuel*, vol. 90, no. 5, pp. 2007–2015, 2011.

[18] S. Cui, P. Ling, H. Zhu, and H. Keener, "Plant pest detection using an artificial nose system: a review," *Sensors*, vol. 18, no. 2, p. 378, 2018.

[19] G. E. Hinton, S. Osindero, and Y.-W. Teh, "A fast learning algorithm for deep belief nets," *Neural Computation*, vol. 18, no. 7, pp. 1527–1554, 2006.

[20] P. Vincent, H. Larochelle, I. Lajoie, Y. Bengio, and P.-A. Manzagol, "Stacked denoising autoencoders: learning useful representations in a deep network with a local denoising criterion," *Journal of Machine Learning Research*, vol. 11, pp. 3371–3408, 2010.

[21] J. Gehring, Y. Miao, F. Metze et al., "Extracting deep bottleneck features using stacked auto-encoders," in *Proceedings of IEEE International Conference on Acoustics, Speech and Signal Processing (IACSSP)*, pp. 3377–3381, Vancouver, BC, Canada, May 2013.

[22] C. Tao, H. Pan, Y. Li, and Z. Zou, "Unsupervised spectral–spatial feature learning with stacked sparse autoencoder for hyperspectral imagery classification," *IEEE Geoscience and Remote Sensing Letters*, vol. 12, no. 12, pp. 2438–2442, 2015.

[23] X. Wang and H. Liu, "Soft sensor based on stacked auto-encoder deep neural network for air preheater rotor deformation prediction," *Advanced Engineering Informatics*, vol. 36, pp. 112–119, 2018.

[24] X. Yuan, B. Huang, Y. Wang, C. Yang, and W. Gui, "Deep learning based feature representation and its application for soft sensor modeling with variable-wise weighted SAE," *IEEE Transactions on Industrial Informatics*, vol. 14, no. 7, pp. 3235–3245, 2018.

[25] P. Vincent, H. Larochelle, Y. Bengio et al., "Extracting and composing robust features with denoising autoencoders," in *Proceedings of 25th international conference on Machine learning*, pp. 1096–1103, Helsinki, Finland, July 2008.

[26] A. Supratak, L. Li, and Y. Guo, "Feature extraction with stacked autoencoders for epileptic seizure detection," in *Proceedings of 36th Annual International Conference of the IEEE Engineering in Medicine and Biology Society*, pp. 4184–4187, Chicago, Illinois, USA, August 2014.

[27] E. Avci, "Selecting of the optimal feature subset and kernel parameters in digital modulation classification by using hybrid genetic algorithm–support vector machines: HGASVM," *Expert Systems with Applications*, vol. 36, no. 2, pp. 1391–1402, 2009.

10

Heuristic Data Placement for Data-Intensive Applications in Heterogeneous Cloud

Qing Zhao,[1] **Congcong Xiong,**[1] **and Peng Wang**[2]

[1] *Tianjin University of Science and Technology, Tianjin 300222, China*
[2] *Tianjin House Fund Management Center, Tianjin 300222, China*

Correspondence should be addressed to Congcong Xiong; xiongcc@tust.edu.cn

Academic Editor: Hui Cheng

Data placement is an important issue which aims at reducing the cost of internode data transfers in cloud especially for data-intensive applications, in order to improve the performance of the entire cloud system. This paper proposes an improved data placement algorithm for heterogeneous cloud environments. In the initialization phase, a data clustering algorithm based on data dependency clustering and recursive partitioning has been presented, and both the factor of data size and fixed position are incorporated. And then a heuristic tree-to-tree data placement strategy is advanced in order to make frequent data movements occur on high-bandwidth channels. Simulation results show that, compared with two classical strategies, this strategy can effectively reduce the amount of data transmission and its time consumption during execution.

1. Introduction

With the arrival of Big Data, many scientific research fields have accumulated vast amounts of scientific data. Cloud computing provides vast amounts of storage and computing resources; however, because the cloud is architected in a distributed environment, a large number of I/O operations can be very time-consuming. There are different correlations between the datasets, and the network conditions between servers are also different. Hence, distributing these datasets intelligently can decrease the cost of data transfers efficiently.

In literature, many works [1–4] show that data placement is very crucial for the overall performance of the cloud system, due to the datasets on it being usually distributed enormously and their tasks having unavoidable complex dependencies [5]. Hence, every cloud platform should automatically and intelligently place the data into nodes to ensure that it can be accessed efficiently. Therefore, both the data correlation and the heterogeneous hardware condition of data centers should be taken into consideration for a reasonable data layout.

In this paper, a heuristic data layout method is proposed. First, both the datasets and the cloud system are abstracted as tree-structured models, respectively, according to data correlations and network bandwidth. And then, a heuristic data allocation method is advanced, so as to make frequent data movements occur on high-bandwidth networks. Therefore, the global time consumption of data communication can be reduced effectively.

The remainder of the paper is organized as follows. Section 2 presents related works. Section 3 illustrates the dataset model and the cloud platform model. Section 4 gives the details of the heuristic data allocation strategy. Section 5 presents and analyzes the simulation results. Finally, Section 6 addresses conclusions and future work.

2. Related Works

Cloud computing [6] offers a promising alternative for data-intensive scientific applications. As cloud platform is distributed and often architected on internet, the strategy of data placement is very significant. Many successful cloud systems, such as Google App Engine [7], Amazon EC2 [8], and Hadoop [9], have automatic mechanisms for storage of user's data but have not given much consideration to data dependencies. Recently, [10] has proposed a data placement strategy for Hadoop in heterogeneous environments, but it is also based on the specific cloud environment and has not considered the heterogynous network conditions. Another research is the Pegasus system which has proposed some data placement strategies [11, 12] based on the RLS system for workflows. These strategies can effectively reduce the overall execution time but only for the runtime stage. Furthermore, in [2], the authors issued a data placement strategy for the distributed systems. It guarantees the reliable and efficient data transfer with different protocols but is not aiming at reducing the total data movement of the whole system.

To reduce the total data movement, modeling the dependencies between datasets is usually the first step. In some literature [13–15], the DAG graph is used to model the data dependencies. And, in addition to the problem of storage resources allocation, other kinds of cloud resources including computing resources also use the similar approaches. For example, in [16], the Tabu Search approach is used for DAG figure partitioning, in order to get size balanced and net-cut minimized scheme of figure partitioning. However, this work is only for the method of graph division; no resource allocation algorithm has been issued. In addition, it only considers how to reduce the frequency of data transmission but did not consider the data amount of transmission. Therefore, it is not suitable for massive amounts of data transmission in Big Data era.

In [17], a matrix based k-means clustering strategy for data placement has been proposed. It groups the data items into k groups in terms of these data dependencies and the value of k is equal to the number of data centers in the cloud. This method can greatly reduce the data movement; nevertheless, it is more suitable for an isomorphic environment. This is because all the differences in the size of datasets, the storage capacities of the servers, and the network transmission speed have not been incorporated. On the other hand, their method is only aiming at decreasing the data transmission frequency, not the data amount of transmissions, or the time consumption by data transmissions.

And in these above methods, after data clustering, the resource allocation algorithms are relatively simple, such as that based on a random distribution principle, and the structure of network is not taken into consideration. In [18], data placement strategy based on a genetic algorithm has been proposed. This method is intended to reduce data movement while balancing the loads of data centers. However, it also lacks the consideration of how to utilize the heterogeneous network conditions more effectively. In our previous work [19, 20], some data placement algorithms have been proposed. In this work, we suppose that the datasets have no fixed-position storage requirements, and the data allocation strategy is also not network-aware. In this paper, the problem of fixed-position data has been considered, and, after data dependency clustering, the clustered datasets are allocated following a principle: frequent data movements occur on high-bandwidth network channels.

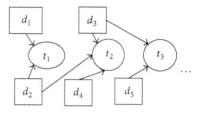

☐ Dataset
◯ Task

FIGURE 1: Tasks and datasets.

3. Data Model and Cloud Platform Model

3.1. Tree-Structure Modeling of the Datasets. In this paper, each application is modeled at a coarse granularity, that is, it is presented as an atomic operation, since data layout is our most significant concern, and the job scheduling can be simplified. Figure 1 provides an example illustration of the tasks and datasets.

Clearly, placing some data items together can decrease data transfer amount. Therefore, the data dependency $c_{i,j}$ between datasets d_i and d_j is defined as how much data transfer amount will be increased if these two datasets are placed on different data centers. This dependency computation method we proposed has improved the method of Yuan [17]. The detail computation algorithm of each dependency item $c_{i,j}$ of the dependency matrix is simply given as follows. This has already been given in our previous work [19, 20], but we have made some improvements.

Because of the problem of different ownership, some of the datasets may have fixed storage location. Here, a symbol D_{fix} is used as the set consisting of all these datasets that have a fixed storage location. For example, any data item i where $i \in D_{\text{fix}}$ must be stationary on a fixed position, and if this fixed position is the jth data center, then this can be expressed as $\text{fix}(i) = j$. Similarly, a data item i with no fixed storage position is expressed as $\text{fix}(i) = 0$. In detail, according to whether fixed-position datasets exist, the calculation method of the data dependency can be divided into two cases.

Case 1 (none of datasets has a fixed storage requirement, i.e., $D_{\text{fix}} = \phi$). We assume that the smaller data item is always moved to the node where the bigger one is stored so as to minimize the cost of data transmission. First, considering the tasks with 2 data items as input, the dependency gain from these tasks is

$$c_{i,j} = \left| T_i \bigcap T_j \right| \times \min \left\{ \text{Size}_{d_i}, \text{Size}_{d_j} \right\},$$

$$d_i, d_j \in D_{\text{in}}(t). \tag{1}$$

Here, $\left| T_i \bigcap T_j \right|$ is the number of tasks which need the datasets d_i and d_j as its whole input data; $\min\{\text{Size}_{d_i}, \text{Size}_{d_j}\}$ is the size of the smaller dataset between d_i and d_j.

And then, for the tasks with more than 2 input data items, the dependency gain is

$$
\begin{aligned}
c_{i,j} = \max \Big\{ &\{ \text{Size}_k \mid d_k \in D_{\text{in}}(t), \ k \neq i \neq j \} \\
&\cup \{ \text{Size}_i + \text{Size}_j \} \Big\} - \max \{ \text{Size}_m \mid d_m \in D_{\text{in}}(t) \}.
\end{aligned} \tag{2}
$$

In this case, the dependency gain between two data items is also defined as how much data transfer amount would be increased when they are put in the same position. For example, a task t requires 3 datasets d_1, d_2, and d_3 sized 3 G, 15 G, and 17 G, respectively. At the beginning, d_1 and d_2 are stored together, d_3 is placed on another node, and then 17 G data transmission at least is needed for running this task. And then consider another situation that the three datasets are stored on three different nodes; the least amount of data movement for this task is $15 + 3 = 18$. This is because moving d_1 and d_2 to the computing center where d_3 is placed on is the optimal approach. Therefore, the dependency gain of d_1 and d_2 for this situation is $18 - 17 = 1$. Therefore, the dependency gain of d_i and d_j can be calculated as

$$
\begin{aligned}
c_{i,j} = &\left(\sum_{d_m \in D_{\text{in}}(t)} \text{Size}_m - \max \{ \text{Size}_m \mid d_m \in D_{\text{in}}(t) \} \right) \\
&- \left(\sum_{d_m \in D_{\text{in}}(t)} \text{Size}_m \right. \\
&\quad - \max \Big\{ \{ \text{Size}_k \mid d_k \in D_{\text{in}}(t), \ k \neq i \neq j \} \\
&\qquad\qquad \left. \cup \{ \text{Size}_i + \text{Size}_j \} \Big\} \right).
\end{aligned} \tag{3}
$$

And this formula can be simplified into (2).

Case 2 (some of datasets have fixed storage requirements, i.e., $D_{\text{fix}} \neq \phi$). We group the datasets with the same storage position requirement first. Therefore, we have $G_j = \{ d_i \mid d_i \in D_{\text{fix}} \text{ and } \text{fix}(i) = j \}$. And if there is no dataset that must be placed on the kth server, then $G_k = \phi$. Therefore, in this case, the groups G_j ($1 \leq j \leq m$) can be seen as a big dataset, and the data dependency can be calculated between these big datasets and the initial data items:

$$
\begin{aligned}
&c_{A,B} \\
&= \begin{cases} 0, & \text{both } A \text{ and } B \text{ are fixed-position data groups} \\ \sum_{(i,j) \in \{A \times B\}} c_{i,j}, & \text{others.} \end{cases}
\end{aligned} \tag{4}
$$

Here, A and B can be either a single data item or a fixed-position data group and $A \times B$ denote the Cartesian product of the two sets A and B. $c_{i,j}$ is the data dependency between two data items and calculated according to (1) and (2). For example, suppose $G_j = \{d_2, d_3, d_4\}$; hence the data dependency between G_j and d_1 is calculated as $c_{d_1, G_j} = c_{1,2} + c_{1,3} + c_{1,4}$. And take another instance where $G_j = \{d_2, d_3, d_4\}$ and $G_k = \{d_5, d_7\}$, since G_j and G_k have different storage position, the dependency c_{G_j, G_k} between them values 0, so they will be separated at an early stage in clustering process.

Based on this dependency derivation, a dependency matrix CM can be generated. After that, BEA transformation is performed on this matrix so as to collect the similar valued items together. And then, recursive partitioning operations are done. For each division, the division point is selected where the following formula reaches its max value:

$$
PM = \frac{\left(\sum_{i=1}^{p} \sum_{j=1}^{p} c'_{ij} + \sum_{i=p+1}^{n} \sum_{j=p+1}^{n} c'_{ij} \right)}{\left(\sum_{i=1}^{p} \sum_{j=p+1}^{n} c'_{ij} \right)}. \tag{5}
$$

The denominator is the total dependency reserved by this partitioning, while the molecule represents the broken dependency. These same partition operations are performed iteratively on each subtree until this following constraint is satisfied: there is at most only one fixed-position data group in the leaf node.

3.2. Tree-Structure Modeling of the Cloud Platform. We assume that there are m geographically distributed servers in the cloud platform. The servers are heterogeneous, have different storage capacities, and also have different network bandwidth among them. For the purpose of reducing the time consumption on data movements, the clustered data groups should be placed to the servers according to the following principles: It is better to place the close related data items on the same server so as to decrease the number of data transfers; and if these data cannot be saved together for the reason of limit storage capacities, they should be allocated to closer nodes with high network bandwidth; therefore, most of the data transmissions can obtain high efficiency benefiting by the high-speed channels. In this section, we build a tree-structure model for the cloud system, since it is suitable for the following data allocation stage.

For the case of the cloud architected on LAN, the platform structure can be easily abstracted to a tree structure based on the server's physical connection structure. Figure 2(a) shows an example illustration of a simple cloud platform. According to its topological structure, it can be directly abstracted as tree structure which is illustrated in Figure 2(b). Otherwise, for the cloud based on WAN, we first build a network condition matrix B and then do BEA transformation and recursive dichotomy on this matrix B. Hence an approximate tree structure can be abstracted. The network bandwidths and the distance between servers will be reflected in $b_{x,y}$ values. And, in order to perform BEA transformation, the items on the diagonal, marked by equivalent indices on the two dimensions, like $b_{1,1}, b_{2,2}$, and so forth, can be simply calculated as the sum of all the other items in this row; that is, $b_{i,i} = \sum_{j \neq i} b_{i,j}$.

4. Data Distribution

The clustered data items are allocated onto the tree-structured cloud servers based on the following idea: for each allocation, try to allocate the highest level subtree in the data tree to the

Function Name: DataAllocation
Input: dtNode: The root of the data item binary-tree
    ctNode: The root of the data center binary-tree
Output: whether the data tree can be allocated to the server tree
(01) /*First, find the smallest server sub-tree that its total storage capacity is more than the total data size of the sub-tree
    dtNode, suppose its root node is r*/
(02) r = nextSmallestServerTree (totalStorageRequirement (dtNode));
(03) while (r != Null) {
(04)   if (DataPlacement (dtNode, r) == True) return True; //DetaPlacement is a recursive function
(05)   else r = nextSmallestServerTree (totalStorageRequirement (dtNode));
(06) }
(07) Return False;

PSEUDOCODE 1: The pseudocode of the heuristic data allocation method: DataAllocation.

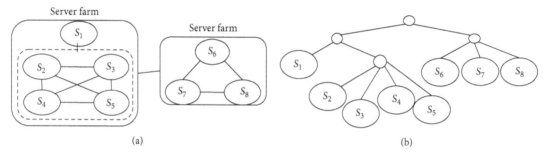

(a)   (b)

FIGURE 2: An example of a simple cloud platform and its tree-structured model.

lowest level subtree in the server tree, as long as the storage space can accommodate. Therefore, the highly associated data items could be assigned into the same node as much times as possible, and if these items could not be stored together due to some storage limits, they could be placed on closer nodes of the tree-structured environment, since these nodes have high-speed network. The detail of the heuristic data allocation method is as follows.

First, we select the highest layer data subtree in a top-down manner to perform the data assignment as higher priorities, and that could retain the data dependency in the group and reduce the frequency of data transmission as much as possible. On the other hand, a bottom-up strategy (assign the data to the lowest level subtree) is adopted for storage location selection and to make sure the storage requirements should be satisfied. This data allocation strategy can effectively guarantee the high-bandwidth requirements, and it can also save resources to facilitate the subsequent data assignments. It is worth noting that the storage space condition must be met during allocation; otherwise it is not a feasible solution. The detailed constraints that should be tested are as follows.

Storage Space Constraint: $RSS_\beta \geq ASS_\alpha$. ASS_α is total Available Storage Space of the subtree α in the server tree, and RSS_β denotes total Required Storage Space of the subtree β in the data tree. These two parameters of every subtree are

recorded in advance, and their detailed computation methods are, respectively, illustrated as follows:

$$ASS_\alpha = \sum_{s_k \in S_\alpha} SS_k \cdot \lambda,$$
$$RSS_\beta = \sum_{d_k \in D_\beta} Size_k. \tag{6}$$

Here, $Size_k$ is the size of the dataset d_k, which is a member of the data subtree β and SS_k is the total storage space of the server s_k which belongs to the server set of the subtree α.

For data-intensive applications, besides the initial data, the generated data can also be very large. We therefore cannot fill the data center with their maximum storage in the build-time stage. Otherwise, newly generated data at the runtime will have no space to be stored. Accordingly, an experiential parameter λ is introduced, which denotes the allowable initial usage of the centers' storage space.

This is the overall strategy of the data allocation method. An allocation example is demonstrated in Figure 3, and the pseudocode is shown in Pseudocodes 1 and 2. In Figure 3(a), the "tree-to-tree" data placement task is described. The data tree (on the left) with a size of 102 GB in all should be allocated into the data center tree (on the right) with the total storage space of 136 GB. Figure 3(b) gives the detailed allocation steps of this heuristic data placement strategy. The allocation steps are numbered as "1", "2", ..., "9" in a top-down order.

```
Function Name: DataPlacement (a recursive function)
Input: dtNode: The root of the data sub-tree prepared to be allocated
   ctNode: The root of the server sub-tree prepared to allocate into
Output: whether this data placement success
(01)  if (ctNode.LeftNode == Null && ctNode.RightNode == Null) //leaf node!
(02)    If (the remainder storage space >= the total size of the current data tree) {
(03)      //Allocate success! And record the allocation result
(04)      for (every node in the tree rooted by ctNode)
(05)            dataPlace[node.number] = ctNode.number;
(06)         update ctNode's Ccr and size; //update the remainder computation and storage value
(07)      Return True; }
(09)  /*Bottom-up server sub-tree selection strategy. First, try to allocate to the left node, and then the right */
(10)  else if (dtNode.size < ctNode.LeftNode.size)
(11)         if (DataPlacement (dtNode, ctNode.LeftNode) == True) return True; //allocated!
(12)  else if (dtNode.size < ctNode.RightNode.size) //try to allocate to the right node
(13)         if (DataPlacement (dtNode, ctNode.RightNode) == True) return True; //allocated!
(14)  /*Top-down data tree selection principle. If the overall current data tree cannot be allocated to any server sub-tree,
      then try to allocate its left sub-tree and right-subtree*/
(15)  Bool LeftSuccess, RightSuccess;
(16)  if (max (dtNode.LeftNode.size, dtNode.RightNode.size) < min (ctNode.LeftNode.size,
(17)  ctNode.RightNode.size)) //the two methods of distributing subtrees (left to left, right to
(18)      //right; or left to right, right to left) are both possible
(19)  /*First try to allocate the data sub-tree with more storage requirements*/
(20)      If (dtNode.LeftNode.size >= dtNode.RightNode.size)
(21)    if (DataPlacement (dtNode.LeftNode, ctNode.LeftNode) == True) LeftSuccess = True;
(22)       else if (DataPlacement (dtNode.LeftNode, ctNode.RightNode) == True) LeftSuccess = True;
(23)       if (LeftSuccess == True ) allocate the reminder data sub-tree to the other server sub-tree, if success,
           RightSuccess = True, else:
(24)    //Bottom-up server sub-tree selection strategy. Try to allocate the data sub-tree to the parent node
        (the higher level sub-tree)
(25)       if (DataPlacement (dtNode.RightNode, ctNode) == True) RightSuccess = True;
(26)          else if (DataPlacement (dtNode.LeftNode, ctNode) == True) LeftSuccess = True;
(27)       /*Else, the right node has more storage requirements, allocate it */
(28)    else      if (dtNode.RightNode.size > dtNode.LeftNode.size)
(29)          if (DataPlacement (dtNode.RightNode, ctNode.LeftNode) == True)    RightSuccess = True;
(31)          else if (DataPlacement (dtNode.RightNode, ctNode.RightNode) == True) RightSuccess = True;
(33)          if (RightSuccess == True ) allocate the reminder data sub-tree to the other server sub-tree, if success,
             LeftSuccess = True, else:
(34)       if (DataPlacement (dtNode.LeftNode, ct Node) == True) LeftSuccess = True;
(35)          else if (DataPlacement (dtNode.RightNode, ctNode) == True) RightSuccess = True;
(36)  if (LeftSuccess == True && RightSuccess == True) return True;
(37)  else return False;
```

PSEUDOCODE 2: The pseudocode of the heuristic data allocation method: DataPlacement.

When the allocation arrives at the bottom leaf node, the judgement of success or nonsuccess will be made. Here, a sign of smiling face means the allocation is feasible. After that, this judgement procedure will trace back to its upper allocation, such as steps (04) and (05).

5. Simulation and Results Analysis

100 random data-task test datasets are generated, and the input dataset of each task includes 1–4 random generated data items sized from 1 G to 100 G, respectively. The dependencies between datasets and tasks are also generated randomly. After running 100 groups of test data for every data placement algorithm, the average performance indicators are calculated and used for comparative performance analysis.

The same test dataset and cloud environments are simulated on other contrast experiments which use the random placement strategy, Yuan's strategy [13], and our previous strategy in CCGrid [20].

In the 1st experiment, we suppose that there are no fixed-position dataset in the model. The simulation results are shown in Figures 4 and 5. In Figure 4, the number of data centers is 8. From this figure we can see that, in contrast to the random algorithm, Yuan's algorithm, and our previous method in CCGrid, both the data movement amount and the time consumption can be reduced by our proposed method. The average reduction percentages of data movement frequency are, respectively, 32.2%, 11.6%, and 1.49% compared with the random strategy, Yuan's strategy, and our previous method in CCGrid. Therefore, we can

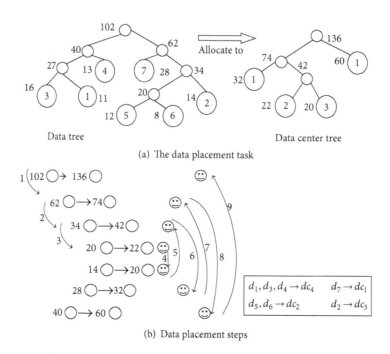

(a) The data placement task

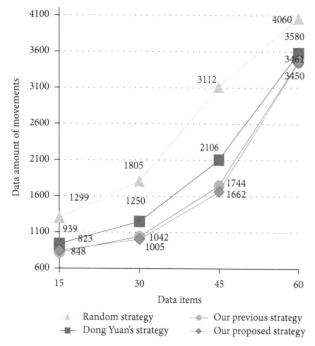

(b) Data placement steps

FIGURE 3: An example of the heuristic data allocation algorithm.

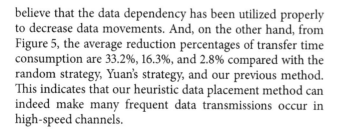

FIGURE 4: Total data movement amount without fixed-position datasets.

FIGURE 5: Total time consumed by data movements without fixed-position datasets.

believe that the data dependency has been utilized properly to decrease data movements. And, on the other hand, from Figure 5, the average reduction percentages of transfer time consumption are 33.2%, 16.3%, and 2.8% compared with the random strategy, Yuan's strategy, and our previous method. This indicates that our heuristic data placement method can indeed make many frequent data transmissions occur in high-speed channels.

In the 2nd experiment, we changed 10% of the input datasets to fixed-location datasets so as to see whether our strategy can be applied to the condition of existing fixed-position datasets. The simulation results are shown in Figures 6 and 7. The average reduction percentages of data movement frequency are, respectively, 24.9% and 8.6% compared with the random strategy and Yuan's strategy. And,

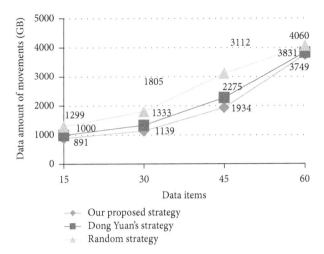

FIGURE 6: Total data movement amount with 10% fixed-position datasets.

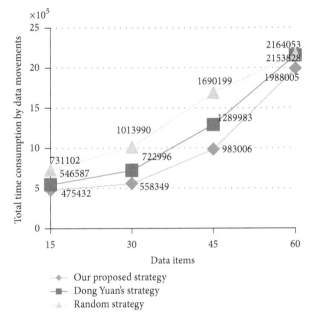

FIGURE 7: Total time consumed by data movements with 10% fixed-position datasets.

on the other hand, the average reduction percentages of transfer time consumption are 28.5% and 15% compared with the random strategy and Yuan's strategy. Therefore, we can believe, with 10% fixed-position datasets, that our proposed method is effective for decreasing data movements and their time consumptions.

6. Conclusions and Future Work

In this paper, we proposed a data placement algorithm for data-intensive applications in cloud system. Compared with previous work, first, both the datasets and the cloud platform are abstracted into tree structures. The contributions of this modeling are as follows. High data dependencies have been retained in the inner group, while the high-speed network groups have been found in a hierarchical manner. And then, a heuristic data allocation method has been issued, and it can make frequent data movements occur in high-bandwidth network environment, so as to achieve the goal of reducing global transmission time. Simulations results indicate that our data placement strategy can effectively reduce data movement amount and time consumption during execution.

In the current work, more placement factors will be taken into consideration, such as the computation capacity of each server and load balance. Furthermore, replication of frequently used data is an effective solution to achieve good performance in terms of system reliability and response time; therefore, this will be another focus of our future research.

Competing Interests

The authors declare that they have no competing interests.

Acknowledgments

This work is supported by the National Natural Science Foundation of China (61272509), the National Natural Science Foundation of China (61402332), the Natural Science Foundation of Tianjin University of Science and Technology (20130124), and the key technologies R & D program of Tianjin no. 15ZCZDGX00200.

References

[1] E. Deelman, G. Singh, M. Livny, B. Berriman, and J. Good, "The cost of doing science on the cloud: the Montage example," in *Proceedings of the ACM/IEEE Conference on Supercomputing (SC '08)*, Austin, Tex, USA, November 2008.

[2] T. Kosar and M. Livny, "A framework for reliable and efficient data placement in distributed computing systems," *Journal of Parallel and Distributed Computing*, vol. 65, no. 10, pp. 1146–1157, 2005.

[3] T. Kosar and M. Livny, "Stork: making data placement a first class citizen in the grid," in *Proceedings of the 24th International Conference on Distributed Computing Systems (ICDCS '04)*, pp. 342–349, Tokyo, Japan, March 2004.

[4] H. Liu and D. Orban, "GridBatch: cloud computing for large-scale data-intensive batch applications," in *Proceedings of the 8th IEEE International Symposium on Cluster Computing and the Grid (CCGRID '08)*, pp. 295–305, Lyon, France, May 2008.

[5] E. Deelman and A. Chervenak, "Data management challenges of data-intensive scientific workflows," in *Proceedings of the 8th IEEE International Symposium on Cluster Computing and the Grid (CCGRID '08)*, pp. 687–692, Lyon, France, May 2008.

[6] A. Weiss, "Computing in the clouds," *netWorker*, vol. 11, no. 4, pp. 16–25, 2007.

[7] Google App Engine, http://code.google.com/appengine/.

[8] Amazon Elastic Computing Cloud, http://aws.amazon.com/ec2/.

[9] Hadoop, http://hadoop.apache.org/.

[10] J. Xie, S. Yin, X. Ruan et al., "Improving MapReduce performance through data placement in heterogeneous Hadoop clusters," in *Proceedings of the IEEE International Parallel & Distributed Processing Symposium*, April 2010.

[11] A. Chervenak, E. Deelman, M. Livny et al., "Data placement for scientific applications in distributed environments," in *Proceedings of the 8th IEEE/ACM International Conference on Grid Computing*, pp. 267–274, IEEE, Austin, Tex, USA, September 2007.

[12] G. Singh, K. Vahi, A. Ramakrishnan et al., "Optimizing workflow data footprint," *Scientific Programming*, vol. 15, no. 4, pp. 249–268, 2007.

[13] Z. Wu, X. Liu, Z. Ni, D. Yuan, and Y. Yang, "A market-oriented hierarchical scheduling strategy in cloud workflow systems," *Journal of Supercomputing*, vol. 63, no. 1, pp. 256–293, 2013.

[14] A. Talukder, M. Kirley, and R. Buyya, "Multiobjective differential evolution for scheduling workflow applications on global grids," *Concurrency & Computation Practice & Experience*, vol. 21, no. 13, pp. 1742–1756, 2009.

[15] X. Liu, Z. Ni, Z. Wu, D. Yuan, J. Chen, and Y. Yang, "A novel general framework for automatic and cost-effective handling of recoverable temporal violations in scientific workflow systems," *Journal of Systems and Software*, vol. 84, no. 3, pp. 492–509, 2011.

[16] T. Ghafarian and B. Javadi, "Cloud-aware data intensive workflow scheduling on volunteer computing systems," *Future Generation Computer Systems*, vol. 51, pp. 87–97, 2014.

[17] D. Yuan, Y. Yang, X. Liu, and J. Chen, "A data placement strategy in scientific cloud workflows," *Future Generation Computer Systems*, vol. 26, no. 8, pp. 1200–1214, 2010.

[18] E.-D. Zhao, Y.-Q. Qi, X.-X. Xiang, and Y. Chen, "A data placement strategy based on genetic algorithm for scientific workflows," in *Proceedings of the 8th International Conference on Computational Intelligence and Security (CIS '12)*, pp. 146–149, Guangzhou, China, November 2012.

[19] Q. Zhao and C. Xiong, "An improved data layout algorithm based on data correlation clustering in cloud," in *Proceedings of the International Symposium on Information Technology Convergence*, October 2014.

[20] Q. Zhao, C. Xiong, X. Zhao, C. Yu, and J. Xiao, "A data placement strategy for data-intensive scientific workflows in cloud," in *Proceedings of the 15th IEEE/ACM International Symposium on Cluster, Cloud and Grid Computing (CCGrid '15)*, pp. 928–934, IEEE, Shenzhen, China, May 2015.

11

Hybrid Model: An Efficient Symmetric Multiprocessor Reference Model

Shupeng Wang,[1] **Kai Huang,**[1] **Tianyi Xie,**[2] **and Xiaolang Yan**[2]

[1]*Department of Information Science and Electronic Engineering, Zhejiang University, Hangzhou 310027, China*
[2]*Institute of VLSI Design, Zhejiang University, Hangzhou 310027, China*

Correspondence should be addressed to Kai Huang; huangk@vlsi.zju.edu.cn

Academic Editor: Marco Platzner

Functional verification has become one of the main bottlenecks in the cost-effective design of embedded systems, particularly for symmetric multiprocessors. It is estimated that verification in its entirety accounts for up to 60% of design resources, including duration, computer resources, and total personnel. Simulation-based verification is a long-standing approach used to locate design errors in the symmetric multiprocessor verification. The greatest challenge of simulation-based verification is the creation of the reference model of the symmetric multiprocessor. In this paper, we propose an efficient symmetric multiprocessor reference model, Hybrid Model, written with SystemC. SystemC can provide a high-level simulation environment and is faster than the traditional hardware description languages. Hybrid Model has been implemented in an efficient 32-bit symmetric multiprocessor verification. Experimental results show our proposed model is a fast, accurate, and efficient symmetric multiprocessor reference model and it is able to help designers to locate design errors easily and accurately.

1. Introduction

Recently, the symmetric multiprocessor (SMP) has become a leading trend in the development of advanced embedded systems. Meanwhile, with the rapid improvement of the hardware manufacturing technologies and the help of computer-aided design (CAD) tools, SMP systems become more and more powerful and complex. As a result, the design verification of SMP systems takes up a large part of the total design period. The verification method directly determines the efficiency of SMP system verification and even the whole design cycle.

A variety of techniques have been deployed to efficiently and effectively detect design errors in SMP systems. These techniques can be divided into three categories: formal verification, simulation-based verification, and hardware emulation [1–3]. Various formal verification methodologies with the relevant environment setup have been proposed and used [4–9]. Formal verification, such as model checking and theorem proving, takes advantage of mathematical methods to judge whether the behavior of the design follows the rules instituted by designers. With the increasing size of system

design, the space needed by formal verification is beyond the ability of tools and the process of formal verification is slow. As a result, the formal verification is not appropriate in large-scale system verification, such as the SMP system verification. Hardware emulation maps a gate level model of the design onto Field-Programmable Gate Array (FPGA) on the emulation system. It is much faster than the simulation-based verification. The main disadvantage of the hardware emulation is that it is difficult to debug when an error takes place. Simulation-based verification [10–14] is the most used method to verify the function of the SMP systems. It generates instruction sequences that are then fed in parallel to the design under test (DUT) and its reference model. Any discrepancy between the two models indicates a design error. Simulation-based verification is able to locate the errors easily and rapidly, and it is not limited by the size of system. As a result, it is widely used in SMP system verification.

The major drawback of the mainstream simulation-based approach is the difficulty of creating an efficient reference model of the DUT in a short time. The success of simulation-based verification depends on the accuracy and the quality of the reference model in use. An efficient and accurate reference model is able to help designers locate errors easily and quickly. Many researchers have already proposed various reference models of the processor at presilicon. During the simulation-based verification, most processors regard the simulator as the reference model. These simulators are normally obtained from earlier stage in processor development, in which simulators are used for performance evaluation under benchmark [15]. Some of these simulators cannot support SMP verification, such as SimpleScalar [16]. Some other simulators, such as MARSS [17] and PTLsim [18], can be implemented to verify SMP systems. However, these simulators are usually timing-accurate; it is time-consuming for design verification by using these simulators to act as the reference model. In addition, the verification of these simulators themselves is often very complicated due to their architectural complexity [19]. As these models are usually timing-accurate, they are called timing-accurate models (TMs). The other type of reference model is Instruction Set Simulator (ISS) that is function-accurate. ISS only cares about the system function and its architecture is simple. These simulators are relatively easy to ensure due to their simpler architectures. This enables them to be used as reference model in the functional verification of the single-core processors. However, as they have no ability to sequence the out-of-order load/store transactions among CPUs perfectly, they cannot be used to verify the SMP system efficiently. As these models are function-accurate, they are called function-accurate models (FMs). It is difficult to test the function of the SMP system by using the timing-accurate models and function-accurate models efficiently. Such difficulties prompt us to create an efficient SMP reference model that is called Hybrid Model (HM). This model is simpler and faster than the timing-accurate model and more accurate than the function-accurate model. SystemC can be very effective in describing the system architecture and functionality to support high-level simulation. So SystemC can be used to obtain the efficient HM. When the reference model has been created, tests are fed in parallel to the DUT and its reference model to check design correctness.

In a simulation process, function coverage analysis is needed to check and show the quality of testing. It helps the verification team to check whether the function points that they want to simulate are covered during the testing phase. Sometime, some direct tests written by hands are needed with the help of function coverage analysis to cover the missing cases. The function coverage analysis is usually achieved from the RTL (Register Transfer Level) code and indicated by one signal or a set of signals. As the verification team is unfamiliar with the RTL code, it is difficult for them to observe the function points in RTL code, especially if the signals needed by the function points do not exist in the RTL code and the verification team has to turn to the designers for help. It is necessary for the designers to add these signals that are useless to the system function. In this way, the function coverage analysis needs the interaction of the verification team and the designers, so it is error-prone. However, the verification team is familiar with the reference model that is created by them. So if they achieve the function coverage analysis from the reference model rather than from the RTL

code, the function coverage result can be more accurate. And the direct tests are able to be written by the verification team more effectively.

The main contribution of our work is that an efficient SMP reference model is proposed. It is written with SystemC. Acting as the SMP reference model, HM is simpler and faster than TM and more accurate than FM. The second contribution is that we define a timing sequence called Dependent Timing Sequence (DTS). The function of DTS is the timing interface between two models. The final contribution is that the function coverage analysis is able to be obtained from HM. In this way, the verification team can achieve more accurate coverage result quickly. Then the direct tests can be written by them more effectively.

2. Hybrid Model

As shown in Figure 1, the Hybrid Model (HM) consists of CPU Pipeline Model (CPM) and Cache Coherence Model (CCM). A common SMP consists of CPU pipelines, Load Store Units (LSUs), caches, and the interconnection between CPUs. The interconnection is responsible for maintaining the cache coherence between CPUs. The reference model of CPU pipeline is the function-accurate CPM. As the interconnection, LSU, and cache are related to load/store transactions, they are called Load Store Module (LSM). LSM is closely related to cache coherence and its reference model is the timing-accurate CCM. CPM and CCM are connected through DTS. The whole SMP system can be verified efficiently with the cooperation of CPM and CCM.

In the validation process, when a test case is stressed on the SMP system and HM simultaneously, the SMP system executes and HM simulates the instructions in this test case one by one. For each single instruction, the CPU pipeline executes it and the execution results of the CPU pipeline are obtained. If this instruction is a load/store instruction, the CPU pipeline needs to send this instruction to LSM. Then LSM executes this instruction and the execution results of the LSM are obtained. In this way, the execution results of the whole SMP system are obtained. On the HM side, first CPM simulates this instruction and the simulation results of CPU pipeline are achieved. If this instruction is a load/store instruction, CPM has to pipe its timing stream to CCM via DTS accordingly. The timing stream makes CCM begin to simulate and the simulation results of LSM are achieved by CCM. In this way, the simulation results of the whole SMP system are achieved. At this time, the tool will compare the execution results with the simulation results to check the correctness. Once any discrepancy occurs, the tool stops the simulation immediately. Then the tool will collect the information of this instruction such as its execution results and simulation results for the verification team. It is convenient for the verification team to locate errors with the help of these messages.

2.1. CPU Pipeline Model. An important part of HM is CPU Pipeline Model (CPM) that is function-accurate. It can be used to act as the reference model of CPU pipeline. CPM

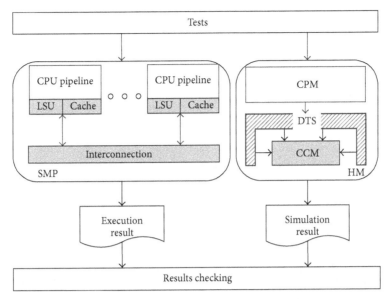

FIGURE 1: Efficient symmetric multiprocessor verification.

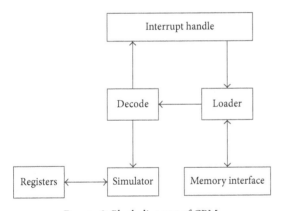

FIGURE 2: Block diagram of CPM.

only cares about the function of CPU pipeline rather than its timing information. As shown in Figure 2, three important modules of CPM are Loader, Decode, and Simulator. When CPM receives a test case needed to be simulated, Loader fetches the instructions in this test case one by one from memory according to the program counter (PC) first. Then Decode is responsible for decoding and interpreting these instructions. The Simulator is implemented with nonpipeline and it simulates these instructions directly. No matter whether instructions in the SMP system are in-order executed or out-of-order executed, they are retired one by one sequentially. As a result, the simulation results achieved by the nonpipeline Simulator directly are the same as the execution results obtained by the processor after going through complex CPU pipeline. For the instructions that are not load/store transactions, there is no need for them to be sent to LSM, as they are irrelevant to the cache coherence. For these transactions, all the simulation results of them

can be achieved by CPM and the simulation is over after updating the value of registers. For load/store transactions, they need not only to go through CPU pipeline but also be sent to LSM. CPM is responsible for piping the timing stream of load/store instructions to CCM via DTS when it has finished its simulation of these instructions. The timing stream makes CCM begin to simulate. The simulation process of a load/store instruction is finished when CPM gets the response from CCM and the value of registers is updated. If an interrupt is found in this process, CPM needs to jump to interrupt handler.

The simulation results of CPU pipeline can be obtained rapidly, including much key information of the SMP system, for example, PC, the value of registers, and the state of the target processor. The tool compares these simulation results achieved by CPM with the execution results obtained by DUT. And any discrepancy indicates an error of the DUT. If no discrepancy occurs and the simulating instruction is not a load/store instruction, the simulation of this instruction is finished successfully. If this instruction is a load/store instruction, CPM has to send the complete timing information of this instruction to CCM via DTS. If an error occurs, the simulation will be stopped at once and the simulation results and the execution results are obtained directly to help the verification team to locate and fix this error.

2.2. Cache Coherence Model. The other important part of HM is Cache Coherence Model (CCM) that is timing-accurate. CCM is the reference model of LSM. As CCM is timing-accurate, it needs to care about the details of LSM. However, only the details that have an effect on the function points that the verification team wants to simulate are considerable. The function points are defined manually by the verification team, and they are the combination of the characteristics

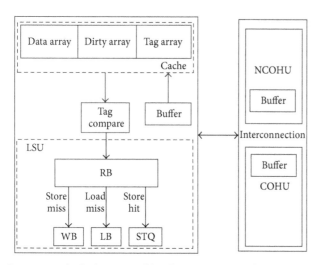

FIGURE 3: Block diagram of hardware. RB is used to preserve load/store transactions and maintain their order. WB keeps store miss transactions, LB is responsible for preserving load miss transactions, and STQ keeps store hit transactions. COHU maintains cache coherence between cores and NCOHU deals with the transactions unrelated to cache coherence.

of the DUT and a series of events that must be verified. In the application, these events are analyzed by observing the signals and states of the DUT. When the verification team has finished listing these events, they would serialize the events that have close relationship and outline their features. Finally the events that have close data relationship are put in one process according to the serialized events and the relationship of data structure between these events. As a result, these processes can be implemented with SystemC and run in parallel. And the processes communicate with each other by FIFO.

Figure 3 shows the common block diagram of the interconnection, cache, and LSU of the SMP system. The load/store transactions are first preserved in the Request Buffer (RB) in LSU. Then these transactions are sent to cache to decide whether the cache lines they want to access are located in cache. Further, they are sent to the appropriate buffers to wait for the chance to access the interconnection. The store miss transactions are sent to Write Buffer (WB), the load miss transactions are sent to Load Buffer (LB), and the store hit transactions are sent to Store Queue (STQ). Then they are sent to the interconnection when they have obtained the permission. The Coherence Unit (COHU) would maintain cache coherence between cores and handle the transactions related to cache coherence. The address domains of these transactions are cacheable and shareable. On the contrary, the function of Noncoherence Unit (NCOHU) is to deal with the transactions unrelated to cache coherence. The address domains of these transactions are other domains. The framework of the LSM is so complex; it is difficult and time-consuming for CCM to be created the same as the hardware. Some unnecessary hardware architectures can be abstracted due to the relationship between the hardware architectures and the function points the verification team wants to simulate. If the abstraction of some hardware

architectures has no effect on the function points and the accuracy, these hardware architectures can be removed in CCM. When the number of cores in the multiprocessor system has been changed, the designers would modify some details of the interconnection according to the specification.

As the main memory has a lower load/store speed, buffers are utilized in the NCOHU to save load/store transactions unrelated to cache coherence. However, it is fast to access software memory. As a result, there is no need to create buffers for memory access in CCM. And sometimes more than one transaction attempts to access cache, whereas cache is a one-port element. So buffers are needed to save the outstanding requests to cache. However, CCM can accept and execute all the requests simultaneously, so no buffer is needed to save these transactions to cache in CCM. The abstraction of these buffers not only has an effect on the function, but also can reduce the implementation time of CCM. However, some hardware architectures cannot be abstracted; even any discrepancy between the hardware and CCM may cause fatal functional mistakes.

The interconnection usually works faster than CPU; some of the transactions related to cache coherence need to be saved in COHU. The order of these transactions is maintained by COHU in order to achieve accurate execution results. CCM has to deal with these load/store transactions in the same way with hardware to obtain the right simulation results. Figure 4 shows the different simulation results caused by the different orders of store transactions. A certain cache line is located in both CPU0 and CPU1 cache. At cycle A, CPU0 and CPU1 send store requests to the interconnection simultaneously. As shown in Figure 4(a), as the arbitration result of these two store transactions is that CPU0 could execute the store transaction before CPU1, the store transaction of CPU0 is accepted by the interconnection at cycle A; however, the store transaction of CPU1 is not accepted which is indicated by the symbol *. Then the store transaction of CPU1 is accepted by the interconnection at cycle B. At cycle C, the cache line in CPU1 cache is invalidated by the interconnection and the state of the store transaction of CPU1 is modified from store hit to store miss. At cycle D, the interconnection accepts the load transaction of CPU2, and the data CPU2 loads is 2. On the other hand, as shown in Figure 4(b), if the arbitration result of these two store transactions is that CPU1 could execute the store transaction before CPU0, the data CPU2 loads would be 1 at cycle D. The data CPU2 gets highly depends on the arbitration of these two store transactions of CPU0 and CPU1. Different execution orders lead to different results; hence, CCM has to achieve timing-accurate for these transactions to avoid errors.

Figure 5 shows the block diagram of CCM. The function of NCOHU is the same as that of SMP. But there are no buffers in NCOHU of CCM. The COHU of CCM is the same as that of SMP, not only their functions but also timing. No buffer is needed for cache in CCM. When the number of cores in the multiprocessor system has been changed, the verification team would modify some details of CCM according to the hardware changes made by the designers. Hence, HM can go to perform well even when the number of cores increases to hundreds.

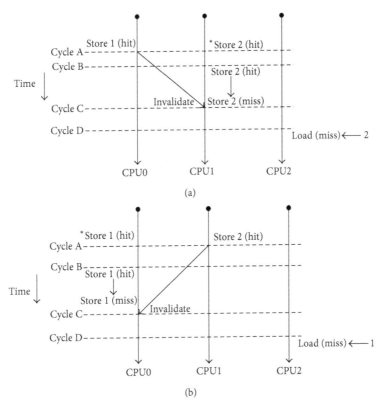

FIGURE 4: The execution result depends on the arbitration. (a) CPU0 executes before CPU1. (b) CPU1 executes before CPU0.

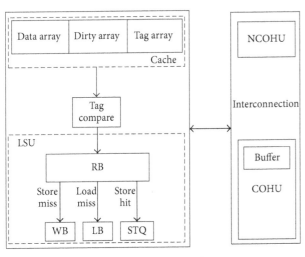

FIGURE 5: Block diagram of CCM.

2.3. Dependent Timing Sequence. Dependent Timing Sequence (DTS) is the timing interface between CPM and CCM. For every single instruction, CPM simulation and CPU pipeline execution proceed simultaneously. The tool compares the simulation results with execution results all the time. If no error is found in CPU pipeline and the simulating instruction is a load/store transaction, CPM is responsible for delivering the timing information of this transaction to DTS. CPM is aware of all the timing information of this transaction except for the cycle number whose function is to notify CCM when to begin its simulation. However, CPM can find this information from the execution results of hardware. In this way, the complete timing sequence of this transaction can be obtained and piped to DTS by CPM. DTS includes all the timing information CCM needs. Then CCM reads the timing information from DTS and begins its simulation. Figure 6 shows the timing information in a simulation process. Transaction type indicates the type of this transaction. Transaction size indicates the byte amount in this transaction. Data means the data CPU stores and x indicates that this transaction is a load transaction. Coherence indicates whether this transaction relates to cache coherence or not. As shown in Figure 6, at cycle number 21, CPU0 stores 1 into address 0x1fff_fee8, and CPU1 stores 2 into the same address. If these two store transactions are both store hit transactions, the condition is similar to what is shown in Figure 4.

As different kinds of CCMs may need different timing information, the information in DTS should be adjusted to meet the timing requirements of CCM.

2.4. Function Coverage Analysis. As HM is written by verification team and only includes the considerable function points, it is fast to obtain the function coverage report. Moreover, the isolation between system design and verification

Cycle number	CPU ID	Transaction type	Transaction size	Address	Data	Coherence

Tail → 112589	2	1	1	0x2020_001c	0	1
○ ○ ○						
156	3	0	3	0x3020_0008	x	0
21	1	1	4	0x1fff_fee8	2	1
21	0	1	4	0x1fff_fee8	1	1
Head → 5	0	0	4	0x1fff_fff0	x	1

FIGURE 6: Timing information in DTS.

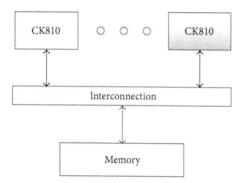

FIGURE 7: Architecture of CK810MP.

due to the proposed function coverage analysis approach can avoid many unnecessary errors in function coverage report and make the analysis more accurate.

3. Experimental Results

3.1. Verification Platform. We selected the CK810MP of Hangzhou C-SKY Microsystems Co., Ltd., to evaluate the feasibility of HM. As shown in Figure 7, CK810MP system consists of several modified CK810 processors, interconnection, and memory. CK810 is a high-performance 32-bit embedded processor based on CSKY v2 instruction set and its LSU is modified to support cache coherence according to the specification. A number of CK810 processors are connected by a bus-based interconnection that is responsible for maintaining cache coherence and dealing with requests to memory. The data channel and instruction channel are separate to increase bandwidth. Finally, an efficient SMP, CK810MP, is obtained with the addition of memory. We made extensive experiments with a CK810 quad-processor system, as the quad-processor is the mainstream of the embedded systems currently, such as mobile phones and personal computers. In addition, the quad-processor can meet the performance requirement of most of embedded

applications, and it is a good tradeoff between performance and power. We chose SystemC to act as our program language and created a timing-accurate model (TM), a function-accurate model (FM), and a Hybrid Model (HM) to act as the reference models of CK810 quad-processor. As FM is only interested in the design function and easy to be created, it took more than 20 days to complete this model. It took almost 6 months to achieve the TM, as it cares about the majority of details of the target CK810 quad-processor. As the HM pays attention to a part of the details of the target processor, it took almost a month to obtain HM. To compare our proposed model with state-of-the-art simulation models, we selected GEM5 [20], which is a popular open-source timing-accurate multiprocessor simulator, to act as the reference model of the target CK810 quad-processor. GEM5 simulator supports a wide range of processor instruction set architectures (ISA), such as Alpha, ARM, MIPS, PowerPC, and x86. However, the GEM5 simulator cannot support the CSKY v2 instruction set. The CSKY v2 instruction set is much less complex than ARM. Moreover, the similar instructions can be found in ARM instruction set for most of the instructions of the CSKY v2 instruction set. Hence, we can use CSKY-to-ARM instruction translation to make GEM5 support the CSKY v2 instruction set and act as the reference model of CK810MP system.

Figure 8 shows the verification platform of CK810MP. DMA (Directly Memory Access) is able to help improve the system performance effectively. TLB (Translation Lookaside Buffer) translates virtual addresses to physical addresses. Each test was generated by a test generator based on random selection from more than 20 types of instructions, such as math, logic, load, store, and jump supported by the CK810 core. The generated tests were stressed on CK810MP system and its four reference models, respectively. The function coverage analysis was performed to direct the verification effort. We obtained four comparison results by comparing execution results of CK810MP system with the simulation results of these four reference models. According to these four comparison results, errors of CK810MP were discovered.

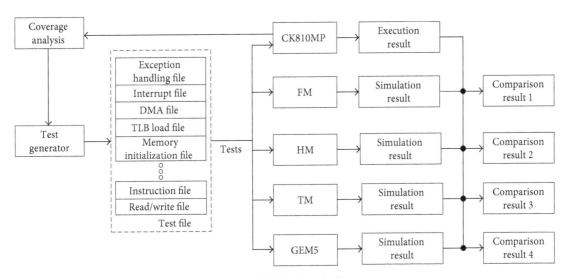

FIGURE 8: Verification platform.

3.2. Simulation Speed. The test generator generated 4000 tests each with 100 instructions, including the boot sequence used to initialize the CK810 core. In the first experiment, we compared the simulation speeds of these four models of CK810MP. To obtain the differential results, these 4000 tests were divided into 10 test groups randomly and each test group has various numbers of tests. The numbers of tests included by these 10 groups gradually increased from the first one to the tenth one. Then these test groups were fed to the reference models of CK810 quad-processor system, respectively, to compare their simulation speeds. Figure 9 shows the average simulation time of these four reference models stressed by these test groups. As shown in Figure 9, the simulation speeds of TM and GEM5 are similar, and they are the slowest in these four reference models as they are both timing-accurate. The simulation speed of FM is about 600 times those of TM and GEM5, and it is the fastest in these four reference models. The simulation speed of HM is about 30 times those of TM and GEM5. In comparison to FM, HM is slower, but it has a much better performance than TM and GEM5 in speed.

Further, we focused on the functional design of CPU pipeline in HM (denoted as CP-FM) and the timing-accurate model of CPU pipeline in TM (denoted as CP-TM) to explain why HM has obvious speed advantages comparing with TM. The test groups were fed to CP-FM and CP-TM to compare their simulation speed. Figure 10 shows the comparison of simulation speeds of CP-FM and CP-TM. The simulation speed of CP-FM is about 720 times as that of CP-TM. This means the speed advantage of HM comes from the functional model of the CPU pipeline.

3.3. Accuracy. In the second experiment, we compared the accuracy of these four models indicated by the number of errors found by them. The 4000 tests in the simulation environment were divided into 10 test groups each with

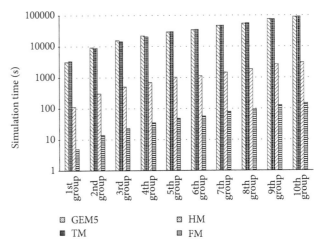

FIGURE 9: Simulation speed.

400 tests randomly. Then these test groups were stressed on CK810MP system and its four reference models, respectively. Figure 11 shows the number of the errors found by these 10 test groups and accumulated errors found by these four reference models. As shown in Figure 11, the abilities of TM and HM to find errors are similar and stronger than those of GEM5 and FM. The accumulated errors found by HM are about 1.5 times as many as those found by GEM5. And the accumulated errors found by HM are about four times as many as those found by FM. The ability of FM to find errors is the weakest in these four reference models. As the GEM5 simulator is developed specifically to evaluate the performance of embedded systems, its details could not be the same as the details of the CK810 quad-processor system. Therefore, the accumulated errors found by GEM5 are much less than those found by TM and HM.

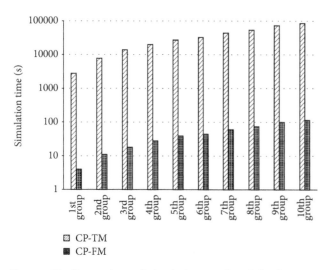

FIGURE 10: Comparison of simulation speeds of the function-accurate model and timing-accurate model of CPU pipeline.

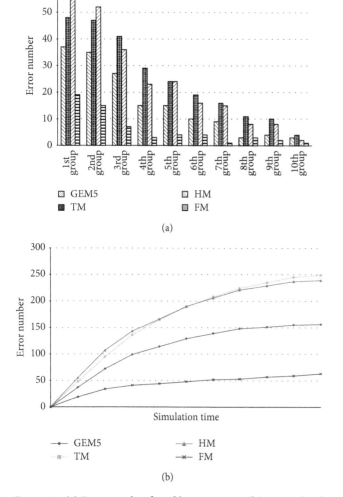

FIGURE 11: (a) Error number found by test groups; (b) accumulated errors.

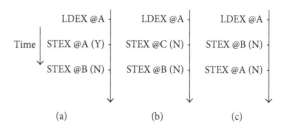

FIGURE 12: An example of exclusive transactions. (a) The correct implementation. (b) The wrong execution result caused by a design error. (c) The wrong simulation result caused by the timing inconsistency.

As soon as these four reference models' writing is finished, they are put into operation in the CK810 quad-processor verification. However, here these models are not exactly the correct golden models defined by the specification, especially the TM. The CPU pipeline of the CK810 quad-processor is a complex dual-emission superscalar 10-stage pipeline; hence some inconsistency between TM and the correct timing-accurate model is unavoidable at the beginning of simulation. The elimination of the inconsistency needs to take a lot of time. Before the TM becomes a correct timing-accurate model, it may obtain wrong simulation results because of some timing inconsistency, whereas the processor achieves the wrong execution results caused by a design error. If the wrong simulation results and the wrong results are the same, unfortunately, TM would take the attitude that the hardware is infallible. Figure 12 shows a simple example, where the results of store exclusive transactions are shown in brackets in red. Y indicates that the store exclusive transaction succeeds, while N shows that the store exclusive transaction fails. Figure 12(a) shows the correct implementation of three exclusive transactions, consisting of a load exclusive transaction and two store exclusive transactions. The first store exclusive transaction is executed successfully, as the exclusive transaction before this store exclusive transaction is a load exclusive transaction and they have the same address. The second store exclusive transaction fails. However, the address of the first store exclusive transaction is modified by a design error in CPU pipeline from address A to address C, as shown in Figure 12(b). As a result, the first store exclusive transaction fails. At the same time, as shown in Figure 12(c), TM inverts the order of two store exclusive transactions and these two store exclusive transactions both fail. In this way, TM cannot find this design error of CPU pipeline. However, HM is able to discover this design error as it can simulate these three exclusive transactions in the right order and obtain the right simulation results as shown in Figure 12(a). Hence, the design errors found by the HM are more than those found by the TM when the first two test groups are simulated.

As the simulation goes on, these models are all modified by the verification team to become the correct golden models gradually. At this time, if some timing errors of CPU pipeline do not influence the function of the CK810 quad-processor, the TM can discover these timing errors but the HM cannot. As an example, the interval between the load

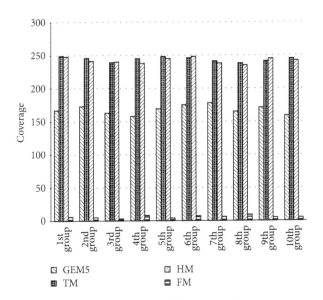

FIGURE 13: Coverage of function points.

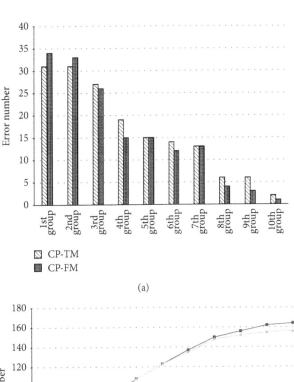

(a)

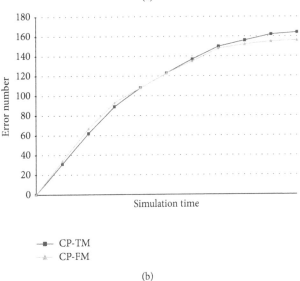

(b)

FIGURE 14: (a) Error number found by test groups; (b) accumulated errors found by the function-accurate model and timing-accurate model of CPU pipeline.

exclusive transaction and the first store exclusive transaction in Figure 12 should be 10 cycles according to plan. However, the store exclusive transaction executed 2 cycles in advance because of the inappropriate change of a request pointer. This store exclusive transaction still succeeds. HM cannot discover this timing error but TM can, as the interval between these two exclusive transactions is ten cycles in TM. As a result, the design errors found by the TM are more than those found by the HM when the last eight test groups are simulated. And the accumulated errors found by the TM are more than those found by the HM at the end of simulation. However, the design errors that HM cannot discover have no effect on the function of processor and most of them can be discovered with the help of assertion checkers.

To compare the accuracy of four reference models further, we analyzed the coverage of function points that we want to simulate. Figure 13 shows the coverage of function points in these four reference models. The interconnection, cache, and LSU have 253 function points. HM and TM are capable of covering all the function points basically and the GEM5 simulator can cover partial function points. However, FM can only cover a few of function points.

Further, we focused on CP-FM and CP-TM to compare their accuracy and explain why HM has obvious speed advantages comparing with TM, while maintaining similar accuracy, by using the test groups used in Figure 11. Figure 14 shows the design errors found by these 10 test groups and the comparison of the accumulated errors found by CP-FM and CP-TM. As shown in Figure 14, 60 to 70 percent of design errors of the CK810 quad-processor are in the CPU pipeline, and the abilities of CP-FM and CP-TM to find errors are similar. The accumulated errors found by CP-TM are a little more than those found by CP-FM, as CP-TM can find the timing errors of CPU pipeline but CP-FM cannot. However, these errors are not functional errors and most of them can be discovered by assertion checkers. The experimental results in Figures 10 and 14 show that the function-accurate model

of the CPU pipeline is much faster than the timing-accurate model of the CPU pipeline, while the accumulated errors found by them are similar. This means the advantages of HM come from the functional design of the CPU pipeline model.

4. Conclusion

An accurate and efficient symmetric multiprocessor reference model is proposed in this paper. The function coverage analysis is able to be achieved from it to help the verification team to write direct tests more accurately. This reference model has been implemented for a 32-bit symmetric multiprocessor verification. The experimental results show that the number of errors found by our proposed model is about 4 times that found by a function-accurate model. Our proposed model has a better performance in finding errors than the function-accurate model. The simulation speed of our proposed model is about 30 times as high as that of a timing-accurate model in the same condition. In comparison to the timing-accurate model, our proposed model is easier to create and faster, whereas their abilities to find errors are similar. The advantages of the proposed model come from the functional design of the CPU pipeline model. With the help of our proposed model, the verification team can locate design errors more quickly and verify the interconnection more efficiently. The time for symmetric multiprocessor verification can be shortened obviously with our proposed model.

Conflict of Interests

The authors declare that there is no conflict of interests regarding the publication of this paper.

Acknowledgment

The authors would like to thank the members of the multiprocessor project team at Hangzhou C-SKY Microsystems Co., Ltd., especially Ke Wang, Xiaomeng Zhang, Teng Hu, and Xiaofei Jin, for their cooperation and help in this work.

References

[1] Y. Chen and V. Dinavahi, "Digital hardware emulation of universal machine and universal line models for real-time electromagnetic transient simulation," *IEEE Transactions on Industrial Electronics*, vol. 59, no. 2, pp. 1300–1309, 2012.

[2] M. Peker, H. Altun, and F. Karakaya, "Hardware emulation of HOG and AMDF based scale and rotation invariant robust shape detection," in *Proceedings of the 1st International Conference on Engineering and Technology (ICET '12)*, pp. 1–5, Cairo, Egypt, October 2012.

[3] F. Ren and Y. R. Zheng, "Hardware emulation of wideband correlated multiple-input multiple-output fading channels," *Journal of Signal Processing Systems*, vol. 66, no. 3, pp. 273–284, 2012.

[4] R. Alur, "Formal verification of hybrid systems," in *Proceedings of the International Conference on Embedded Software (EMSOFT '11)*, pp. 273–278, Taipei, Taiwan, October 2011.

[5] M. Amrani, L. Lúcio, G. Selim et al., "A tridimensional approach for studying the formal verification of model transformations," in *Proceedings of the 5th IEEE International Conference on Software Testing, Verification and Validation (ICST '12)*, pp. 921–928, IEEE, Montreal, Canada, April 2012.

[6] S. F. Siegel and T. K. Zirkel, "Automatic formal verification of MPI-based parallel programs," in *Proceedings of the 16th ACM Symposium on Principles and Practice of Parallel Programming (PPoPP '11)*, pp. 309–310, San Antonio, Tex, USA, February 2011.

[7] M. L. Bolton, E. J. Bass, and R. I. Siminiceanu, "Using formal verification to evaluate human-automation interaction: a review," *IEEE Transactions on Systems, Man, and Cybernetics Part A: Systems and Humans*, vol. 43, no. 3, pp. 488–503, 2013.

[8] R. Zhou, R. Min, Q. Yi, C. Li, and Y. Sheng, "Formal verification of fault-tolerant and recovery mechanisms for safe node sequence protocol," in *Proceedings of the 28th IEEE International Conference on Advanced Information Networking and Applications (AINA '14)*, pp. 813–820, Victoria, Canada, May 2014.

[9] H. Chockler, A. Ivrii, A. Matsliah, S. Moran, and Z. Nevo, "Incremental formal verification of hardware," in *Proceedings of the Formal Methods in Computer-Aided Design (FMCAD '11)*, pp. 135–143, Austin, Tex, USA, October 2011.

[10] E. Guralnik, M. Aharoni, A. J. Birnbaum, and A. Koyfman, "Simulation-based verification of floating-point division," *Institute of Electrical and Electronics Engineers. Transactions on Computers*, vol. 60, no. 2, pp. 176–188, 2011.

[11] S. Seidel, U. Donath, and J. Haufe, "Approach to a simulation-based verification environment for material handling systems," in *Proceedings of the IEEE 17th International Conference on Emerging Technologies & Factory Automation (ETFA '12)*, pp. 1–4, Krakow, Poland, September 2012.

[12] A. Braun, O. Bringmann, D. Lettnin, and W. Rosenstiel, "Simulation-based verification of the MOST netinterface specification revision 3.0," in *Proceedings of the Design, Automation and Test in Europe Conference and Exhibition (DATE '10)*, pp. 538–543, Leuven, Belgium, March 2010.

[13] A. S. Kamkin and M. M. Chupilko, "Survey of modern technologies of simulation-based verification of hardware," *Programming and Computer Software*, vol. 37, no. 3, pp. 147–152, 2011.

[14] E. Clarke, A. Donzé, and A. Legay, "On simulation-based probabilistic model checking of mixed-analog circuits," *Formal Methods in System Design*, vol. 36, no. 2, pp. 97–113, 2010.

[15] J. An, X. Fan, and S. Zhang, "A fast virtual device framework for improving RTL verification efficiency," in *Proceedings of the IEEE 3rd International Conference on Communication Software and Networks (ICCSN '11)*, pp. 73–75, IEEE, Xi'an, China, May 2011.

[16] T. Austin, E. Larson, and D. Ernest, "SimpleScalar: an infrastructure for computer system modeling," *Computer*, vol. 35, no. 2, pp. 59–67, 2002.

[17] A. Patel, F. Afram, S. Chen, and K. Ghose, "MARSS: a full system simulator for multicore x86 CPUs," in *Proceedings of the 48th ACM/EDAC/IEEE Design Automation Conference (DAC '11)*, pp. 1050–1055, New York, NY, USA, June 2011.

[18] M. T. Yourst, "PTLsim: a cycle accurate full system x86-64 microarchitectural simulator," in *Proceedings of the IEEE International Symposium on Performance Analysis of Systems & Software (ISPASS '07)*, pp. 23–34, San Jose, Calif, USA, April 2007.

[19] B. Glamm and D. J. Lilja, "Automatic verification of instruction set simulation using synchronized state comparison," in *Proceedings of the 34th Annual Simulation Symposium*, pp. 72–77, Seattle, Wash, USA, April 2001.

[20] N. Binkert, B. Beckmann, G. Black et al., "The gem5 simulator," *ACM SIGARCH Computer Architecture News*, vol. 39, no. 2, pp. 1–7, 2011.

12

Reordering Features with Weights Fusion in Multiclass and Multiple-Kernel Speech Emotion Recognition

Xiaoqing Jiang,[1,2] Kewen Xia,[1] Lingyin Wang,[2] and Yongliang Lin[1,3]

[1]School of Electronics and Information Engineering, Hebei University of Technology, Tianjin 300401, China
[2]School of Information Science and Engineering, University of Jinan, Shandong, Jinan 250022, China
[3]Information Construction and Management Center, Tianjin Chengjian University, Tianjin 300384, China

Correspondence should be addressed to Kewen Xia; kwxia@hebut.edu.cn

Academic Editor: Andreas Spanias

The selection of feature subset is a crucial aspect in speech emotion recognition problem. In this paper, a Reordering Features with Weights Fusion (RFWF) algorithm is proposed for selecting more effective and compact feature subset. The RFWF algorithm fuses the weights reflecting the relevance, complementarity, and redundancy between features and classes comprehensively and implements the reordering of features to construct feature subset with excellent emotional recognizability. A binary-tree structured multiple-kernel SVM classifier is adopted in emotion recognition. And different feature subsets are selected in different nodes of the classifier. The highest recognition accuracy of the five emotions in Berlin database is 90.549% with only 15 features selected by RFWF. The experimental results show the effectiveness of RFWF in building feature subset and the utilization of different feature subsets for specified emotions can improve the overall recognition performance.

1. Introduction

Feature selection is a crucial aspect in pattern recognition problems. In multiclass SVM classifier, for example, the structure of the classifier can be one-to-one, one-to-all, hierarchy, or tree structure, so several SVM nodes or models exist in the multiclass classifier [1–3]. There are two questions in speech emotion recognition (SER): (1) how to seek the optimal feature subset from the acoustic features; (2) whether the same acoustic feature subset is proper in all nodes of the multiclass classifier. These questions are researched in this paper. A novel algorithm named Reordering Features with Weights Fusion (RFWF) is proposed to select feature subsets. And in emotion recognition procedure, different feature subsets are adopted in SVM nodes to recognize different emotions.

In SER field, the dimension of feature set ranges from tens to hundreds. However, the increasing dimension does not mean a radical improvement of the recognition accuracy, because the variety and redundancy between more and more features influence the overall performance and complexity

of the system [4]. And there is not a categorical assertion about the most effective feature set in SER nowadays. Feature selection algorithms used in machine learning widely can choose the optimal feature subset with the least generalization error. There are three types of feature selection methods: the wrapper method, the embedded method, and the filter method [5]. Compared with the wrapper method and the embedded method, the filter method is simpler and faster in calculation and its learning strategy is more robust to overfitting. Additionally, because the selection result of the filter method is independent of the learning model, the filter method can be adopted in a variety of leaning tasks. The criteria in filter methods mainly focus on the relevance, the redundancy, and the complementarity. For example, Joint Mutual Information (JMI) [6] considers the relevance between features and classes. Fast correlation-based filter (FCBF) [7] takes the redundancy between features into account. Max-Relevance Min-Redundancy (MRMR) [8] gives consideration to both relevance and redundancy to find the balance between the two properties. In Conditional Information Feature Extraction (CIFE) [9], the information

TABLE 1: Feature set.

Type	Feature	Statistic parameters
Prosodic feature	Pitch	Maximum (1), minimum (2), range (3), mean (4), Std (5), first quartile (6), median (7), third quartile (8), interquartile range (9)
	Energy	Maximum (10), minimum (11), range (12), mean (13), Std (14), first quartile (15), median (16), third quartile (17), interquartile range (18)
	Time	Total frames (19), voiced frames (20), unvoiced frames (21), ratio of voiced frames versus unvoiced frames (22), ratio of voiced frames versus total frames (23), ratio of unvoiced frames versus total frames (24)
Voice quality feature	Formant	F_1:mean (25), Std (26), median (27) F_2: mean (28), Std (29), median (30) F_3: mean (31), Std (32), median (33)
Spectral feature	MFCC	12 MFCC (34–45)

provided by the features is divided into two parts: the class-relevant information that benefits the classification and the class-redundant information that disturbs the classification. And the key idea of Double Input Symmetrical Relevance (DISR) [10] is the utilization of symmetric relevance to consider the complementarity between two input features. In the SER field, various feature selection criteria are often adopted [7, 11–13], and different criterion emphasizes different aspects. Reordering Features with Weights Fusion (RFWF) algorithm proposed in this paper aims to consider relevance, redundancy, and complementarity comprehensively.

Traditionally the same feature subset is adopted in all emotional classes for training and testing [14]. In [11], different feature subsets are adopted on two emotional speech databases, but the emotional recognizability of the features to different emotions has not been considered. Research has shown that acoustic features have different recognizability to specific emotions. For example, pitch related features are usually essential to classify happy and sad [15], while they are often weak in the recognition between happy and surprise because of their high values in these emotions [16]. In order to improve the performance of the whole system, different feature subsets are selected and adopted on the different nodes of the multiclass classifier in this paper.

The content of the paper is arranged as follows: Section 2 gives the basic concepts of filter feature selection and the method of RFWF; Section 3 introduces the structure of the multiclass and multiple-kernel SVM classifier; Section 4 is the analysis of experiments including the results of RFWF and recognition accuracies of emotions; and the final section is devoted to the conclusions.

2. Features and Feature Selection Methods

2.1. Acoustic Features. Speech acoustic features usually used in SER are the prosodic features, voice quality features, and spectral features. In this paper, 409 utterances in Berlin database [17] of 5 emotions including happy (71 samples), angry (127 samples), fear (69 samples), sad (63 samples), and neutral (79 samples) are studied. These samples are separated into training and testing categories randomly. The training samples are 207 including happy (36 samples), angry (64

samples), fear (35 samples), sad (32 samples), and neutral (40 samples), and the rest 202 ones are the test samples.

Pitch, energy, time, formant, and Mel Frequency Cepstrum Coefficient (MFCC) and their statistics parameters are extracted. The total dimension the feature set is 45. Table 1 lists the acoustic features and their sequence indices in this paper.

2.2. Mathematical Description of Feature Selection. Relevance, redundancy, and complementarity are considered in feature selection methods. If a feature can provide information about the class, the relevance exists between the feature and class. The redundancy is based on the dependency between the selected and unselected features. And complementarity means that the interaction between an individual feature and the selected feature subset is beneficial to the classification. Complementarity is important in the cases of null relevance, such as XOR problem [10, 18].

The concepts of information theory, such as mutual information denoted by I and entropy denoted by H, are widely used in feature selection. Mathematically, F_i ($i = 1, \ldots, 409$) is the feature vector of ith sample, and the $f_{i,j}$ is the jth feature of the ith sample in the feature set $\mathbf{F}$. The selected subset and unselected subset are $\mathbf{F}_s$ and $\mathbf{F}_{-s}$ with the mathematic relation of $\mathbf{F}_s \cap \mathbf{F}_{-s} = \varnothing$ and $\mathbf{F}_s \cup \mathbf{F}_{-s} = \mathbf{F}$. C_n, $n = 1, \ldots, 5$ is the specified emotion in Berlin database. In the following content, the mathematical description of relevance, redundancy, and complementarity is interpreted through introduction of MRMR and DISR.

In MRMR $\mathbf{F}_s = \{f_p\}$, $p = 1, \ldots, d$ and $f_q \in \mathbf{F}_{-s}$, $q = 1, \ldots, 45 - d$, the relevance term $u_q = I(f_q; C)$ and the redundancy term $z_q = 1/d \sum_{f_p \in \mathbf{F}_s} I(f_p; f_q)$ are used in the criterion:

$$f_q^{\text{MRMR}} = \arg\max_{f_q \in \mathbf{F}_{-s}} \{u_q - z_q\}, \tag{1}$$

where $I(f_q; C)$ can represent the relevance between an unselected feature and the class and $I(f_p; f_q)$ can represent the redundancy between the unselected and selected features. The detailed computation can be found in [8].

The key idea of DISR depends on the consideration of the second average sub-subset information criterion in (2) to consider the complementarity between an unselected feature f_q and a selected feature f_p given the specific class C.

$$f_q^{\text{DISR}} = \arg\max_{f_q \in \mathbf{F}_{-s}} \left\{ \sum_{f_p \in \mathbf{F}_s} I\left(f_{p,q}; C\right) \right\}. \qquad (2)$$

Equation (2) also can be modified by a normalized relevance measure named symmetric relevance calculated by the following:

$$\text{SR} = \frac{I\left(f_{p,q}; C\right)}{H\left(f_{p,q}; C\right)}. \qquad (3)$$

In DISR, $I(f_{p,q}; C)$ is the complementarity calculated by

$$I\left(f_{p,q}; C\right) = I\left(f_p; C\right) + I\left(f_q; C\right) - A\left(f_p; f_q; C\right), \qquad (4)$$

where $A(f_p; f_q; C)$ stands for the interaction among f_p, f_q, and C. From its general meaning, for n sets of random variables $X_1, X_2, \ldots, X_n$, the interaction can be defined as

$$A\left(X_1, X_2, \ldots, X_n\right) = \sum_{k=1}^{n} \sum_{S \subseteq \{1,\ldots,n\}: S=k} (-1)^{k+1} H\left(X_S\right). \qquad (5)$$

The detailed definition and proof can be found in [10].

2.3. Reordering Features with Weights Fusion. For the comprehensive consideration of relevance, redundancy, and complementarity, the following criterion named Reordering Features with Weights Fusion (RFWF) is proposed to fuse the intrinsic properties of the features:

$$f_q^{\text{RFWF}} = \arg\max_{f_q \in \mathbf{F}_{-s}} \left\{ W_1 \left(I\left(f_q; C\right)\right) \right.$$

$$\left. + W_2 \left(\sum_{f_p \in \mathbf{F}_s} I\left(f_{p,q}; C\right)\right) - W_3 \left(\sum_{f_p \in \mathbf{F}_s} I\left(f_p; f_q\right)\right) \right\}, \qquad (6)$$

where W_1, W_2, and W_3 are the fusing weights of the unselected feature f_q and they are combined in (6) to reflect the contribution of f_q to given class. The procedure of RFWF algorithm described in the following is illustrated in Figure 1:

(1) $L_m(f_q)$ ($m = 1, 2, 3$) is the sequence number of the feature f_q ranked in order of the values of $I(f_q; C)$, $\sum_{f_p \in \mathbf{F}_s} I(f_{p,q}; C)$ and $\sum_{f_p \in \mathbf{F}_s} I(f_p; f_q)$, respectively. If the dimension of the feature set is 45, $L_m(f_q)$ is an integer value ranging within 1~45. For example, if the $I(f_q; C)$ is the largest, $L_1(f_q)$ is 1. And if the $\sum_{f_p \in \mathbf{F}_s} I(f_{p,q}; C)$ is the lowest, $L_2(f_q)$ is 45. The initial selected feature f_p in $\mathbf{F}_s$ is confirmed by the largest value of $I(f_p; C)$.

(2) Weighted values can be calculated by the following formula:

$$W_m\left(f_q\right) = 45 - L_m\left(f_q\right) + 1,$$
$$m = 1, 2, 3, \quad q = 1, \ldots, 45. \qquad (7)$$

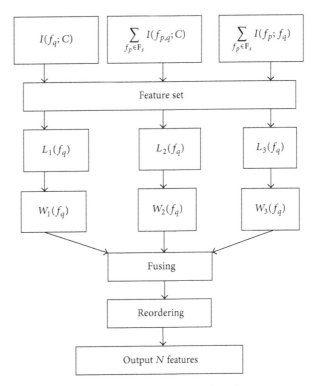

FIGURE 1: Procedure of RFWF algorithm.

For example, if $L_1(f_q)$ is 1, the corresponding weight about the relevance between feature and class is $W_1(I(f_q; C)) = 45$.

(3) All of the features can be reordered by the fusing result using W_1, W_2, and W_3.

(4) The top N features can be selected to construct the optimal feature subset.

Because this algorithm fuses three weights to consider the contribution of features in the classification and a reordering process exists in the process, the algorithm is named Reordering Features with Weights Fusion (RFWF).

3. Multiclass and Multiple-Kernel SVM Classifier with Binary-Tree Structure

The Support Vector Machine (SVM) is a discriminative classifier proposed for binary classification problem and based on the theory of structural risk minimization. The performance of a single-kernel method depends heavily on the choice of the kernel. If a dataset has varying distributions, a single kernel may not be adequate. Kernel fusion has been proposed to deal with this problem [19].

The simplest kernel fusion is a weighted combination of M kernels:

$$\mathbf{K} = \sum_{s=1}^{M} \mu_s \mathbf{K}_s, \qquad (8)$$

where μ_s is the optimal weights and $\mathbf{K}_s$ is the sth kernel matrix. The selection of μ_s is an optimal question, and the

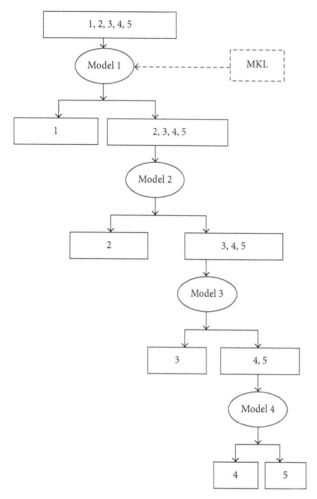

FIGURE 2: The binary-tree structured multiclass and multiple-kernel SVM classifier.

4. Experiments and Analysis

4.1. The Experimental Results of RFWF. Table 2 lists the reordering results of features for the four SVM models in Figure 2 according to the fusing results of W_1, W_2, and W_3. In Table 2, the numbers are the indices of the features listed in Table 1.

It is clear that, in the four SVM models, the contribution of different features to emotional recognizability is distinct. For example, the standard deviation of pitch (feature sequence index is 5) is the most essential feature to classify happy and the other emotions in Berlin database, while ratio of voiced frames versus total frames (feature sequence index is 23) is the most important feature to recognize neutral and sad. The results show that it is necessary to adopt different feature subsets to recognize different emotions.

4.2. Experimental Results of SER and Analysis. In the SER experiments, LibSVM package is adopted. Three basis Radial Basis Functions (RBF) kernel functions with parameters of $\gamma_1 = 0.01$, $\gamma_2 = 0.1$, $\gamma_3 = 1$ are combined in Model 1. YALMIP toolbox is used to solve the SDP problem and find three μ_s with the features listed in Table 1. In single-kernel SVM models, the value of γ is $1/k$, where k is the selected feature number in the recognition procedure. When the selected feature number is specified, the same γ is adopted for all single-kernel models.

Recognition accuracies, Root Mean Square Error (RMSE) and Maximum Error (MaxE) are used to evaluate the performance of the SVM classifier. RMSE and MaxE are calculated by following equations:

$$P_{\text{RMSE}} = \sqrt{\frac{1}{5}\sum_{i=1}^{5} e_i^2}$$

$$Q_{\text{MaxE}} = \max\{e_i\}, \tag{9}$$

where e_i is the recognition error (%) of ith emotion. Obviously, the higher the recognition accuracies and the lower the values of RMSE and MaxE, the better the performance of the classifier.

If the dimension of feature subset is N, then the top N features in the Table 2 are selected to construct the feature subset. N ranging within 1–45 achieves different recognition performance. Figure 3 plots the curves of total emotion recognition accuracies of MRMR, DISR, and RFWF features selection algorithms, respectively, where RFWF is adopted in multiple-kernel (RFWF MK) and single-kernel (RFWF SK) SVM classifiers. Different feature subsets are selected for Models 1–4. Figure 4 gives the RMSE and MaxE corresponding to Figure 3. In Figures 3 and 4, the horizontal axis describes the different number of the selected features or the dimension of the selected feature subset. Table 3 lists the detailed experimental data of the highest total accuracies of MRMR, DISR, RFWF MK, and RFWF SK methods.

The recognition results show DISR and MRMR algorithms reach their highest accuracies with 39 features. However, the highest accuracy of RFWF MK is 90.594% with only 15 features. The accuracies of DISR and MRMR are 70.792%

objective function and constraints of the problem can be formulated as the Semidefinite Programming (SDP) form. The detailed proof of can be found in [20].

In this paper, a multiple-kernel SVM classifier with an unbalance binary-tree structure illustrated in Figure 2 is adopted. In Figure 2, there are five emotions to be recognized. The first classifying node (Model 1) is improved by multiple-kernel SVM to recognize the most confusable emotion while the subsequent classifying nodes still retain single-kernel SVM. This arrangement attributes the reduction of recognition error accumulation and the computing complexity required in the calculation of the multiple-kernel matrices for all nodes.

According to the previous works [2, 11, 21, 22], happy is the most confusable emotion and its recognition accuracy is the main factor influencing the total performance in Berlin database. Thus in the classifier shown in Figure 2, happy is 1, angry is 2, fear is 3, neutral is 4, and sad is 5. Feature subset selected by RFWF is adopted in the SVM training and testing, where Model 1 is learned by multiple kernels. Models 2, 3, and 4 are still single-kernel SVM models.

Table 2: RFWF results of the feature set in different models of the classifier.

						Indices of features									
	5	37	38	42	8	1	9	20	40	33	26	3	4	45	18
Model 1	44	15	24	21	13	29	10	6	7	14	16	19	23	17	35
	41	22	34	25	2	12	31	43	36	39	28	30	32	11	27
	36	34	20	43	42	7	5	14	18	41	16	8	4	15	1
Model 2	6	33	37	24	19	23	45	9	3	31	13	17	21	10	32
	22	39	40	2	30	28	35	12	38	11	29	27	44	26	25
	4	20	43	35	36	45	8	16	7	18	9	23	34	11	25
Model 3	19	21	2	6	5	22	44	27	10	24	38	32	29	42	12
	26	40	14	17	39	13	31	15	37	41	28	30	1	33	3
	23	7	39	41	14	10	15	19	24	22	13	21	40	35	11
Model 4	16	42	25	27	38	8	18	33	36	43	12	20	6	29	5
	30	17	31	4	2	37	28	9	44	1	26	34	3	32	45

Table 3: Emotion recognition accuracies of different feature selection methods with the best feature number.

Selection methods	Feature number	SER accuracies (%)					
		Total	Angry	Fear	Happy	Neutral	Sad
DISR	39	88.614	93.651	79.412	97.143	74.359	96.774
MRMR	39	90.099	92.063	67.647	97.143	94.872	96.774
RFWF MK	15	90.594	90.476	79.412	97.143	87.179	100
RFWF SK	39	79.208	95.238	73.529	28.571	87.179	100

and 77.723%, respectively, when the selected feature number is 15. When the selected feature number is 45, it means that no feature selection algorithms are utilized. In this situation, the performances of DISR, MRMR, and RFWF MK are the same and the total accuracy is 83.663%. These results show that the RFWF algorithm has the best performance with the lowest dimension of feature subset. The corresponding RMSE and MaxE curves of RFWF are the lowest when the selected feature number N is below 30. If the dimension of the feature subset increases, the three feature selection methods with multiple-kernel classifier have similar performance. This is mainly because RFWF uses the same weighing methods for the relevance, redundancy, and complementarity. From this aspect, it is an average strategy in the procedure of weights fusion. The results show that when the dimension feature subset is close to 45, the RFWF degrades to handle with the complex inherent properties between the features and more optimal feature fusion method should be studied.

The highest total accuracy of RFWF SK is 79.208%, which is much lower than accuracy of RFWF MK. The recognition accuracies of happy are 97.143% steadily in the three methods when Model 1 is improved by multiple-kernel SVM. The experimental results demonstrate that multiple-kernel classifier can solve the confusion between happy and other emotions effectively, which cannot be dealt with by single-kernel SVM. The highest SER accuracies of RFWF MK can be compared to the results of the Enhanced Sparse Representation Classifier (Enhanced-SRC) in [11] and feature fusion based on MKL in [23]. The experimental comparison is listed in Table 4, where the symbol "N" denotes no relating experimental results in the reference.

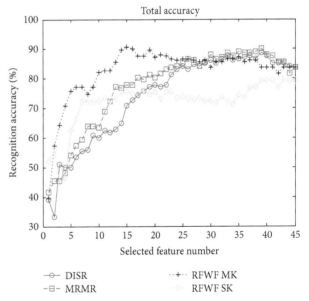

Figure 3: Emotional recognition accuracies.

If Models 2–4 use the same feature subset as in Model 1 with the dimension of 15, the accuracy of RFWF MK is only 63.861%. And when all models use the same feature subset of 39, the highest accuracy of RFWF MK is 85.149%. The data confirms that the utilization of the same feature subset in all models influences the emotion recognition performance negatively. These experimental results demonstrate that different feature subset is necessary in the recognition of

TABLE 4: Comparison on SER accuracies (%) of 5 emotions in Berlin database.

Methods	Anger	Fear	Happy	Neutral	Sad
Enhanced-SRC	98.55	83.16	57.73	70.08	96.71
Feature fusion based on MKL	81	83	*N*	65	95
RFWF MK	90.476	79.412	97.143	87.179	100

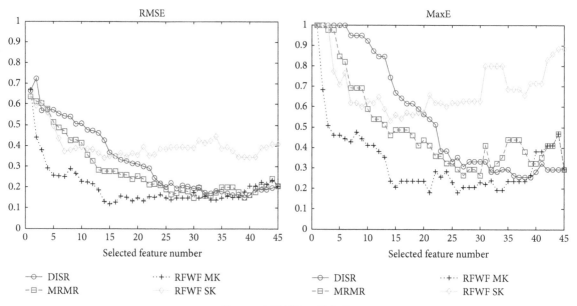

FIGURE 4: RMSE and MaxE.

different emotions, which also indicates the difficulty to build a robust and effective feature subset for all emotions.

5. Conclusions

In this paper, a RFWF feature selection method is proposed for building more effective feature subset in SER. A binary-tree structured multiclass and multiple-kernel SVM classifier is adopted to recognize emotions in a public emotional speech database. The experimental results indicate the effectiveness of the whole system.

The conclusions of this paper are as follows: (1) intrinsic properties of features about relevance, redundancy, and complementarity can be considered comprehensively by weights fusion. (2) Feature subset selected by RFWF achieves higher total accuracy than MRMR and DISR with lower dimension. (3) In multiclass classifier, different feature subsets adopted in different nodes can improve the recognizability of the whole system. (4) Multiple-kernel SVM classifier is robust and effective in recognizing the most confusable emotion.

The next work can focus on the research about more optimal feature fusion algorithms and automatic acquisition of optimal dimension of feature subset.

Conflicts of Interest

The authors declare that they have no conflicts of interest.

Acknowledgments

This work was supported by the National Natural Science Foundation of China (no. 61501204 and no. 61601198), Hebei Province Natural Science Foundation (no. E2016202341), Hebei Province Foundation for Returned Scholars (no. C2012003038), Shandong Provincial Natural Science Foundation (no. ZR2015FL010), and Science and Technology Program of University of Jinan (no. XKY1710).

References

[1] L. Chen, X. Mao, Y. Xue, and L. L. Cheng, "Speech emotion recognition: features and classification models," *Digital Signal Processing*, vol. 22, no. 6, pp. 1154–1160, 2012.

[2] S. Chandaka, A. Chatterjee, and S. Munshi, "Support vector machines employing cross-correlation for emotional speech recognition," *Measurement: Journal of the International Measurement Confederation*, vol. 42, no. 4, pp. 611–618, 2009.

[3] C.-C. Lee, E. Mower, C. Busso, S. Lee, and S. Narayanan, "Emotion recognition using a hierarchical binary decision tree approach," *Speech Communication*, vol. 53, no. 9-10, pp. 1162–1171, 2011.

[4] J. Yuan, L. Chen, T. Fan, and J. Jia, "Dimension reduction of speech emotion feature based on weighted linear discriminate analysis," in *Image Processing and Pattern Recognition*, vol. 8, pp. 299–308, International Journal of Signal Processing, 2015.

[5] Y. Saeys, I. Inza, and P. Larrañaga, "A review of feature selection techniques in bioinformatics," *Bioinformatics*, vol. 23, no. 19, pp. 2507–2517, 2007.

[6] H. Hua Yang and J. Moody, "Data visualization and feature selection: new algorithms for nongaussian data," *Advances in Neural Information Processing Systems*, vol. 12, pp. 687–693, 1999.

[7] D. Gharavian, M. Sheikhan, A. Nazerieh, and S. Garoucy, "Speech emotion recognition using FCBF feature selection method and GA-optimized fuzzy ARTMAP neural network," *Neural Computing and Applications*, vol. 21, no. 8, pp. 2115–2126, 2012.

[8] H. Peng, F. Long, and C. Ding, "Feature selection based on mutual information: criteria of max-dependency, max-relevance, and min-redundancy," *IEEE Transactions on Pattern Analysis and Machine Intelligence*, vol. 27, no. 8, pp. 1226–1238, 2005.

[9] D. Lin and X. Tang, "Conditional infomax learning: an integrated framework for feature extraction and fusion," in *Proceedings of the 9th European Conference on Computer Vision*, pp. 68–82, Graz, Austria, 2006.

[10] P. E. Meyer, C. Schretter, and G. Bontempi, "Information-theoretic feature selection in microarray data using variable complementarity," *IEEE Journal on Selected Topics in Signal Processing*, vol. 2, no. 3, pp. 261–274, 2008.

[11] X. Zhao, S. Zhang, and B. Lei, "Robust emotion recognition in noisy speech via sparse representation," *Neural Computing and Applications*, vol. 24, no. 7-8, pp. 1539–1553, 2014.

[12] A. Mencattini, E. Martinelli, G. Costantini et al., "Speech emotion recognition using amplitude modulation parameters and a combined feature selection procedure," *Knowledge-Based Systems*, vol. 63, pp. 68–81, 2014.

[13] D. Ververidis, C. Kotropoulos, and I. Pitas, "Automatic emotional speech classification," in *Proceedings of the IEEE International Conference on Acoustics, Speech, and Signal Processing*, pp. I-593–596, Quebec, CA, USA, 2004.

[14] J. Liu, C. Chen, J. Bu et al., "Speech emotion recognition based on a fusion of all-class and pairwise-class feature selection," in *Proceedings of the ICCS*, pp. 168–175, Beijing, China, 2007.

[15] X. Xu, Y. Li, X. Xu et al., "Survey on discriminative feature selection for speech emotion recognition," in *Proceedings of the 9th International Symposium on Chinese Spoken Language Processing, ISCSLP 2014*, pp. 345–349, Singapore, Singapore, September 2014.

[16] L. Tian, X. Jiang, and Z. Hou, "Statistical study on the diversity of pitch parameters in multilingual speech," *Control and Decision*, vol. 20, no. 11, pp. 1311–1313, 2005.

[17] F. Burkhardt, A. Paeschke, M. Rolfes et al., "A database of German emotional speech," in *Proceedings of the 9th European Conference on Speech Communication and Technology*, pp. 1517–1520, Lisbon, Portugal, 2005.

[18] J. R. Vergara and P. A. Estévez, "A review of feature selection methods based on mutual information," *Neural Computing and Applications*, vol. 24, no. 1, pp. 175–186, 2014.

[19] C.-Y. Yeh, W.-P. Su, and S.-J. Lee, "An efficient multiple-kernel learning for pattern classification," *Expert Systems with Applications*, vol. 40, no. 9, pp. 3491–3499, 2013.

[20] G. R. G. Lanckriet, N. Cristianini, P. L. Bartlett et al., "Learning the kernel matrix with semidefinite programming," *Machine Learning Research*, vol. 5, no. 1, pp. 27–72, 2004.

[21] X. Jiang, K. Xia, X. Xia, and B. Zu, "Speech emotion recognition using semi-definite programming multiple-kernel SVM," *Journal of Beijing University of Posts and Telecommunications*, vol. 38, no. S1, pp. 67–71, 2015.

[22] B. Yang and M. Lugger, "Emotion recognition from speech signals using new harmony features," *Signal Processing*, vol. 90, no. 5, pp. 1415–1423, 2010.

[23] Y. Jin, P. Song, W. Zheng, and L. Zhao, "Novel feature fusion method for speech emotion recognition based on multiple kernel learning," *Journal of Southeast University*, vol. 29, no. 2, pp. 129–133, 2013.

13

Acoustic Log Prediction on the Basis of Kernel Extreme Learning Machine for Wells in GJH Survey, Erdos Basin

Jianhua Cao, Yancui Shi, Dan Wang, and Xiankun Zhang

College of Computer Science and Information Engineering, Tianjin University of Science and Technology, Tianjin, China

Correspondence should be addressed to Jianhua Cao; caojh@tust.edu.cn

Academic Editor: Hui Cheng

In petroleum exploration, the acoustic log (DT) is popularly used as an estimator to calculate formation porosity, to carry out petrophysical studies, or to participate in geological analysis and research (e.g., to map abnormal pore-fluid pressure). But sometime it does not exist in those old wells drilled 20 years ago, either because of data loss or because of just being not recorded at that time. Thus synthesizing the DT log becomes the necessary task for the researchers. In this paper we propose using kernel extreme learning machine (KELM) to predict missing sonic (DT) logs when only common logs (e.g., natural gamma ray: GR, deep resistivity: REID, and bulk density: DEN) are available. The common logs are set as predictors and the DT log is the target. By using KELM, a prediction model is firstly created based on the experimental data and then confirmed and validated by blind-testing the results in wells containing both the predictors and the target (DT) values used in the supervised training. Finally the optimal model is set up as a predictor. A case study for wells in GJH survey from the Erdos Basin, about velocity inversion using the KELM-estimated DT values, is presented. The results are promising and encouraging.

1. Introduction

Oil and gas exploration in sedimentary basins is very complicated, since all the targets are buried underground and they cannot be viewed or touched directly. So all the properties for the buried targets have to be predicted or estimated by using modern electrical or magnetic tools. The physical properties of the geologic formations include pore-fluid pressure, rock lithology, porosity, permeability, and oil or water saturation. Nowadays the conventional tool for characterizing these geophysical properties is well logging, and some logs such as gamma ray (GR), dual induction log, formation density (DEN) compensated, deep resistivity (REID), self-potential (SP), and sonic log (DT) are usually recorded. Among them, the sonic log (DT) has largely been used to predict rock porosity, to perform petrophysical analysis, or to carry out well-to-seismic inversion.

Owing to historical operation mistakes or recording loss, the sonic log may not be available in well logging suites. The traditional way solving this problem is to transform the DEN or REID log to DT log based on some experimental formula

built between these logs. It might be feasible for some area, but sometimes the errors are unacceptable.

Artificial intelligence techniques have the advantage in connecting unrelated parameters and solving nonlinear problems. Such techniques, including BP neural network, fuzzy reasoning, or evolutionary computing for data analysis and interpretation have become effective tools in the workflow for well drilling and reservoir characterization [1–10]. However, traditional neural networks have many known drawbacks in the learning process, such as multiple local minima, slow learning speed, and poor generalization performances [11].

Extreme learning machine (ELM) is a single-hidden layer feed-forward neural network (SLFN) proposed by Huang et al. [12, 13]. The ELM approach to training SLFN consists in the random generation of the hidden layer weights, followed by solving a linear system of equations by least-squares for the estimation of the output layer weights. This learning strategy is very fast and gives good prediction accuracy. Theoretically and practically, this algorithm can produce good generalization performance in most cases and can learn thousands of times faster than conventional popular learning algorithms for feed-forward neural networks [14]. A lot of real-life applications [15–18] have already demonstrated advantages of using basic ELM. A kernel-based ELM (KELM) has also been developed lately [19], where the hidden layer feature mapping is determined by the kernel matrix. In this version, only the kernel function and its parameters are needed to be defined; the number of hidden nodes is not required. With the use of kernel function, KELM is expected to achieve better generalization performance than basic ELM. Furthermore, as randomness does not occur in KELM, the chance of result variations could be reduced [20].

In this paper, kernel-based extreme learning machine is used to predict missing sonic (DT) logs when only common logs (e.g., natural gamma ray—GR, bulk density—DEN, or deep resistivity—REID) are available. By using KELM, we first create and train a supervised network model based on experimental data and then confirm and validate the model by blind-testing the results. The optimal model is at last applied to wells containing the predictor data but with lack of DT log. We use this workflow in GJH survey from Erdos Basin and the KELM-estimated DT logs are then integrated in the seismic inversion to identify the sandstone reservoir.

The rest of this paper proceeds as follows. Section 2 gives a short review of ELM and KELM. Section 3 describes the experiments using KELM, including the data preparation, parameter selection, and model validation. Section 4 gives the prediction application in GJH survey. Finally, Section 5 gives the conclusion of this work.

2. Methodology

In this study, the kernel extreme learning machine (KELM) is employed to predict the DT logs for the wells in GJH survey. So we present an overview of the ELM and kernel-based ELM as follows.

2.1. ELM. The classical ELM was proposed for SLFNs by Huang et al. [12, 13]. Different from BP network, the input weights and biases of ELM are randomly assigned and need not be fine-tuned within the training phase, and the output weights can be determined analytically by finding the least-square solution. The prediction of ELM is given by

$$f_L(\mathbf{x}) = \sum_{i=1}^{L} \boldsymbol{\beta}_i \mathbf{h}_i(\mathbf{x}) = \mathbf{h}(\mathbf{x})\,\boldsymbol{\beta}, \qquad (1)$$

where $\boldsymbol{\beta} = [\boldsymbol{\beta}_1, \ldots, \boldsymbol{\beta}_L]^T$ is the weight vector connecting the hidden node and the output nodes and $\mathbf{h}(\mathbf{x}) = [\mathbf{h}_1(\mathbf{x}), \ldots, \mathbf{h}_L(\mathbf{x})]^T$ is the output of the hidden layer with respect to the sample $\mathbf{x}$. Since the weights and biases are initially assigned for the hidden layer, when the activation function is set, $\mathbf{h}(\mathbf{x})$ is determined and need not be tuned. And the only unknown parameter is $\boldsymbol{\beta}$, which can be solved as constrained optimization problem:

$$\text{Minimize:} \quad \|\mathbf{H}\boldsymbol{\beta} - T\|_p^{\alpha 1} + \frac{C}{2}\|\boldsymbol{\beta}\|_q^{\alpha 2}, \qquad (2)$$

where C is control parameter for a tradeoff between structural risk and empirical risk, T is the target output for the network.

And when $p, q = F$ and $\alpha 1, \alpha 2 = 2$, a popular and efficient closed-form solution for $\boldsymbol{\beta}$ is

$$\boldsymbol{\beta} = \begin{cases} \mathbf{H}^T\left(C\mathbf{I} + \mathbf{HH}^T\right)^{-1} T & N \geq L \\ \left(C\mathbf{I} + \mathbf{HH}^T\right)^{-1}\mathbf{H}^T T & N \leq L \end{cases} \qquad (3)$$

2.2. KELM. As proposed in Huang et al. [19], if $\mathbf{h}(\cdot)$ is unknown, that is, an implicit function, one can apply Mercer's conditions on ELM and define a kernel matrix for ELM that takes the form

$$\mathbf{K}_{\mathrm{ELM}} = \mathbf{HH}^T :$$
$$\mathbf{K}_{\mathrm{ELM}_{i,j}} = \mathbf{h}(\mathbf{x}_i) \cdot \mathbf{h}(\mathbf{x}_j) = \mathbf{k}(\mathbf{x}_i, \mathbf{x}_j), \qquad (4)$$

where $\mathbf{k}(\mathbf{x}_i, \mathbf{x}_j)$ is a kernel function. Many kernel functions can be used in kernel-based ELM, such as linear, polynomial, and radial basis function, so that we can obtain the kernel form of the output function as follows:

$$f_L(\mathbf{x}) = \begin{bmatrix} \mathbf{k}(\mathbf{x}, \mathbf{x}_1) \\ \vdots \\ \mathbf{k}(\mathbf{x}, \mathbf{x}_N) \end{bmatrix} (C\mathbf{I} + \mathbf{K}_{\mathrm{ELM}})^{-1} T \qquad (5)$$

Similar to the SVM, $\mathbf{h}(\mathbf{x})$ need not be known; instead, its kernel can be provided (e.g., Gaussian kernel $\mathbf{k}(\mathbf{u}, \mathbf{v}) = \exp(\|\mathbf{u}-\mathbf{v}\|^2/\sigma)$). The optimal penalty parameter C and kernel width s are determined by try and error way. Node number of the hidden layer L need not be available beforehand either. The experimental and theoretical analysis of Huang et al. showed that KELM produces improved generalization performance over the SVM/LS-SVM [21].

For the given type of the kernel function, the training dataset, and the initial parameters of the network, the following steps are considered.

Step 1. Initiate the population based on the kernel function.

Step 2. Evaluate the fitness function of each parameter.

Step 3. The optimal parameters of kernel function can be determined. Then, based on the optimized parameters, the hidden layer kernel matrix is computed.

Step 4. Determine the final output weights.

3. Experimental Study

3.1. Problem Description and Related Work. Well logging is the practice of making a detailed record of the geologic formations penetrated by a borehole. Normally the log is based on the physical measurements made by instruments lowered into the borehole. According to the geophysical properties of the rocks, the logs are always classified as follows: electrical logs, porosity logs, lithology logs, and miscellaneous logs. Sonic log (DT) belongs to the porosity logs, and it provides a formation interval transit time, which typically varies lithology and rock texture, especially porosity for the rocks. Gamma ray log is a log of the natural radioactivity of the formation along the borehole, measured in API units, particularly useful for distinguishing between sands and shales in a siliciclastic environment. This is because sandstones are usually nonradioactive quartz, whereas shales are naturally radioactive due to potassium isotopes in clays and adsorbed uranium and thorium.

The main datasets used in this study include acoustic log (DT), the gamma ray (GR), the resistivity log (REID), which represents the variation of the electric resistivity, the density (DEN), which records the density variation with depth in the borehole, and the self-Potential (SP), a measurement of natural electric potential. These geophysical parameters DT, GR, REID, DEN, and SP are intrinsically linked, since each of them reflects some physical property of the same rock layer. Take sandstone as an example. Pores are sure to exist at the sandstone interval, and if the pores are not filled with other types of tight materials, fluid is the only also important stuffing. There might be oil or gas and water as well. Since the fluid has different physical parameters than the surrounding sandstone, obvious differences will be recorded on the measuring logs: lower GR, lower DT, higher REID, lower DEN, and abnormal change on SP. Thus just observing the characters of the logs, especially those abnormal changes, the experienced researchers have confidence to tell the geological information along the borehole. And then some researchers try to build theoretical relationships between the logs. Thousands of experiments result in empirical equations. For example, DEN could be transformed using DT log when DEN is missing and the relation is defined as Gardener formula [6]:

$$DEN = \alpha DT^{-\beta}, \tag{6}$$

where, α, β are the coefficients and their values are up to the core tests for the studied area.

In this study, the key we focus on is the DT log, and we want to find the optimal way to get the DT log when it is missing.

The sonic log (DT) is very important in petroleum exploration phase. One way for using DT is to estimate rock porosity, which is the critical parameter for the reservoir evaluation, and identify the fluid information along the borehole. Additionally, since DT log has both time and velocity information, it becomes the reliable key for the time-depth conversion when using seismic data to interpret structures and geological mapping. In one word, the DT log is indispensable for the geophysical and geological study.

But there has always been imperfection, and sometimes, owing to operation mistake or recording loss, DT log may not be available in some wells. One solution for obtaining the DT log is to carry out empirical transformation from other logs, and the model is built by experiment analysis. The formula is just for specific field condition, and it can not be used for all the formation conditions. For instance, Faust formula is just for DT calculation using REID log, and cases [7] have shown that the formula is not suitable when fluid exits in the formation. So another study to synthesize

missing DT is to use soft-computing methods, such as artificial neural network, gene expressing programming, and fuzzy reasoning. ANN (artificial neural network) has been frequently used in petrophysical properties estimation, and results show satisfied performances when choosing proper models and parameters [8, 9, 16]. The most important property of ANNs is their ability to approximate virtually any function in a stable and efficient way. By using ANNs, it is possible to create a platform on which different models can be constructed. Baziar et al. [22] tested coactive neurofuzzy inference system which combines fuzzy model and neural network in permeability prediction in a tight gas reservoir and gained convincing results.

Since DT has intrinsic links with the other geophysical logs, researchers often use logs like GR, REID, and so forth as the original inputs and the DT as outputs. Linear and nonlinear relationships have been set up using the soft-computing methods. But the results are not always satisfied. Thus our purpose is to build an optimal and reliable relationship between those geophysical logs and DT log.

In this paper, we investigate the capability of a kernel extreme learning machine in building the nonlinear mathematical model that best explains DT (target) as a function of GR, REID, DEN, and SP (predictors).

3.2. Data Preparation. In order to validate the use of KELM in the context of log data recorded in oil and gas wells, we employed datasets obtained from seven wells drilled in the GJH survey in Erdos Basin.

The study involves the following well logging parameters: gamma ray (GR), deep resistivity (REID), self-potential (SP), formation density (DEN), and sonic log (DT). Among the wells, wells of YQ2, Y209, S211, S212, and S215 have full suites of well logs, while DT log is not available in the other two wells (S219 and S205). According to the evaluation conclusion for the logging process, we choose the farther four wells as training dataset sources and well S215 as the testing dataset. Shanxi group of the Permian formation is set as the analysis interval. Logs of GR, REID, SP, DEN, and DT in the interval from the mentioned four wells are collected and grouped as training dataset, while logs of well S215 as the validation target.

Figure 1 is the example of logs showing of well YQ2 in the Shanxi group of Permian formation ranging from 2700 to 2798 meters. The lithology includes sandstone, mudstone, and thin coal layer, and it is easy to differentiate them from the GR log. Coal layer has very low GR and DEN response and abnormal high DT and REID. Thus, for the same type of rocks, these logs have close geophysical link, which is the foundation for DT prediction using these logs.

We select data in the same interval from the four wells of YQ2, Y209, S210, and S212 as the training samples. To ensure the quality of the logs, we use caliper log (CAL) as the reference. Constant diameter of the wellbore (described by CAL) means good environment for the other suite of logs. Totally about 40,000 data items are available for the training process.

To speed up the convergence of the gradient descent algorithm, data normalization is mandatory for the performance. And the above-mentioned logs have different measurement units. All of the logs are normalized before formally inputting

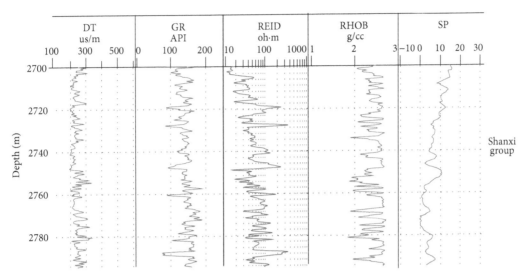

FIGURE 1: Logs showing of well YQ2 in the Shanxi group of Permian formation.

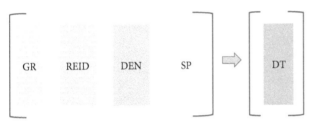

FIGURE 2: Example of multi-input versus single-output sonic log prediction using KELM. Details about the well logging parameters depicted in the figure are given in text.

into the network. The normalized variable has the following form:

$$X_{new} = \frac{X_{old} - \min X}{\max X - \min X}, \tag{7}$$

where X stands for logs of GR, AC, DEN, REID, and SP. The new normalized variable X_{new} takes the range from 0 to 1 for all the parameters.

In KELM network learning, the output model is created by learning patterns from the training examples provided. Therefore, the training dataset should be carefully chosen in order to provide correct examples. And noise should be removed from the samples; otherwise errors may affect the final performance.

3.3. KELM Model Training. For the KELM network model, there are totally four input neurons and one target at the output layer. The four inputs include GR, REID, SP, and DEN logs, and the main task is to build reliable prediction model between these inputs logs and DT log (shown as Figure 2). Gaussian radial basis kernel function is used because it usually produces good results and outperforms other functions for regression.

In the algorithms of KELM, two hyperparameters, namely, the regularization factor (C) and the basis width

parameter of the kernel function ($s2$), are necessary. To select the best values for these hyperparameters, leave-one-out cross-validation (LOOCV) is usually applied [9]. In the preliminary experiment, the KELM model achieves the best performance when the values of C and s are set to (10, 1), so these values are finally chosen in our experiment.

The quality of the trained model is evaluated based on the prediction accuracy. The Mean Squared Error (MSE) is computed as the average over all squared deviations of the predictions from the real values.

After training, the model could be presented in the following form:

$$Y = \begin{bmatrix} K(X, x_1) \\ \cdots \\ K(X, x_n) \end{bmatrix} \beta, \tag{8}$$

where $K(*)$ is the Gaussian radial basis kernel function, n is the number of training data, and β is the trained weight matrix of the model based on the training data. By providing unseen input data X to the model, the corresponding model output Y can be predicted.

Furthermore, in order to testify the advantages of KELM, BP network algorithm is used in the model training and testing process to compare with KELM. Backpropagation (BP) feed-forward network is the most commonly used ANN approach, and it is also criticized on its difficulty to decide learning rates, being easy to be stuck on local minimums, overfit problems, and being time-consuming [11].

Table 1 shows the results on testing data. Accuracy, MSE, and training time are three factors in comparison, and the values are obtained by averaging estimations of the samples in well YQ2. The table shows the accuracy, Mean Squared Error (MSE), and total time in seconds for the two processing approaches, respectively. Best results are achieved by KELM with an accuracy of 0.906, mean absolute error of 0.423%, and fast learning speed (23 seconds).

TABLE 1: Comparison of porosity prediction performance results on KELM against BP methodology for well YQ2. The comparison strata belong to the Shanxi group of the Permian formation.

Algorithm	Accuracy	MSE (%)	Training time (s)
BP	0.752	1.812	912
KELM	0.906	0.423	23

3.4. KELM Model Validation and Prediction. Through the above-mentioned training process, the KELM model for predicting DT is established finally. Although the training dataset has almost 40,000 data points, the training task costs very short time and the performance is satisfying. To validate the KELM model, we use well S215 as blind well. The four logs are collected and processed for the well, and then we input them into the model and keep the network parameters. Since the data for validation is small group with nearly 6000 samples, the process only costs 6 seconds and one predicted DT is generated. In well S215, there has been DT log, so that the predicted DT can be used in comparison with the real DT. Figure 3 shows the comparison result. The curve with the red color is the predicted one from KELM model, and the curve with the blue color stands for the recorded DT log. It is easy to see that the total changing trend and the finest part are almost the same; thus the model is qualified in this study and is reliable to be a predictor.

In this study, DT log is missing in the two wells of S219 and S205. Here the KELM model is then recommended to do the prediction task for the two wells. Luckily, the four input logs (GR, REID, DEN, and SP) are guaranteed in both of the wells. Using the same noise-filtering and normalization step in the training and validating step, we firstly input the four predictor logs of well S219 into the model and generate DT log for this well. And then we repeat the steps for the well S205 and also get the DT log. Figure 4 shows the predicted DT log for well S219 in the Shanxi group of Permian formation.

4. KELM-Estimated DT Application

The above analysis has shown the reliability and accuracy of the KELM-based prediction model. All of the 7 wells in the studied area have DT logs now, although two of them are generated using KELM model.

In reservoir description phase, seismic profiles are just wiggle-based and not so convenient for researchers to understand and identify the potential fluid zone. Thus transforming the wiggle shape of seismic sections into velocity or lithological profiles are the necessary step in seismic interpretation. That goal of transformation in geophysical process is the seismic inversion. Since DT log has time unit and velocity information, while seismic data is just in time unit, in the inversion task, DT can be used to do the well-to-seismic calibration and mark the reservoir interval. Here we just focus on the KELM-estimated DT application in the seismic inversion other than discussing the complex inversion technique.

Figure 5 shows part section of the seismic inversion result for line 400 using the predicted DT log of well S205.

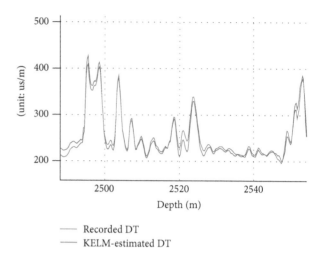

Recorded DT
KELM-estimated DT

FIGURE 3: Logs comparison in Shanxi group of Permian formation in well S215.

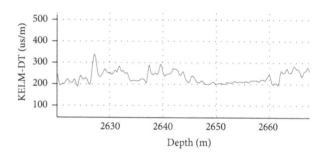

FIGURE 4: Estimated DT log using KELM model (colored in blue) for S219.

The inversion result is colored, and the color stands for the velocity change within the Permian formation. Warm color of red and yellow is the high velocity area, while the cold color of green and blue is the relatively low velocity area. Since the rocks within the interval have the difference in velocity reference, the color changes can be viewed as the lithology component difference. Normally sandstone has higher velocity than mudstone, and coal layer has the lowest velocity character. Therefore warm color in the section represents the sandstone area, while the pure blue color is the index of coal layer. So when interpreting the inversion result with the geological reference, we may divide the interval into three parts: the upper part-I, which is mainly composed of sandstone and mudstone and the farther is richer, the middle part-II, with upper half-dominant coal layer and lower half-dominant sandstone, and the lower part-III, which has almost the same bedding principal as the middle part, with thinner sandstone and coal layer. The estimated DT log is inserted as color plot and the meaning of color ranges is the same as the inversion section. It almost matches the section in color resolution, and that is the normal phenomenon. DT log has finer sample interval than the section, and, for the section, more focus will be directed to the horizontal color difference interpretation. The continuous horizontal color zones mean a lot for the geologists and engineers.

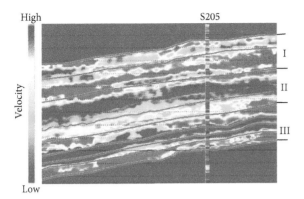

FIGURE 5: KELM-based inverted velocity section crossing well S205.

5. Conclusions

This paper discusses kernel extreme learning machine as a tool for predicting the sonic log in gas/oil wells based on other available common logs. Strict steps including data normalization, training set selection, and optimization of the ELM parameters are very important for deciding the prediction power, the generalization capability, and the complexity of the derived regression model. Extensive applications are carried on to investigate the prediction power of model-predicted DT log use for seismic inversion.

The method presented here is not limited to modeling DT logs only. It can be extended, with appropriate modifications of the algorithm, in any area of well logging studies, where missing log values are needed. Thus, we offer a blueprint for future similar applications.

Competing Interests

The authors declare that they have no conflict of interests.

Acknowledgments

This work is supported by National Natural Science Foundation of China (no. 61402331). The Foundation of Educational Commission of Tianjin City, China (Grant no. 20140803) also funded this research.

References

[1] A. F. Al-Anazi and I. D. Gates, "Support vector regression to predict porosity and permeability: effect of sample size," *Computers and Geosciences*, vol. 39, pp. 64–76, 2012.

[2] J. Asadisaghandi and P. Tahmasebi, "Comparative evaluation of back-propagation neural network learning algorithms and empirical correlations for prediction of oil PVT properties in Iran oilfields," *Journal of Petroleum Science and Engineering*, vol. 78, no. 2, pp. 464–475, 2011.

[3] M. Baneshi, M. Behzadijo, M. Schaffie, and H. Nezamabadi-Pour, "Predicting log data by using artificial neural networks to approximate petrophysical parameters of formation," *Petroleum Science and Technology*, vol. 31, no. 12, pp. 1238–1248, 2013.

[4] C. Cranganu and M. Breaban, "Using support vector regression to estimate sonic log distributions: a case study from the Anadarko Basin, Oklahoma," *Journal of Petroleum Science and Engineering*, vol. 103, pp. 1–13, 2013.

[5] S. Chikhi and M. Batouche, "Probabilistic neural method combined with radial-bias functions applied to reservoir characterization in the Algerian Triassic province," *Journal of Geophysics and Engineering*, vol. 1, no. 2, pp. 134–142, 2004.

[6] H. Khoshdel and M. A. Riahi, "Multi attribute transform and neural network in porosity estimation of an offshore oil field—a case study," *Journal of Petroleum Science and Engineering*, vol. 78, no. 3-4, pp. 740–747, 2011.

[7] J. R. Hearst, P. H. Nelson, and F. L. Paillet, *Well Logging for Physical Properties*, John Wiley & Sons, 2000.

[8] A. Kouider El Ouahed, D. Tiab, A. Mazouzi, and A. J. Safraz, "Application of artificial intelligence to characterize naturally fractured reservoirs," Paper SPE 84870, 2013.

[9] A. Ouenes, "Practical application of fuzzy logic and neural networks to fractured reservoir characterization," *Computers & Geosciences*, vol. 26, no. 8, pp. 953–962, 2000.

[10] R. S. Zazoun, "Fracture density estimation from core and conventional well logs data using artificial neural networks: the Cambro-Ordovician reservoir of Mesdar oil field, Algeria," *Journal of African Earth Sciences*, vol. 83, pp. 55–73, 2013.

[11] R. B. C. Gharbi and G. A. Mansoori, "An introduction to artificial intelligence applications in petroleum exploration and production," *Journal of Petroleum Science and Engineering*, vol. 49, no. 3-4, pp. 93–96, 2005.

[12] G.-B. Huang, Q.-Y. Zhu, and C.-K. Siew, "Extreme learning machine: a new learning scheme of feedforward neural networks," in *Proceedings of the IEEE International Joint Conference on Neural Networks*, pp. 985–990, Budapest, Hungary, July 2004.

[13] G.-B. Huang, Q.-Y. Zhu, and C.-K. Siew, "Extreme learning machine: theory and applications," *Neurocomputing*, vol. 70, no. 1–3, pp. 489–501, 2006.

[14] H. Zhong, C. Miao, Z. Shen, and Y. Feng, "Comparing the learning effectiveness of BP, ELM, I-ELM, and SVM for corporate credit ratings," *Neurocomputing*, vol. 128, pp. 285–295, 2014.

[15] J. B. Butcher, D. Verstraeten, B. Schrauwen, C. R. Day, and P. W. Haycock, "Reservoir computing and extreme learning machines for non-linear time-series data analysis," *Neural Networks*, vol. 38, pp. 76–89, 2013.

[16] J. Cao, J. Yang, Y. Wang, D. Wang, and Y. Shi, "Extreme learning machine for reservoir parameter estimation in heterogeneous sandstone reservoir," *Mathematical Problems in Engineering*, vol. 2015, Article ID 287816, 10 pages, 2015.

[17] R. Minhas, A. Baradarani, S. Seifzadeh, and Q. M. Jonathan Wu, "Human action recognition using extreme learning machine based on visual vocabularies," *Neurocomputing*, vol. 73, no. 10–12, pp. 1906–1917, 2010.

[18] R. Moreno, F. Corona, A. Lendasse, M. Graña, and L. S. Galvão, "Extreme learning machines for soybean classification in remote sensing hyperspectral images," *Neurocomputing*, vol. 128, pp. 207–216, 2014.

[19] G.-B. Huang, D. H. Wang, and Y. Lan, "Extreme learning machines: a survey," *International Journal of Machine Learning and Cybernetics*, vol. 2, no. 2, pp. 107–122, 2011.

[20] S. Shamshirband, K. Mohammadi, H.-L. Chen, G. N. Samy, D. Petković, and C. Ma, "Daily global solar radiation prediction from air temperatures using kernel extreme learning machine: a case study for Iran," *Journal of Atmospheric and Solar-Terrestrial Physics*, vol. 134, pp. 109–117, 2015.

[21] G.-B. Huang, H. Zhou, X. Ding, and R. Zhang, "Extreme learning machine for regression and multiclass classification," *IEEE
Transactions on Systems, Man, and Cybernetics, Part B: Cybernetics*, vol. 42, no. 2, pp. 513–529, 2012.

[22] S. Baziar, M. Tadayoni, M. Nabi-Bidhendi, and M. Khalili, "Prediction of permeability in a tight gas reservoir by using three soft
computing approaches: a comparative study," *Journal of Natural
Gas Science and Engineering*, vol. 21, pp. 718–724, 2014.

14

Speaker Recognition using Wavelet Packet Entropy, I-Vector, and Cosine Distance Scoring

Lei Lei and She Kun

Laboratory of Cyberspace, School of Information and Software Engineering, University of Electronic Science and Technology of China, Chengdu 610054, China

Correspondence should be addressed to She Kun; kun@uestc.edu.cn

Academic Editor: Lei Zhang

Today, more and more people have benefited from the speaker recognition. However, the accuracy of speaker recognition often drops off rapidly because of the low-quality speech and noise. This paper proposed a new speaker recognition model based on wavelet packet entropy (WPE), i-vector, and cosine distance scoring (CDS). In the proposed model, WPE transforms the speeches into short-term spectrum feature vectors (short vectors) and resists the noise. I-vector is generated from those short vectors and characterizes speech to improve the recognition accuracy. CDS fast compares with the difference between two i-vectors to give out the recognition result. The proposed model is evaluated by TIMIT speech database. The results of the experiments show that the proposed model can obtain good performance in clear and noisy environment and be insensitive to the low-quality speech, but the time cost of the model is high. To reduce the time cost, the parallel computation is used.

1. Introduction

Speaker recognition refers to recognizing the unknown persons from their voices. With the use of speech as a biometric in access system, more and more ordinary persons have benefited from this technology [1]. An example is the automatic speech-based access system. Compared with the conventional password-based system, this system is more suitable for old people whose eyes cannot see clearly and figures are clumsy.

With the development of phone-based service, the speech used for recognition is usually recorded by phone. However, the quality of phone speech is low for recognition because the sampling rate of the phone speech is only 8 KHz. Moreover, the ambient noise and channel noise cannot be completely removed. Therefore, it is necessary to find a speaker recognition model that is not sensitive to those factors such as noise and low-quality speech.

In a speaker recognition model, the speech is firstly transformed into one or many feature vectors that represent unique information for a particular speaker irrespective of the speech content [2]. The most widely used feature vector is the short vector, because it is easy to compute and yield good

performance [3]. Usually, the short vector is extracted by Mel frequency cepstral coefficient (MFCC) method [4]. This method can represent the speech spectrum in compacted form, but the extracted short vector represents only the static information of the speech. To represent the dynamic information, the Fused MFCC (FMFCC) method [5] is proposed. This method calculates not only the cepstral coefficients but also the delta derivatives, so the short vector extracted by this method can represent both the static and dynamic information.

Both of the two methods use discrete Fourier transform (DFT) to obtain the frequency spectrum. DFT decomposes the signal into a global frequency domain. If a part of frequency is destroyed by noise, the whole spectrum will be strongly interfered [6]. In other words, the DFT-based extraction methods, such as MFCC and FMFCC, are insensitive to the noise. Wavelet packet transform (WPT) [7] is other type of tool used to obtain the frequency spectrum. Compared with the DFT, WPT decomposes the speech into many small frequency bands that are independent of each other. Because of those independent bands, the ill effect of noise cannot be transmitted over the whole spectrum. In other words, WPT has antinoise ability. Based on WPT, wavelet packet entropy

(WPE) [8] method is proposed to extract the short vector. References [8–11] have shown that the short vector extracted by WPE is insensitive to noise.

I-vector is another type of feature vector. It is a robust way to represent a speech using a single high-dimension vector and it is generated by the short vectors. I-vector considers both of the speaker-dependent and background information, so it usually leads to good accuracy. References [12–14] have used it to enhance the performance of speaker recognition model. Specially, [15] uses the i-vector to improve the discrimination of the low-quality speech. Usually, the i-vector is generated from the short vectors extracted by the MFCC or FMFCC methods, but we employ the WPE to extract those short vectors, because the WPE can resist the ill effect of noise.

Once the speeches are transformed into the feature vectors, a classifier is used to recognize the identity of speaker based on those feature vectors. Gaussian mixture model (GMM) is a conventional classifier. Because it is fast and simple, GMM has been widely used for speaker recognition [4, 16]. However, if the dimension of the feature vector is high, the curse of dimension will destroy this classifier. Unfortunately, i-vector is high-dimensional vector compared with the short vector. Cosine distance scoring (CDS) is another type of classifier used for the speaker recognition [17]. This classifier uses a kernel function to deal with the problem of high-dimension vector, so it is suitable for the i-vector. In this paper, we employ the CDS for speaker classification.

The main work of this paper is to propose a new speaker recognition model by using the wavelet packet entropy (WPE), i-vector, and cosine distance scoring (CDS). WPE is used to extract the short vectors from speeches, because it is robust against the noise. I-vector is generated from those short vectors. It is used to characterize the speeches used for recognition to improve the discrimination of the low-quality speech. CDS is very suitable for high-dimension vector such as i-vector, because it uses a kernel function to deal with the curse of dimension. To improve the discrimination of the i-vector, linear discriminant analysis (LDA) and the covariance normalization (WCNN) are added to the CDS. Our proposed model is evaluated by TIMIT database. The result of the experiments show that the proposed model can deal with the low-quality speech problem and resist the ill effect of noise. However, the time cost of the new model is high, because extracting WPE is time-consuming. This paper calculates the WPE in a parallel way to reduce the time cost.

The rest of this paper is organized as follows. In Section 2, we describe the conventional speaker recognition model. In Section 3, the speaker recognition model based on i-vector is described. We propose a new speaker recognition model in Section 4, and the performance of the proposed model is reported in Section 5. Finally, we give out a conclusion in Section 6.

2. The Conventional Speaker Recognition Model

Conventional speaker recognition model can be divided into two parts such as short vector extraction and speaker classification. The short vector extraction transforms the speech into the short vectors and the speaker classification uses a classifier to give out the recognition result based on the short vectors.

2.1. Short Vector Extraction. Mel frequency cepstral coefficient (MFCC) method is the conventional short vector extraction algorithm. This method firstly decomposes the speech into 20–30 ms speech frames. For each frame, the cepstral coefficient can be calculated as follows [18]:

(1) Take DFT of the frame to obtain the frequency spectrum.

(2) Map the power of the spectrum onto Mel scale using the Mel filter bank.

(3) Calculate the logarithm value of the power spectrum mapped on the Mel scale.

(4) Take DCT of logarithmic power spectrum to obtain the cepstral coefficient.

Usually, the lower 13-14 coefficients are used to form the short vector. Fused MFCC (FMFCC) method is the extension of MFCC. Compared with MFCC, it further calculates the delta derivatives to represent the dynamic information of speech. The derivatives are defined as follows [5]:

$$d_i = \frac{\sum_{p=1}^{2} p\left(cc_{i-p} + cc_{i+p}\right)}{2\sum_{p=1}^{2} p^2},$$

$$dd_i = \frac{\sum_{p=1}^{2} p\left(d_{i-p} + d_{i+p}\right)}{2\sum_{p=1}^{2} p^2}; \quad (1)$$

$$i = 1, 2, 3, \ldots,$$

where cc_i is the ith cepstral coefficient obtained by the MFCC method and p is the offset. d_i is the ith delta coefficient and dd_i is the ith delta-delta coefficient. If the short vector extracted by MFCC is denoted as $[cc_1, cc_2, cc_3, \ldots, cc_I]^T$, then the short vector extracted by FMFCC is denoted as $[cc_1, cc_2, cc_3, \ldots, cc_I; d_1, d_2, \ldots, d_I; dd_1, dd_2, \ldots, dd_I]^T$.

2.2. Speaker Classification. Gaussian mixture model (GMM) is a conventional classifier. It is defined as

$$p(\mathbf{x}) = \sum_{m=1}^{M} \alpha_m G\left(\mathbf{x}; \boldsymbol{\mu}_m, \boldsymbol{\Sigma}_m\right), \quad (2)$$

where $\mathbf{x}$ is a short vector extracted from an unknown speech. $G(\mathbf{x}; \boldsymbol{\mu}_m, \boldsymbol{\Sigma}_m)$ is the mth Gaussian function in GMM, where $\boldsymbol{\mu}_m, \boldsymbol{\Sigma}_m$ are its mean vector and variance matrix, respectively. α_m is the combination weight of the Gaussian function and satisfies $\sum_{m=1}^{M} \alpha_m = 1$. M is the mixture number of the GMM. All of the parameters, such as weights, mean vectors, and variance matrices, are estimated by the famous EM algorithm [19] using the speech samples of a known speaker. In other words, $p(\mathbf{x})$ represents the characteristic of the known speaker's voice, so we use $p(\mathbf{x})$ to recognize the author of

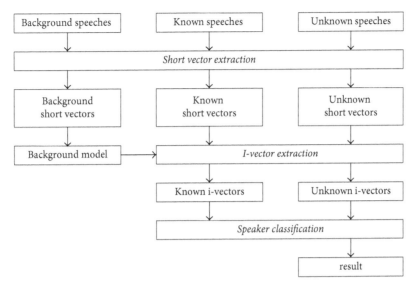

FIGURE 1: The structure of the speaker recognition using i-vector.

the unknown speeches. Assume that an unknown speech is denoted by $\mathbf{Y} = \{\mathbf{y}_1, \mathbf{y}_2, \ldots, \mathbf{y}_N\}$, where $\mathbf{y}_i$ represents the ith short vector extracted from $\mathbf{Y}$. Also, assume that the parameters of $p(\mathbf{x})$ are estimated using the speech samples of a known speaker s. The result of recognition is defined as

$$r = \frac{1}{N} \sum_{i=1}^{N} \log \left[p\left(\mathbf{y}_i\right)\right] + \theta, \tag{3}$$

where $\theta > 0$ is the decision threshold and should be adjusted beforehand to obtain the best recognition performance. If $r \leq 0$, then the GMM decides that the author of the unknown speech is not the known speaker s; if the $r > 0$, then the GMM decides that the unknown speech is spoken by the speaker s.

3. The Speaker Recognition Model Using I-Vector

The speaker recognition model using i-vector can be decomposed into three parts such as short vector extraction, i-vector extraction, and speaker classification. Figure 1 shows the structure of the model.

There are three types of speeches used for this model. Background speeches contains thousands of speeches spoken by lots of people, the known speeches are the speech samples of known speakers, and the unknown speeches are spoken by the speaker to be recognized. In the short vector extraction, all of the speeches are transformed into the short vectors by a feature extraction method. In the i-vector extraction, the background short vectors are used to train the background model. The background model is usually represented by a GMM with 2048 mixtures, and all covariance matrices of the GMM are assumed the same for easy computation. Based on the background model, the known and unknown short vectors are used to extract the known and unknown i-vectors, respectively. Note that one i-vector refers to only one speech. In the speaker classification, a classifier is used to match the

known i-vector with the unknown i-vector and give out the recognition result.

4. The Proposed Speaker Recognition Model

The accuracy of recognition system usually drops off rapidly because of the low-quality speech and noise. To deal with the problem, we propose a new speaker recognition model based on wavelet packet entropy (WPE), i-vector, and cosine distance scoring (CDS). In Section 4.1, we describe the WPE method and use it to extract the short vector. Section 4.2 describes how to extract the i-vector using the above short vectors. Finally, the details of CDS are described in Section 4.3.

4.1. Short Vector Extraction. This paper uses WPE to extract the short vector. The WPE is based on the wavelet packet transform (WPT) [20], so the WPT is firstly described. WPT is a local signal processing approach that is used to obtain the frequency spectrum. It decomposes the speech into many local frequency bands at multiple levels and obtains the frequency spectrum based on the bands. For the discrete signal such as digital speech, WPT is usually implemented by the famous Mallat fast algorithm [21]. In the algorithm, WPT is realized by a low-pass filter and a high-pass filter, which are generated by the mother wavelet and the corresponding scale function, respectively. Through the two filters, the speech is iteratively decomposed into a low-frequency and a high-frequency components. We can use a full binary tree to describe the process of WPT. The three structures are shown in Figure 2.

In Figure 2, root is the speech to be analyzed. Each nonroot node represents a component. The left child is the low-frequency component of its parent and the right child is the high-frequency component of its parent. The left branch and the right branch are the low-pass and high-pass filtering

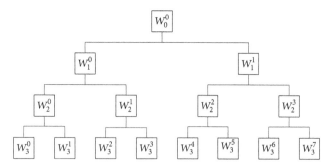

FIGURE 2: The wavelet packet transform at 2 levels.

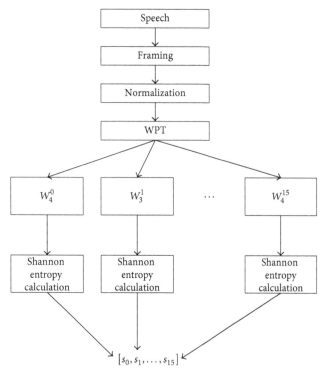

FIGURE 3: The flow chart of wavelet packet entropy.

processes followed by $2:1$ downsampling, respectively. The filtering processes are defined as

$$\mathbf{W}_{j+1}^{2k}(n) = \mathbf{W}_j^k * \mathbf{h}(2n),$$

$$\mathbf{W}_{j+1}^{2k+1}(n) = \mathbf{W}_j^k * \mathbf{g}(2n); \qquad (4)$$

$$0 \le k \le 2^j, \ 0 \le j \le J, \ 0 \le n \le N_j,$$

where $\mathbf{h}$ and $\mathbf{g}$ are the low-pass and high-pass filter, respectively. N_j is the length of the frequency component at level j. $*$ is the convolution operation. J is the total number of the decomposition levels. Because the WPT satisfies the conservation of energy, each leaf node denotes the spectrum of the frequency bands obtained by WPT. Based on the WPT, the wavelet packet entropy (WPE) method is proposed to extract the short vector and we add a normalization step into the method to reduce the ill effect of the volume in this paper. The flow chart of WPE used in this paper is shown in Figure 3.

Assume that there is a digital speech signal that has finite energy and length. It is firstly decomposed into 20 ms frames, and then each frame is normalized. The normalization process is defined as

$$\overline{f}[m] = \frac{f[m] - \mu}{\sigma}; \quad i = 1, 2, 3, \ldots, M, \qquad (5)$$

where f is a signal frame and M is its length. μ is the mean value of the frame and σ is its standard variance. $\overline{f}$ is the normalized frame. After the normalization process, the WPT decomposes the frame at 4 levels using (4). Therefore, we finally obtain 16 frequency bands, and the frequency spectrums in those bands are denoted as $W_4^0, W_4^1, \ldots, W_4^{15}$, respectively. For each spectrum, the Shannon entropy is calculated. The Shannon entropy is denoted as

$$s_k = -\sum_{n=1}^{N} p_{k,n} \log(p_{k,n}); \quad k = 0, 2, 3, \ldots, 7 \qquad (6)$$

with

$$p_{k,n} = \frac{\left| W_4^k(n) \right|^2}{e_k},$$

$$e_k = \sum_{n=1}^{N} \left| W_4^k(n) \right|^2, \qquad (7)$$

where e_k is the energy of the kth spectrum. $p_{k,n}$ is the energy distribution of the kth spectrum. N is the length of each frequency spectrum. Finally, all of Shannon entropies of all spectrums are calculated and are collected to form a feature vector that is denoted as $[s_0, s_1, \ldots, s_7]^T$.

4.2. I-Vector Extraction. I-vector is a robust feature vector that represents a speech using a single high-dimension vector. Because it considers the background information, i-vector usually improves the accuracy of recognition [22]. Assume that there is a set of speeches. Those speeches are supplied by different speakers and the all speeches are transformed into the short vectors. In the i-vector theory, the speaker- and channel-dependent feature vector is assumed as

$$\overline{\mathbf{m}} = \mathbf{m} + \mathbf{Tw}(\mathbf{U}), \qquad (8)$$

where $\overline{\mathbf{m}}$ is the speaker- and channel-dependent feature vector. $\mathbf{m}$ is the background factor. Usually, it is generated by stacking the mean vectors of a background model. Assume that the mean vectors of the background model are denoted by $\boldsymbol{\mu}_1^T, \boldsymbol{\mu}_2^T, \ldots, \boldsymbol{\mu}_N^T$, where each mean vector is a row vector. $\mathbf{m}$ is denoted by $[\boldsymbol{\mu}_1, \boldsymbol{\mu}_2, \ldots, \boldsymbol{\mu}_N]^T$. $\mathbf{T}$ is named the total variability matrix and represents a space that contains the speaker- and channel-dependent information. $\mathbf{w}(\mathbf{U})$ is a random vector having standard normal distribution $N(0, 1)$. The i-vector is the expectation of the $\mathbf{w}(\mathbf{U})$. $\mathbf{U}$ is a set of speeches and all of speeches are transformed into the short vectors. Assume that a background model is given, and $\mathbf{\Sigma}$ is initialized by covariance matrix of the background model. $\mathbf{T}$ and $\mathbf{w}(\mathbf{U})$ are initialized randomly. $\mathbf{T}$ and $\mathbf{w}(\mathbf{U})$ are estimated by an iteratively process described as follows:

(1) E-step: for each speech in the set $\mathbf{U}$, calculate the parameters of the posterior distribution of $\mathbf{w}(\mathbf{U})$ using the current estimates of $\mathbf{T}$, $\mathbf{\Sigma}$, and $\mathbf{m}$.

(2) M-step: update $\mathbf{T}$ and $\mathbf{\Sigma}$ by a linear regression in which $\mathbf{w}(\mathbf{U})$s play the role of explanatory variables.

(3) Iterate until the expectation of the $\mathbf{w}(\mathbf{U})$ is stable.

The details of the estimation processes of $\mathbf{T}$ and $\mathbf{w}(\mathbf{U})$ are described in [23].

4.3. Speaker Classification. Cosine distance scoring (CDS) is used as the classifier in our proposed model. It uses a kernel function to deal with the curse of dimension, so CDS is very suitable for the i-vector. To describe this classifier easily, we take a two-classification task, for example. Assume that there are two speakers denoted as s_1 and s_2. The two speakers, respectively, speak N_1 and N_2 speeches. All speeches are represented by i-vectors and are denoted by $X^1 = \{\mathbf{x}_1^1, \mathbf{x}_2^1, \ldots, \mathbf{x}_{N_1}^1\}$ and $X^2 = \{\mathbf{x}_1^2, \mathbf{x}_2^2, \ldots, \mathbf{x}_{N_2}^2\}$, where $\mathbf{x}_j^i$ is i-vector representing the jth speech sample of the speaker s_i. We also assume there is an unknown speech represented by i-vector $\mathbf{y}$. The purpose of the classifier is to match the unknown i-vector with the known i-vectors and determine which one speaks the unknown speech. the result of the recognition is defined as

$$D_i(\mathbf{y}) = \frac{1}{N_i} \sum_{n=1}^{N_i} K(\mathbf{x}_n^i, \mathbf{y}) + \theta; \quad i = 1, 2, \qquad (9)$$

where N_i is the total number of speeches supported by the speaker s_i. θ is the decision threshold. If $D_i(\mathbf{y}) \leq \mathbf{0}$, the unknown speeches are not spoken by the known speaker s_i; if $D_i(\mathbf{y}) > \mathbf{0}$, then author of the unknown speeches is the speaker s_i. $K(\cdot, \cdot)$ is the cosine kernel and is defined as

$$K(\mathbf{x}, \mathbf{y}) = \frac{\mathbf{x}\mathbf{y}^T}{\sqrt{\mathbf{x}\mathbf{x}^T}\sqrt{\mathbf{y}\mathbf{y}^T}}, \qquad (10)$$

where $\mathbf{x}$ is the known i-vector and $\mathbf{y}$ is the unknown i-vector. Usually, the linear discriminant analysis (LDA) and within class covariance normalization (WCCN) are used to implement the discrimination of the i-vector. Therefore, the kernel function is rewritten as

$$K(\mathbf{x}, \mathbf{y}) = \frac{\left(\mathbf{A}^T\mathbf{x}\right)\mathbf{W}^{-1}\left(\mathbf{A}^T\mathbf{y}\right)}{\sqrt{\left(\mathbf{A}^T\mathbf{x}\right)\mathbf{W}^{-1}\left(\mathbf{A}^T\mathbf{x}\right)}\sqrt{\left(\mathbf{A}^T\mathbf{y}\right)\mathbf{W}^{-1}\left(\mathbf{A}^T\mathbf{y}\right)}}, \qquad (11)$$

where $\mathbf{A}$ is the LDA projection matrix and $\mathbf{W}$ is WCCN matrix. $\mathbf{A}$ and $\mathbf{W}$ are estimated by using all of the i-vectors and the details of LAD and WCCN are described in [24].

5. Experiment and Results

In this section, we report the outcome of our experiments. In Section 5.1, we describe the experimental dataset. In Section 5.2, we carry on an experiment to select the optimal mother wavelet for the WPE algorithm. In Section 5.3, we evaluate the recognition accuracy of our model. In Section 5.4, we evaluate the performance of the proposed model. Finally, the time cost of the model is count in Section 5.5.

5.1. Experimental Dataset. The results of our experiments are performed on the TIMIT speech database [25]. This database contains 630 speakers (192 females and 438 males) who come from 8 different English dialect regions. Each speaker supplies ten speech samples that are sampled at 16 KHz and last 5 seconds. All female speeches are used to obtain background models that represent the common characteristic of the female voice. Also, all male speeches are used to generate another background model characterizing the male voice. 384 speakers (192 females and 192 males) are randomly selected and their speeches are used as the known and unknown speeches. The test results presented in our experiments are collected on a computer with 2.5 GHz Intel Core i5 CPU and 8 GM of memory and the experimental platform is MATLAB R2012b.

5.2. Optimal Mother Wavelet. A good mother wavelet can improve the performance of the WPE algorithm. The performance of a mother wavelet is based on two important elements such as the support size and the number of vanishing moments. If a mother wavelet has large number of vanish moments, the WPE would ignore much of unimportant information; if the mother wavelet has small support size, the WPE would accurately locate important information [26]. Therefore, an optimal mother wavelet should have a large number of vanishing moments and a small support size. In this view, the Daubechies and Symlet wavelets are good wavelets, because they have the largest number of vanishing moments for a given support size. Moreover, those wavelets are orthogonal and are suitable for the Mallat fast algorithm.

In is paper, we use the Energy-to-Shannon Entropy Ratio (ESER) to evaluate those Daubechies and Symlet wavelets to find out the best one. ESER is a way to analyze the performance of mother wavelet and has been employed to select the best mother wavelet in [27]. The ESER is defined as

$$r = \frac{E}{S}, \qquad (12)$$

where S is the Shannon entropy of the spectrum obtained by WPT and E was the energy of the spectrum. The high energy means the spectrum obtained by WPT contained much enough information of the speech. The low entropy means that the information in the spectrum is stable. Therefore, the optimal mother wavelet should maximize the energy and meanwhile minimize the entropy.

In this experiment, 8 Daubechies and 8 Symlet wavelets, which are, respectively, denoted as db1–8 and sym1–8, are employed to decompose speeches that are randomly selected from the TIMIT database. We run the experiment 100 times and record the average WSER of those mother wavelets in Table 1.

In Table 1, We find that db4 and sym6 obtain the highest ESER. In other words, the db4 and sysm6 are the best mother wavelets for the speech data. Reference [28] suggests that the sym6 can improve the performance of the speaker recognition model. However, the Symlet wavelets produce the complex coefficients whose imaginary parts are redundant for the real signal such as digital speech, so we abandon the sym6 and choose the db4.

TABLE 1: The average WSER of the mother wavelets.

Mother wavelet	ESER
db1	888.37
db2	890.32
db3	897.44
db4	**908.49**
db5	901.41
db6	896.53
db7	891.69
db8	890.84
sym1	888.35
sym2	890.36
sym3	894.93
sym4	899.75
sym5	903.82
sym6	**908.59**
sym7	902.44
sym8	898.37

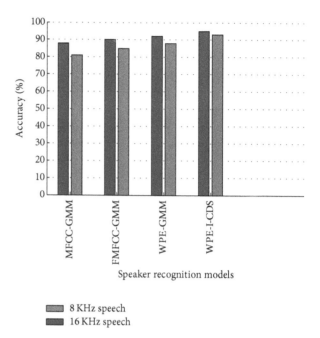

FIGURE 4: The mean accuracy of 4 models in clean environment.

5.3. The Accuracy of Speaker Recognition Model in Clear Environment. This experiment evaluates the accuracy of the speaker recognition model. We randomly select 384 speakers (192 females and 192 males). For each speaker, half of speeches are used as the unknown speech and the other half of speeches are used as the known speeches. For each speaker, the speaker recognition model matches the his/her unknown speeches with all of the known speeches of the 384 speakers and determines who speaks the unknown speeches. If the result is right, the model obtains one score; if the result is wrong, the model gets zero score. Finally, we count the score and calculate the mean accuracy that is defined as

$$\text{accuray} = \frac{\text{score}}{384} \times 100\%. \tag{13}$$

In this experiment, we use four types of speaker recognition models for comparison. The first one is the MFCC-GMM model [4]. This model uses MFCC method to extract 14D short vectors and uses the GMM with 8 mixtures to recognize speaker based on those short vectors. The second one is FMFCC-GMM model [16]. This model is very similar to the MFCC-GMM model, but it uses the FMFCC method to extract the 52D short vectors. The third one is the WPE-GMM model [10]. This model firstly uses WPE to transform the speeches into 16D short vectors and then uses GMM for speaker classification. The last one was the WPE-I-CDS model proposed in this paper. Compared with WPE-GMM model, our model uses the 16D short vectors to generate 400D i-vector and uses CDS to recognize speaker based on the i-vector. We carry on each experiment in this section 25 times to obtain the mean accuracy. The mean accuracy of the above 4 models is shown in Figure 4.

In Figure 4, we find that MFCC-GMM obtains the lowest accuracy of 88.46%. The result of [4] shows the MFCC-GMM model can obtain accuracy of higher than 90%. This is because we use the GMM with 8 mixtures as the classifier, but [4] uses the GMM with 32 mixtures as the classifier. Large

mixture number can improve the performance of the GMM, but it also causes the very high computational expense. WPE-I-CDS obtain the highest accuracy of 94.36%. This interprets the achievements of i-vector theory. On the other hand, when the 8 KHz speeches (low-quality speeches) are used, all accuracy of speaker recognition models is decreased. The accuracy of MFCC-GMM, FMFCC-GMM, and WPE-GMM decrease by about 6%. Comparatively, the accuracy of WPE-I-CDS decreases by about 1%. This is because the i-vector considers the i-vector to improve the accuracy of the speaker recognition model, and the CDS used the LDA and WCCN to improve the discrimination of the i-vector. Reference [29] also reports that the combination of the i-vector and the CDS can enhance the performance of speaker recognition model used for low-quality speeches such as phone speeches.

5.4. The Accuracy of Speaker Recognition Model in Noisy Environment. It is hard to find a clean speech in the real applications, because the noise in the transmission channel and environment cannot be controlled. In this experiment, we add 30 dB, 20 dB, and 10 dB Gaussian white noise into the speeches to simulate the noisy speeches. All noises are generated by the MATLAB's Gaussian white noise function.

For comparison, this experiment employed three i-vector based models such as MFCC-I-CDS [30], FMFCC-I-CD [31], and our WPE-I-CDS. The two models are very similar to our proposed model, but they use the MFCC and FMFCC to extract the short vectors, respectively. The accuracy of the 3 models in noisy environment is shown in Figure 5.

In Figure 5, the three models obtained high accuracy in clean environment. This also shows that the i-vector can improve the recognition accuracy effectively. However, when we use the noisy speeches to test the 3 models, their accuracies decrease. When 30 dB noise is added to the speeches, the

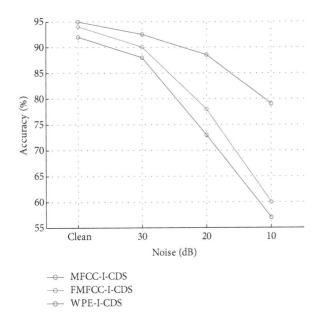

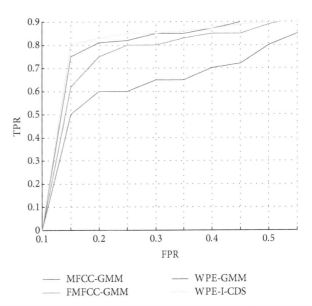

FIGURE 5: The accuracy of the 3 models in noisy environment.

FIGURE 6: The ROC curves of TPR versus FPR.

accuracy of the three models decreases by about 4%. This shows that all of the models can resist weak noise. However, when we enhance the power of noise, the accuracy of MFCC-I-CDS and FMFCC-I-CDS drops off rapidly. In particular, when the noise increases into 10 dB, the accuracy of the above two models decreases by more than 30%. Comparatively, the WPE-I-CDS's accuracy decreases by less than 12%. Those show that the WPE-I-CDS is robust in noisy environment compared with MFCC-I-CDS and FMFCC-I-CDS. This is because the WPE uses the WPT to obtain the frequency spectrum but MFCC and FMFCC use the DFT to do that. The WPT decomposes the speech into many local frequency bands that can limit the ill effect of noise, but the DFT decomposes the speech into a global frequency domain that is sensitive to the noise.

5.5. The Performance of the Speaker Recognition Model. Usually, the speaker recognition model is used in the access control system. Therefore, a good speaker recognition model should have ability to accept the login of the correct people and meanwhile to reject the access of the imposter, as a gatekeeper does. In this experiment, we use the receiver operating characteristic (ROC) curve to evaluate the ability of our model. The ROC curve shows the true positive rate (TPR) as a function of the false positive rate (FPR) for different values of the decision threshold and has been employed in [2].

In this experiment, we randomly select 384 speakers (192 males and 192 females) to calculate the ROC curve. Half of those speakers are used as the correct people and another half of the speakers are used as the imposters. We firstly use the speeches of the correct people to test the speaker recognition model to calculate the TPR, and then we use the speeches of the imposters to attack the speaker recognition

model to calculate the FPR. The 4 models, such as MFCC-GMM, FMFCC-GMM, WPE-GMM, and our WPE-I-CDS, are used for comparison. To plot the ROC curve, we adjusted the decision thresholds to obtain different ROC points. The ROC curves of those 4 models were shown in Figure 6.

Low FPR shows that the speaker recognition model can effectively resist the attack coming from the imposters, and high TPR shows that the speaker recognition model can accurately accept the correct speakers' login. In other words, a speaker recognition model can be useful if its TPR is high for a low FPR. In Figure 6, when FPR is higher than 0.45, all models obtain the high TPR, but WPE-I-CDS obtain higher TPR than other 3 models for a given FPR that is less than 4.5. This shows that the WPE-I-CDS can more effectively achieve the access control task than other models.

5.6. Time Cost. This section tests the time cost of the fast MFCC-GMM, the conventional MFCC-I-CDS, and our WPE-I-CDS. We used 200 5-second-long speeches to test each model and calculated the average time cost. The result of this experiment was shown in Table 2.

In Table 2, MFCC-GMM does not employ the i-vector for speech representation, so it does not cost time to extract the i-vector. Comparatively, the WPE-I-CDS should cost time to extract the i-vector. The WPE-I-CDS cost the most time to extract the short vector compared with the MFCC-GMM. This is because the WPT used by WPE is more complex than the DFT used by the MFCC. On the other hand, the parameters of GMM should be estimated beforehand, as MFCC-GMM cost time to train the classifier. CDS needs not cost time to estimate the parameters, but it should cost time to estimate the matrices of the LDA and WCNN in the training classifier step. In all, the i-vector can improve the recognition accuracy at cost of increasing the time consumption and calculating the WPE costs too much time compared with

TABLE 2: The time cost of the different speaker recognition models.

Speaker recognition model	Feature extraction (s/speech)		Speaker classification (s/speech)	
	Short vector extraction	I-vector extraction	Training classifier	Recognition
MFCC-GMM	0.46	—	1.92	0.64
MFCC-I-CDS	0.45	2.37	1.81	0.73
WPE-I-CDS	2.81	2.24	1.82	0.75
WPE-I-CDS (parallel computation)	0.78	2.23	1.82	0.74

calculating the MFCC. Therefore, it is very important to find way to reduce the time cost of the WPE.

Parallel computation is an effective way to reduce the time cost, because the loops in the linear computation can be finished at once using a parallel algorithm. For example, a signal, whose length is N, is decomposed by WPT at M levels. In the conventional linear algorithm of WPT, we have to run a filtering process whose time complexity was $O(\log N)$ $M \times N$ times for each decomposition level, so the total time cost of WPT is $O(MN \log N)$. If we used N independent computational cores to implant the WPT using a parallel algorithm, the time complexity of WPT can reduce to $O(M \log N)$. This paper uses 16 independent computational cores to implement the WPE parallel algorithm, and the last line of Table 2 shows that the time cost of WPE is reduced very much.

6. Conclusions

With the development of the computer technique, the speaker recognition has been widely used for speech-based access system. In the real environment, the quality of the speech may be low and noise in the transformation channel cannot be controlled. Therefore, it is necessary to find a speaker recognition model that is not sensitive to those factors such as noise and low-quality speech.

This paper proposes a new speaker recognition model by employing wavelet packet entropy (WPE), i-vector, and CDS, and we name the model WPE-I-CDS. WPE used a local analysis tool named WPT rather than the DFT to decompose the signal. Because WPT decomposes the signal into many independent frequency bands that limit the ill effect of noise, the WPE is robust in the noisy environment. I-vector is a type of robust feature vector. Because it considers the background information, i-vector can improve the accuracy of recognition. CDS uses a kernel function to deal with the curse of dimension, so it is suitable for the high-dimension feature vector such as i-vector. The result of the experiments in this paper shows that the proposed speaker recognition models can improve the performance of recognition compared with the conventional models such as MFCC-GMM, FMFCC-GMM, and WPE-GMM in clean environment. Moreover, the WPE-I-CDS obtains higher accuracy than other i-vector-based models such as MFCC-I-CDS and FMFCC-I-CDS in noisy environment. However, the time cost of the proposed model is very higher. To reduce the time cost, we employ the parallel algorithm to implement the WPE and i-vector extraction methods.

In the future, we will combine audio and visual feature to improve the performance of the speaker recognition system.

Conflicts of Interest

The authors declare that they have no conflicts of interest.

Acknowledgments

The authors also thank Professor Kun She for their assistance in preparation of the manuscript. This paper is supported by the Project of Sichuan Provincial Science Plan (M112016GZ0073) and National Nature Foundation (Grant no. 61672136).

References

[1] H. Perez, J. Martinez, and I. Espinosa, "Using acoustic paraliguistic information to assess the interaction quality in speech-based system for elder users," *International Jounrnal of Human-Computer Studies*, vol. 98, pp. 1–13, 2017.

[2] N. Almaadeed, A. Aggoun, and A. Amira, "Speaker identification using multimodal neural networks and wavelet analysis," *IET Biometrics*, vol. 4, no. 1, pp. 18–28, 2015.

[3] T. Kinnunen and H. Li, "An overview of text-independent speaker recognition: from features to supervectors," *Speech Communication*, vol. 52, no. 1, pp. 12–40, 2010.

[4] D. A. Reynolds and R. C. Rose, "Robust text-independent speaker identification using gaussian mixture speaker models," *IEEE Transactions on Speech and Audio Processing*, vol. 3, no. 1, pp. 72–83, 1995.

[5] K. S. Ahmad, A. S. Thosar, J. H. Nirmal, and V. S. Pande, "A unique approach in text-independent speaker recognition using mfcc feature sets and probabilistic neural network," in *Proceedings of the 8th International Conference on Advances in Pattern Recognition (ICAPR '15)*, Kolkata, India, 2015.

[6] X.-Y. Zhang, J. Bai, and W.-Z. Liang, "The speech recognition system based on bark wavelet MFCC," in *Proceedings of the 8th International Conference on Signal Processing (ICSP '06)*, pp. 16–20, Beijing, China, 2006.

[7] A. Biswas, P. K. Sahu, and M. Chandra, "Admissible wavelet packet features based on human inner ear frequency response for Hindi consonant recognition," *Computer & Communication Technology*, vol. 40, pp. 1111–1122, 2014.

[8] K. Daqrouq and T. A. Tutunji, "Speaker identification using vowels features through a combined method of formants, wavelets, and neural network classifiers," *Applied Soft Computing*, vol. 27, pp. 231–239, 2015.

[9] D. Avci, "An expert system for speaker identification using adaptive wavelet sure entropy," *Expert Systems with Applications*, vol. 36, no. 3, pp. 6295–6300, 2009.

[10] K. Daqrouq, "Wavelet entropy and neural network for text-independent speaker identification," *Engineering Applications of Artificial Intelligence*, vol. 24, no. 5, pp. 796–802, 2011.

[11] M. K. Elyaberani, S. H. Mahmoodian, and G. Sheikhi, "Wavelet packet entropy in speaker-identification emotional state detection from speech signal," *Journal of Intelligent Procedures in Electrical Technology*, vol. 20, pp. 67–74, 2015.

[12] M. Li, A. Tsiartas, M. Van Segbroeck, and S. S. Narayanan, "Speaker verification using simplified and supervised i-vector modeling," in *Proceedings of the 38th IEEE International Conference on Acoustics, Speech, and Signal Processing (ICASSP '13)*, pp. 7199–7203, Vancouver, Canada, 2013.

[13] D. Garcia-Romero and A. McCree, "Supervised domain adaptation for i-vector based speaker recognition," in *Proceedings of the IEEE International Conference on Acoustics Speech and Signal Processing*, pp. 4047–4051, Florence, Italy, 2014.

[14] A. Kanagasundaram, D. Dean, and S. Sridharan, "I-vector based speaker recognition using advanced channel compensation techniques," *Computer Speech & Labguage*, vol. 28, pp. 121–140, 2014.

[15] M. H. Bahari, R. Saeidi, H. Van Hamme, and D. Van Leeuwen, "Accent recognition using i-vector, gaussian mean supervector and gaussian posterior probability supervector for spontaneous telephone speech," in *Proceedings of the IEEE International Conference on Acoustics, Speech and Signal Processing*, pp. 7344–7348, IEEE, Vancouver, Canada, 2013.

[16] B. Saha and K. Kamarauslas, "Evaluation of effectiveness of different methods in speaker recognition," *Elektronika ir Elektrochnika*, vol. 98, pp. 67–70, 2015.

[17] K. K. George, C. S. Kumar, K. I. Ramachandran, and A. Panda, "Cosine distance features for robust speaker verification," in *Proceedings of the 16th Annual Conference of the International Speech Communication Association (INTERSPEECH '15)*, pp. 234–238, Dresden, Germany, 2015.

[18] B. G. Nagaraja and H. S. Jayanna, "Efficient window for monolingual and crosslingual speaker identification using MFCC," in *Proceedings of the International Conference on Advanced Computing and Communication Systems (ICACCS '13)*, pp. 1–4, Coimbatore, India, 2013.

[19] M. Medeiros, G. Araújo, H. Macedo, M. Chella, and L. Matos, "Multi-kernel approach to parallelization of EM algorithm for GMM training," in *Proceedings of the 3rd Brazilian Conference on Intelligent Systems (BRACIS '14)*, pp. 158–165, Sao Paulo, Brazil, 2014.

[20] H. R. Tohidypour, S. A. Seyyedsalehi, and H. Behbood, "Comparison between wavelet packet transform, Bark Wavelet & MFCC for robust speech recognition tasks," in *Proceedings of the 2nd International Conference on Industrial Mechatronics and Automation (ICIMA '10)*, pp. 329–332, Wuhan, China, 2010.

[21] X.-F. Lv and P. Tao, "Mallat algorithm of wavelet for time-varying system parametric identification," in *Proceedings of the 25th Chinese Control and Decision Conference (CCDC '13)*, pp. 1554–1556, Guiyang, China, 2013.

[22] D. Marthnez, O. Pichot, and L. Burget, "Language recognition in I-vector space," in *Proceedongs of the Interspeech*, pp. 861–864, Florence, Italy, 2011.

[23] P. Kenny, G. Boulianne, and P. Dumouchel, "Eigenvoice modeling with sparse training data," *IEEE Transactions on Speech and Audio Processing*, vol. 13, no. 3, pp. 345–354, 2005.

[24] M. McLaren and D. Van Leeuwen, "Improved speaker recognition when using i-vectors from multiple speech sources," in *Proceedings of the 36th IEEE International Conference on Acoustics, Speech, and Signal Processing (ICASSP '11)*, pp. 5460–5463, Prague, Czech Republic, 2011.

[25] A. Biswas, P. K. Sahu, A. Bhowmick, and M. Chandra, "Feature extraction technique using ERB like wavelet sub-band periodic and aperiodic decomposition for TIMIT phoneme recognition," *International Journal of Speech Technology*, vol. 17, no. 4, pp. 389–399, 2014.

[26] S. G. Mallat, *A Wavelet Tour of Signal Processing*, ELsevier, Amsterdam, Netherlands, 2012.

[27] Q. Yang and J. Wang, "Multi-level wavelet shannon entropy-based method for single-sensor fault location," *Entropy*, vol. 17, no. 10, pp. 7101–7117, 2015.

[28] T. Ganchev, M. Siafarikas, I. Mporas, and T. Stoyanova, "Wavelet basis selection for enhanced speech parametrization in speaker verification," *International Journal of Speech Technology*, vol. 17, no. 1, pp. 27–36, 2014.

[29] M. Seboussaoui, P. Kenny, and N. Dehak, "An i-vector extractor suitable for speaker recognition with both microphone and telephone speech," *Odyssey*, vol. 6, pp. 1–6, 2011.

[30] N. Dehak, R. Dehak, P. Kenny, N. Brummer, P. Ouellet, and P. Dumouchel, "Support vector machines versus fast scoring in the low-dimensional total variability space for speaker verification," in *Proceedings of the 10th Annual Conference of the International Speech Communication Association (INTERSPEECH '09)*, pp. 1559–1562, Brighton, United Kingdom, 2009.

[31] M. I. Mandasari, M. McLaren, and D. Van Leeuwen, "Evaluation of i-vector speaker recognition systems for forensic application," in *12th Annual Conference of the International Speech Communication Association (INTERSPEECH '11)*, pp. 21–24, Florence, Italy, 2011.

15

Detection and Visualization of Android Malware Behavior

Oscar Somarriba,[1,2] Urko Zurutuza,[1] Roberto Uribeetxeberria,[1] Laurent Delosières,[3] and Simin Nadjm-Tehrani[4]

[1]Electronics and Computing Department, Mondragon University, 20500 Mondragon, Spain
[2]National University of Engineering (UNI), P.O. Box 5595, Managua, Nicaragua
[3]ExoClick SL, 08005 Barcelona, Spain
[4]Department of Computer and Information Science, Linköping University, 581 83 Linköping, Sweden

Correspondence should be addressed to Oscar Somarriba; oscar.somarriba@gmail.com

Academic Editor: Aniket Mahanti

Malware analysts still need to manually inspect malware samples that are considered suspicious by heuristic rules. They dissect software pieces and look for malware evidence in the code. The increasing number of malicious applications targeting Android devices raises the demand for analyzing them to find where the malcode is triggered when user interacts with them. In this paper a framework to monitor and visualize Android applications' anomalous function calls is described. Our approach includes platform-independent application instrumentation, introducing hooks in order to trace restricted API functions used at runtime of the application. These function calls are collected at a central server where the application behavior filtering and a visualization take place. This can help Android malware analysts in visually inspecting what the application under study does, easily identifying such malicious functions.

1. Introduction

Collecting a large amount of data issued by applications for smartphones is essential for making statistics about the applications' usage or characterizing the applications. Characterizing applications might be useful for designing both an anomaly-detection system and/or a misuse detecting system, for instance.

Nowadays, smartphones running on an Android platform represent an overwhelming majority of smartphones [1]. However, Android platforms put restrictions on applications for security reasons. These restrictions prevent us from easily collecting traces without modifying the firmware or rooting the smartphone. Since modifying the firmware or rooting the smartphone may void the warranty of the smartphone, this method cannot be deployed on a large scale.

From the security point of view, the increase in the number of internet-connected mobile devices worldwide, along with a gradual adoption of LTE/4G, has drawn the attention of attackers seeking to exploit vulnerabilities and mobile infrastructures. Therefore, the malware targeting

smartphones has grown exponentially. Android malware is one of the major security issues and fast growing threats facing the Internet in the mobile arena, today. Moreover, mobile users increasingly rely on unofficial repositories in order to freely install paid applications whose protection measures are at least dubious or unknown. Some of these Android applications have been uploaded to such repositories by malevolent communities that incorporate malicious code into them. This poses strong security and privacy issues both to users and operators. Thus, further work is needed to investigate threats that are expected due to further proliferation and connectivity of gadgets and applications for smart mobile devices.

This work focuses on monitoring Android applications' suspicious behavior at runtime and visualizing their malicious functions to understand the intention behind them. We propose a platform-independent behavior monitoring infrastructure composed of four elements: (i) an Android application that guides the user in selecting, instrumenting, and monitoring of the application to be examined, (ii) an embedded client that is inserted in each application to be

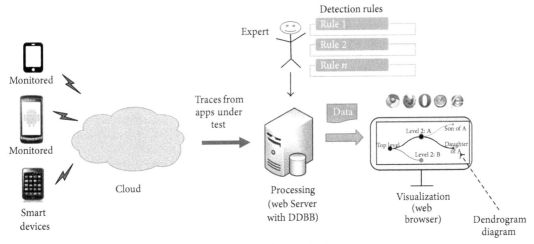

FIGURE 1: Overview of the monitoring system.

monitored, (iii) a cloud service that collects the application to be instrumented and also the traces related to the function calls, (iv) and finally a visualization component that generates behavior-related dendrograms out of the traces. A dendrogram [2] consists of many U-shaped nodes-lines that connect data of the Android application (e.g., the package name of the application, Java classes, and methods and functions invoked) in a hierarchical tree. As a matter of fact, we are interested in the functions and methods which are frequently seen in malicious code. Thus, malicious behavior could be highlighted in the dendrogram based on a predefined set of anomaly rules. An overview of the monitoring system is shown in Figure 1.

Monitoring an application at runtime is essential to understand how it interacts with the device, with key components such as the provided application programming interfaces (APIs). An API specifies how some software components (routines, protocols, and tools) should act when subject to invocations by other components. By tracing and analyzing these interactions, we are able to find out how the applications behave, handle sensitive data, and interact with the operating system. In short, Android offers a set of API functions for applications to access protected resources [3].

The remainder of the paper is organized as follows. Section 2 provides the notions behind the components used in the rest of the paper. Next, the related work is discussed in Section 3. Next we describe the monitoring and visualization architecture in Section 4, while we provide the details of the implementational issues of our system in Section 5. Later, in Section 6, we evaluate the proposed infrastructure and the obtained results by using 8 malware applications. Limitations and Conclusions are presented in Sections 7 and 8, respectively.

2. Background

Web Services extend the World Wide Web infrastructure to provide the means for software to connect to other software applications [4]. RESTFul Web Services are Web Services that use the principles of REpresentational State Transfer (REST) [5]. In other words, they expose resources to clients that

can be accessed through the Hypertext Transfer Protocol (HTTP).

Regarding the Android operating system (OS), it is divided into four main layers: applications, application framework, middleware, and Linux kernel.

(i) Applications. The top layer of the architecture is where the applications are located. An Android application is composed of several components, amongst which we have Activities and Services. Activities provide a user interface (UI) of the application and are executed one at a time, while Services are used for background processing such as communication, for instance.

(ii) Application Framework. This layer is a suite of Services that provides the environment in which Android applications run and are managed. These programs provide higher-level Services to applications in the form of Java classes.

(iii) Middleware. This layer is composed of the Android runtime (RT) and C/C++ libraries. The Android RT is, at the same time, composed of the Dalvik Virtual Machine (DVM) (Android version 4.4. launches a new virtual machine called Android runtime (ART). ART has more advanced performance than DVM, among other things, by means of a number of new features such as the ahead-of-time (OTA) compilation, enhanced garbage collection, improved application debugging, and more accurate high-level profiling of the apps [6]) and a set of native (core) Android functions. The DVM is a key part of Android as it is the software where all applications run on Android devices. Each application that is executed on Android runs on a separate Linux process with an individual instance of the DVM, meaning that multiple instances of the DVM exist at the same time. This is managed by the Zygote process, which generates a fork of the parent DVM instance with the core libraries whenever it receives a request from the runtime process.

(iv) Linux Kernel. The bottom layer of the architecture is where the Linux kernel is located. This provides basic system functionality like process and memory management.

The kernel also handles a set of drivers for interfacing Android and interacting with the device hardware.

In standard Java environments, Java source code is compiled into Java bytecode, which is stored within .class format files. These files are later read by the Java Virtual Machine (JVM) at runtime. On Android, on the other hand, Java source code that has been compiled into .class files is converted to .dex files, frequently called Dalvik Executable, by the "dx" tool. In brief, the .dex file stores the Dalvik bytecode to be executed on the DVM.

Android applications are presented on an Android application package file (APK) .apk, the container of the application binary that contains the compiled .dex files and the resource files of the app. In this way, every Android application is packed using zip algorithm. An unpacked app has the following structure (several files and folders) [7]:

(i) an *AndroidManifest.xml* file: it contains the settings of the application (meta-data) such as the permissions required to run the application, the name of the application, definition of one or more components such as Activities, Services, Broadcasting Receivers, or Content Providers. Upon installing, this file is read by the *PackageManager*, which takes care of setting up and deploying the application on the Android platform.

(ii) a *res* folder: it contains the resources used by the applications. By resources, we mean the app icon, its strings available in several languages, images, UI layouts, menus, and so forth.

(iii) an *assets* folder: it stores noncompiled resources. This is a folder containing applications assets, which can be retrieved by *AssetManager*.

(iv) a *classes.dex* file: it stores the classes compiled in the dex file format to be executed on the DVM.

(v) a *META-INF* folder: this directory includes *MANIFEST.MF* which contains a cryptographic signature of the application developer certificate to validate the distribution.

The resulting .apk file is signed with a keystore to establish the identity of the author of the application. Besides, to build Android applications, a software developer kit (SDK) is usually available allowing access to APIs of the OS [8]. Additionally, two more components are described in order to clarify the background of this work: the Android-apktool [9] and the Smali/Backsmali tools. The Android-apktool is generally used to unpack and disassemble Android applications. It is also used to assemble and pack them. It is a tool set for reverse engineering third party Android apps that simplifies the process of assembling and disassembling Android binary .apk files into Smali .smali files and the application resources to their original form. It includes the Smali/Baksmali tools, which can decode resources (i.e., .dex files) to nearly original form of the source code and rebuild them after making some modifications. This enables all these assembling/disassembling operations to be performed automatically in an easy yet reliable way.

However, it is worth noting that the repackaged Android binary .apk files can only possess the same digital signature if the original keystore is used. Otherwise, the new application will have a completely different digital signature.

3. Related Work

Previous works have addressed the problem of understanding the Android application behavior in several ways. An example of inspection mechanisms for identification of malware applications for Android OS is presented by Karami et al. [10] where they developed a transparent instrumentation system for automating the user interactions to study different functionalities of an app. Additionally, they introduced runtime behavior analysis of an application using input/output (I/O) system calls gathered by the monitored application within the Linux kernel. Bugiel et al. [11] propose a security framework named *XManDroid* that extends the monitoring mechanism of Android, in order to detect and prevent application-level privilege escalation attacks at runtime based on a given policy. The principal disadvantage of this approach is that the modified framework of Android has to be ported for each of the devices and Android versions in which it is intended to be implemented. Unlike [10, 11], we profile only at the user level and therefore we do not need to root or to change the framework of Android smartphones if we would like to monitor the network traffic, for example.

Other authors have proposed different security techniques regarding permissions in Android applications. For instance, Au et al. [12] present a tool to extract the permission specification from Android OS source code. Unlike the other methods, the modules named Dr. Android and Mr. Hide that are part of a proposed and implemented app by Jeon et al. [13] do not intend to monitor any smart phones. They aim at refining the Android permissions by embedding a module inside each Android application. In other words, they can control the permissions via their module. We also embed a module inside each Android application but it is used to monitor the Android application instead.

In the work by Zhang et al. [3], they have proposed a system called *VetDroid* which can be described as a systematic analysis technique using an app's permission use. By using real-world malware, they identify the callsites where the app requests sensitive resources and how the obtained permission resources are subsequently utilized by the app. To do that, *VetDroid* intercepts all the calls to the Android API and synchronously monitors permission check information from Android permission enforcement system. In this way, it manages to reconstruct the malicious (permission use) behaviors of the malicious code and to generate a more accurate permission mapping than PScout [12]. Briefly this system [3] applies dynamic taint analysis to identify malware. Different from *VetDroid*, we do not need to root or jailbreak the phone nor do we conduct the permission-use approach for monitoring the smartphone.

Malware detection (MD) techniques for smart devices can be classified according to how the code is analyzed, namely, static analysis and dynamic analysis. In the former case, there is an attempt to identify malicious code by decompiling/disassembling the application and searching for suspicious strings or blocks of code; in the latter case the behavior of the application is analyzed using execution information. Examples of the two named categories are *Dendroid* [2] as an example of a static MD for Android OS devices and *Crowdroid* as a system that clusters system call frequency of applications to detect malware [14]. Also, hybrid approaches have been proposed in the literature for detection and mitigation of Android malware. For example, Patel and Buddhadev [15] combine Android applications analysis and machine learning (ML) to classify the applications using static and dynamic analysis techniques. Genetic algorithm based ML technique is used to generate a rules-based model of the system.

A thorough survey by Jiang and Zhou [16] charts the most common types of permission violations in a large data set of malware. Furthermore, in [17], a learning-based method is proposed for the detection of malware that analyzes applications automatically. This approach combines static analysis with an explicit feature map inspired by a linear-time graph kernel to represent Android applications based on their function call graphs. Also, Arp et al. [18] combine concepts from broad static analysis (gathering as many features of an application as possible) and machine learning. These features are embedded in a joint vector space, so typical patterns indicative of malware can be automatically identified in a lightweight app installed in the smart device. Shabtai et al. [19] presented a system for mobile malware detection that takes into account the analysis of deviations in application networks behavior (app's network traffic patterns). This approach tackles the challenge of the detection of an emerging type of malware with self-updating capabilities based on runtime malware detector (anomaly-detection system) and it is also standalone monitoring application for smart devices.

Considering that [17] and Arp et al. [18] utilize static methods, they suffer from the inherent limitations of static code analysis (e.g., obfuscation techniques, junk code to evade successful decompilation). In the first case, their malware detection is based upon the structural similarity of static call graphs that are processed over approximations, while our method relies upon real functions calls that can be filtered later on. In the case of Debrin, transformation attacks that are nondetectable by static analysis, as, for example, based on reflection and bytecode encryption, can hinder an accurate detection.

Although in [19] we have a detection system that continuously monitors app executions. There is a concern about efficiency of the detection algorithm used by this system. Unfortunately, in this case, they could not evaluate the Features Extractor and the aggregation processes' impact on the mobile phone resources, due to the fact that an extended list of features was taken into account. To further enhance the system's performance, it is necessary to retain only the most effective features in such a way that the runtime malware detector system yields relatively low overhead on the mobile phone resources.

Our proposed infrastructure is related to the approaches mentioned above and employs similar features for identifying malicious applications, such as permissions, network addresses, API calls, and function call graphs. However, it differs in three central aspects from previous work. First, we have a runtime malware detection (dynamic analysis) but abstain from crafting detection in protected environment as the dynamic inspections done by *VetDroid*. While this system provides detailed information about the behavior of applications, they are technically too involved to be deployed on smartphones and detect malicious software directly. Second, our visual analysis system is based on accurate API call graphs, which enables us to inspect directly the app in an easy-to-follow manner in the cloud. Third, we are able to monitor not just the network traffic, but most of the restricted and suspicious API calls in Android. Our platform is more dynamic and simpler than other approaches mentioned above.

General overview of the state of security in mobile devices and approaches to deal with malware can be found in [20], and in the work by Suarez-Tangil et al. in [21], as well as in recent surveys by Faruki et al. in [7] and Sufatrio et al. [6]. Malware in smart devices still poses many challenges and, in different occasions, a tool for monitoring applications at a large scale might be required. Given the different versions of Android OS, and with a rising number of device firmwares, modifying each of the devices might become a nontrivial task. This is the scenario in which the proposed infrastructure in this paper best fits. The core contribution of this work is the development of a monitoring and instrumentation system that allows a visual analysis of the behavior of Android applications for any device on which an instrumented application can run. In particular, our work results in a set of dendrograms that visually render existing API calls invoked by Android malware application, by using dynamic inspection during a given time interval, and visually highlighting the suspicious ones. Consequently, we aim to fill the void of visual security tools which are easy to follow for Android environments in the technical literature.

4. Platform Architecture

When Android applications are executed, they call a set of functions that are either defined by the developer of the application or are part of the Android API. Our approach is based on monitoring a desired subset of the functions (i.e., hooked functions) called by the application and then uploading information related to their usage to a remote server. The hooked function traces are then represented in a graph structure, and a set of rules are applied to color the graphs in order to visualize functions that match known malicious behavior.

For this, we use four components: the *Embedded client* and the *Sink* on the smartphone side, and the *Web Service* and the *Visualization component* on the remote server side.

A work flow depicting the main elements of the involved system is shown in Figure 2. In Stage 1, the application under study and a set of permissions are sent to the Web Service. Next, the main processing task of Stage 2, labeled as hooking process, is introduced. In this case, hooks or logging codes are inserted in the functions that require at least one of the permissions specified at the previous stage.

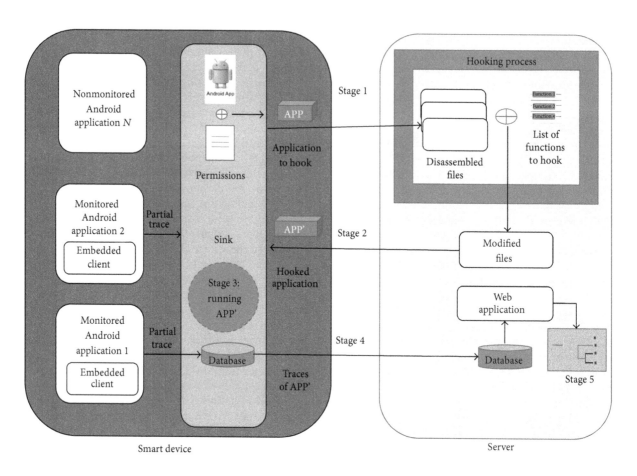

FIGURE 2: Schematics and logical stages of the system.

The new "augmented" application will be referred to as APP' from now on. Stages 3, 4, and 5 consist of running APP', saving the traces generated by APP' in the server's database, and showing the results as visualization graphs, respectively. The aforementioned infrastructure for platform-independent monitoring of Android applications is aimed to provide behavioral analysis without modifying the Android OS or root access to the smart device.

4.1. Embedded Client and Sink. The monitoring system consists of two elements: an embedded client that will be inserted into each application to be monitored and a Sink that will collect the hooked functions that have been called by the monitored applications. The embedded client simply consists of a communication module that uses the User Datagram Protocol (UDP) for forwarding the hooked functions to the Sink. Here, JavaScript Object Notation (JSON) is used when sending the data to the Sink, which allows sending dynamic data structures. In order to know the origin of a hooked function that has been received by the Sink, the corresponding monitored application adds its application hash, its package name, and its application name to the hooked function which we call a partial trace before sending it to the Sink.

The partial traces are built by the prologue functions (i.e., hook functions) that are placed just before their hooked

functions and which modify the control flow of the monitored applications in order to build the partial traces corresponding with their hooked functions and passing the partial traces as parameter to the embedded client. Only the partial traces are built by the monitored application so that we add little extra overhead to the monitored application. The insertion of the embedded client and of the prologue functions in the Android application that is to be monitored is explained in Section 4.3.

The embedded client is written using the Smali syntax and is included on each of the monitored applications at the Web Service, at the same time that the functions hooks are inserted, before the application is packed back into an Android binary .apk file.

The Sink, on the other hand, is implemented as an Android application for portability both as a service and an activity whose service is started at the boot time. It is responsible for receiving the partial traces issued from all the monitored applications clients via a UDP socket, augmenting the partial traces to get a trace (i.e., adding a timestamp and the hash of the ID of the phone), storing them, and sending them over the network to the Web Service. As for the activity, it is responsible for managing the monitored applications via a UI, sending the applications to hook to the Web Service, and downloading the hooked applications from the Web Service. By hooked applications, we mean the applications in which hooks have been inserted. Once an application has been hooked then we can monitor it.

Before storing the traces in a local database, the Sink first stores them in a circular buffer which can contain up to 500 traces. The traces are flushed to the local database when any of the following conditions are met: (i) when the buffer is half full, (ii) when the Sink service is shutting down, or (iii) upon an activated timeout expiring. This bulk flushing enables the Sink to store the traces more efficiently. Unfortunately, if the service is stopped by force, we lose the traces that are present in the circular buffer. Once the traces are persisted in the local database, the timeout is rescheduled. Every hour, the Sink application tries to send the traces that remain in the local database out to the Web Service. A trace is removed locally upon receiving an acknowledgment from the Web Service. An acknowledgment is issued when the Web Service has been able to record the trace in a SQL database with success. If the client cannot connect to the Web Service, it will try again at the next round.

When a user wants to monitor an application, a message with the package name as payload is sent to the Sink service which keeps track of all the applications to monitor in a list. When a user wants to stop monitoring a given application, a message is sent to the Sink service which removes it from its list of applications to monitor.

4.2. The Web Service. This server provides the following services to *Sink*: upload applications, download the modified applications, and send the traces. Now the key part of the whole system, where the logic of the method presented lies, is the tool that implements the application, a process known as "hooking." In the following, we explain it. The Web Service, implemented as a Servlet on a Tomcat web application server, is a RESTful Web Service which exposes services to clients (e.g., Android smartphone) via resources. The Web Service exposes three resources which are three code pages enabling the Sink to upload an application to hook, download a hooked application, and send traces. The hooking process is explained in more detail in Section 4.3.1.

The file upload service allows the Sink to send the target application to monitor and triggers the command to insert all the required hooks and the embedded client to the application. Also, it is in charge of storing the submitted Android binary .apk file on the server and receiving a list of permissions. This set of permissions will limit the amount of hooks to monitor, hooking only the API function calls linked to these permissions. Conversely, the file download service allows the Sink to download the previously sent application, which is now prepared to be monitored. A ticket system is utilized in order to keep tracking of the current application under monitoring. The trace upstream service allows the Sink to upload the traces stored on the device to the server database and remove the traces from the devices local SQLite database. Upon receiving traces, the Web Service records them in a SQL database and sends an acknowledgment back to the Sink. In case of failure in the server side or in the communication channel, the trace is kept locally in the SQLite database until the trace is stored in the server and an acknowledgment is received by the

Sink. In both cases, it might occur that the trace has just been inserted in the SQL database and no answer is sent back. Then the Sink would send again the same trace and we would get a duplication of traces. However, the mechanism of primary key implemented in the SQL database prevents the duplication of traces. A primary key is composed of one or more data attributes whose combination of values must be unique for each data entry in the database. When two traces contain the same primary key, only one trace is inserted while the insertion of the other one throws an exception. When such an exception is thrown, the Web Service sends back an acknowledgment to the Sink so as to avoid the Sink resending the same trace (i.e., forcing the Sink to remove from its local database the trace that has already been received by the Web Service).

4.3. Instrumenting an Application. In this section, we first describe the process of inserting hooks into an Android application and then we show an example of a hook implementation. A tutorial on instrumentation of Android applications is presented by Arzt et al. in [22].

However, before proceeding with the insertion of instrumentation code to the decompiled APK below, we would like to clarify the effect of disassembling the uploaded applications, that is, the differences between the original code and code generated after instrumentation. Briefly, the disassembling of the uploaded application is performed by using the Smali/Baksmali tool which is assembler/disassembler, respectively, for the dex-format (https://source.android.com/devices/tech/dalvik/dex-format.html). This is the format used by Dalvik, one of the Android's JVM implementations. Thus, the disassembling is able to recover an assembler-like representation of the Java original code. This representation is not the original Java source code (Baksmali is a disassembler, not a decompiler after all). However, Baksmali creates both an exact replica of the original binary code behavior and high-level enough to be able to manipulate it in an easy way. This is why we can add additional instructions to instrument the original code for our purposes and then reassemble it back to a dex file that can be executed by Android's JVM. On the other hand, as discussed in [22], instrumentation of applications outperforms static analysis approaches, as instrumentation code runs as part of the target app, having full access to the runtime state. So, this explains the rationale behind introducing hooks in order to trace core sensitive or restricted API functions used at runtime of the apps. In other words, the Smali code reveals the main restricted APIs utilized by the apps under test, even in the presence of source code obfuscation. We can therefore resort to monitoring these restricted APIs and keep tracking of those Android suspicious programs' behavior.

4.3.1. Hooks Insertion. The hooking process is done in 6 steps: (i) receiving the application to hook from the smartphone, (ii) unpacking the application and disassembling its Dalvik byte code via the Android-apktool, (iii) modifying the application files, (iv) assembling Dalvik byte code and packing the hooked application via the Android-apktool, (v) signing the

```
(1) .class public Lcom/mainactivity/MainActivity;
(2) ...
(3) invoke-static/range {v2 ··· v6}, log_sendTextMessage(···)
(4) invoke-virtual/range {v1 ··· v6}, sendTextMessage(···)
(5) ...
```

LISTING 1: Main activity class.

```
(1) .class public Lorg/test/MonitorLog;
(2) ...
(3) .method public static log_sendTextMessage(···)
(4) ...
(5) const-string v0, "packageName: com.testprivacy,..."
(6) invoke-static {v0}, sendLog(Ljava/lang/String;)
(7) return-void
(8) .end method
(9)
(10) .method public static sendLog(Ljava/lang/String;)
(11) .locals 3
(12) .parameter payload
(13) move-object v0, p0
(14) ...
(15) new-instance v1, Ljava/lang/Thread;
(16) new-instance v2, Lorg/test/EmbeddedClient;
(17) invoke-direct {v2, v0}, init(Ljava/lang/String;)
(18) invoke-direct {v1, v2}, init(Ljava/lang/Runnable;)
(19) invoke-virtual {v1}, start()
(20) return-void
(21) .end method
```

LISTING 2: Monitor log class.

hooked application, and (vi) sending the hooked application upon request of the smartphone.

Step (iii) can be subdivided into several substeps:

(1) adding the Internet permission in the *AndroidManifest* to enable the embedded client inserted in the application to hook to communicate with the Sink via UDP sockets,

(2) parsing the code files and adding invocation instructions to the prologue functions before their corresponding hooked functions: when the monitored application is running, before calling the hooked function, its corresponding prologue function will be called and will build its corresponding partial trace. The list of desired functions to hook is provided by the administrator of the Web Service. For instance, if the administrator is interested in knowing the applications usage, it will hook the functions that are called by the application when starting and when closing,

(3) adding a class that defines the prologue functions: it is worth noting that there will be as many prologue

functions as functions to hook. Each prologue function builds its partial trace. Since we do not log the arguments of the hooked functions, the partial traces that are issued by the same monitored application will only differ by the name of the hooked function. It is also worth noting that the prologue functions are generated automatically.

Since every Android application must be signed by a certificate for being installed on the Android platform, we use the same certificate to check if the hooked application comes from our Web Service. For this, the certificate used in the Web Service has been embedded in the Sink application. This prevents attackers from injecting malicious applications by using a man-in-the-middle attack between the smartphone and the Web Service.

4.3.2. Hook Example. Consider a case where the function *sendTextMessage*, used to send short messages (SMS) on the Android platform, is to be logged in a monitored application. This function is called in the main activity class of the application corresponding to the code Listing 1. As for the class shown in Listing 2, it defines the prologue functions and the function responsible for passing the partial traces, built by the prologue functions, to the embedded client. For space reasons, we will not show the embedded client.

In the main activity class corresponding to the class shown in Listing 1, the function *sendTextMessage* is called at line (4) with its prologue function *log_sendTextMessage* which has been placed just before at line (3). Since the hooked function may modify common registers used for storing the parameters of the hooked function and for returning objects, we have preferred placing the prologue functions before their hooked functions. The register *v1* is the object of the class *SmSManager* needed to call the hooked function. As for the registers *v2* to *v6*, they are used for storing the parameters of the hooked function. Since our prologue functions are declared as static, we can call them without instantiating their class 2, and therefore we do not need to use the register *v1*.

An example of the monitor log class is shown in Listing 2. The name of the class is declared at line (1). At lines (3) and (10), two functions are defined, namely, *log_sendTextMessage* and *sendLog*. The former function, prologue function of the hooked function *sendTextMessage*, defines a constant string object containing the partial trace at line (5) and puts it into the register *v0*. Then the function *sendLog* is called at line (6) with the partial trace as parameter. The latter function saves the partial trace contained in the parameter *p0* into the register *v0* at line (13). At lines (15) and (16), two new instances are created, respectively: a new thread and new instance of the class *EmbeddedClient*. Their instances are initialized, respectively, at lines (17) and (18). Finally, the thread is started at line (19) and the partial trace is sent to the Sink. It is worth noting that, in these two examples, we have omitted some elements of the code which are replaced by dots to facilitate the reading of the code.

4.4. Visualization. The visualization of anomalous behavior is the last component of the proposed architecture. In order to perform a visual analysis of the applications' behavior in a simplified way, a D3.js (or just D3 for Data-Driven Documents (JavaScript library available at http://d3.org/)) graph was used. D3 is an interactive and a browser-based data visualizations library to build from simple bar charts to complex infographics. In this case, it stores and deploys graph oriented data on a tree-like structure named dendrograms using conventional database tables. Generally speaking, a graph visualization is a representation of a set of nodes and the relationships between them shown by links (*vertices* and *edges*, resp.).

This way, we are able to represent each of the analyzed application's behaviors with a simple yet illustrative representation. In general, the graphs are drawn according to the schema depicted in Figure 3. The first left-hand (root) node, "Application," contains the package name of the application, which is unique to each of the existing applications. The second middle node (parent), "Class," represents the name of the Android component that has called the API call. The third node, "Function" (the right-hand or child node), represents the names of functions and methods invoked by the application. It is worth noting that each application can include several classes and each class can call various functions or methods.

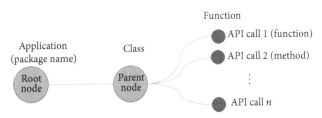

FIGURE 3: Schema used for the dendrograms.

In other words, function calls are located in the right-hand side of the dendrogram. For each node at this depth we are looking for known suspicious functions derived from a set of predefined rules as described below.

4.4.1. Rules "Generation". The rules aim to highlight restricted API calls, which allow access to sensitive data or resources of the smartphone and are frequently found in malware samples. These could be derived from the static analysis where the classes.dex file is converted to Smali format, as mentioned before, to get information considering functions and methods invoked by the application under test. On the other hand, it is well know that many types of malicious behaviors can be observed during runtime only. For this reason we utilize dynamic analysis; that is, Android applications are executed on the proposed infrastructure (see Figure 2) and interact with them. As a matter of fact, we are only interested in observing the Java based calls, which are mainly for runtime activities of the applications. This includes data accessed by the application, location of the user, data written to the files, phone calls, sending SMS/MMS, and data sent and received to or from the networks.

For the case that an application requires user interactions, we resort to do that manually so far. Alternatively, for this purpose one can use MonkeyRunner toolkit, which is available in Android SDK.

In [18, 23], authors list API functions calls that grant access to restricted data or sensible resources of the smartphone, which are very often seen in malicious code. We base our detection rules in those suspicious APIS calls. In particular, we use the following types of suspicious APIs:

(i) API calls for accessing sensitive data, for example, IMEI and USIMnumbeleakage, such as *getDeviceId()*, *getSimSerialNumber()*, *getImei()*, and *getSubscriberId()*,

(ii) API calls for communicating over the network, for example, *setWifiEnabled()* and *execHttpRequest()*,

(iii) API calls for sending and receiving SMS/MMS messages, such as *sendTextMessage()*, *SendBroadcast()*, and *sendDataMessage()*,

(iv) API calls for location leakage, such as *getLastKnownLocation()* and *getLatitude()*, *getLongitude()*, and *requestLocationUpdates()*,

(v) API function calls for execution of external or particular commands like *Runtime.exec()*, and *Ljava/lang/Runtime; -> exec()*,

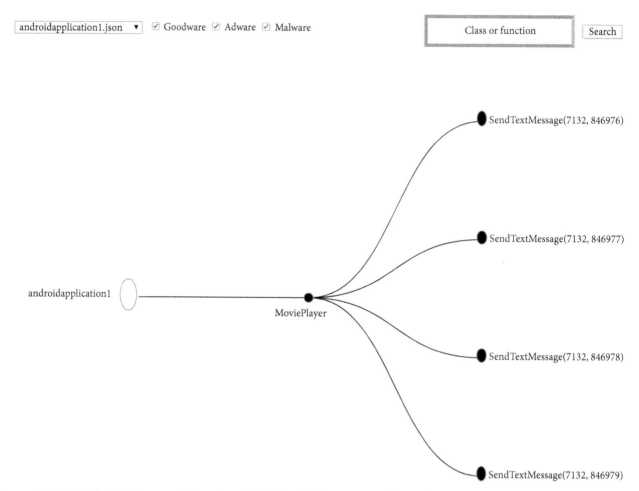

FIGURE 4: The simplified dendrogram of the malware *FlakePlayer* has been generated using the D3. Note that at the upper left corner of the figure there is a combobox to select the monitored malware (here, for simplicity, we use a shortened version of package name of the app, i.e., *androidapplication1*). Besides, lining up to the right of the combobox, there are three activated checkboxes, labeled as Goodware in blue, Adware in orange, and Malware in red. Also, at the upper right corner of the figure, there is a *search button* that allows us to look for classes or functions. The complete package name of the malware *FakePlayer* is *org.me.androidapplication1.MoviePlayer*.

(vi) API calls frequently used for obfuscation and loading of code, such as *DexClassLoader.Loadclass()* and *Cipher.getInstance()*.

Here the rule module uses the above-mentioned API calls to classify the functions and methods invoked on the runtime of the applications into three classes, that is, Benign, Adware, or Malware. So in this way, we can generate IF-THEN rules (cf. rules-based expert systems). Next we show example rules that describe suspicious behavior. Some of the rules generated by us are similar or resemble the ones in [24], namely,

(1) a rule that shows that the examined app is not allowed to get the location of the smart device user:

IF Not (*ACCESS_FINE_LOCATION*) AND *CALL_getLastKnownLocation* THEN Malware,

(2) another rule which might detect that the application is trying to access sensitive data of the smartphone without permission:

IF Not (*READ_PHONE_STATE*) AND *CALL_getImei* THEN Malware.

Our approach selects from the database those functions that have been executed that match the suspicious functions described in the rules. Package name and class name of such function are colored accordingly to the "semaphoric" labeling described in Section 6.1.

To illustrate the basic idea we choose a malware sample, known as *FakePlayer*, in order to draw its graph. Thus, by means of running the filtering and visualization operations we end up with the graph of the malware, shown in Figure 4.

The system allows adding new rules in order to select and color more families of suspicious functions.

5. Testbed and Experimentation

Before introducing the reader into the results of using the monitoring and visualization platform, we need to explain the testbed. We first describe the experiment setup; then we follow the steps of running the client-side Sink.

5.1. Experiment Set Up. All the experiments have been realized on a Samsung Nexus S with Android Ice Cream

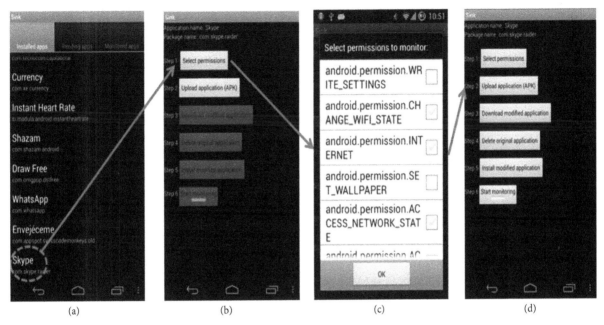

FIGURE 5: User interface of the Sink. (a) Choosing the application, (b) selecting the menu for permissions, (c) electing the permissions, and (d) steps of the monitoring process.

Sandwich (ICS). The Nexus S has a 1 GHz ARM Cortex A8 based CPU core with a PowerVR SGX 540 GPU, 512 MB of dedicated RAM, and 16 GB of NAND memory, partitioned as 1 GB internal storage and 15 GB USB storage.

We have explored different Android applications in order to evaluate the whole framework; some of these samples have been taken from the Android Malware Genome Project (The Android Malware Genome Project dataset is accessible at http://www.malgenomeproject.org/):

(i) *FakePlayer malware*,

(ii) *SMSReplicator malware*,

(iii) *iMatch malware*,

(iv) *DroidKungFu1 malware*,

(v) *DroidKungfu4 malware*,

(vi) *The spyware GoldDream in two flavors*,

(vii) *GGTracker malware*.

5.2. Client-Side Monitoring. The activities in Figure 5(a) display all the applications installed on the device that did not come preinstalled, from which the user selects a target application to monitor. Once an application is selected, the next step is to choose which permission or permissions the user wants to monitor. This can be observed in the third snapshot (white background) of Figure 5(c). Following the permissions clearance, the interface guides the user along several activities starting with the uploading of the selected application which is sent to the Web Service where the hooks are inserted. After this hooking process has finished, the modified application is downloaded from the Web Service. Afterwards, the original application is uninstalled and replaced by the modified application. Finally, a toggle allows starting and stoping monitoring of the application at any time by the user.

We focus on the functions of the Android API that require, at least, one permission. This allows the user to select from the Sink those permissions that are to be monitored at each application. This allows understanding how and when these applications use the restricted API functions. The PScout [12] tool was used to obtain the list of functions in the "API permission map." This way, the permission map obtained contains (Android 4.2 version API level 17) over thirty thousand unique function calls and around seventy-five different permissions. Besides, it is worth mentioning here that we refer to those associated with a sensitive API as well as sensitive data stored on device and privacy-sensitive built-in sensors (GPS, camera, etc.) as "restricted API functions." The first group is any function that might generate a "cost" for the user or the network. These APIs include [8], among others, Telephony, SMS/MMS, Network/Data, In-App Billing, and NFC (Near Field Communication) Access. Thus, by using the API map contained in the server's database, we are able to create a list of restricted ("suspicious") API functions.

The trace managing part is a service that runs in background with no interface and is in charge of collecting the traces sent from the individual embedded clients, located on each of the monitored applications. It adds a timestamp and the hash of the device ID and stores them on a common circular buffer. Finally, the traces are stored in bulk on a common local SQLite database and are periodically sent to the Web Service and deleted from the local database.

In summary, the required steps to successfully run an Android modified instrumented application are listed in Figure 5(d) and comprise the following.

Step 1 (select permissions). Set up and run the platform. Choose an application APP to be monitored on the device. Elect the permission list.

Step 2 (upload the application (APK)). Then, when this command is launched to upload the applications to the Web Service, the hooking process is triggered.

Step 3 (download modified application). This starts the downloading of the hooked application.

Step 4 (delete original application). This command starts the uninstallation process of the original application.

Step 5 (install modified application). This command starts the installation process of the modified application using Android's default application installation window.

Step 6 (start monitoring). Finally, a toggle is enabled and can be activated or disabled to start or stop monitoring that application as chosen by the user.

6. Results

To evaluate our framework, in this section we show the visualization results for several different applications to both benign and malicious. Then we proceed to evaluate the Sink application in terms of CPU utilization and ratio of partial traces received. Finally, we estimate the CPU utilization of a monitored application and its responsiveness.

6.1. Visual Analysis of the Traces. As mentioned before, a set of predefined rules allows us to identify the suspicious API functions and depending on its parameters (e.g., application attempts to send SMS to a short code that uses premium services) we assign colors to them. This enables us to quickly identify the functions and associate them with related items. On top of that, by applying the color classification of each node of the graph associated with a function in accordance with the color code (gray, orange, and red) explained below, it allows a "visual map" to be partially constructed. Furthermore, this graph is suitable to guide the analyst during the examination of a sample classified as dangerous because, for example, the red shading of nodes indicates malicious structures identified by the monitoring infrastructure.

In particular, to give a flavor to this analysis, the dendrogram of *FakePlayer* in Figure 4 provides the user with an indication of the security status of the malware. Different colors indicate the level of alarm associated with the currently analyzed application:

(i) Gray indicates that no malicious activity has been detected, as of yet.

(ii) Orange indicates that no malicious behavior has been detected in its graph, although some Adware may be presented.

(iii) Red indicates in its graph that a particular application has been diagnosed as anomalous, meaning that it contained one or more "dangerous functions"

described in our blacklist. Moreover, it could imply the presence of suspicious API calls such as *sendTextMessage* with forbidden parameters, or the case of using restricted API calls for which the required permissions have not been requested (root exploit).

So, it is possible to conduct a visual analysis of the permissions and function calls invoked per application, where using some kind of "semaphoric labeling" allows us to identify easily the benign (in gray and orange colors) applications. For instance, in Figure 4 there is a presence of malware, and the nodes are painted in red.

The dendrogram shown for *FakePlayer* confirms its sneaky functionality by forwarding all the SMS sent to the device to the previously set phone number remaining unnoticed. For the sake of simplicity, we reduce the API function call *sendTextMessage*(phoneNo, null, SMS Content, null, null) to *sendTextMessage*(phoneNo, SMS Content). It uses the API functions to send four (see Figure 4) premium SMS messages with digit codes on it in a matter of milliseconds. Of course, sending a SMS message does not have to be malicious per se. However, for example, if this API utilizes numbers less that 9 digits in length, beginning with a "7" combined with SMS messages, this is considered a costly premium-rate service and a malware that sends SMS messages without the user's consent. The malware evaluated sends SMS messages that contain the following strings: 846976, 846977, 846978, and 846979. The message may be sent to a premium SMS short code number "7132," which may charge the user without his/her knowledge. This implies financial charges. Usually, when this malware is installed, malicious Broadcast Receiver is enrolled directly to broadcast messages from malicious server to the malware, so that user cannot understand whether specific messages are delivered or not. This is because the priority of malicious Broadcast Receiver is higher than SMS Broadcast Receiver. Once the malware is started, sending the function call *sendTextMessage* of SMS Manager API on the service layer, a message with premium number is sent which is shown in Figure 4.

6.2. Interactive Dendrograms. In general, it is needed to conduct the visual analysis from different perspectives. To do that we have developed an interactive graph visualization. So, we have four options or features in the D3 visualization of the application to monitor, namely, (a) selection of full features of the application (Goodware checkbox, Adware checkbox, and Malware checkbox), (b) the Goodware checkbox indicating that the app is assumed to be Goodware, (c) the Adware checkbox of the application, and (d) the Malware checkbox to look for malicious code. The analyst can choose to observe a particular Java class or function by typing the name of it inside the search box and clicking on the related search button.

Figures 6 and 7 illustrate a big picture of the whole behavioral performance of the malware *DroidKungFu1* whose package name is *com.nineiworks.wordsXGN*, and the malicious function calls are invoked. For the sake of simplicity, we shorten the package name of *DroidKungFu1* to *wordsXGN* in the dendrogram. As a matter of fact, we apply a similar

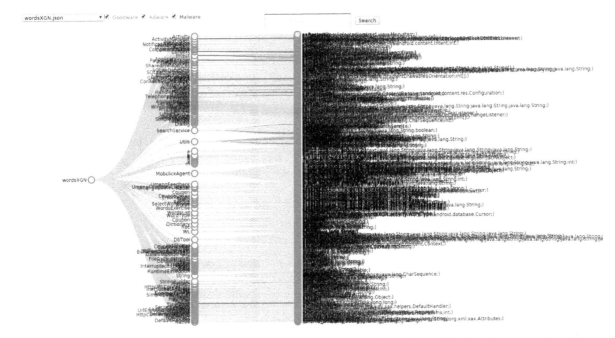

FIGURE 6: Visualization of the *DroidKungFu1* malware with full features chosen (i.e., all the checkboxes are activated).

TABLE 1: Malware family, detection rules, and suspicious functions.

Malware family	Detection rules	Suspicious functions
FakePlayer	IF (SEND_SMS) && (CALL_sendTextMessage() with preset numbers) THEN Malware	sendTextMessage(7132, null, 846976, null, null)
SMSReplicator	IF (SEND_SMS) && (CALL_sendTextMessage() with preset numbers) THEN Malware	sendTextMessage(1245, null, {From: 123456789 Hi how are you}, null, null)
iMatch	IF Not (ACCESS_FINE_LOCATION) && IF (SEND_SMS) THEN Malware	requestLocationUpdates(); sendTextMessage()
DroidKungFu1	[IF (INTERNET) && IF Not (ACCESS_FINE_LOCATION)] ‖ [IF (READ_PHONE_STATE) && IF (INTERNET)] THEN Malware	getLatitude(); getLongitude(); getDeviceid(); getLIne1Number(); getImei()
DroidKungFu4	IF (INTERNET) && IF (READ_PHONE_STATE) THEN Malware	getDeviceid(); getLIne1Number(); getSimSerial(); getImei();
GoldDream (Purman)	[IF (READ_PHONE_STATE) && IF Not (SEND_SMS)] ‖ [IF Not (READ_PHONE_STATE) && IF (INTERNET)] THEN Malware	getDeviceId(); getLIne1Number(); getSimSerial(); sendTextMessage(); getImei()
GoldDream (Dizz)	[IF (READ_PHONE_STATE) && IF Not (SEND_SMS)] ‖ [IF Not (ACCESS_FINE_LOCATION) && IF (INTERNET)] THEN Malware	getDeviceId(); getLIne1Number(); getSimSerial(); sendTextMessage(); requestLocationUpdates(); getImei()
GGTracker	[IF (READ_PHONE_STATE) && Not (SEND_SMS)] ‖ [IF Not (ACCESS_FINE_LOCATION) && IF (INTERNET)] THEN Malware	getDeviceId(); getLIne1Number(); getSimSerial(); sendTextMessage(); requestLocationUpdates(); getImei()

labeling policy to the other dendrograms. Moreover, we have the dendrograms for the *DroidKungFu4* in Figure 8. In particular, in the graph of Figure 8(a), we conduct the visual inspection by using full features (i.e., all the checkboxes active simultaneously) looking for red lines (presence of malware, if that is the case). Furthermore, in the graph of Figure 8(b), now we can focus our visual examination in the malicious functions carried out by the application. The visual analysis of the *DroidKungFu1* and *DroidKungFu4* includes encrypted

root exploits, Command & Control (C & C) servers which in the case of *DroidKungFu1* are in plain text in a Java class file, and shadow payload (embedded app). In Table 1, we have some of the suspicious function calls utilized by the malware which pop up from the dendrograms. Regarding the IF-THEN rules, the allowed clauses or statements in our infrastructure are permissions and API functions calls. The fundamental operators are Conditional-AND which is denoted by &&, Conditional-OR which is denoted by ‖,

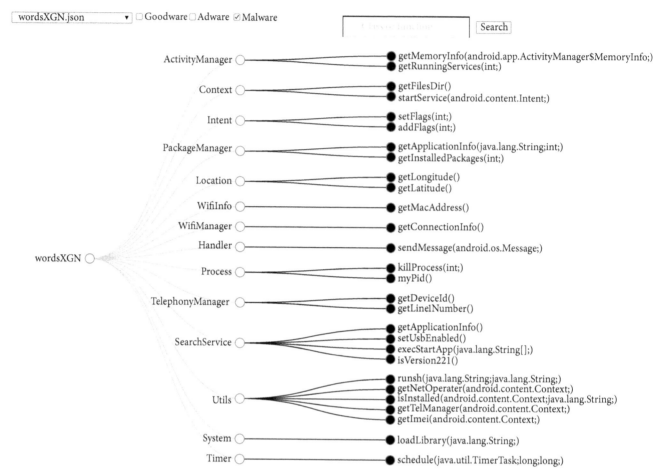

FIGURE 7: Visualization of the malicious API calls detected by our system for *DroidKungFu1*. Note the chosen options of the monitored malware in the dendrogram at the upper left side. First, we shorten version of the package name (*wordsXGN*) of the malware in the combobox. Next we have three checkboxes, namely, Goodware, Adware, and Malware. In this graph, only the red checkbox has been activated in order to conduct the visual analysis. The full package name of *DroidKungFu1* is *com.nineiworks.wordsXGN*.

and Not. For example, if the examined app does not have permission to send SMS messages in the *AndroidManifest* file and that app trys to send SMS messages with the location of the smartphone THEN that application may have malicious code. The rule generated for this case is shown below:

>   IF Not (*SEND_SMS*) && (*ACCESS_FINE_LOCA-TION*) THEN Malware.

Here, malicious code and malware are interchangeable terms. The possible outcomes are Goodware or Malware. Nevertheless, the proposed infrastructure might be capable of evaluating a third option, Adware, in a few cases. In this paper we do not describe the IF-THEN rules for the third kind of outcome. In this work, we restrain the possible outcomes to the two mentioned options.

We have used 7 rules in our experimentation which are listed in Table 1 (note that rules 1 and 2 are the same). We have listed in Table 1 the most frequently used rules. They mainly cover cases of user information leakage.

The most frequently used detection rules that we have utilized in our experimentation are listed in Table 1 (second column).

6.3. Client-Side CPU Use Analysis. We define the CPU utilization of a given application as the ratio between the time when the processor was in busy mode only for this given application at both the user and kernel levels and the time when the processor was either in busy or idle mode. The CPU times have been taken from the Linux kernel through the files "/proc/stat" and "/proc/pid/stat" where pid is the process id of the given application. We have chosen to sample the CPU utilization every second.

The CPU utilization of the Sink application has been measured in order to evaluate the cost of receiving the partial traces from the diverse monitored applications, processing them, and recording them in the SQLite database varying the time interval between two consecutive partial traces sent. We expect to see that the CPU utilization of the Sink increases as the time interval between two consecutive partial traces sent decreases. Indeed, since the Sink must process more partial traces, it needs more CPU resource. This is confirmed by the curve in Figure 9. The CPU utilization has a tendency towards 30% when the time interval between two consecutive partial traces received tends to 10 ms because the synthetic application takes almost 30% of the CPU for building and

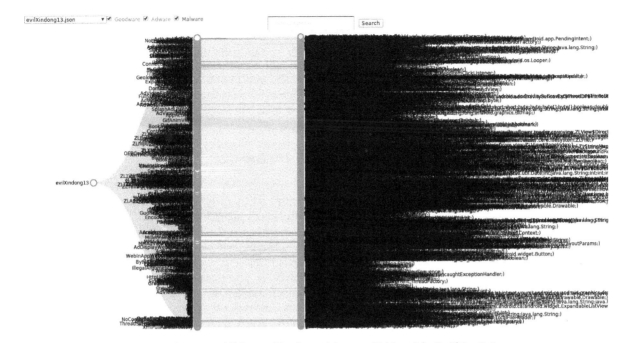

(a) Dendrogram in full features (Goodware, Adware, and Malware) for *DroidKungFu4*

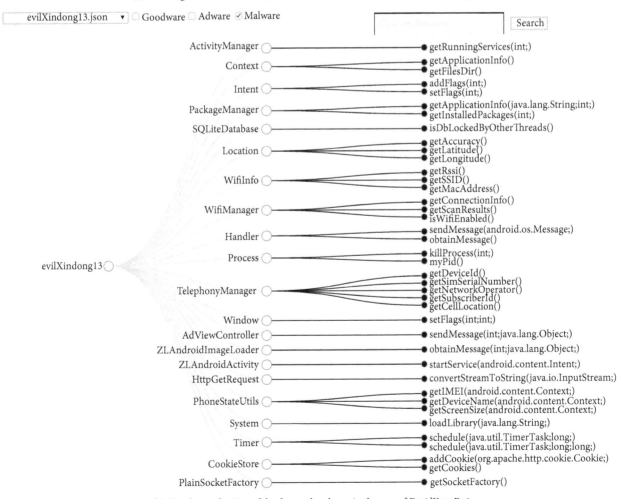

(b) Graph visualization of the detected malware in the case of *DroidKungFu4*

FIGURE 8: Dendrograms of the tested application. (a) Graph of the *DroidKungFu4* in full features, and (b) graph of the malicious functions invoked by *DroidKungFu4*. The full package name of DroidKungFu4 is com.evilsunflower.reader.evilXindong13.

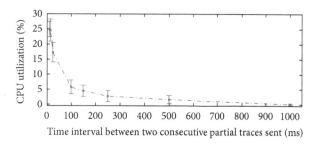

FIGURE 9: CPU utilization of the Sink.

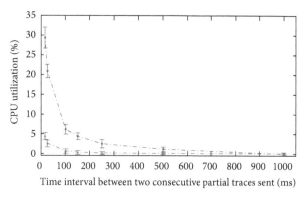

-●- Synthetic application monitored
-▲- Synthetic application nonmonitored

FIGURE 10: Difference of CPU utilization between an application monitored and nonmonitored.

sending partial traces, and the rest of applications utilize the rest of the CPU resource. When no monitored applications send partial traces to the Sink and the Sink is running in the background (i.e., its activity is not displayed on the screen), it consumes about 0% of the CPU.

The CPU utilization of a synthetic application has also been measured in order to evaluate the cost of building and sending the partial traces to the Sink while the time interval between two consecutive partial traces sent was varied. We expect to see a higher CPU utilization when the application is monitored. Indeed, since the synthetic application must build and send more partial traces, it needs more CPU resources. This is confirmed by Figure 10. We note that the increase of CPU utilization of the application can be up to 28% when it is monitored. The chart shows an increase in application CPU utilization to a level up to 38% which is justified when the monitoring is fine-grained at 10 ms. However, this high frequency is not likely to be needed in real applications.

6.4. Responsiveness. We define an application as responsive if its response time to an event is short enough. An event can be a button pushed by a user. In other words, the application is responsive if the user does not notice any latency while the application is running. In order to quantify the responsiveness and see the impact of the monitoring on the responsiveness of monitored applications, we have measured the time spent for executing the prologue function of the synthetic application. We have evaluated the responsiveness

of the monitored application when the Sink was saturated by partial traces requests, that is, in its worst case. The measured response time was on average less than 1 ms. so, the user does not notice any differences when the application is monitored or not, even though the Sink application is saturated by partial traces. This is explained by the fact that UDP is connectionless and therefore sends the partial traces directly to the UDP socket of the Sink without waiting for any acknowledgments.

7. Limitations

So far we illustrated the possibilities of our visual analysis framework by analyzing 8 existing malicious applications. We successfully identified different types of malware accordingly to the malicious payload (e.g., privilege escalation, financial charges, and personal information stealing) of the app while using only dynamic inspection in order to obtain the outcomes. Even though the results are promising, they only represent a few of the massive malware attacking today's smart devices. Of course, the aim of this system is not to replace existing automated Android malware classification systems because the final decision is done by a security analyst.

Although, here, we propose a malware detector system based on runtime behavior, this does not have detection capabilities to monitor an application's execution in real time, so this platform cannot detect intrusions while running. It only enable detecting past attacks.

Also, one can figure out that malware authors could try avoiding detection, since they can gain knowledge whether their app has been tampered with or no. As a result, the actual attack might not be deployed, which may be considered a preventive technique. Moreover, it is possible for a malicious application to evade detection by dynamically loading and executing Dalvik bytecode at runtime.

One of the drawbacks of this work could be the manual interactions with the monitored application during runtime (over some time interval). Also, the classification needs a more general procedure to get the rule-based expert system. The natural next step is to automate these parts of the process. For example, in the literature there are several approaches that can be implemented in order to automatically generate more IF-THEN rules [15] or to resort to the MonkeyRunner kit available in Android SDK to simulate the user interactions. Of course, the outcomes of the 8-sample malware presented here are limited to longest time interval used in the study, which was 10 minutes. Extending this "playing" time with the app using tools for the automation of user's interactions could provide a more realistic graph and better pinpoint the attacks of the mobile malware.

Another limitation of this work is that it can only intercept Java level calls and not low level functions that can be stored as libraries in the applications. Thus, a malicious app can invoke native code through Java Native Interface (JNI), to deploy attacks to the Android ecosystem. Since our approach builds on monitoring devices that are not rooted, this approach is out of the scope of our research.

It is worth mentioning that our API hooking process does not consider the Intents. The current version of the infrastructure presented in this paper is not capable of monitoring the Intents sent by the application, as sending Intents does not require any kind of permission. Not being able to monitor Intents means that the infrastructure is not able to track if the monitored application starts another app for a short period of time to perform a given task, for instance, opening a web browser to display the end-user license agreement (EULA). Also, adding this feature would allow knowing how the target application communicates with the rest of the third party and system applications installed on the device.

Ultimately, this framework could be useful for final users interested in what apps are doing in their devices.

8. Conclusions

We provide a monitoring architecture aiming at identifying harmful Android applications without modifying the Android firmware. It provides a visualization graph named dendrograms where function calls corresponding to predefined malware behaviors are highlighted. Composed of four components, namely, the embedded client, the Sink, the Web Service, and the visualization, any Android application can be monitored without rooting the phone or changing its firmware.

The developed infrastructure is capable of monitoring simultaneously several applications on various devices and collecting all the traces in the same place. The tests performed in this work show that applications can be prepared to be monitored in a matter of minutes and that the modified applications behave as they were originally intended to, with minimal interference with the permissions used for. Furthermore, we have shown that the infrastructure can be used to detect malicious behaviors by applications, such as the monitored *FakePlayer*, *DroidKungFu1* and *DroidKungFu4*, and the *SMSReplicator* and many others taken from the dataset of the Android Malware Genome Project.

Evaluations of the Sink have revealed that our monitoring system is quite reactive, does not lose any partial traces, and has a very small impact on the performance of the monitored applications.

A major benefit of the approach is that the system is designed as platform-independent so that smart devices with different versions of Android OS can use it. Further improvements on the visualization quality and the user interface are possible, but the proof of concept implementation is demonstrated to be promising. For future work, we plan to extend the current work in order to develop a real-time malware detection infrastructure based on network traffic and on a large number of apps.

Competing Interests

The authors declare that they have no competing interests.

Acknowledgments

This research has been partially funded by Basque Governments Elkartek Program under Grant no. KK-2015/0000080. Also, the last author would like to acknowledge the support by the RICS Centre for Resilient Information and Control Systems (http://www.rics.se/) financed by the Swedish civil contingencies agency.

References

[1] Gartner, "Gartner says worldwide traditional PC, tablet, ultramobile and mobile phone shipments on pace to grow 7.6 percent in 2014," October 2015, http://www.gartner.com/newsroom/id/2645115.

[2] G. Suarez-Tangil, J. E. Tapiador, P. Peris-Lopez, and J. Blasco, "Dendroid: a text mining approach to analyzing and classifying code structures in Android malware families," *Expert Systems with Applications*, vol. 41, no. 4, pp. 1104–1117, 2014.

[3] Y. Zhang, M. Yang, B. Xu et al., "Vetting undesirable behaviors in android apps with permission use analysis," in *Proceedings of the ACM SIGSAC Conference on Computer and Communications Security (CCS '13)*, pp. 611–622, ACM, Berlin, Germany, November 2013.

[4] Microsoft, "Web services," 2014, http://msdn.microsoft.com/en-us/library/ms950421.aspx.

[5] R. T. Fielding, *Architectural styles and the design of network-based software architectures [Ph.D. thesis]*, University of California, Irvine, Calif, USA, 2000.

[6] Sufatrio, D. J. J. Tan, T.-W. Chua, and V. L. L. Thing, "Securing android: a survey, taxonomy, and challenges," *ACM Computing Surveys*, vol. 47, no. 4, article 58, 2015.

[7] P. Faruki, A. Bharmal, V. Laxmi et al., "Android security: a survey of issues, malware penetration, and defenses," *IEEE Communications Surveys & Tutorials*, vol. 17, no. 2, pp. 998–1022, 2015.

[8] Android.com, "Android system permissions," 2014, http://developer.android.com/guide/topics/security/permissions.html.

[9] R. Winsniewski, "Android-apktool: a tool for reverse engineering android apk files," 2012.

[10] M. Karami, M. Elsabagh, P. Najafiborazjani, and A. Stavrou, "Behavioral analysis of android applications using automated instrumentation," in *Proceedings of the 7th International Conference on Software Security and Reliability (SERE-C '13)*, pp. 182–187, Gaithersburg, Md, USA, June 2013.

[11] S. Bugiel, L. Davi, A. Dmitrienko, T. Fischer, and A.-R. Sadeghi, "Xmandroid: a new android evolution to mitigate privilege escalation attacks," Tech. Rep. TR-2011-04, Technische Universität Darmstadt, Darmstadt, Germany, 2011.

[12] K. W. Y. Au, Y. F. Zhou, Z. Huang, and D. Lie, "PScout: analyzing the Android permission specification," in *Proceedings of the 2012 ACM Conference on Computer and Communications Security (CCS '12)*, pp. 217–228, ACM, Raleigh, NC, USA, October 2012.

[13] J. Jeon, K. K. Micinski, J. A. Vaughan et al., "Dr. android and Mr. hide: fine-grained permissions in android applications," in *Proceedings of the 2nd ACM Workshop on Security and Privacy in Smartphones and Mobile Devices (SPSM '12)*, pp. 3–14, ACM, Raleigh, NC, USA, October 2012.

[14] I. Burguera, U. Zurutuza, and S. Nadjm-Tehrani, "Crowdroid: behaviorbased malware detection system for android," in *Proceedings of the 1st ACM Workshop on Security And Privacy in Smartphones and Mobile Devices*, pp. 15–26, ACM, 2011.

[15] K. Patel and B. Buddhadev, "Predictive rule discovery for network intrusion detection," in *Intelligent Distributed Computing*,

vol. 321 of *Advances in Intelligent Systems and Computing*, pp. 287–298, Springer, Basel, Switzerland, 2015.

[16] X. Jiang and Y. Zhou, *Android Malware*, Springer, New York, NY, USA, 2013.

[17] H. Gascon, F. Yamaguchi, D. Arp, and K. Rieck, "Structural detection of android malware using embedded call graphs," in *Proceedings of the ACM Workshop on Artificial Intelligence and Security*, pp. 45–54, ACM, 2013.

[18] D. Arp, M. Spreitzenbarth, M. Hübner, H. Gascon, K. Rieck, and C. Siemens, "Drebin: effective and explainable detection of android malware in your pocket," in *Proceedings of the Annual Symposium on Network and Distributed System Security (NDSS '14)*, San Diego, Calif, USA, February 2014.

[19] A. Shabtai, L. Tenenboim-Chekina, D. Mimran, L. Rokach, B. Shapira, and Y. Elovici, "Mobile malware detection through analysis of deviations in application network behavior," *Computers & Security*, vol. 43, pp. 1–18, 2014.

[20] M. La Polla, F. Martinelli, and D. Sgandurra, "A survey on security for mobile devices," *IEEE Communications Surveys & Tutorials*, vol. 15, no. 1, pp. 446–471, 2013.

[21] G. Suarez-Tangil, J. E. Tapiador, P. Peris-Lopez, and A. Ribagorda, "Evolution, detection and analysis of malware for smart devices," *IEEE Communications Surveys & Tutorials*, vol. 16, no. 2, pp. 961–987, 2014.

[22] S. Arzt, S. Rasthofer, and E. Bodden, "Instrumenting android and java applications as easy as abc," in *Runtime Verification*, pp. 364–381, Springer, Berlin, Germany, 2013.

[23] S.-H. Seo, A. Gupta, A. M. Sallam, E. Bertino, and K. Yim, "Detecting mobile malware threats to homeland security through static analysis," *Journal of Network and Computer Applications*, vol. 38, no. 1, pp. 43–53, 2014.

[24] K. Patel and B. Buddadev, "Detection and mitigation of android malware through hybrid approach," in *Security in Computing and Communications*, vol. 536 of *Communications in Computer and Information Science*, pp. 455–463, Springer, Basel, Switzerland, 2015.

16

SVM Intrusion Detection Model based on Compressed Sampling

Shanxiong Chen,[1] **Maoling Peng,**[2] **Hailing Xiong,**[1] **and Xianping Yu**[1]

[1]*College of Computer and Information Science, Southwest University, Chongqing 400715, China*
[2]*Chongqing City Management Vocational College, Chongqing 400055, China*

Correspondence should be addressed to Shanxiong Chen; csxpml@163.com

Academic Editor: Michele Vadursi

Intrusion detection needs to deal with a large amount of data; particularly, the technology of network intrusion detection has to detect all of network data. Massive data processing is the bottleneck of network software and hardware equipment in intrusion detection. If we can reduce the data dimension in the stage of data sampling and directly obtain the feature information of network data, efficiency of detection can be improved greatly. In the paper, we present a SVM intrusion detection model based on compressive sampling. We use compressed sampling method in the compressed sensing theory to implement feature compression for network data flow so that we can gain refined sparse representation. After that SVM is used to classify the compression results. This method can realize detection of network anomaly behavior quickly without reducing the classification accuracy.

1. Introduction

With the rapid development of network technology, various Internet-based technologies are widely applied in various industries, leading to great improvement of productive forces. People are enjoying convenience and efficiency brought about by network, and a variety of potential threats are jeopardizing the security of network communication at the same time. At the beginning of network design, people paid more attention to data transmission efficiency and communication convenience and paid less attention to the security of network protocol [1]. Many network protocols are lacking secure communication mechanism; thus, there are naturally a lot of security vulnerabilities in Internet based on these network protocols [2, 3]. With the development of e-commerce, e-government affairs, and other businesses having high demand for security, a variety of network-based security communication protocols appeared, but these protocols are based on TCP/IP architecture, which is a kind of unsafe open system from the basic communication layer [4]. The existing attack techniques and technologies have unceasingly developed with the enhancement of security technology, so in the case of all kinds of inevitable network threats, a current research hotspot on network security is to timely and correctly detect security threats and to take appropriate treatment, so as to reduce the loss caused by network attacks [5–7].

Compressed sensing is a new data processing theory; there are many important applications in medical image [8] and signal processing [9], communications [10], harmonic detection [11], and so forth. Data acquisition and processing method of compressed sensing theory give rise to great performance improvement of intrusion detection technology [12, 13]. Currently, massive data processing is the performance bottleneck of network software and hardware equipment. In the phase of data acquisition, if the dimension of data can be reduced and characteristic information of network data can be directly obtained, the efficiency of the detection will be greatly improved [14, 15]. SVM intrusion detection technology based on compressed sensing uses the compressed sampling technology of compressed sensing theory to get a small amount of data concerning network behavior characteristics and then uses the support vector machine (SVM) to establish an intrusion detection model, so as to realize rapid judgment of intrusion behavior.

2. Compressed Sensing Theory

If there are only K nonzero elements in a discrete signal, the signal is considered to be K sparse. In view of a nonsparse discrete signal u, the signal can obtain the sparse or nearly sparse representation in the condition of a proper sparse base $\Psi \in R^{N \times L}$:

$$u = \Psi x. \tag{1}$$

x is the sparse or nearly sparse representation of signal u. According to the CS (compressed sensing) theory, the sampling process of discrete signal is described as below: The signal u with a length of N is projected M times on the sensing matrix $\Phi\{\Phi_i, i = 1, 2, \ldots, M\}$, and then the compressed form of the signal can be obtained [16]. Its expression is $y_i = \Phi_i^T u, i = 1, 2, \ldots, M$. In order to improve the efficiency of sampling, the frequency of sampling should be reduced as much as possible; usually, $M < N$. It can be seen that the length of y is less than that of u, so it is called compressed sensing. It is different from traditional data acquisition method that includes acquisition, compression, transmission, and decompression; the compressed sensing theory merely collects the information that best represents data characteristic rather than obtaining a complete signal and high resolution images. Compressed sampling method saves storage space and reduces transmission cost to a great extent. The biggest difference between compressed sensing and traditional data sampling mode is that compressed sensing has realized the compression in the process of data acquisition and reconstruction in the later phase; the traditional mode is to collect complete data information first and then to compress data for storage and transmission. Therefore, the CS theory provides an undersampling mode for data acquisition and can get information in the slower rate compared to Nyquist. The mathematical model of compressed sensing is expressed as below.

For signal $u \in R^{N \times 1}$, find a linear measurement matrix $\Phi \in R^{M \times N}$ ($M < N$) for projection algorithm

$$y = \Phi u, \tag{2}$$

where

$$\Phi = \begin{bmatrix} \Phi_1^T \\ \Phi_2^T \\ \ldots \\ \Phi_M^T \end{bmatrix},$$

$$x = \begin{bmatrix} u_1 \\ u_2 \\ \ldots \\ u_N \end{bmatrix}, \tag{3}$$

$$y = \begin{bmatrix} y_1 \\ y_2 \\ \ldots \\ y_M \end{bmatrix}.$$

y represents the collected signals. The crux of the problem is to recover signal u from signal y, and Φ is not a square

matrix ($M < N$), so it gets involved in a problem of solving an underdetermined equation. And u to be solved can have a solution set. Furthermore, the compressed sensing theory shows that, under the specific conditions, u is the uniqueness solution, and this solution is obtained through reconstructing y that is acquired by compressed sampling [17, 18].

Equation (2) shows the signal sampling mode, and the CS theory suggests that the solution of (2) must ensure that x is sparse, so as to solve the equation through $L0$ norm minimization problem. In reality, most of the signals are not sparse. The existing theory shows that when a signal is projected on the orthogonal transformation matrix, the absolute value of most transform coefficients is small [19], and the obtained transform vector is sparse or approximately sparse, which is considered as a concise expression of original signal, a prior condition of compressed sensing; namely, the signal must have a sparse representation under some type of transformation. Therefore, sparse transformation base Ψ is established, and the sparse representation of nonsparse signals is completed according to (1). Combined with (1) and (2), compression sampling of the signal u can be described as below: equation (2) is used for compressed sampling of the signal u to obtain y, and then (4) is used for x sparse solution; ultimately, x is used for sparse inverse transformation, so as to reconstruct the signal u. Consider

$$y = \Phi \Psi x = \Theta x, \tag{4}$$

where $\Theta = \Phi \Psi$, which is still an underdetermined equation; however, under certain constraints, y is used to solve x. Of course, if the signal is sparse, there is no need for sparse transformation; at this point $\Theta = \Phi$. In compressed sensing, the signal needs to meet the conditions; one constraint condition is sparse representation, and the other important one is to satisfy the RIP (Restricted Isometry Property) [20]; namely, there is a restricted isometry constant δ_s for the matrix Θ.

δ_s is defined as the minimum value to make the equation true. Consider

$$(1 - \delta_s) \|v_s\|_2^2 \le \|\Theta v_s\|_2^2 \le (1 + \delta_s) \|v_s\|_2^2. \tag{5}$$

Herein v_s represents s-order sparse vector.

3. SVM Intrusion Detection Model Based on Compressed Sensing

The SVM intrusion detection method based on compressed sensing is to carry out compressed sampling of the tagged training dataset, so as to obtain compressed characteristic data and then to input it into SVM classifier for training, so as to obtain the classification model. In the detection phase, carry out compressed sampling of the untagged dataset, and then reuse the built SVM classification model to classify data, to obtain normal or abnormal access behaviors, and then reconstruct the detected data of normal behaviors, to obtain the complete normal network data flow.

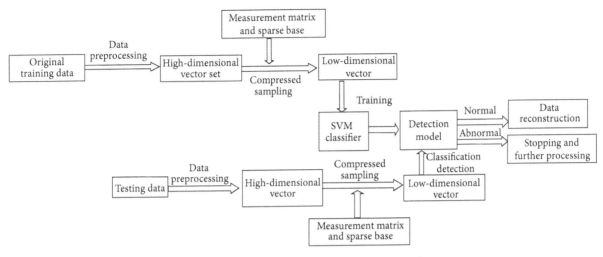

FIGURE 1: Intrusion detection process based on compressed sensing.

As shown in Figure 1, the steps for intrusion detection based on compressed sensing include the following:

(1) Pretreatment of dataset: the compressed sensing theory is to directly sample vector data, so training data and testing data should be expressed in the form of vector.

(2) Selection of proper measurement matrix and sparse matrix: measurement matrix and sparse base should meet the conditions of RIP, and data resulting from their compressed sampling must effectively express the original data at the same time.

(3) Construction of the SVM classifier: the SVM classifier can use compressed sampling to obtain low-dimensional data, so as to complete classification training, and testing dataset has high detection precision.

(4) After performing detection, if network access is normal, the reconstruction algorithm is used to restore detection data to full form before sampling.

4. Experiments and Analysis

The experiments used KDD CUP99 dataset. The dataset was collected in a network environment which was established in MIT Lincoln Laboratory, simulating local area network (LAN) of the US Air Force. It includes 9-week TCP dump network connections and system audit data, simulating various types of users, network traffic, and attack technique.

The compressed sensing theory request data must be expressed in the form of vector; therefore, each nonnumerical attribute must be converted into a numerical value, and herein the numerical value can simply replace category attributes. Furthermore, in order to eliminate the influence of characteristic dimension on the experimental results, continuous data need to be standardized. The following equation is used for standardization. $S = \{s_{ij} \mid i = 1, \ldots, N, \ j = 1, \ldots, D\}$ is input data, N represents the number of sample datasets,

and D represents the characteristic digit of sample data, μ represents mean value, and σ is standard deviation of the sample. Therefore, the normalization expression of sample data is as below:

$$S'_{ij} = \frac{S_{ij} - \mu}{\sigma}, \tag{6}$$

where

$$\mu = \frac{1}{N} \sum_{i=1}^{N} S_{ij},$$

$$\sigma = \sqrt{\frac{1}{N-1} \sum_{i=1}^{N} \left(X_{ij} - \mu \right)^2}. \tag{7}$$

In order to clearly observe the experimental results, we introduced the following indicators for detection performance.

Detection rate refers to the ratio between the number of correct attack datasets detected in the testing set and the number of total actual attack datasets; that is, the equation is as below:

$$\text{DR} = \frac{\text{the number of attacks detected}}{\text{the number of attacks}} \%. \tag{8}$$

False positive rate refers to the ratio between the number of attack datasets being identified by mistake after the test set is detected through the algorithm and the number of total attack datasets detected; that is, the equation is as below:

$$\text{FPR} = \frac{\text{the number of false positive}}{\text{false positive} + \text{true positive}} \%. \tag{9}$$

The experiments adopted 10% training subsets of the KDD CUP99 dataset as training data of the classifier and the test subset tagged correct as test data. We first considered the classifier learning and detection without compressed sampling and then carried out compressed sampling of

TABLE 1: Detection result of the support vector machine (SVM) as the classifier.

Detection type		Normal	Probe	Dos	U2R	R2L
Noncompressed sampling	Detection rate (%)	98.73	97.34	99.27	94.21	99.35
	False positive rate (%)	0.87	1.03	0.92	1.08	0.92
Compressed sampling						
Gaussian random matrix	Detection rate (%)	98.23	96.42	97.08	90.37	97.64
	False positive rate (%)	0.82	1.19	0.96	1.26	0.98
Random Bernoulli matrix	Detection rate (%)	97.31	97.07	99.14	88.39	98.71
	False positive rate (%)	1.13	1.21	1.07	1.86	0.92
Partial Hadamard measurement matrix	Detection rate (%)	98.12	96.94	98.71	90.84	97.75
	False positive rate (%)	0.93	1.05	0.92	1.49	1.04
Toeplitz matrix measurement	Detection rate (%)	97.86	96.93	98.49	89.15	98.73
	False positive rate (%)	0.88	1.06	0.91	2.12	0.94
Structure random matrix	Detection rate (%)	96.57	96.72	97.87	87.35	98.76
	False positive rate (%)	1.15	1.23	0.97	2.34	0.96
Chirp measurement matrix	Detection rate (%)	97.33	96.24	98.39	90.08	99.01
	False positive rate (%)	1.08	1.33	1.15	1.13	0.94

(i) Probe: surveillance or probe, (ii) DoS: Denial of Service, (iii) U2R: User to Root, and (iv) R2L: Remote to Local.

training data and test data and input it into the SVM classifier for learning and detection. The experimental procedure is as follows:

(1) We extract test data from 10% training subsets of the KDD CUP99 dataset. Compressed sampling is to deal with numeric data; it is required to convert nonnumeric data into numeric data in the procedure, except data with attack attribute; namely, attack-type data cannot be converted to numeric data; otherwise, attack-type data cannot be recognized. So the corresponding relation between attribute value of attack-type data and each record should be kept.

(2) The KDD CUP99 dataset refers to normal and attack data collected for a long time; from the perspective of the entire data sample, there is a small number of attack datasets, so the standardized dataset is a sparse set, the formed matrix is a sparse matrix, and there is no need for sparsification.

(3) In the experiment, multiple measurement matrices are directly used for compressed sampling of training set: Gaussian random matrix, random Bernoulli matrix, partial Hadamard measurement matrix, Toeplitz measurement matrix, structure random matrix, and Chirp measurement matrix.

(4) The compressed data obtained are, respectively, input into the SVM-constructed classifier for training, thus forming a training model.

(5) The corrected subsets of KDD CUP99 dataset are selected as test set. Herein carry out normalized conversion of test data; namely, convert nonnumeric data into numerical data for compressing sampling, and then input compressed data into the training model for detection.

Table 1 shows the results of using the SVM-constructed classifier for intrusion detection of different sampling matrixes through 30 times of sampling.

Table 1 showed the results of using the compressed sampling method for intrusion detection and of using the noncompressed sampling method to directly input it into the classifier for training and detection. It can be seen from Table 1 that the results obtained through two methods were similar. For the traditional method of compressed sampling, the detection rate of five types, that is, Normal, Probe, Dos, U2R and R2L, was more than 98% except that of U2R. Under the condition of compressed sensing, the detection rate obtained by using different sampling matrixes was around 98%. Only the detection rate obtained by using the compressed sampling method for U2R attack-type data was lower, and the false positive rate was higher. After further analysis, it was found that the traditional method for U2R attack-type data had a low detection rate, which was related to dataset itself, less U2R type data, and deviation of the training model. In reality, the use of compressed sensing method cannot greatly improve the detection rate but can increase the efficiency of training and detection by reducing dimension data. Figure 2 showed training and detection time under different sampling matrixes after 30 times of sampling.

Figure 2 showed that, after the method of compressed sampling was used for information processing of KDD CUP99 dataset, time used for training and inspection was reduced. In particular, it can be found that for data obtained through using the Gaussian random matrix for compressed sampling its training and detection time is decreased greatly for four classifiers of detection.

Besides attack-type attribute, the KDD CUP99 dataset has 41D characteristics, and matrixes are used for compressed sampling of 41D characteristics. However, compressed sampling also affects detection precision. In theory, the higher the degree of compression is, the shorter the model's training and detection time is, affecting detection precision. In further

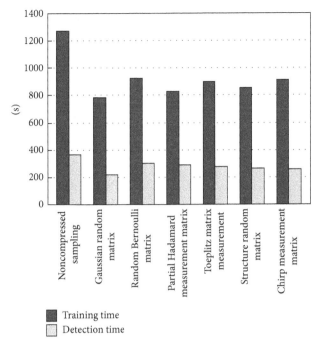

FIGURE 2: Training and detection time.

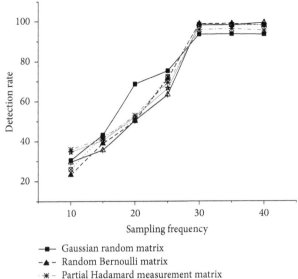

FIGURE 3: Detection rate of the K-nearest neighbor algorithm as a classifier for DoS attack.

experiments, we analyzed the relationship between compression degree and detection precision. For convenience of representation, the detection rate for DoS attack was selected for analysis. In the experiments, there are six sampling matrixes, respectively, under different sampling frequencies, so SVM method was used to obtain the detection rate of the corrected dataset according to sampling matrixes. Sampling frequencies were $10, 15, 20, \dots, 40$. The dimension of KDD CUP99 data was 41D, so there was basically no compressed sampling under the condition of sampling frequency of 40.

It can be seen from Figure 3 that, under the condition of low sampling frequency, the SVM-constructed classifier had lower DoS detection precision. Based on the compressed sensing theory, in order to perfectly express data, sampling frequency M must have particular relations; that is, $M \geq C \cdot k \cdot \log N$. In general, four times of data sparseness are selected as the sampling frequency. The figure showed that, under the low sampling frequency, the detection rate was lower; with the increase of sampling frequency, the detection rate was increased accordingly. When the sampling frequency was up to 30 or so, the detection rate tended to be stable. At this time, the low-dimensional data obtained through compressed sampling of KDD CUP99 dataset can effectively express the original high-dimensional data. Thus, DoS detection rate is approximate to the detection rate obtained by using the method of noncompressed sampling. However, with the further increase of sampling frequency, there was no significant change of detection rate.

5. Conclusion

Intrusion detection needs to deal with massive network data, leading to low detection efficiency. In the paper, the compressed sensing technology was applied to realize network data compression, and the SVM method was used to anomalously detect the compressed data. We have arrived at a conclusion that, relative to direct use of the classifier for learning and detection of training set and testing set, the intrusion detection model established through compressed sensing had no significant change of detection rate and false positive rate, but training and detection time was greatly reduced, which is the key to detect network data flow. A large number of network datasets need rapid and real-time detection, so it can be seen that intrusion detection based on compressed sensing has provided a real-time network security protection mechanism.

Competing Interests

The authors declare that they have no competing interests.

Acknowledgments

This work was supported by the National Natural Science Foundation of China (61303227), the Fundamental Research Funds for the Central Universities (XDJK2014C039, XDJK2016C045), and Postdoctoral Fund of Southwestern University (swu114033).

References

[1] A. P. Lauf, R. A. Peters, and W. H. Robinson, "A distributed intrusion detection system for resource-constrained devices in ad-hoc networks," *Ad Hoc Networks*, vol. 8, no. 3, pp. 253–266, 2010.

[2] S. Raza, L. Wallgren, and T. Voigt, "SVELTE: Real-time intrusion detection in the Internet of Things," *Ad Hoc Networks*, vol. 11, no. 8, pp. 2661–2674, 2013.

[3] T. Zhang, E. Lee, and J. K. Seo, "Anomaly depth detection in trans-admittance mammography: a formula independent of anomaly size or admittivity contrast," *Inverse Problems*, vol. 30, no. 4, Article ID 045003, 2014.

[4] D.-S. Pham, S. Venkatesh, M. Lazarescu, and S. Budhaditya, "Anomaly detection in large-scale data stream networks," *Data Mining and Knowledge Discovery*, vol. 28, no. 1, pp. 145–189, 2014.

[5] R. Puzis, M. Tubi, Y. Elovici, C. Glezer, and S. Dolev, "A decision support system for placement of intrusion detection and prevention devices in large-scale networks," *ACM Transactions on Modeling and Computer Simulation*, vol. 22, no. 1, 2011.

[6] S. Chen, S. Wu, Y. Cao, and D. Tang, "An intrusion detection model based on non-negative matrix factorization," *Applied Mechanics and Materials*, vol. 148-149, pp. 895–899, 2012.

[7] V. Chandola, A. Banerjee, and V. Kumar, "Anomaly detection: a survey," *ACM Computing Surveys*, vol. 41, no. 3, article 15, 2009.

[8] J. Haupt, W. U. Bajwa, G. Raz, and R. Nowak, "Toeplitz compressed sensing matrices with applications to sparse channel estimation," *IEEE Transactions on Information Theory*, vol. 56, no. 11, pp. 5862–5875, 2010.

[9] L. B. Montefusco, D. Lazzaro, S. Papi, and C. Guerrini, "A fast compressed sensing approach to 3D MR image reconstruction," *IEEE Transactions on Medical Imaging*, vol. 30, no. 5, pp. 1064–1075, 2011.

[10] Y. Wiaux, G. Puy, and P. Vandergheynst, "Compressed sensing reconstruction of a string signal from interferometric observations of the cosmic microwave background," *Monthly Notices of the Royal Astronomical Society*, vol. 402, no. 4, pp. 2626–2636, 2010.

[11] F. Bonavolontà, M. D'Apuzzo, A. Liccardo, and G. Miele, "Harmonic and interharmonic measurements through a compressed sampling approach," *Measurement*, vol. 77, pp. 1–15, 2016.

[12] D. L. Donoho, "Compressed sensing," *IEEE Transactions on Information Theory*, vol. 52, no. 4, pp. 1289–1306, 2006.

[13] D. L. Donoho, A. Maleki, and A. Montanari, "The noise-sensitivity phase transition in compressed sensing," *IEEE Transactions on Information Theory*, vol. 57, no. 10, pp. 6920–6941, 2011.

[14] R. Bhargavi and V. Vaidehi, "Semantic intrusion detection with multisensor data fusion using complex event processing," *Sadhana—Academy Proceedings in Engineering Sciences*, vol. 38, no. 2, pp. 169–185, 2013.

[15] W. J. An and M. G. Liang, "A new intrusion detection method based on SVM with minimum within-class scatter," *Security and Communication Networks*, vol. 6, no. 9, pp. 1064–1074, 2013.

[16] E. J. Candès, "The restricted isometry property and its implications for compressed sensing," *Comptes Rendus Mathematique*, vol. 346, no. 9-10, pp. 589–592, 2008.

[17] K. Takeda and Y. Kabashima, "Statistical mechanical assessment of a reconstruction limit of compressed sensing: toward theoretical analysis of correlated signals," *EPL*, vol. 95, no. 1, Article ID 18006, 2011.

[18] L. Zelnik-Manor, K. Rosenblum, and Y. C. Eldar, "Sensing matrix optimization for block-sparse decoding," *IEEE Transactions on Signal Processing*, vol. 59, no. 9, pp. 4300–4312, 2011.

[19] Y. Zhao, Y. H. Hu, and H. Wang, "Enhanced random equivalent sampling based on compressed sensing," *IEEE Transactions on Instrumentation and Measurement*, vol. 61, no. 3, pp. 579–586, 2012.

[20] E. J. Candes and Y. Plan, "A probabilistic and RIPless theory of compressed sensing," *IEEE Transactions on Information Theory*, vol. 57, no. 11, pp. 7235–7254, 2011.

17

A New Feature Extraction Algorithm based on Orthogonal Regularized Kernel CCA and its Application

Xinchen Guo,[1] Xiuling Fan,[2] Xiantian Xi,[3] and Fugeng Zeng ⓘ[1]

[1]College of Ocean Information Engineering, Hainan Tropical Ocean University, Sanya, China
[2]Henan Xuehang Education and Information Service Co., Zhengzhou, China
[3]Shanghai Renyi Technology Co., Ltd., Shanghai, China

Correspondence should be addressed to Fugeng Zeng; zengfugeng@foxmail.com

Academic Editor: Jar Ferr Yang

In this paper, an orthogonal regularized kernel canonical correlation analysis algorithm (ORKCCA) is proposed. ORCCA algorithm can deal with the linear relationships between two groups of random variables. But if the linear relationships between two groups of random variables do not exist, the performance of ORCCA algorithm will not work well. Linear orthogonal regularized CCA algorithm is extended to nonlinear space by introducing the kernel method into CCA. Simulation experimental results on both artificial and handwritten numerals databases show that the proposed method outperforms ORCCA for the nonlinear problems.

1. Introduction

Canonical correlation analysis (CCA) is a technique of multivariate statistical analysis, which deals with the mutual relationships of two sets of variables [1–3]. This method extracts the representative variables which are the linear combination of the variables in each group. The relationships between new variables can reflect the overall relationships between two groups of variables [4].

The orthogonal regularization canonical correlation analysis (ORCCA) algorithm [5] is that the original formula of CCA algorithm with orthogonal constraints is substituted for CCA conjugate orthogonalization [6, 7]. When the number of samples is less and the sample distribution patterns of different classifications are different, the ORCCA algorithm has the better ability of classification. A suboptimal solution to eigenvalue decomposition problem can be obtained by introducing two regularization parameters [8]. So, the complexity of time and space for the quadratic optimization problem should be considered at the same time. ORCCA algorithm is the same as CCA algorithm that both their goals look for the linear combinations of the variables in each group. But when the nonlinear

relationships between the variables exist, ORCCA algorithm cannot extract effectively the comprehensive variables.

In this paper, the kernel method [9–11] is introduced into ORCCA algorithm, and ORKCCA algorithm is presented. The kernel method maps the linear inseparable data in the low-dimensional space into a higher-dimensional space [12, 13]. In the higher-dimensional space, the characteristics of the data can be extracted and analyzed through the linear method. By introducing kernel function, the computation of the orthogonal regularization canonical correlation analysis extends to a nonlinear feature space. Experimental results show that the accuracies of classification of our method in the nonlinear space are significantly improved. The experimental results show ORKCCA is feasible.

2. Orthogonal Regularized CCA Algorithm

Given n pairs of pairwise samples $\mathbf{X} = (\mathbf{x}_1, \mathbf{x}_2, \ldots, \mathbf{x}_n)^T$ and $\mathbf{Y} = (\mathbf{y}_1, \mathbf{y}_2, \ldots, \mathbf{y}_n)^T$, where $\mathbf{x}_i \in R^p$, $\mathbf{y}_i \in R^q$ ($i = 1, 2, \ldots, n$). We assume that the samples have been centered. ORCCA algorithm aims at finding a pair of projection directions **a** and **b** which satisfy the following optimal problem [5].

$$\min_{\mathbf{a},\mathbf{b}} \quad \frac{1}{n} \sum_{i=1}^{n} \left\| \mathbf{a}^T \mathbf{x}_i - \mathbf{b}^T \mathbf{y}_i \right\|^2,$$

$$\text{s.t.} \quad \mathbf{a}^T \mathbf{a} = 1, \tag{1}$$

$$\mathbf{b}^T \mathbf{b} = 1.$$

The objective function in Equations (1) can be expanded as follows:

$$\frac{1}{n} \sum_{i=1}^{n} \left\| \mathbf{a}^T \mathbf{x}_i - \mathbf{b}^T \mathbf{y}_i \right\|^2 = \mathbf{a}^T \mathbf{S}_{xx} \mathbf{a} + \mathbf{b}^T \mathbf{S}_{yy} \mathbf{b} - 2\mathbf{a}^T \mathbf{S}_{xy} \mathbf{b}, \tag{2}$$

where $\mathbf{S}_{xx} = (1/n)\mathbf{X}^T\mathbf{X}$, $\mathbf{S}_{yy} = (1/n)\mathbf{Y}^T\mathbf{Y}$, and $\mathbf{S}_{xy} = (1/n)\mathbf{X}^T\mathbf{Y}$.

The optimal model in Equation (1) can be rewritten as

$$\max_{\mathbf{a},\mathbf{b}} \quad 2\mathbf{a}^T \mathbf{S}_{xy} \mathbf{b} - \mathbf{a}^T \mathbf{S}_{xx} \mathbf{a} - \mathbf{b}^T \mathbf{S}_{yy} \mathbf{b},$$

$$\text{s.t.} \quad \mathbf{a}^T \mathbf{a} = 1, \tag{3}$$

$$\mathbf{b}^T \mathbf{b} = 1.$$

According to the Lagrange multipliers method, Lagrange function is as follows:

$$L(\mathbf{a},\mathbf{b}) = 2\mathbf{a}^T \mathbf{S}_{xy} \mathbf{b} - \mathbf{a}^T \mathbf{S}_{xx} \mathbf{a} - \mathbf{b}^T \mathbf{S}_{yy} \mathbf{b} - \lambda_1 \left(\mathbf{a}^T \mathbf{a} - 1 \right)$$
$$- \lambda_2 \left(\mathbf{b}^T \mathbf{b} - 1 \right), \tag{4}$$

where both λ_1 and λ_2 are Lagrange multipliers.

The solutions to Equation (4) are given as follows:

$$\left(\mathbf{S}_{xy} \left(\mathbf{S}_{yy} + \lambda_2 \mathbf{I}_q \right)^{-1} \mathbf{S}_{xy}^T - \mathbf{S}_{xx} \right) \mathbf{a} = \lambda_1 \mathbf{a}, \tag{5}$$

$$\left(\mathbf{S}_{xy}^T \left(\mathbf{S}_{xx} + \lambda_1 \mathbf{I}_p \right)^{-1} \mathbf{S}_{xy} - \mathbf{S}_{yy} \right) \mathbf{b} = \lambda_2 \mathbf{b}, \tag{6}$$

where $\mathbf{I}_p$ and $\mathbf{I}_q$ denote identity matrices of size $p * p$ and $q * q$, respectively.

Both λ_1 and λ_2 in Equations (5) and (6) are called regularization parameters. By solving Equation (5), the eigenvalues $\lambda_1^{(1)}, \lambda_1^{(2)}, \ldots, \lambda_1^{(p)}$ and their corresponding eigenvectors $\mathbf{a}_1, \mathbf{a}_2, \ldots, \mathbf{a}_p$ can be obtained. The eigenvalues $\lambda_2^{(1)}, \lambda_2^{(2)}, \ldots, \lambda_2^{(q)}$ and their corresponding eigenvectors $\mathbf{b}_1, \mathbf{b}_2, \ldots, \mathbf{b}_q$ can be obtained from Equation (6).

3. Orthogonal Regularized Kernel CCA Algorithm (ORKCCA)

ORCCA algorithm can give the linear relationships between two groups of random variables. But if the linear relationships between two groups of random variables do not exist, the performance of ORCCA will not work well. The kernel method is an effective way to analyze the nonlinear pattern problem. So, the kernel method is introduced into ORCCA algorithm, and ORKCCA algorithm is proposed.

Both Φ_x and Φ_y are nonlinear mappings which map original random variables $\mathbf{x}_i$ and $\mathbf{y}_i$ into $\Phi_x(\mathbf{x}_i)$ and $\Phi_y(\mathbf{y}_i)$ in P-dimensional space $F_x (P > p)$ and Q-dimensional space $F_y (Q > q)$, $i = 1, 2, \ldots, n$. Let $\mathbf{a} = \Phi_x(\mathbf{X})^T \boldsymbol{\alpha}$, $\mathbf{b} = \Phi_y(\mathbf{Y})^T \boldsymbol{\beta}$, where $\Phi_x(\mathbf{X}) \in R^{n \times P}$, $\Phi_y(\mathbf{Y}) \in R^{n \times Q}$ $\boldsymbol{\alpha}, \boldsymbol{\beta} \in R^n$.

ORCCA is implemented in higher-dimensional spaces F_x and F_y. So, Equation (7) can be obtained by substituting $\mathbf{a}$, $\mathbf{b}$, $\Phi_x(\mathbf{x}_i)$, and $\Phi_y(\mathbf{y}_i)$ into Equation (1) as follows:

$$\min_{\boldsymbol{\alpha},\boldsymbol{\beta}} \quad \frac{1}{n} \sum_{i=1}^{n} \left\| \boldsymbol{\alpha}^T \Phi_x(\mathbf{X}) \Phi_x(\mathbf{x}_i) - \boldsymbol{\beta}^T \Phi_y(\mathbf{Y}) \Phi_y(\mathbf{y}_i) \right\|^2,$$

$$\text{s.t.} \quad \boldsymbol{\alpha}^T \Phi_x(\mathbf{X}) \Phi_x(\mathbf{X})^T \boldsymbol{\alpha} = 1, \tag{7}$$

$$\boldsymbol{\beta}^T \Phi_y(\mathbf{Y}) \Phi_y(\mathbf{Y})^T \boldsymbol{\beta} = 1.$$

Expanding the objective function in Equation (7), we get

$$\frac{1}{n} \sum_{i=1}^{n} \left\| \boldsymbol{\alpha}^T \Phi_x(\mathbf{X}) \Phi_x(\mathbf{x}_i) - \boldsymbol{\beta}^T \Phi_y(\mathbf{Y}) \Phi_y(\mathbf{y}_i) \right\|^2$$

$$= \boldsymbol{\alpha}^T \frac{1}{n} \Phi_x(\mathbf{X}) \Phi_x(\mathbf{X})^T \Phi_x(\mathbf{X}) \Phi_x(\mathbf{X})^T \boldsymbol{\alpha}$$

$$+ \boldsymbol{\beta}^T \Phi_y(\mathbf{Y}) \Phi_y(\mathbf{Y})^T \Phi_y(\mathbf{Y}) \Phi_y(\mathbf{Y})^T \boldsymbol{\beta} \tag{8}$$

$$- 2\boldsymbol{\alpha}^T \frac{1}{n} \Phi_x(\mathbf{X}) \Phi_x(\mathbf{X})^T \Phi_y(\mathbf{Y}) \Phi_y(\mathbf{Y})^T \boldsymbol{\beta}.$$

Applying the kernel trick to Equation (8), $\mathbf{K}_x$ and $\mathbf{K}_y \in R^{n \times n}$ can be computed, namely, $\mathbf{K}_x = \Phi_x(X)\Phi_x(X)^T = (\Phi_x(x_i)^T \Phi_x(x_j))_{n \times n} = (k(x_i, x_j))_{n \times n}$ $\mathbf{K}_y = \Phi_y(Y)\Phi_y(Y)^T = (\Phi_y(y_i)^T \Phi_y(y_j))_{n \times n} = (k(y_i, y_j))_{n \times n}$, where $k(\cdot, \cdot)$ is kernel function. Centralization is exerted on $\mathbf{K}_x$ and $\mathbf{K}_y$. The optimal model in which the kernel method is introduced can be given by using Equation (9):

$$\max_{\boldsymbol{\alpha},\boldsymbol{\beta}} \quad 2\boldsymbol{\alpha}^T \mathbf{M}_{xy} \boldsymbol{\beta} - \boldsymbol{\alpha}^T \mathbf{M}_{xx} \boldsymbol{\alpha} - \boldsymbol{\beta}^T \mathbf{M}_{yy} \boldsymbol{\beta},$$

$$\text{s.t.} \quad \boldsymbol{\alpha}^T \mathbf{K}_x \boldsymbol{\alpha} = 1, \tag{9}$$

$$\boldsymbol{\beta}^T \mathbf{K}_y \boldsymbol{\beta} = 1,$$

where $\mathbf{M}_{xy} = (1/n)\mathbf{K}_x^T \mathbf{K}_y$, $\mathbf{M}_{xx} = (1/n)\mathbf{K}_x^T \mathbf{K}_x$, and $\mathbf{M}_{yy} = 1/n\mathbf{K}_y^T \mathbf{K}_y$.

According to the Lagrange multiplier method, the Lagrange function is as follows

$$L'(\boldsymbol{\alpha},\boldsymbol{\beta}) = 2\boldsymbol{\alpha}^T \mathbf{M}_{xy} \boldsymbol{\beta} - \boldsymbol{\alpha}^T \mathbf{M}_{xx} \boldsymbol{\alpha} - \boldsymbol{\beta}^T \mathbf{M}_{yy} \boldsymbol{\beta} - \zeta_1 \left(\boldsymbol{\alpha}^T \mathbf{K}_x \boldsymbol{\alpha} - 1 \right)$$
$$- \zeta_2 \left(\boldsymbol{\beta}^T \mathbf{K}_y \boldsymbol{\beta} - 1 \right), \tag{10}$$

where ζ_1 and ζ_2 are Lagrange multipliers. Taking the partial derivatives of $L'(\boldsymbol{\alpha}, \boldsymbol{\beta})$ with respect to $\boldsymbol{\alpha}$ and $\boldsymbol{\beta}$ and letting them zero, we get

$$\begin{cases} \dfrac{\partial L'}{\partial \boldsymbol{\alpha}} = 2 \left(\mathbf{M}_{xy} \boldsymbol{\beta} - \mathbf{M}_{xx} \boldsymbol{\alpha} - \zeta_1 \boldsymbol{\alpha} \right) = 0, \\[2mm] \dfrac{\partial L'}{\partial \boldsymbol{\beta}} = 2 \left(\mathbf{M}_{xy}^T \boldsymbol{\alpha} - \mathbf{M}_{yy} \boldsymbol{\beta} - \zeta_2 \boldsymbol{\beta} \right) = 0, \end{cases} \tag{11}$$

where $\mathbf{M}_{xx}$ and $\mathbf{M}_{yy}$ are positive semidefinite matrices and ζ_1 and ζ_2 are positive numbers.

So, α and β can be obtained from Equation (11):

$$\alpha = \left(M_{xx} + \zeta_1 I_P\right)^{-1} M_{xy}\beta, \qquad (12)$$

$$\beta = \left(M_{yy} + \zeta_2 I_Q\right)^{-1} M_{xy}^T \alpha, \qquad (13)$$

where I_P and I_Q are the identity matrices of size $P * P$ and $Q * Q$, respectively.

Equations (14) and (15) can be obtained through replacing α and β with their expressions in Equations (12) and (13), respectively.

$$\left(M_{xy}\left(M_{yy} + \zeta_2 I_Q\right)^{-1} M_{xy}^T - M_{xx}\right)\alpha = \zeta_1 \alpha, \qquad (14)$$

$$\left(\mathbf{M}_{xy}^T\left(\mathbf{M}_{xx} + \zeta_1 \mathbf{I}_P\right)^{-1}\mathbf{M}_{xy} - \mathbf{M}_{yy}\right)\beta = \zeta_2 \beta. \qquad (15)$$

As like before, both λ_1 and λ_2 in Equations (14) and (15) are called regularization parameters. By solving Equation (14), the eigenvalues $\zeta_1^{(1)}, \zeta_1^{(2)}, \ldots, \zeta_1^{(n)}$ and their corresponding eigenvectors $\alpha_1, \alpha_2, \ldots, \alpha_P$ can be obtained. The eigenvalues $\zeta_2^{(1)}, \zeta_2^{(2)}, \ldots, \zeta_2^{(Q)}$ and their corresponding eigenvectors $\beta_1, \beta_2, \ldots, \beta_Q$ can be obtained from Equation (15).

4. Simulation Experiments

In this section, we evaluate our method compared with ORCCA on artificial and handwritten numerals databases.

4.1. Experiment on Artifical Databases. The pairwise samples $\mathbf{X}$ and $\mathbf{Y}$ are generated from the expressions in Equations (16) and (17), respectively.

$$\mathbf{x} = \begin{pmatrix} \theta \\ \cos\dfrac{\theta}{2} \\ \sin 3\theta \\ \sin\theta\cos\theta \end{pmatrix} + \boldsymbol{\varepsilon}_1, \qquad (16)$$

$$\mathbf{y} = e^{2\theta}\begin{pmatrix} \cos\theta^2 \\ \sin\dfrac{\theta}{3} \end{pmatrix} + \boldsymbol{\varepsilon}_2, \qquad (17)$$

where θ obeys uniform distribution on $[-\pi, \pi]$ and $\boldsymbol{\varepsilon}_1$ and $\boldsymbol{\varepsilon}_2$ are Gaussian noise with standard deviation 0.05. The radial basis function $k(\mathbf{x}, \mathbf{y}) = \exp\left(-|\mathbf{x} - \mathbf{y}|^2/2\sigma^2\right)$ is chosen as kernel function, where $\sigma = 1.0$.

4.1.1. Determining Regularization Parameters. For the selection of the regularization parameters, by far there is no reliable method to determine the optimal values. In this paper, in order to simplify the calculation, let $\lambda = \lambda_1 = \lambda_2$ and $\zeta = \zeta_1 = \zeta_2$. The regularization parameters were chosen from 10^{-5}, 10^{-4}, 10^{-3}, 10^{-2}, 10^{-1}, and 1. This method is used in the literature [5].

According to Equations (16) and (17), 100 pairs of data are randomly generated as the training samples. Canonical variables are calculated from the ORCCA and ORKCCA algorithms for the different values of regularization parameters. The correlation coefficients of canonical variables are sorted by the descending order. Many pairs of canonical variables can be gained from the two algorithms. For the sake of simplicity, the most representative of the former two groups of canonical variables are examined.

The average value of the correlation coefficients of the former two groups of canonical variables is regarded as criterion that judges the regularization parameters is good or not. The larger the average value is, the better the regularization parameters are.

Table 1 lists the average value of the correlation coefficients of the former two groups of canonical variables for the different values of the regularization parameters.

Table 1 shows that the optimal values of the regularization parameters for the ORCCA and ORKCCA algorithms are 10^{-3} and 10^{-1}, respectively. The optimal regularization parameters are used to perform simulations in the next section.

4.1.2. Simulation Experiment 1. According to Equations (16) and (17), 200 pairs of data are randomly generated as the test samples. For the regularization parameters $\lambda = 10^{-3}$ and $\zeta = 10^{-1}$ in the ORCCA and ORKCCA algorithms, the canonical variables are obtained for test samples, respectively. The correlation coefficients of the canonical variables are sorted in the descending order.

Tables 2 and 3 list the correlation coefficients of the first two groups of canonical variables for ORCCA and ORKCCA algorithms. u_1 and v_1 denote the first group of canonical variables. u_2 and v_2 are the second group of canonical variables.

The experimental results in Tables 2 and 3 show that the correlationships between the same pair of the canonical variables are better than that between the different pairs of canonical variables, especially for nonlinear data.

4.1.3. Simulation Experiment 2. According to Equations (16) and (17), 5 pairs of data are randomly generated as the sample data. Each pair of sample data represents the center data of each class. 100 pairs of data for each class are given by adding Gaussian noise with standard deviation of 0.05 to each class center data. So we have five class data, which contains 100 samples for each class.

100, 175, and 250 pairs of data are chosen from the 500 pairs of the whole data as the training samples, respectively. The rest 400, 325, and 250 pairs of data are the test samples, respectively. The classification experiments based on K-neighbors algorithm are carried out on the test samples data which are preprocessed in the above way. And, the accuracies of classification are given. For the test samples with 400, 325, and 250 pairs of data, the experiments are performed 15 times, respectively. The accuracies of classification for 400, 325, and 250 pairs of data are the averages of the accuracies of classification for the 15 experiments results,

TABLE 1: The mean values of the correlation coefficients of the former two groups of canonical variables for the different values of the regularization parameters from ORCCA and ORKCCA.

Regularization parameters	Mean values of the correlation coefficients	
	ORCCA	ORKCCA
10^{-5}	0.74	0.80
10^{-4}	0.77	0.84
10^{-3}	**0.82**	0.89
10^{-2}	0.81	0.92
10^{-1}	0.79	**0.93**
1	0.80	0.92

TABLE 2: The correlation coefficients of the first two groups of canonical variables for ORCCA.

	v_1	v_2
u_1	0.58	0.14
u_2	0.21	0.36

TABLE 3: The correlation coefficients of the first two groups of canonical variables for ORkCCA.

	v_1	v_2
u_1	0.91	0.08
u_2	0.06	0.83

respectively. Table 4 gives the accuracies of classification for ORCCA and ORKCCA for the test samples with the different number.

In Table 4, the first column is the numbers of the training samples and the second column and the third column are the accuracies of classification for ORCCA and ORKCCA for the training samples with the different number. The experimental results show that the accuracies of classification for ORKCCA are higher than those for ORCCA. So, the performance of ORKCCA outperforms that of ORCCA for the nonlinear problem. The comparison curves of the accuracies of classification for ORCCA and ORKCCA are given in Figure 1.

4.2. Experiments on Handwritten Numerals Databases. The Concordia University CENPARMI database of handwritten Arabic numerals have 10 classes, that is, 10 digits (from 0 to 9), and 600 samples for each. The first 400 samples are used as the training set, and the remaining samples as the test set in each class. Then, the training samples and the test samples are 4000 and 2000, respectively. The handwritten digital images are preprocessed by the method given in [14]. Four kinds of features are extracted as follows: X^G (256-dimensional Gabor transformation feature), X^L (121-dimensional Legendre moment feature), X^P (36-dimensional Pseudo-Zernike moment feature), and X^Z (30-dimensional Zernike moment feature).

For the choice of the regularization parameters, let $\lambda = \lambda_1 = \lambda_2$ and $\zeta = \zeta_1 = \zeta_2$. The regularization parameters were chosen from 10^{-5}, 10^{-3}, and 1. The results of our method are

TABLE 4: Comparisons of the accuracies of classification for ORCCA and ORKCCA.

Numbers of the training samples	ORCCA (%)	ORKCCA (%)
100	65.0	73.1
175	72.4	77.8
250	76.5	83.6

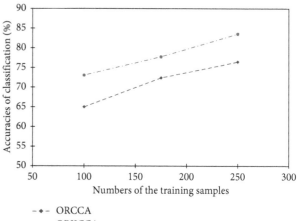

FIGURE 1: Comparison curves of the accuracies of classification for ORCCA and ORKCCA.

TABLE 5: Comparisons of the accuracies of classification for ORCCA and ORKCCA in different feature combinations and regularization parameters.

Feature combinations	ORCCA			ORKCCA		
	$\lambda = 10^{-5}$	$\lambda = 10^{-3}$	$\lambda = 1$	$\zeta = 10^{-5}$	$\zeta = 10^{-3}$	$\zeta = 1$
X^G-X^L	0.9314	0.9300	0.9375	0.9625	0.9681	0.9687
X^G-X^P	0.9230	0.9228	0.9248	0.9511	0.9525	0.9536
X^G-X^Z	0.9180	0.9196	0.9196	0.9482	0.9518	0.9520
X^L-X^P	0.9187	0.9187	0.9190	0.9500	0.9533	0.9545
X^L-X^Z	0.9200	0.9205	0.9235	0.9574	0.9600	0.9615
X^P-X^Z	0.7413	0.7413	0.7525	0.8436	0.8450	0.8450

compared with the results of ORCCA in order to verify the effectiveness of ORKCCA. Table 5 lists the accuracies of classification for ORCCA and ORKCCA in different feature combinations and regularization parameters. Experimental results show that (1) the classification effect of the two methods is the best as the regularization parameter is 1; (2) the classification accuracies of ORKCCA are higher than that of ORCCA for different features combinations; (3) the classification accuracies of ORKCCA in the regularization parameters 10^{-5} and 10^{-3} are higher than those of ORCCA in the regularization parameters 1.

5. Conclusions

An orthogonal regularized kernel CCA algorithm for nonlinear problem is presented. By introducing the kernel function, our proposed algorithm is more suitable for solving nonlinear problem. Contrast experiments of ORCCA and ORKCCA are performed on artificial and handwritten numerals databases. Experimental results show that the proposed method outperforms ORCCA for the correlation coefficients of canonical variables and the accuracies of classification on the test data. The experimental results show ORKCCA is feasible.

Conflicts of Interest

The authors declare that they have no conflicts of interest.

Acknowledgments

The authors are grateful to the support of the Hainan Provincial Natural Science Foundation (117150) and the Scientific Research Foundation of Hainan Tropical Ocean University (RHDXB201624).

References

[1] Q. H. Ran, Z. N. Shi, and Y. P. Xu, "Canonical correlation analysis of hydrological response and soil erosion under moving rainfall," *Journal of Zhejiang University-SCIENCE A*, vol. 14, no. 5, pp. 353–361, 2013.

[2] B. K. Sarkar and C. Chakraborty, "DNA pattern recognition using canonical correlation algorithm," *Journal of Biosciences*, vol. 40, no. 4, pp. 709–719, 2015.

[3] R. R. Sarvestani and R. Boostani, "FF-SKPCCA: kernel probabilistic canonical correlation analysis," *Applied Intelligence*, vol. 46, no. 2, pp. 438–454, 2016.

[4] E. Sakar, H. Ünver, S. Keskin, and Z. M. Sakar, "The investigation of relationships between some fruit and kernel traits with canonical correlation analysis in ankara region walnuts," *Erwerbs-Obstbau*, vol. 58, no. 1, pp. 19–23, 2015.

[5] S. D. Hou and Q. S. Sun, "An orthogonal regularized CCA learning algorithm for feature fusion," *Journal of Visual Communication and Image Representation*, vol. 25, no. 5, pp. 785–792, 2014.

[6] X. Shen and Q. Sun, "Orthogonal multiset canonical correlation analysis based on fractional-order and its application in multiple feature extraction and recognition," *Neural Process Letters*, vol. 42, no. 2, pp. 301–316, 2015.

[7] Y. H. Yuan, Y. Li, X. B. Shen, Q. S. Sun, and J. L. Yang, "Laplacian multiset canonical correlations for multiview feature extraction and image recognition," *Multimedia Tools and Applications*, vol. 76, no. 1, pp. 731–755, 2015.

[8] X. Xing, K. Wang, T. Yan, and Z. Lv, "Complete canonical correlation analysis with application to multi-view gait recognition," *Pattern Recognition*, vol. 50, pp. 107–117, 2016.

[9] H. Joutsijoki and M. Juhola, "Kernel selection in multi-class support vector machines and its consequence to the number of ties in majority voting method," *Artificial Intelligence Review*, vol. 40, no. 3, pp. 213–230, 2013.

[10] S. Wang, Z. Deng, F. L. Chung, and W. Hu, "From Gaussian kernel density estimation to kernel methods," *International Journal of Machine Learning and Cybernetics*, vol. 4, no. 2, pp. 119–137, 2013.

[11] X. Chen, R. Tharmarasa, T. Kirubarajan, and M. Mcdonald, "Online clutter estimation a Gaussian kernel density estimator for multitarget tracking," *Radar Sonar and Navigation IET*, vol. 9, no. 1, pp. 1–9, 2014.

[12] O. Taouali, I. Jaffel, H. Lahdhiri, M. F. Harkat, and H. Messaoud, "New fault detection method based on reduced kernel principal component analysis (RKPCA)," *International Journal of Advanced Manufacturing Technology*, vol. 85, no. 5, pp. 1547–1552, 2016.

[13] K. Yoshida, J. Yoshimoto, and K. Doya, "Sparse kernel canonical correlation analysis for discovery of nonlinear interactions in high-dimensional data," *BMC Bioinformatics*, vol. 18, no. 1, pp. 108–118, 2017.

[14] Z. Hu, Z. Lou, J. Yang, K. Liu, and C. Suen, "Handwritten digital recognition based on multi-classifier combination," *Chinese Journal Computers*, vol. 22, no. 4, pp. 369–374, 1999.

18

Cloud Multidomain Access Control Model based on Role and Trust-Degree

Lixia Xie and Chong Wang

School of Computer Science and Technology, Civil Aviation University of China, No. 2898, Jinbei Road, Tianjin 300300, China

Correspondence should be addressed to Lixia Xie; lxxie@126.com

Academic Editor: Hui Cheng

In order to solve the problem of access control among different security domains in cloud networks, this paper presents an access control model based on role and trust-degree. The model combines role-based access control and trust-based access control. The role assessment weights are defined based on the user's role classes, and the trust-degree is calculated according to the role assessment weights and the role's behavior. In order to increase the accuracy of access control, the model gives the concept and calculation methods of feedback trust-degree. To achieve fine-grained access control, the model introduces direct trust-degree, recommendation trust-degree, and feedback trust-degree, all of which participate in comprehensive trust-degree by adjusting their weights. A simulation experiment was conducted in the LAN environment, and a web system was used to construct an access control model with multisecurity domains in the experiment. The experimental results demonstrate that our model has higher security, expansibility, and flexibility.

1. Introduction

With the rapid development of network technology and cloud computing, attacks and interactions are becoming more and more frequent; complex network security situation will be more serious. By controlling the access permission of the key resources, access control achieves the protection of system resources, ensuring that all of the main direct entrances to the object are authorized and preventing legitimate users from using illegal access to system resources at the same time. Access control policy is one of the main strategies of network security and the main method to realize data confidentiality and integrity [1]; it has become the important subject in the area of network security.

At present the commonly used access control policy includes discretionary access control, mandatory access control, and role-based access control [1]. Due to the arbitrariness in users' privileges transfer, discretionary access control is unable to ensure the security of the system, and it is not conducive to achieving a unified global access control. In addition, it is easy for the protected information to leak, and it can not resist the Trojan horse attacks in this access control policy [2]. However, the mandatory access control is no interference access control. Due to its reinforcement in access restrictions, the system flexibility declines, and the application is limited. At present, this policy is mainly used in military and the field which has obvious hierarchies and the high security requirement. Role-based access control is different from the above two kinds of access control policy and develops rapidly. It combined with existing security technologies. A variety of access control models emerged. Reference [3] proposed a C/S structure of trust decentralized access control (TDAC) framework: through the client's temporary monitors and server-side assessment of the primary monitor application access request in the subject context-aware access control to protect private data. The defects of this method are increasing the burden to clients and servers. When error occurs in the clients, the servers will not easily detect and repair it. Reference [4] proposed a flexible access control strategy, and the strategy ensures that when users are offline, independent user groups still have the right to perform critical tasks, but the performance of this strategy should be improved. Reference [5] proposed a comprehensive encryption-based access control framework for the content

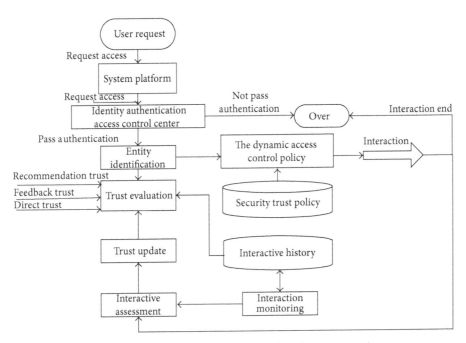

FIGURE 1: Framework of role and trust-based access control.

centric network; it was also extensible and flexible. The design of the framework mostly relied on secure content objects' concept. It also implemented two access control schemes, group-based access control and broadcast access control, to demonstrate the flexibility. Reference [5] proposed a hybrid access control model. It combined the advantage of both type enforcement model and role-based access control. It enabled unified access control and authorization for IaaS clouds and the permission transition framework was also provided to dynamically assign permission to virtual machines. This paper puts forward the access control that is based on roles and trust method, the concept of feedback credibility, and the role of trust evaluation weight. It also combined with direct trust and recommended trust to evaluate the user's access behaviors [6]. It realizes the dynamic fine-grained access control.

2. Model Framework

The framework which is based on role and trust entity access control is shown in Figure 1. It describes the relationship of each component. The framework mainly includes the entity recognition and trust management. The following paragraphs will give instructions about the two parts.

2.1. Entity Recognition. The framework of the entity recognition [6] is mainly used to identify the login entity components (user) level, so as to obtain the trust evaluation weights used in the subsequent fine-grained trust evaluation. Entity recognition features include the foreign entity visit and entity mapping, in the process, if the entity for anonymous entity will not affect the interaction with other entities.

If the anonymous entity has the identity of the lowest level, conforming to the resource access trust threshold can

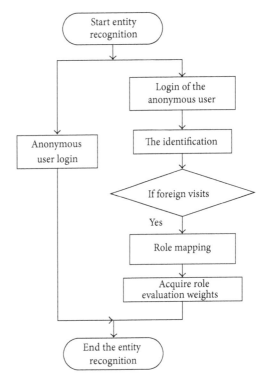

FIGURE 2: Entity recognition process.

also be carried out in accordance with the established process interaction. The anonymous entity in the process of the session by the trust through the above framework participates in the trust evaluation; in order to avoid malicious slander, anonymous users' trust evaluation will not be involved. Entity recognition process is shown in Figure 2.

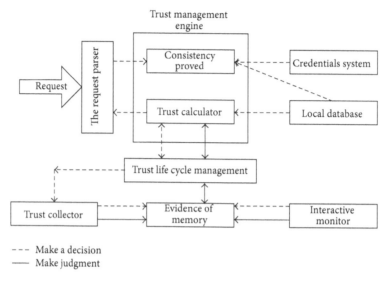

FIGURE 3: Trust management model structures.

2.2. Trust Management.

2.2. Trust Management. Trust management include computing, collecting, and updating the trust. Trust management model structure is shown in Figure 3. Trust computation can be divided into three parts: interactive entity directly trusted computing, feedback trust computation, and other entities in the recommendation trust computing network. In the process of the above calculation, it gives three kinds of calculation results of different weight coefficient.

If interactive entities are new members of the network, we give an initial trust value and assign certain access permissions through a third-party authority. The entities that are out of the system also can use anonymous entity. The system automatically assigned a smaller trust value and the role of a minimal operation.

At present the commonly used access control models mainly include discretionary access control, mandatory access control, and role-based access control. Due to discretionary access control permissions to users with the transfer of the arbitrariness result in the decrease of the safety of the system. This is not conducive to achieving a unified global access control. The information leaks easily. It can not resist the Trojan horse attacks in the access control model. However the mandatory access control has no interference of access control, due to its access restrictions for the reinforcement, thus affecting the flexibility of the system. Role-based access control is different from the above two kinds of model. It obtained a rapid development and combined with some existing security technologies derived from a variety of access control model.

3. Role and Trust

Principal component analysis (PCA) is a mathematical transformation method [3], and it is used to reduce data dimension. It can switch the multidimensional data into several major dimensional data. The main problems that need to be solved in the role management include the role mapping, the strategy of role adding and deleting, and role

conflict resolution strategy. Set up the weight of participation trust-degree evaluation according to the level and this is role evaluation weight:

(1) Role mapping: when two equivalent security domains visit each other's resources, each should map the role in this domain to target resources domain's role. In access control model system proposed in this paper, the distrust security domain and trust security domain take different role mapping strategies.

(2) Adding the role: upon adding new roles, new role mapping's strategy is automatically generated according to the model's mapping strategy.

(3) Deleting the role: upon deleting a domain role, the mapping will be replaced until mapping this role to its subrole.

(4) Role conflict resolution: in this paper, the solution of role conflict of access control is to allow the outland role to have the right of the highest conversion role mapping.

(5) The role of trust evaluation: set up different roles according to the user in the access control security domain model and the role of the various security domains, each role assigned different weights of evaluation, and the higher weights reflect the higher user level permissions.

Table 1 is a sample which is set in the simulation experiments depending on the set role rank and role evaluation weight values, in a real environment, according to the need to set more user levels and evaluation weights which are fit for the level.

According to literature [4], the time t node n_i direct trust-degree is defined as $D(n_i, n_j, t)$. A direct trust table is distributed to the network nodes. Each cell in the table is the node for direct interaction. According to the direct trust table of all nodes to build a two-dimensional direct trust

TABLE 1: Example of rolegrade and role weight evaluation.

Role level	Role description	Evaluation weights
1	Total access control center administrator	1.00
2	Access control security domain administrator	0.95
3	Security component user	0.90
4	Anonymous users or components	none

relationship matrix [3], defining it as M_1, nodes n_i to node n_j direct trust is represented by $M_1(n_i, n_j)$.

At time t, if nodes n_i and n_j have an interaction, the direct trust $D(n_i, n_j, t)$ is

$$D\left(n_i, n_j, t\right) = M_1\left(n_i, n_j\right) e^{-(t-t_{ij})}, \quad t - t_{ij} \geq 0, \quad (1)$$

where $e^{-(t-t_{ij})}$ is time decay function. It describes the case that direct trust declines with time passing by.

If nodes n_i and nodes n_j have had interactions many times at time t, the direct trust is shown by mean value

$$D\left(n_i, n_j, t\right) = \frac{\sum_{k=1}^{I(k)} S\left(n_i, n_j, t_k\right) e^{-(t-t_k)}}{I(k)}, \quad t - t_k \geq 0, \quad (2)$$

where $\sum_{k=1}^{I(k)} S(n_i, n_j, t_k) e^{-(t-t_k)}$ is interaction evaluation expectations of nodes n_i and n_j after every interaction evaluation, $I(k)$ represents the times when nodes n_i and n_j have interactions frequency in time t. Based on literature [5], define recommendation trust $R(n_i, n_j, t)$ at time t of node n_i to node n_j:

$$R\left(n_i, n_j, t\right) = W_i \times D\left(n_i, n_j, t\right). \quad (3)$$

Recommendation trust of node n_j is given by recommended node n_i's evaluation of n_j. Trust evaluation weight is represented by w_i, defined as follows:

$$W_i = e^{-1/\sum_{k=1}^{I(k)} S(n_i, n_j, t_k) e^{-(t-t_k)}}. \quad (4)$$

On the basis of direct trust, this paper puts forward the concept of feedback trust and gives the calculation method of feedback credibility. Different from direct trust and recommendation trust, feedback trust is the evaluation which represents the feedback of their own behaviors. The feedback helps users adjust trust behavior quickly.

Definition 1. Feedback trust is a kind of excitation mechanism that users are responsible for their access behavior [6]. According to regulations, users can use information resources in the system safely and reliably; this will improve their trust and have permissions of enjoying more safe and reliable services.

In the access control model proposed in this paper, for every node n_i establish a two-dimensional feedback trust matrix. It records all the feedback trust between all nodes.

The feedback trust of node n_i to node n_j is represented by $M_2(n_i, n_j)$.

At time t, the feedback trust of node n_i to node n_j is defined as $F(n_i, n_j, t)$:

$$F\left(n_i, n_j, t\right) = M_2\left(n_i, n_j\right) e^{-(t-t_{ij})}, \quad t - t_{ij} \geq 0, \quad (5)$$

where $e^{-(t-t_{ij})}$ is time decay function.

Formula (5) is considering that the interaction time is only once. If nodes n_i and n_j interact many times, the users' operations feedback trust computing takes interaction average:

$$F\left(n_i, n_j, t\right) = \frac{\sum_{k=1}^{I(k)} X\left(n_i, n_j, t_k\right) e^{-(t-t_k)}}{I(k)}, \quad t - t_k \geq 0. \quad (6)$$

$X(n_i, n_j, t_k)$ represent moment t_k and node n_i feedback operation evaluation to n_j, taking value interval as $[0, 1]$. In formula (6), $\sum_{k=1}^{I(k)} X(n_i, n_j, t_k) e^{-(t-t_k)}$ is the evaluation of each interaction expectation after nodes n_i and n_j interaction evaluation and attenuation. $I(k)$ represent node n_j and n_i interactions times within the time t. Direct trust, recommendation trust, and feedback trust describe the user's trust from different views [7]. All are defined as comprehensive trust. It can describe user trust comprehensively and accurately. For arbitrary nodes n_i and n_j, then

$$T\left(n_i, n_j, t\right) = D\left(n_i, n_j, t\right) + R\left(n_i, n_j, t\right) + F\left(n_i, n_j, t\right), \quad (7)$$

where the comprehensive trust of node n_i to node n_j is represented by $T(n_i, n_j, t)$ at time t. When there are third-party authentication institutions to participate in the trust evaluation, nodes n_i, n_j formula of comprehensive trust at time t can be expressed as

$$
\begin{aligned}
T&\left(n_i, n_j, t\right) \\
&= \text{status}\left(n_i, n_j, t\right) \\
&\quad \wedge \left[D\left(n_i, n_j, t\right) + R\left(n_i, n_j, t\right) + F\left(n_i, n_j, t\right)\right],
\end{aligned} \quad (8)
$$

where $\text{status}(n_i, n_j, t)$ is a state function, representing the allowance of n_i to n_j at time t. $\text{status}(n_i, n_j, t)$'s value is 0 representing identity permission, 1 indicating identity is not allowed. If the interaction time is too long, the trust declines with time. The status of the current network node can not reflect trust by direct trust $D(n_i, n_j, t)$, and recommendation trust $R(n_i, n_j, t)$ and feedback credibility $F(n_i, n_j, t)$ can accurately reflect the current state of the node [8]. After calculating the direct trust $D(n_i, n_j, t)$, recommendation trust $R(n_i, n_j, t)$, and feedback credibility $F(n_i, n_j, t)$, comprehensive trust is calculated:

$$
\begin{aligned}
T&\left(n_i, n_j, t\right) \\
&= \text{status}\left(n_i, n_j, t\right) \\
&\quad \wedge \left[\alpha D\left(n_i, n_j, t\right) + \beta R\left(n_i, n_j, t\right) + \gamma F\left(n_i, n_j, t\right)\right],
\end{aligned} \quad (9)
$$

where $\alpha + \beta + \gamma = 1, \alpha \geq 0, \beta \geq 0, \gamma \geq 0$.

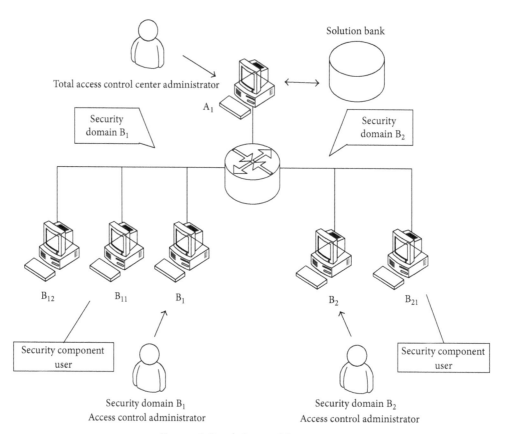

FIGURE 4: Simulation model structures.

If the security component is the service provider, it does not have feedback trust in practical situation [9]. Under this condition, the comprehensive trust is

$$T\left(n_i, n_j, t\right) = \text{status}\left(n_i, n_j, t\right)$$
$$\wedge \left[\alpha D\left(n_i, n_j, t\right) + \beta R\left(n_i, n_j, t\right)\right], \quad (10)$$

where $\alpha + \beta = 1$, $\alpha \geq 0$, $\beta \geq 0$. Similarly, if a certain security component does not provide services and resources, it does not have direct trust [10]. Under this condition the trust is

$$T\left(n_i, n_j, t\right) = \text{status}\left(n_i, n_j, t\right)$$
$$\wedge \left[\beta R\left(n_i, n_j, t\right) + \gamma F\left(n_i, n_j, t\right)\right]. \quad (11)$$

Among them, $\beta + \gamma = 1$, $\beta \geq 0$, $\gamma \geq 0$.

4. Experiments

The experiments are done in the laboratory's LAN environment. A server is the general access control center, two PC represent two different domain management centers, and the other three PC represent the security components of different domains. Simulation model structure is shown as in Figure 4. In Figure 4, A_1 is model access control center which is responsible for user management and providing safe trust policy, dynamic access control, interactive assessment, and trust evaluation. B_1 and B_2 are the domain management

centers which manage their security domain. B_{11}, B_{12}, and B_{21} belong to the security domain security components of security domains B_1 and B_2.

Simulation model is using B/S structure, so the B_{11}, B_{12}, and B_{21} do not need to deploy any function module, simply by IE login and connecting to the corresponding access control center module and interacting with other security components.

In the process of simulation experiment, by different user login access control system and other security components interaction access and access control center do corresponding actions in the process of access control. In order to achieve the legitimate users access to legal resources, illegal user cannot access resources, and the legal user cannot access illegal resources.

5. Experimental Process and Results

In the simulation model, userb_{12} and userb_{11} were two security components in security domain B_1. In the process of creating security component of model, users were given 0.7 as initial recommendation trust.

Different user roles grading to ascertain the weight of character evaluation values is according to Table 1 and, in the initial stages, defined on the relationship between the credibility and trust, as shown in Table 2.

At this time the direct trust and feedback trust were 0. In the model the user creates immediate access to the test,

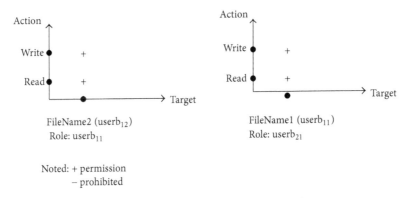

FIGURE 5: Access policies of userb$_{11}$ and userb$_{12}$.

TABLE 2: Definition of trust status.

Trust *value t*	Trust situation
$0 \le t < 0.5$	Do not *trust*
$0.5 \le t < 1$	Relative *trust*
$t = 1$	Total *trust*

TABLE 3: Weights of the three trust degrees.

Right to direct trust value α	Recommendation trust weights β	Feedback trust weights γ
0.35	0.3	0.35
0.6	0.4	0.0
0.0	0.5	0.5
0.0	1.0	0.0

so at this time of attenuation it is negligible (the results approximately equal 0.7), so the first degree of trust visits is

$$T\left(n_i, n_j, t\right) = \alpha D\left(n_i, n_j, t\right) + \beta R\left(n_i, n_j, t\right) + \gamma F\left(n_i, n_j, t\right), \quad (12)$$

where $\alpha + \beta + \gamma = 1$, $a \ge 0$, $\beta \ge 0$, $\gamma \ge 0$.

Calculated by formula (1)–(11) $T(\text{userb}_{11}, \text{userb}_{12}, t_0) = T(\text{userb}_{12}, \text{userb}_{11}, t_0) \approx 0.7$; that is, at time t_0, component userb$_{11}$ access to components userb$_{12}$ trust is 0.7; at the same time userb$_{12}$ access to userb$_{11}$ trust was 0.7. Based on the model set userb$_{11}$ resources "document 1" literacy reading and writing trust-degree threshold were 0.5 and 0.7. userb$_{12}$ have the read and write permissions to "document 1."

Userb$_{11}$ is used for designing experiment of userb$_{12}$ access control policy as shown in Figure 5. Ordinate Action represents access Action, including two operations which are write and read. Abscissa represents the Target resources.

userb$_{11}$, for resources "document 2" after the read operation, calculated userb$_{12}$ providing services for direct trust evaluation of 0.9, according to type (12) to calculate the trust at this time $T(\text{userb}_{11}, \text{userb}_{12}, t_1) = 0.788$. According to "document 1" userb$_{11}$ setting threshold, userb$_{12}$ still have permissions to read and write. If userb$_{12}$ provides the unsafe service, on a visit to "document 2" again, after access to direct trust evaluation is set to 0.5, according to type (10) one gets $T(\text{userb}_{11}, \text{userb}_{12}, t_2) = 0.644$. At this point, according to userb$_{11}$ access to resources "document 1" trust threshold setting, userb$_{12}$ has only permissions to read and lost permissions to write, and it is through this mechanism that users are motivated to provide more safe and reliable service. If userb$_{12}$ has access components provided by certain standard judged to be extremely dangerous, relevant access components or the administrator can delimit userb$_{12}$ directly

into the blacklist, causing its loss of the appropriate minimum component resources access.

userb$_{11}$ to userb$_{12}$ resources for access to the direct trust evaluation are calculated; at the same time, userb$_{12}$ feedback on userb$_{11}$ for trust evaluation is calculated by formula (9) trust and synchronous update in the database. Through this mechanism they can exercise the power of their own incentive component, safer permissions to read and write, and so forth.

The detailed testing results of all kinds of trust weight value are shown in Table 3. For different access requirements of the system, the setting of the weight of all kinds of trusts is also different. It reflects the flexibility of the model. Based on the definition of various types of trust, the following conclusion can be drawn.

The test results can be seen from Table 3; when evaluating trust gradually reduced, the trust declined. On the contrary, when a user provided good service and safe and reliable resources or used their legal rights, it had the higher credibility evaluation. Thus the total trust increased. The experimental results showed the feasibility and effectiveness of the proposed access control mode.

Experiments of all kinds of trust weight value settings are shown in Table 3. For different access requirements of the system, the setting of the weight of all kinds of trust also is different; it also reflects the flexibility of the model. Based on the definition of various types of trust one can draw the following conclusion. When direct trust weight value is bigger, the user's comprehensive trust continued volatility may occur; for example, for some security component trust evaluation is more matching and for other components trust is completely opposite. When the recommendation trust

TABLE 4: Test result.

Users	Comprehensive trust	Target resource	Operation	Result	Trust evaluation/role level
$Userb_{11}$	0.7000	Document 2	Read	0: action succeeded	0.90/1, 0.90/3
$Userb_{12}$	0.8200	Document 1	Read	0: action succeeded	0.85/1, 0.85/3
$Userb_{11}$	0.8225	Document 2	Write	0: action succeeded	0.80/1, 0.80/3
$Userb_{12}$	0.8050	Document 1	Write	0: action succeeded	0.75/1, 0.75/3
$Userb_{11}$	0.7875	Document 2	Read	0: action succeeded	0.70/1, 0.70/3
$Userb_{12}$	0.7452	Document 1	Read	0: action succeeded	0.65/1, 0.65/3
$Userb_{11}$	0.6378	Document 2	Write	1: action is not allowed	0.60/1, 0.60/3
$Userb_{12}$	0.5968	Document 1	Write	1: action is not allowed	0.55/1, 0.55/3
$Userb_{11}$	0.4968	Document 2	Read	1: action is not allowed	0.50/1, 0.50/3
$Userb_{12}$	0.4658	Document 1	Read	1: action is not allowed	0.45/1, 0.45/3
$Userb_{11}$	0.3847	document 2	Write	1: action is not allowed	0.40/1, 0.40/3

weight value is bigger, the user's comprehensive trust value is relatively stable.

When feedback trust weight value is larger, comprehensive trust users access to the current user behavior is more sensitive and can quickly reflect the current access behavior trust situation. In general according to the different requirements of different systems all kinds of trust weight value can be set. This also can make all kinds of trust weight values roughly equal. The weights of three kinds of trust assignment are shown in Table 3.

In Table 3, the first line says three types of trust are the weights of evaluation. The second line indicates only direct trust and recommendation trust weights. The third line showed only recommendation trust and feedback trust weights. In the fourth row only recommendation trust weights are shown. Recommendation trust in the building of a role is given, so it is inevitable.

Detailed test results are shown in Table 4. Initial conditions are as follows: system building role given recommended trust being 0.7, the name of documents 1 and 2, and speaking, reading, and writing trust threshold being 0.5 and 0.7. Detailed test of read and write operations alternates, initial interaction evaluation value is 0.9; read and write interactive evaluation is reduced to 0.05.

6. Conclusions

This paper puts forward a kind of access control method based on the character and credibility. It also puts forward the concept of feedback credibility and the role of trust evaluation weight, combined with direct trust and recommendation trust. Direct trust and recommendation trust all evaluate the user's access comprehensive action. The effectiveness of the proposed model is verified by simulation.

The test results can be seen from Table 4; when evaluating trust gradually reduced, the trust will drop. On the other hand, when a user provides good service and safe and reliable resources or exercises their GeFaQuan period, it will get higher credibility evaluation; thus the total trust will be increased.

Design of access control model in this paper is through such mechanism incentive component users with better service and more safe and reliable resources and more effective

exercise of their rights and increase of their trust, so as to enjoy a higher authority. Based on user roles we set different weights of evaluation and give the weight of different trust to achieve fine-grained trust evaluation and credibility in order to achieve the fair and reasonable evaluation purpose. The test results of Table 4 show that the access control model proposed in this paper is feasible and effective.

Competing Interests

The authors declare that they have no financial and personal relationships with other people or organizations that can inappropriately influence their work, and there is no professional or other personal interest of any nature or kind in any product, service, and/or company that could be construed as influencing the position presented in, or the review of, this paper.

References

[1] G. Jun, *Research on the Hierarchical Authorization Management of Role-Based Access Control*, Xidian University, Xi'an, China, 2012.

[2] S. Barker, M. J. Sergot, and D. Wijesekera, "Status-based access control," *ACM Transactions on Information and System Security*, vol. 12, no. 1, pp. 1–47, 2008.

[3] W. Han, M. Xu, W. Zhao, and G. Li, "A trusted decentralized access control framework for the client/server architecture," *Journal of Network and Computer Applications*, vol. 33, no. 2, pp. 76–83, 2010.

[4] N.-H. Li, M. V. Tripunitara, and Q.-H. Wang, "Resiliency policies in access control," in *Proceedings of the 13th ACM Conference on Computer and Communications Security*, pp. 113–123, ACM Press, 2009.

[5] J. Kuriharay, E. Uzun, and C. A. Wood, "An encryption-based access control framework for content-centric networking," in *Proceedings of the 14th IFIP Networking Conference*, pp. 1–9, IEEE, Toulouse, France, May 2015.

[6] C. Zhou and B. Li, "iHAC: a hybrid access control framework for IaaS clouds," in *Proceedings of the IEEE/ACM 7th International Conference on Utilty and Cloud Computing (UCC '14)*, pp. 853–858, London, UK, December 2014.

[7] W. Tolone, G. J. Ahn, and T. Pai, "Access system," *Journal of ACM Computing Surveys*, vol. 37, no. 1, pp. 29–41, 2005.

[8] S. Barker, M. J. Sergot, and D. Wijesekera, "Status-based access control," *ACM Transactions on Information and System Security*, vol. 12, no. 1, article 1, 2008.

[9] W. Liang and G. Ya-Jun, "Reputation-based on trust evaluation mechanism for P2P system," *Computer Engineering and Applications*, vol. 45, no. 15, pp. 136–138, 2009.

[10] S. Ma, J. He, and F. Gao, "An access control model based on multi-factors trust," *Journal of Networks*, vol. 7, no. 1, pp. 173–178, 2012.

19

Behavior Intention Derivation of Android Malware using Ontology Inference

Jian Jiao ⓘ,[1,2] Qiyuan Liu ⓘ,[1,2] Xin Chen ⓘ,[2] and Hongsheng Cao[1,2]

[1]Beijing Key Laboratory of Internet Culture and Digital Dissemination Research, Beijing Information Science and Technology University, Beijing, China
[2]School of Computer Science, Beijing Information Science and Technology University, Beijing, China

Correspondence should be addressed to Jian Jiao; jiaojian@bistu.edu.cn

Academic Editor: Ahmad K. Malik

Previous researches on Android malware mainly focus on malware detection, and malware's evolution makes the process face certain hysteresis. The information presented by these detected results (malice judgment, family classification, and behavior characterization) is limited for analysts. Therefore, a method is needed to restore the intention of malware, which reflects the relation between multiple behaviors of complex malware and its ultimate purpose. This paper proposes a novel description and derivation model of Android malware intention based on the theory of intention and malware reverse engineering. This approach creates ontology for malware intention to model the semantic relation between behaviors and its objects and automates the process of intention derivation by using SWRL rules transformed from intention model and Jess inference engine. Experiments on 75 typical samples show that the inference system can perform derivation of malware intention effectively, and 89.3% of the inference results are consistent with artificial analysis, which proves the feasibility and effectiveness of our theory and inference system.

1. Introduction

Android malware forms a gray interest industrial chain for the purpose of tariff consumption, malicious chargeback, malicious promotion, and privacy trafficking (privacy theft). Security companies face a large number of suspicious samples to analyze every day. The workload of manual analysis is huge, and the extraction efficiency of malicious features is low, which worsens the security situation of Android [1]. Therefore, the analysis of malware samples has become a top priority of Android security. Traditional malware analyses rely on the analysts' experience, and analysts can cope with limited number of new malicious samples, while being unable to handle it when the scale is too large. In addition, though detection tools based on malware characteristics and behavior patterns can detect some malicious behavior of malware, there are still some problems:

(i) The detected results only give a preliminary judgment of malware's malice. For example, this application may cause your privacy to be stolen or your cost loss. But they did not explain what kind of privacy was stolen and which kind of fee deduction happened.

(ii) Detection of malicious behavior may not reflect the ultimate intention of malware, such as remote control.

(iii) The detected information of behavior is limited and the granularity of the hint is too thick to carry out the whole malicious software intention analysis, and there are also some uncertain factors such as false positive rate.

Therefore, the traditional methods of malware detection combined with manual analysis are facing severe challenges. It has become the bottleneck of the development of Android security to some extent. We need to transform the traditional thinking pattern of research, focus on how to present malicious software intention to ordinary users, and allow users to obtain high readable software analysis results.

Behavior intention is defined as a *sequence of software behaviors* directed at a particular *purpose*. The definition contains two key components: sequence of software behaviors and purpose. We think that sensitive behaviors can be extracted from a program using sensitive APIs invocation (security relevant API invocation, usually controlled by sensitive permission) as a clue. But what is the purpose? How to represent the purpose of malware to users? We use one of our examples to illustrate the problem. This malware involves sensitive API calls, such as getMessageBody() and getDeviceId(), setEntity(), connect(), and execute(). It first accesses user's short message and device ID number; after encrypting them, it connects to a remote server and transmits the information to the server. We use access, encrypt, connect, and transmit to represent these behaviors, but the semantic of access (behavior) depends on its object (SMS, DeviceId); thus we use these objects to represent behaviors. After these APIs execution, the state of the objects will change; we use the final states of these objects to describe the purpose of intention. Now the key components in the definition of intention have been illustrated. We use this idea as motivation example to put forward our theory.

The aims of this research are as follows: firstly, extracting security sensitive semantic layer behaviors depending only on the semantic information (sensitive APIs) of the program; secondly, proposing a derivation and description method of security centric behavior chain that does not care about unrelated software behavior; thirdly, the final intention results based on the combination of natural language and formal representation. The advantage of formalization is that automatic behavior reasoning can be implemented and natural language description of behaviors can help users understand the semantics of program. The reasoning results can be represented by graphical method easily, so that the end-users can get concise and intuitive software intention information.

We propose a new description and derivation model of malware intention using the existing reverse analysis results [2–4] of Android malware and the theory of intention [5, 6]. On this basis, we complete the deduction of behavioral intention at semantic level with the help of ontology reasoning technology [7] and realize the reverse reduction from low-level Android malicious code to high-level intention finally. The main work of this paper is divided into two aspects: Firstly, the definition and formalized model of malware intention are given and the rationality of this model is proved. Secondly, we use ontology to model the semantic relationship between behaviors and objects and automate the process of intention derivation using SWRL [8] rules and Jess engine [9]. SWRL is a semantic web rule language combining OWL and RuleML and also a language that presents rules in a semantic way. Jess engine is the rule engine for Java platform, which can be used to complete many complex logical reasoning tasks.

The reasons for introducing ontology are as follows: (1) the conceptual system based on ontology is computable, and the automatic deduction of intentions can be achieved by the computing between concepts; (2) the ontology model of the elements and their relationships in malware behavior intention domain can standardize domain knowledge and make it shareable [10]; (3) the extensibility of ontology enables us to extend the conceptual model at any time according to the emergence of new features of malware.

The rest of the paper is organized as follows. Section 2 introduces related works about the research status of malware detection, reverse analysis, and the theory of intention. Section 3 elaborates the modeling process of the intention. Section 4 defines ontology model and SWRL rule and describes the establishment process of Fact Base. Section 5 shows the experimental results of our representative sample of malware. Finally, the paper concludes with Section 6.

2. Related Works

The essence of malware intention reduction is behavior analysis and software intention is divorced from the specific API function call. It is a behavior abstraction of semantic layer and can describe the behavior semantics intuitively. From the perspective of reverse engineering, ApkRiskAnalyzer [11] uses commercial disassembly tool IDA Pro [12] to collect the disassembly information. It constructs taint analysis engine and constant analysis engine to detect privacy disclosure behavior and constant use malicious behavior based on collected information. Jian and Qing [13] use the program slice of sensitive API to obtain the calling sequence of malicious code and then return the use case diagram of the whole malicious code. They restore the functional semantics of malicious behavior to some extent and help users locate malicious code quickly, but they do not consider the specific relationship between behaviors and cannot reflect the real intention of malware.

Android malware research mainly focuses on the determination of malicious behavior and the extraction of malicious features. Although the semantic relations between APIs are considered in [14–16] and certain results have been achieved, they come to the direction of malware detection eventually and cannot provide complete analysis and presentation of malware intention. AppContext [14] judges whether the behavior is benign or malicious according to the context of the sensitive API. It is believed that the trigger of security sensitive behavior can be judged by context, such as trigger events that lead to sensitive behavior or external environmental conditions. DroidADDMiner [15] gives the construction method of feature vectors required for machine learning through the extraction of data dependence paths between sensitive APIs and combines constant usage and context information, which can detect, classify, and characterize Android malware eventually. DroidSIFT [16] constructs weighted contextual API dependency graph based on semantics and then gives the corresponding weight according to the risk of sensitive API. After constructing the data set of behavior graph, similarity value of graph is used as the element of machine learning feature vector and the feature construction is completed finally.

The research of intention recognition is widely used in network security defense, artificial intelligence, natural language understanding, and so on. Intrusion intention recognition [17] is an analysis of a large amount of underlying alarm information to explain and determine what attackers want to achieve. It is essentially a process of implementing a reasonable interpretation of a large number of attack data. The identification of attacker's intention can determine the true intention of attackers and predict the subsequent behavior of attackers. It is the premise and foundation of threat analysis and decision response and is an important component of network security situational awareness. Shirley and Evans [6] get the malicious judgment of software behavior according to the matching degree of user's operation intention and software behavior. In the field of artificial intelligence [18], the human intention identified by agents is that of formal representation. These studies provide a theoretical basis for our malware intention modeling.

3. Model of Malware Intention

This chapter focuses on the modeling process of malware intention. First, the formalized definition of software intention is given according to the abstract of the problem and related literature. Then the key component in the definition of intention has been defined and explained. Finally, the inference process of intention model has been proved using mathematical theorem.

3.1. Formalization of Software Intention. In the study of behavioral theory, Bratman Michael [5] believes that intention should be a basic unit of behavior research and suggests that intention is behavior sequence based on future orientation; that is, the intention will influence the behavior of the next step. After the synthesis and analysis of a large number of definitions of intention, the connotation of intention as a sequence of actions directed at a particular purpose is obtained.

To obtain the formalized definition of software intention, program is regarded as combination of data structure and algorithm. Then the problem can be abstracted as follows: Abstracting a function call or program operation of a sensitive API into an action, a sequence of actions that contain specific relations can perform certain functions. They operate on a set of input data, including event messages, user input, privacy data, and constant arguments. The semantics of input data are abstracted into an object description of action. When trigger condition is satisfied a malware starts its process of operations. This set of data (objects) reaches a certain state (data in final) after a series of operations eventually while these final states reflect the purpose of the program's execution.

Definition 1. Software intention is a sequence of software behaviors directed at a particular purpose, formally represented as

$$\vec{\omega}\,(\text{Intention})$$
$$= (\langle \omega_1\,(P_1), \omega_2\,(P_2), \dots, \omega_n(P_n)\rangle, \text{Goal})\,. \tag{1}$$

In formula (1), "$\vec{\omega}$" refers to directionality, which indicates the behavior sequence $\langle \omega_1(P_1), \omega_2(P_2), \dots, \omega_n(P_n)\rangle$ points to the purpose Goal; ω represents temporal and spatial attributes of behavior, and temporal attributes describe specific temporal relationships between actions; spatial attributes indicate the impact of behavior on external objects.

3.2. Intention Elements. The elements of software intention include software behavior sequence, behavior objects (behavior facts), and software goals, which are defined below separately. They are the theoretical basis for the derivation of Section 3.3, and the extraction method of behavior facts is described in Section 4.3.

Definition 2. Behavior object is an abstract description of the data or device objects that Android API invocation can operate on. It is a three-tuple:

$$\text{Beh\_object} = (\text{obj\_name}, \text{attribute}, \text{attri\_value}) \tag{2}$$

In tuple (2), obj_name represents object name, attribute refers to the object's property, and attri_value represents the property value. Different behaviors act on different objects, and these objects correspond to different entities in the program.

Behavior objects usually presented in the form of a class object (system resource management, network connection objects, and network buffer objects), constants (SP number, advertising link, URL, and file address), local executable files (system command, local library (.so) file), and passed variables (parameter, data path). The abstract semantics of these objects can be determined by certain mapping rules.

Definition 3. Software behavior is an abstract software operation that can operate on the object and change its property value, formally represented as

$$\text{Behavior} = (\text{beh\_name}, \text{Input}, \text{Output})$$
$$\text{Input} = \{\text{Beh\_object}\} \tag{3}$$
$$\text{Output} = \{\text{Beh\_object}'\}\,.$$

In formula (3), beh_name represents the name of a behavior, Input represents the input object descriptions of this behavior, and Output represents the output object descriptions of this behavior. These behaviors can be divided into two types temporarily according to the number of their input in this paper: B1 (single input, single output); B2 (double input, double output).

We have discovered 102 significant behaviors involving 115 sensitive APIs, via sensitive API mining in Genome's Android apps and the summary of related literature [15, 19–21]. We also refer to Android's official API document and a database of sensitive API behavior is established based on the information collected. These APIs are controlled by 30 Android sensitive permissions and have detailed descriptions in official documents.

We generate behavior facts for API patterns based on their internal program logics. There are APIs whose semantics are similar and can be classified as a class of behavior. We further study the extraction mechanism; Table 1 presents the three major logics that we used. (1) Sequential relation APIs constitute a special workflow. For instance, connect() always happens before execute(), since the first provides the

TABLE 1: The rules of behavior semantic extraction.

Program structure	Location of behavior semantic
(1) Sequential relation	Extracting both of these APIs.
(2) Prepared for the latter	Extracting the latter API.
(3) Multilevel data access	Extracting the former API.

second with necessary inputs. In this case, we study the document of both APIs and extract behaviors from both of them. (2) A former object is retrieved for latter operations. For example, a SmsMessage.createFromPdu(pdus) is always invoked prior to SmsMessage.getMessageBody() because the former fetches the default object SmsMessage that the latter needs. We then only extract behaviors from the latter APIs. (3) Multilevel data is accessed through multiple levels of APIs. For example, when accessing location data, we first call getLastKnownLocation() to return a location object and then call getLongitude() and getLatitude() to get the longitude and latitude from this object. As these higher level APIs are meaningful enough, we hence only extract behaviors from the former APIs.

According to the example analysis of malware samples and the description of related literature, we summarize a variety of malware behaviors and give the behavior set E:

$$E ::= \{ \varphi_{\text{right\_gain}}, \varphi_{\text{access}}, \varphi_{\text{store}}, \varphi_{\text{encrypt}}, \varphi_{\text{monitor}}, \varphi_{\text{intercept}}, $$

$$\varphi_{\text{connect}}, \varphi_{\text{transmit}}, \varphi_{\text{send}}, \varphi_{\text{dial}}, \varphi_{\text{decode}}, \varphi_{\text{install}}, \varphi_{\text{popup}}, \quad (4)$$

$$\varphi_{\text{tamper}}, \varphi_{\text{delete}}, \varphi_{\text{hide}}, \varphi_{\text{remote\_control}} \} .$$

Taking the monitoring and interception of broadcast message as an example explains how behavior is described. Behavior can be described as a mapping relationship:

(i) Broadcast message monitoring:

$$\varphi_{\text{monitor}} : \text{Broadcast\_info} \longrightarrow \text{Broadcast\_info}'$$

$$\text{Broadcast\_info} = (\text{Broadcast\_info}, \text{is\_monitored}, \text{No})$$

$$\text{Broadcast\_info}' \quad (5)$$

$$= (\text{Broadcast\_info}, \text{is\_monitored}, \text{Yes}) .$$

(ii) Broadcast message interception:

$$\varphi_{\text{intercept}} : \text{Broadcast\_info}' \longrightarrow \text{Broadcast\_info}''$$

$$\text{Broadcast\_info}'$$

$$= (\text{Broadcast\_info}, \text{is\_monitored}, \text{Yes}) \quad (6)$$

$$\text{Broadcast\_info}''$$

$$= (\text{Broadcast\_info}, \text{is\_intercepted}, \text{Yes}) .$$

Behavior is not independent and irrelevant; there is always a relation between the outputs of one behavior corresponding to the inputs of another behavior. One of the most common relationships is data dependence; that

is, the execution input of the later behavior needs the execution output of the previous behavior. Another common relationship is control dependence; although two behaviors have no direct data flow relationship, the execution of the latter behaviors needs the execution of the previous one as a trigger condition. In former example, the relation between *monitor* and *intercept* is data dependence relation and can be described as follows:

$$\text{Output} \left(\varphi_{\text{monitor}} \right) \longrightarrow \text{Input} \left(\varphi_{\text{intercept}} \right)$$

$$\text{Broadcast\_info} \longrightarrow \text{Broadcast\_info}' \quad (7)$$

$$\longrightarrow \text{Broadcast\_info}''$$

Definition 4. Software purpose is the final state of all input objects that act in an intention, formally represented as

$$\text{Goal} = (\text{object}_1, \text{attribute}, \text{attri\_value}) \times \cdots$$

$$\times (\text{object}_n, \text{attribute}, \text{attri\_value}) . \quad (8)$$

In purpose representation, all input objects, $\text{object}_1 \cdots \text{object}_n$, represent the objects involved in the intention. For example, after the extraction of sensitive behaviors in a malware and having a formal semantic representation, we use the ontology reasoning engine to automate the reasoning. We can eventually get the description of the relationship between behaviors and the final states of all the objects. For instance, we use "(SMS, position, "1062568")" to illustrate that the SMS is sent to "1062568"; (URL, is_used, Yes) represents the fact that the URL is used in the related function, and (DeviceId, is_encrypt, Yes) illustrates that the DeviceId has been encrypted.

3.3. Proof of Model. If intention is viewed as a system [22], the basic component of intention is therefore the behavior. After the inputs and outputs involved in these behaviors are defined, a series of basic mapping relationships are obtained which reflects the influence on external object of the basic behavior. The overall nature of an intention system can be determined by a set of mappings between a set of inputs and a set of outputs. Lemmas 5 and 6 are the basic mathematical theory of our behavior deduction.

Lemma 5 (function combination). *The union of mapping set φ_i is a mapping $\varphi : A \to B$:*

$$\varphi = \bigcup_{i=1}^{n} \varphi_i,$$

$$A = \bigcup_{i=1}^{n} A_i,$$

$$B = \bigcup_{i=1}^{n} B_i$$

$$\varphi_i : A_i \rightarrow B_i, \quad 1 \le i \le n$$

$$(9)$$

when $(\forall A_i)(\forall A_j)(A_i \subseteq A \wedge A_j \subseteq A \wedge A_i \ne A_j \rightarrow A_i \cap A_j = \varnothing).$

Lemma 6 (function compound). *Two-tuple* φ *consisted of a set of mappings* Φ *and its compound relation* ξ° *is a mapping* $\varphi : \mathrm{dom}(\varphi_1) = \mathrm{ran}(\varphi_n)$:

$$\varphi = (\Phi, \xi^\circ)$$

$$\Phi = \{\varphi_i \mid \varphi_i : A_i \rightarrow B_i, \; A_i = \mathrm{dom}(\varphi_i), \; B_i$$

$$= \mathrm{ran}(\varphi_i), \; 1 \le i \le n\}$$

$$(10)$$

$$\xi^\circ = \{\varphi_{i+1} \circ \varphi_i \mid \varphi_i, \; \varphi_{i+1} \in \Phi, \; 1 \le i \le n-1\}$$

when $(\forall i)((1 \le i \le n-1) \rightarrow \mathrm{ran}(\varphi_i) \subseteq \mathrm{dom}(\varphi_{i+1})).$

According to Lemmas 5 and 6, we proved Corollaries 7 and 8.

Corollary 7 (compound intention deduction). $\{\varphi_1, \varphi_2, \ldots, \varphi_n\}$ *represents a set of behaviors that are involved in an intention. If the relation between these behaviors is* $Output(\varphi_i) = Input(\varphi_{i+1})$, $1 \le i \le n-1$, *the output* $Output(\varphi_n)$ *of behavior* φ_n *is therefore the representation of final goal; behavior sequence is denoted as* $\xi_i = (\varphi_1, \varphi_2, \ldots, \varphi_n).$

Proof. $\{\varphi_1, \varphi_2, \ldots, \varphi_n\}$ are a set of behaviors. By the definition of φ, behavior satisfies the mapping relation between objects and can be regarded as function mapping. φ_i and φ_{i+1} satisfy the former output corresponding to the latter input; that is, the range of φ_i is equal to the domain of φ_{i+1}, which satisfies $(\forall i)((1 \le i \le n-1) \rightarrow \mathrm{ran}(\varphi_i) \subseteq \mathrm{dom}(\varphi_{i+1}))$. According to Lemma 6, Corollary is proved. □

Corollary 8 (combination-compound intention deduction). $\{\varphi_1, \varphi_2, \ldots, \varphi_n\}$ *represents a set of behaviors that are involved in an intention. If there is an input to output relation* $Output(\varphi_m) = Input(\varphi_u)$, $1 \le m, u \le n$, *and parallel relationship* $Output(\varphi_i) \cup Output(\varphi_j) = Input(\varphi_k)$, $1 \le i, j, k \le n$, *at the same time, then the output* $Output(\varphi_u) \cup Output(\varphi_k)$ *of* φ_u *and* φ_k *is the final goal. Behavior sequences are denoted as* $\xi_i = (\Phi, R)$. Φ *is behavior set; R is the relationship between these behaviors.*

Proof. $\{\varphi_1, \varphi_2, \ldots, \varphi_n\}$ is known as a set of behaviors. By the definition of φ, behavior satisfies the mapping relation between objects and can be regarded as function mapping. φ_m and φ_u satisfy the former's output corresponding to the latter's input; that is, the range of φ_m is equal to the domain of φ_u. $\mathrm{dom}(\varphi_u)$ is the compound output according to Lemma 6. φ_i and φ_j satisfy both of their outputs as the input of φ_k; because the intersection of the inputs of φ_i and φ_j is empty $(\mathrm{ran}(\varphi_i) \cup \mathrm{ran}(\varphi_j) = \varnothing)$, they satisfy Lemma 5. φ_i and φ_j

satisfy combination relation, which could be combined into a new mapping:

$$\varphi' : \mathrm{ran}(\varphi_i) \cup \mathrm{ran}(\varphi_j) \longrightarrow \mathrm{dom}(\varphi_i) \cup \mathrm{dom}(\varphi_j). \quad (11)$$

Then, φ' and φ_k satisfy the condition of Lemma 6; $\mathrm{dom}(\varphi_k)$ is the compound output. Corollary is proved according to Lemma 6. □

4. Ontology Inference System

This chapter elaborates the construction process of ontology inference system. Section 1 gives the construction specification of ontology model [10]. Section 2 gives SWRL rules used in inference engine. Section 3 is the description of mapping methods from Data Source to Fact Base. Section 4 elaborates the framework of inference system.

4.1. Ontology Model. The reasons for using ontology in our inference system are as follows: (1) The conceptual system based on ontology is computable, and the automatic deduction of intentions can be achieved by the computing between concepts. The system has reduced the workload of code writing accordingly. (2) The extensibility of ontology enables us to extend the conceptual model at any time according to the emergence of new features of malware. Once new malware knowledge appears we only need to modify the ontology model based on the knowledge. In this way, we have reduced the amount of code update and maintenance. (3) The ontology model of the elements and their relationships in malware behavior intention domain can standardize domain knowledge and make it shareable [10]. It can provide a standardized representation for malware intention.

The ontology model of malware behavior intention uses the following knowledge: the definition and classification of behavior and behavior object, intention model, and Corollaries 7 and 8. The concepts and the relation are shown in Figure 1. The definitions of each concept are given in Section 3. We use Pellet engine reasoning to verify the consistence of ontology.

The definitions of object attributes and data attributes are illustrated in Table 2.

4.2. SWRL Inference Rules. This section uses the knowledge of Corollaries 7 and 8 and Definition 4 in Section 3. Before writing inference rules, we need to define the format of basic facts. The fact is a composition description of basic behavior. There are two categories of basic facts (in our research): B1: the behavior with single input and single output; B2: the behavior with double input and double output. See Box 1.

(1) Inference Rules of the Relationship between Behaviors

Premise 1. Any two B1 behaviors are B11 and B12; B11(in) represents the input of B11, and B11(out) represents its output. If any two B1 behaviors B11 and B12 have the relation of B11's

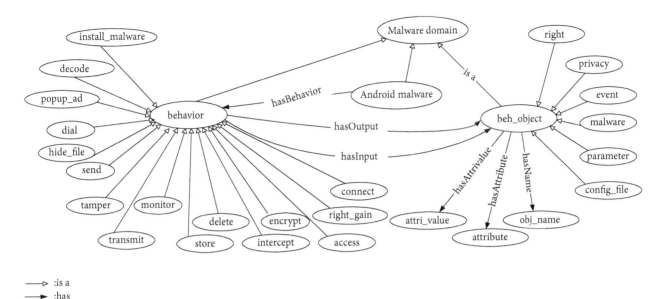

FIGURE 1: Semantic ontology of behavior intention.

FIGURE 2: SWRL inference rules of the relationship between behaviors and final goal.

output object corresponding to B12's object input, Rule-1 is the inference rule corresponding to this condition. See Box 1.

Premise 2. Any two B1 behaviors are B11 and B12; one B2 behavior is B2. B11(in) represents the input to B11, and B11(out) represents its output. B2(1in), B2(2in), B2(1out), and B2(2out) represent the input and output of B2, respectively.

If the output's union of any two B1 behaviors is the input of a certain B2 behavior and the input intersection of these two B1 behaviors is empty, then B11 and B12 have a compound relation with the B2 behavior, respectively. There is also a combination relation between B11 and B12. The rule is B1-B2-Rule-1 shown in Figure 2 and the rest of the rules are similar.

(2) Inference Rules of the Final Goal. On the basis of behavior's inference rules and Definition 4, the inference rules of final goal are summarized as in Figure 2, such as Goal-Rule-1. The outputs are the descriptions of object's final state. Due to the limited space, other rules are no longer presented.

4.3. Extraction of Behavior Facts. The basic facts include B1 and B2 behavior, and the behavior's elements which should be extracted from Data Source are as follows:

(1) Behavior (name): extracting the behavior description in a program according to the mapping between the

behaviors defined in our sensitive API database and sensitive APIs (or code segment) in program.

(2) Input (behavior object): we determine objects description based on the parameters of sensitive APIs and the official document definition.

(3) Output (behavior object): object after a behavior operates on it, its object name, and attribute will not change while its attribute value will be affected. Therefore, we can determine the changes in attribute values based on this behavior's definition.

The mapping from Data Source to behavior facts is divided into two stages: the first stage is behavior recognition; the second includes object identification and relation analysis between objects. Detailed process is as follows.

First Stage. Use reverse tool to decompile these malware samples and then generate its call graph (CG) and control flow graph (CFG). The leaf nodes of the call graph are traversed to find sensitive API and identify the corresponding behavior according to the mapping relation between behavior and sensitive API calls. Partial mapping relations between behaviors and sensitive API calls and object descriptions are shown in Table 3.

Second Stage. For each identified behavior, the behavior's object is identified according to the usage of parameter in

TABLE 2: Specification of object attributes and data attributes.

Attribute name	Specification
hasCombinationwith	Behaviors have combination relation
hasCompoundwith	Behaviors have compound relation
hasInput(x, y)	The behavior's single input is "y"
hasOutput(x, z)	The behavior's single output is "z"
hasFirstInput(x, y1)	The first input of double input is "y1"
hasSecondInput(x, y2)	The second input of double input is "y2"
hasFirstOutput(x, z1)	The first output of double input is "z1"
hasSecondOutput(x, z2)	The second output of double input is "z2"
hasBehavior(x, y)	The behavior belonging to malware is "y"
hasObjectName(x, y)	The name of the object is "y"
hasAttribute(x, y)	The attributes of an object are "y"
hasAttributeValue(x, y)	The object's attributes value is "y"

Rule-1: behavior_B1(?B11) ∧ behavior_B1(?B12) ∧ has
BehaviorName(?B11, ?bn1)∧hasBehaviorName (?B12, ?bn2)
∧ hasOutput(?B11,?op) ∧ hasInput(?B12,?ip)∧ hasObject
name(?op, ?on1) ∧ hasObjectname(?ip, ?on2)∧swrlb:equal
(?on1,?on2) ∧ hasAttribute(?op, ?att1) ∧ has Attribute
(?ip, ?att2) ∧ hasValue(?att1, ?attri1) ∧ hasValue
(?att2, ?attri2) ∧ swrlb:equal (?attri1, ?attri2) ∧ hasAttribute
Value(?op,?attv1) ∧ hasAttributeValue (?ip, ?attv2) ∧ hasValue
(?attv1, ?attriv1) ∧ hasValue(?attv2,?attriv2) ∧ swrlb:equal
(?attriv1,?attriv2) → hasCompoundwith(?bn1, ?bn2).

Box 1

sensitive API (two categories: the first obtains behavior object based on the class object and the definition of API, such as getDeviceId(); the second obtains behavior object based on the parameter usage of API and the definition of API, such as Runtime.exec (RootExploit.file)). Data dependence between behaviors is analyzed using FlowDroid [4].

4.4. Framework of Inference System. The framework of intention inference system is shown in Figure 3.

We use the knowledge of intention definition and Corollaries 7 and 8 to construct SWRL rules (the rules are represented in ontology language). Extracting Data Source from Android applications uses reverse engineering technology [15]. The extraction methods of facts are illustrated in Section 4.3. Jess inference engine completes the reasoning process using the Facts Base and SWRL rules and gives the inference output (the description of malware intention) finally.

4.5. Motivation Example. Take Zitmo [16] as an example to show the facts extracted from these samples, as shown in Table 4. Among these extracted facts, *access* and *transmit* are B2 behavior; B2's double input indicates that the execution of the behavior needs to meet the condition of the two key inputs.

After the rules and facts are imported to Jess engine, the inference results are exported; they are the formalized

descriptions of intentions of each malicious sample. The results of Zitmo's behavior relations are shown in Figure 4. Other results of intention reasoning are analyzed separately and show reasonable efficiency.

We extract behavior relations and goal representation from Figure 4, which are shown in Table 5.

Zitmo's intention includes behavior sequence (consisting of behavior set and behavior relation) and the representation of goal (output object description). To visually demonstrate the reasoning results, we display them in Figure 5 graphically. In Figure 5, rectangle represents the behavior, ellipse represents the input or output object of the behavior, and arrow indicates the relationship between object and behavior. The ellipse with a black font represents the raw input of objects involved in the intention, respectively, as broadcast information, text messages, and URL addresses. These final states are as follows: broadcast message is monitored and intercepted, the contents of the messages are transmitted to remote server, and the URL is used as the destination address of the transmission. They represent the goal of the intention together.

5. Evaluation

We have implemented the ontology inference system described in Section 4.4 in a prototype inference system for identifying and describing malware intention in behavior

TABLE 3: Partial mappings between behavior and sensitive APIs.

Behavior	Behavior object	sensitiveAPI
right_gain	Root permission	Runtime.exec()
access	Device ID	getDeviceId()
	Carrier name	getNetworkOperatorName()
	Phone position	getCellLocation()
	Short Message	createFromPdu()
send	Number and contents	sendTextMessage()
intercept	Broadcast information	abortBroadcast()
connect	URL-parameter	URLConnection.connect()
transmit	Parameter	execute()
encrypt	Parameter	setEntity()
store	Parameter	writeRec()

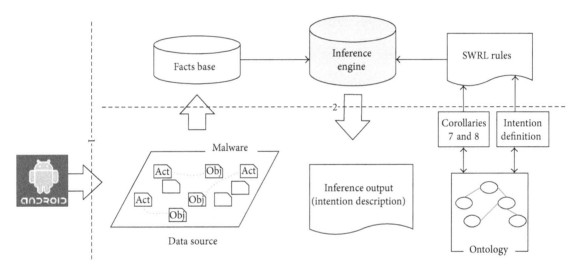

FIGURE 3: The framework of intention inference system.

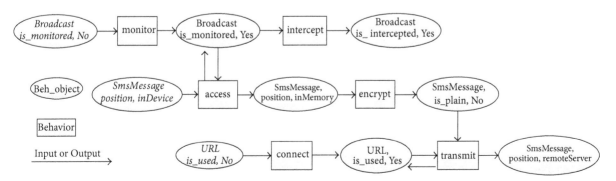

FIGURE 4: Inference results of Zitmo's behavior relations.

FIGURE 5: Visualization of Zitmo's inference results.

TABLE 4: Behavior facts extracted from Zitmo.

Behavior	Code segment or function	Behavior object
monitor	onReceive()	Broadcast
intercept	abortBroadcast()	Broadcast'
access	createFrompdu(), getMessageBody(), getOriginatingAddress()	Broadcast', SmsMessage
connect	new HttpPost(URL)	URL
encrypt	setEntity()	SmsMessage
transmit	execute()	URL', SmsMessage

TABLE 5: The inference results of Zitmo.

Behavior relationship	Final goal representation
hasCompoundwith(monitor, intercept)	(Broadcast, is_monitored, Yes), (Broadcast, is_intercepted, Yes)
hasCompoundwith(monitor, access)	(SmsMessage, position, inMemory)
hasCompoundwith(access, encrypt)	(SmsMessage, is_plain, No)
hasCombinationwith(connect, encrypt)	No
hasCompoundwith(encrypt, transmit)	(URL, is_used, Yes)
hasCompoundwith(connect, transmit)	(SmsMessage, position, remoteServer)

facts. In this section, we evaluate the following aspects: First, we verify whether the sensitive API library we build can cover the behavior facts that exist in malware samples and give the coverage rate analysis. Second, to verify the effectiveness of artificial extraction (semiautomated) behavior facts, we compare our manual analysis results with the results generated by automated tool CopperDroid [19]. Thirdly, the effectiveness and reasoning performance of the ontology inference system are shown. Finally, the correctness, readability, and effectiveness of the results of intention reasoning are tackled.

We have selected 75 typical malware samples (1 real-world ransomware sample and 9 real-world samples from Genome's 1260 samples and 65 DroidBench samples) for evaluation, which are shown in Table 6. Among these 10 real-world samples, 9 samples are collected from Android malware database established by Zhou and Jiang [23] in North Carolina State University. We use these real-world samples because they are typical and representative of their family. Other samples in Genome are in same family, so the vulnerabilities and threats in the program are similar. For efficiency consideration, we do not add the remaining samples to experimental sample set. DroidBench [4] samples are designed to assess the correctness of static analyses on Android apps. We use these samples as the ground truths because they have open-sourced programs with clear semantics [20]. Thus we can make an adequate analysis of these samples. In fact, static analysis technique in general often lacks capability of extracting runtime behaviors and can be evaded accordingly, but it has incomparable advantages over dynamic technology. Nevertheless, this paper focuses

on the research of software intention reduction; that is, the emphasis is to study the extraction and semantic mapping methods of malware's behavior, the extraction of relationship between behaviors, and the representation of malware's final goal.

5.1. Effectiveness of Behavior Facts Extraction. In general, we have discovered 102 significant behaviors involving 115 sensitive APIs, via sensitive API mining in Genome's Android apps and the summary of related literature [15, 19–21]. We also refer to Android's official API document and based on the information collected a database of sensitive API behavior is established. These APIs are controlled by 30 Android sensitive privileges and have detailed descriptions in official documents.

To evaluate the effectiveness and validity of behavior facts extracting, we compare the description of our behavior facts extraction and CopperDroid's [19] behavior description. CopperDroid is an automatic VMI-based dynamic analysis system to reconstruct the behaviors of Android malware; the novelty of CopperDroid lies in its agnostic approach to identify interesting OS- and high-level Android-specific behaviors. We perform a user study on CopperDroid platform and our extraction methods; the goal is twofold. First, we give a comparative analysis on the behavior coverage rate of these samples. Second, we hope to know whether the behavior description generated by our methods is readable to average audience. To this end, we compare the behavior description of our methods and CopperDroid's Public Reports [24]. We have collected 150 copies of CopperDroid's public malware sample analysis report and make a statistical analysis. As

TABLE 6: Malware samples and their behavior information.

Sample family	Number	Ours (Copper)	Major behavior	Intention classification
Zitmo	1	6 (2)	monitor, intercept, access, connect, encrypt, transmit	Privacy stealing
GoldDream	1	9 (4)	monitor, access, store, connect, transmit	Privacy stealing
DroidDream	1	5 (3)	right_gain, access, connect, transmit	Privacy stealing
DroidDeluxe	1	3 (2)	monitor, right_gain, access, connect, transmit	Privacy stealing
HippoSMS	1	4 (2)	send, monitor, access, intercept	Tariff consumption
Geinimi	1	6 (3)	remote_control, send, connect, transmit	Tariff consumption
RogueSPPush	1	6 (2)	send, monitor, access, intercept, delete	Malicious chargeback
GGTracker	1	9 (4)	access, connect, transmit, store, encrypt, monitor, send, intercept	Malicious chargeback
DroidKungFu-Update	1	4 (2)	connect, transmit, install_mal, popup	Malware propagation
Love buckle word	1	4 (1)	popup, tamper, connect, transmit, right_gain	Extortion user
Aliasing	1	2 (2)	access, send	Privacy leak
AndroidSpecific	9	3 (2)	access, logging, send	Privacy leak
ArraysAndLists	7	2 (2)	access, send	Privacy leak
Callbacks	4	2 (2)	access, send	Privacy leak
EmulatorDetection	3	3 (2)	access, logging, send	Privacy leak
FieldAndObjectSensitivity	3	3 (2)	access, logging, send	Privacy leak
GeneralJava	14	3 (2)	access, logging, send	Privacy leak
ImplicitFlows	4	2 (2)	access, logging	Privacy leak
InterAppCommunication	3	2 (2)	access, send	Privacy leak
Lifecycle	11	4 (2)	access, connect, send, logging	Privacy leak
Reflection	4	2 (2)	access, send	Privacy leak
Threading	2	3 (2)	access, logging, send	Privacy leak

TABLE 7: Behavior semantics between ours and CopperDroid.

Behavior class	Objects	Copper	Ours	Similar
Access personal info	SMS phone accounts location	4	18	90%
FS access	Open Write	2	2	100%
Network access	Generic HTTP DNS	3	3	100%
Send SMS	SMS	1	1	100%
Execute external file	Generic Priv. Esc Shell Inst. APK	6	8	75%
Encrypt info	File info	0	2	0%
Intercept SMS	SMS	0	2	0%
Store info	Privacy info	0	1	0%

TABLE 8: Intention generation results for samples.

Sample set	False status	Missing desc	Correct	T#
Genome	1	1	8	10
DroidBench	4	2	59	65
Total	5	3	67	75

shown in Table 6, the third column (ours/Copper) indicates the number of behaviors' extraction using our methods and the number of behaviors extracted by CopperDroid for the same sample. In terms of the number of extracted behaviors, our extraction mechanism (87) is 77.6% more than CopperDroid's behavior number (49).

We further study whether the behavior description generated by our methods is readable to average audience. As behavior facts extraction is the basis of this study, we thus produce 75 behavior descriptions reports for these 75 samples. The result, illustrated in Table 7, depicts that the descriptions derived from ours are richer than CopperDroid, while the ratio of behavior similarity ranges from 75% to 100%. CopperDroid failed to extract some of the behaviors we extract, such as encrypt, intercept, and store personal info. Thus we argue that the behaviors we extract can reflect the common program semantics and programming conventions effectively.

Notice that though it may take artificial effort to generate behavior facts description, behavior extraction is a technology that has already been realized. We refer to the work of predecessors extracting malware behaviors though automatic extraction technology is not so mature. The focus of this work is to propose a framework for the description and deduction of behavioral intentions. We argue that any analysis tools, both static and dynamic, can be utilized in our framework to achieve the described malware intention.

5.2. Validity of Ontology Inference System. Next, we evaluate the validity of ontology inference system. Ontology inference experiment reveals that the workload of manual writing code reduced significantly and Pellet engine reasoning verified that the ontology is complete and consistent. We evaluate the runtime performance and ontology validity for 75 samples; preparation for behavior facts (add ontology instance)

dominates the runtime, while the intention results generation is usually fairly fast (under 200 milliseconds). The average inference runtime is 2 seconds, while the analysis for a majority (85%) of apps can be completed within 5 seconds. The validation of the reasoning results indicates that 89.3% of the sample's reasoning results are correct and the intention results of graphical display show high readability; Table 9 shows the readability ratings of 75 apps.

5.3. Correctness, Readability, and Effectiveness

Correctness. To evaluate the correctness, we produce intention descriptions for 75 malware sample apps (10 typical real-world samples and 65 DroidBench samples) using our behavior facts extraction algorithm and ontology inference engine. First, we use artificial methods to simulate automation tools to extract the behavior facts in these samples. The extraction mechanism is to construct the environment dependence graph first and then use the methods in Section 4.3 to map the sensitive APIs to behavior facts. Second, the extracted behavior facts are instantiated in the tools provided by protégé 3.4.7, and then the instances that are obviously wrong are filtered. Finally, we use Jess inference engine for reasoning the behavior facts, and the SWRL rules are imported to inference engine at the same time. The inference results give the output of behavior sequence and final goal representation (see the definition of malware intention); finally, the framework is shown in Figure 3.

Results. Table 8 presents the experimental results, which show that our inference system achieves a true positive rate of 89.3%. We must reiterate that the basis of our reasoning is the sensitive API database we built can fully map sensitive behaviors in malware. Although it is not perfect, it can be

TABLE 9: Precision results for Appscan and intention reports.

Judgment	Appscan report			Intention description		
	geno	Droid	All	geno	Droid	All
(1) Ineffective	5	0	5	1	2	3
(2) Uncertain	1	65	66	1	4	5
(3) Effective	4	0	4	8	59	67
Total	10	65	75	10	65	75

fully covered in the 75 selected samples. Inference system misses intention descriptions due to two major reasons: (1) Artificial behavior facts extraction lacks accuracy. We rely on our environment dependence graph and extraction algorithm to perform simulation analysis. However, it is not precise enough to handle the data flow propagation that cannot be solved by existing static analysis technology (such as exception handler code, reflective calls). (2) The program logic in real-world malware is more complex and with semantic ambiguity, and there are too many independent sensitive behaviors (in the form of user defined functions). This is not the result of the lack of theory and only technical problem.

In fact, static analysis in general lacks the capability of extracting runtime behaviors and can be evaded accordingly. Nevertheless, we argue that our focus is to construct a framework which produces description and derivation model of malware intention.

Readability and Effectiveness. To evaluate the readability and effectiveness of inference output (Intention), we perform a user study on our malware intention inference results. The goal is twofold. First, we hope to know whether the generated intentions are readable to average audience. Second, we expect to see whether our intention descriptions can actually help users avoid risky apps.

Methodology. 360 microscopes' Appscan platform [25] is an online security scanning system which focuses on the security scan of Android apps. The system will provide a scan report after the scanning and describe possible malicious intent of the app to users. We uploaded all the samples to 360 microscopes' Appscan platform and got 75 security reports of these samples. We also collate ontology inference results and show them in the form of formalization and graphics; 75 samples' intention reports are produced. We use both 75 Appscan reports and 75 intention reports to measure user reaction and the number of vulnerabilities provided by 360 microscopes' Appscan platform is compared with the intention description. Furthermore, due to the objective evaluation consideration, we perform the user study based on the official intents descriptions of 75 apps. We use these official descriptions as a reference standard.

We have recruited participant directly from our laboratory group and we require participant that must be smartphone users. We also make sure that participants have experiences with Android malware analysis and understand basic smartphone events, such as "intercept SMS" or "access GPS location." We provide a rating for each sample report (Appscan and intention) with respect to its effectiveness. The rating ranges from 1 to 3, where 1 means ineffective, 2 means uncertain, and 3 means effective, as shown in Table 9.

Results and Implications. Eventually, the results are shown in Table 9, 360 microscopes' Appscan platform provides a coarser grained description, and users can only judge the true intents of 4 samples according to the Appscan report. While users can judge the malice of 67 samples using intention description report. This indicates our intention report is readable, even compared to Appscan report created by 360 microscopes' Appscan platform. The results also reveal that the readability and granularity of intention description are relatively important while Appscan-generated ones sometimes confuse users; 66 samples cannot be judged correctly through Appscan report. In a further investigation, we notice that Appscan report provides a coarse intent description of the sample, while our security centered intention report provides a fairly fine-grained display of intention. We believe that this can be further utilized during threat analysis.

Threat Analysis. Analysts are able to understand the relationships between malware behaviors (including trigger process of behaviors, data transfer relation, and the change in object characteristics) according to the intention description. This is of great practical significance for users to understand the implementation mechanism of malware, evaluate its possible losses, and provide preventive solutions.

6. Conclusion

In this paper, a novel description and derivation model of Android malware intention based on the theory of intention and malware reverse engineering is proposed to restore the intention of malware and automate the process of intention reasoning process. In order to standardize the new conceptual system and automate the intent derivation, we create ontology of malware intention. As ontology is computable, we import SWRL rules represented in ontology language and Fact Base to Jess engine, and Jess's outputs are the description of malware intention. We evaluate our system using 75 typical malware samples (5 kinds). Experiments show that our inference system is capable of achieving the desired results of intention description, which proved its feasibility and effectiveness. In addition, by using existing reverse technology and data flow analysis tools we can extract behavioral facts effectively.

Methods of mapping from Data Source to facts are divided into two forms: artificial extraction and automatic extraction. We mainly use the methods of artificial facts extraction. There are many opportunities for future works, such as the implementation of automatic facts extraction methods and the automatic visualization of the reasoning results.

Conflicts of Interest

The authors declare that there are no conflicts of interest regarding the publication of this article.

Acknowledgments

This work was partly supported by Beijing Key Laboratory of Internet Culture and Digital Dissemination Research Project (no. ICDDXN001), National Key Technology Research and Development Program of the Ministry of Science and Technology of China (no. 2015BAK12B03-03), Special Project of Central Government to Guide the Development of Local Science and Technology (no. Z171100004717002), and National Natural Science Foundation of China (nos. 61370065, 61502040).

References

[1] P. Guojun, L. Jingwen, and S. Runkang, "Research and Progress of Android malware detection," *Journal of Wuhan University (Science Edition)*, vol. 61, no. 1, pp. 21–33, 2015.

[2] A. Kharraz, S. Arshad, C. Mulliner et al., "A Large-Scale, Automated Approach to Detecting," in *Proceedings of the 25th USENIX Security Symposium (USENIX Security 16)*, pp. 757–772, USENIX Association, 2016.

[3] M.-Y. Su and K.-T. Fung, "Detection of android malware by static analysis on permissions and sensitive functions," in *Proceedings of the 8th International Conference on Ubiquitous and Future Networks, ICUFN 2016*, pp. 873–875, Austria, July 2016.

[4] S. Arzt, S. Rasthofer, C. Fritz et al., "FlowDroid: precise context, flow, field, object-sensitive and lifecycle-aware taint analysis for Android apps," *ACM Sigplan Notices*, vol. 49, no. 6, pp. 259–269, 2014.

[5] E. Bratman Michael, "What is intention?" in *Intentions in communication*, P. R. Cohen, Ed., pp. 15–32, the MIT Press, 1990.

[6] J. Shirley and D. Evans, "The user is not the enemy: Fighting malware by tracking user intentions," in *Proceedings of the New Security Paradigms Workshop 2008, NSPW '08*, pp. 33–45, USA, September 2008.

[7] C.-T. Jung, C.-H. Sun, and M. Yuan, "An ontology-enabled framework for a geospatial problem-solving environment," *Computers, Environment and Urban Systems*, vol. 38, no. 1, pp. 45–57, 2013.

[8] I. Horrocks, F. P. Patel-Schneider, H. Boley et al., *SWRL: A Semantic Web Rule Language Combining OWL and RuleML*, W3C Member Submission, 2004.

[9] J. Bak, C. Jedrzejek, and M. Falkowski, "Usage of the jess engine, rules and ontology to query a relational database," *Lecture Notes in Computer Science (including subseries Lecture Notes in Artificial Intelligence and Lecture Notes in Bioinformatics): Preface*, vol. 5858, pp. 216–230, 2009.

[10] X.-Y. Du, M. Li, and S. Wang, "Survey on ontology learning research," *Ruan Jian Xue Bao/Journal of Software*, vol. 17, no. 9, pp. 1837–1847, 2006.

[11] S. Cheng, S. Luo, Z. Li et al., "Static Detection of Dangerous Behaviors in Android Apps," in *Proceedings of the the the 5th international symposium on cyberspace safety and security*, Springer International Publishing, 2013.

[12] IDA pro. http://www.hex-rays.com/products/ida.

[13] J. Jian and X. Qing, "On case auto generation using reverse analysis for Android malware," *Journal of HeFei University of Technology (Natural Science Edition)*, vol. 39, no. 4, pp. 466–470, 2016.

[14] W. Yang, X. Xiao, B. Andow, S. Li, T. Xie, and W. Enck, "AppContext: differentiating malicious and benign mobile app behaviors using context," in *Proceedings of the 37th IEEE/ACM International Conference on Software Engineering (ICSE '15)*, vol. 1, pp. 303–313, IEEE, May 2015.

[15] Y. Li, T. Shen, X. Sun et al., "Detection, Classification and Characterization of Android Malware Using API Data Dependency," in *Proceedings of the International Conference on Security and Privacy in Communication Systems*, vol. 164, pp. 23–40, Springer International Publishing, 2015.

[16] M. Zhang, Y. Duan, H. Yin, and Z. Zhao, "Semantics-aware Android malware classification using weighted contextual API dependency graphs," in *Proceedings of the 21st ACM Conference on Computer and Communications Security (CCS '14)*, pp. 1105–1116, ACM, Scottsdale, Ariz, USA, November 2014.

[17] P. Wu, H. Changzhen, and Y. Shuping, "A dynamic intrusive intention recognition method based on timed automata," *Journal of Computer Research and Development*, vol. 48, no. 7, pp. 1288–1297, 2011.

[18] J.-H. Han, S.-J. Lee, and J.-H. Kim, "Behavior Hierarchy-Based Affordance Map for Recognition of Human Intention and Its Application to Human-Robot Interaction," *IEEE Transactions on Human-Machine Systems*, vol. 46, no. 5, pp. 708–722, 2016.

[19] K. Tam, S. J. Khan, A. Fattori et al., "CopperDroid: automatic reconstruction of android malware behaviors," in *Proceedings of the Network and Distributed System Security Symposium*, San Diego, Calif, USA, 2015.

[20] M. Zhang and H. Yin, "Automatic Generation of Security-Centric Descriptions for Android Apps," in *Android Application Security*, Springer International Publishing, 2016.

[21] Z. Wang, C. Li, Z. Yuan, Y. Guan, and Y. Xue, "DroidChain: A novel Android malware detection method based on behavior chains," *Pervasive and Mobile Computing*, vol. 32, pp. 3–14, 2016.

[22] X. Guozhi, *System science and Engineering Research*, Shanghai science and Technology Education Press, 2001.

[23] Y. Zhou and X. Jiang, "Dissecting android malware: characterization and evolution," in *Proceedings of the 33rd IEEE Symposium on Security and Privacy*, pp. 95–109, IEEE, 2012.

[24] http://copperdroid.isg.rhul.ac.uk/copperdroid/index.php.

[25] http://appscan.360.cn/.

20

Enhancing the Cloud Computing Performance by Labeling the Free Node Services as Ready-to-Execute Tasks

Radwan S. Abujassar and Moneef Jazzar

Information Technology and Computing, Arab Open University, Kuwait Branch, Al-Ardiya, Kuwait

Correspondence should be addressed to Radwan S. Abujassar; radwanbr@hotmail.com

Academic Editor: Marimuthu Karuppiah

The huge bandwidth and hardware capacity form a high combination together which leads to a vigorous development in the Internet. On the other hand, different problems will come up during the use of the networks such as delay and node tasks load. These problems lead to degrade the network performance and then affect network service for users. In cloud computing, users are looking to be provided with a high level of services from the service provider. In addition, cloud computing service facilitates the execution of complicated tasks that needed high-storage scale for the computation. In this paper, we have implemented a new technique to retain the service and assign tasks to the best and free available node already labeled by the manager node. The Cloud Computing Alarm (CCA) technique is working to provide all information about the services node and which one is ready to receive the task from users. According to the simulation results, the CCA technique is making good enhancements on the QoS which will increase the number of users to use the service. Additionally, the results showed that the CCA technique improved the services without any degrading of network performance by completing each task in less time.

1. Introduction

In the earlier days, the online services started to be desirable from the end users; many promotions about new productions show a great challenge for public and private companies to attract users. Cloud computing is starting to be used widely according to the rapid development of the Internet with new modern devices such as smart phones, tablets, and others. Businesses have increasingly invested in cloud computing services. According to International Data Corporation (IDC), cloud computing services were used up to 42 billion times in 2012, compared with 16 billion in 2008. Public companies such as Google, Yahoo, Microsoft, and Amazon are already invested in cloud computing services. Hence, the network bandwidth and developing hardware are leading to create new technologies related to cloud computing [1–3]. Cloud computing allows users to use more applications and software from any place because many nodes can cooperate to perform the request services. On the other hand, the Internet applications keep on getting updated and developing with high-performance multimedia and high quality devices in

the network [2, 4]. In the cloud computing environment, players can log in and access Internet applications software. Also, cloud computing can offer a different environment according to the services need, and the infrastructure for the Internet is growing more which leads to allocating the computing system services to different places. The advantages of cloud computing by offering access to services for users also encourage distributed system design and application to support user-oriented services applications. The busy and load CPU node in cloud computing was always considered to be a problem requiring a load balancing mechanism or a technique that can distribute the job tasks between the service nodes; hence, CCA technique is one of the solutions to alleviate the impact of loads on the service nodes in the network. Recent researchers are devoted to find out different solutions by involving several techniques to make load balancing on the service nodes that they need to execute the job task which is required by the users. The aim of cloud computing is to get high-performance computing power, which is normally used by a huge number of users (e.g., in military applications) to perform tens of trillions of computations/sec.

The cloud computing forms large groups of servers typically running with low-cost consumers. Many services are running through cloud computing over the Internet. These services are broadly divided into three terms: Infrastructure-as-a-Service (IaaS), Platform-as-a-Service (PaaS), and Software-as-a-Service (SaaS) [2, 5–7].

The Infrastructure-as-a-Service (IaaS) (e.g., https://www.amazon.com) provides the customer with virtual server instances and storage as well as Application Software (S/W) Interfaces. Application Program Interface (API) allows users to access and configure their virtual servers and storage. The Platform-as-a-Service (PaaS) is a set of tools hosted on the service provider's infrastructure. Through PaaS, users can create applications on the provider's platform over the Internet. Some APIs need to be installed by customers on their Personal Computer (PC). The Google applications (GoogleApp) are a good pattern of PaaS. On the other hand, Software-as-a-Service (SaaS) provides hardware infrastructure by interacting with the users [8, 9]. All services can be used through a front-end portal. SaaS is widely used and it can be anything from web-based and database processing and the user can access and use the services anytime. The cloud computing is considered a distributed system because it has the capabilities to provide multiple external customers by using internal technologies. Service providers provide many services to end customers. They have service level agreement (SLA), according to which service providers must deliver services with a better performance to the end users. The service may suffer disruptions for short durations due to the many factors that affect the network, causing economic damage and degrading network performance. Therefore, researchers proposed a number of different solutions for the cloud computing services in the network. This is because flooding and load over flow are common and varied in the everyday operation of the cloud computing network. When load occurs, it causes undesired behaviour such as the delay for the completed task is increased because the preprocessors in the service nodes cannot execute many high complexity jobs during a short time. Therefore, the aim of this paper is to develop and propose a potential solution for the cloud computing network through alleviating and allocating job task based on the service node availability. The proposed algorithm should reduce the time to complete each task required by the users.

The main contribution of this paper is how to make the manager node determine and label the free service node based on its response by running the CCA technique. The free service node will state as ready to receive any task which is demanded by the user to reduce execution time and make the service faster.

The rest of the paper is organized as follows. In Section 2, we describe the related works about incentive schemes. In Section 3, taxonomy of cloud computing is divided into two sections; the first is about the combination between hardware and software in the cloud networks and the second part of this section is about the cloud computing services. In Section 4, we have discussed our proposed technique and its mechanism. Section 5 shows some mathematical modeling and theoretical analysis for the CCA technique. The results

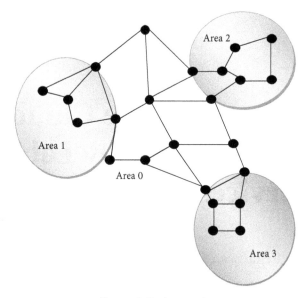

FIGURE 1: Real network.

have been showed and evaluated the performance of the proposed technique in Section 6. Finally, the conclusion and the future work have been discovered in Section 7.

2. Related Works

The network protocols form a very important factor to build the network information which lead to construct the best routes between the nodes. This routing table leads to transmitting the data from source to destination via the best path. Some protocols such as Open Shortest Path is widely used in the networks. The OSPF protocol uses Dijkstra algorithm [10] as a routing algorithm in the network. All routers use the Dijkstra algorithm to compute the shortest path tree (SPT). The IP packets are routed by OSPF protocol based on the IP destination address, which is in the IP packet header [11]. When OSPF is used in the network, each router discovers and maintains a full picture view of the network topology by flooding Link State Advertisements (LSAs), which form the complete topology graph for the routers in their memories, known as a link state database. This database contains information about Autonomous System's topology, and each router will have an identical copy of this information to ensure that data packets will be forwarded over the adjacent routers interface without creating loops in the network topology [12]. The OSPF can divide networks into a set of groups called areas, as shown in Figure 1. The cloud computing networks also can be divided into areas and each area can has head nodes called also the manager nodes. In all companies that provide the cloud services, they are using the routing protocol which aims to make the user executes his task with its all networks services [13]. Many products can be offered by cloud computing services. Each service might be required a different open web OS, which is one of the web applications that shows various environments. In cloud computing environments, the

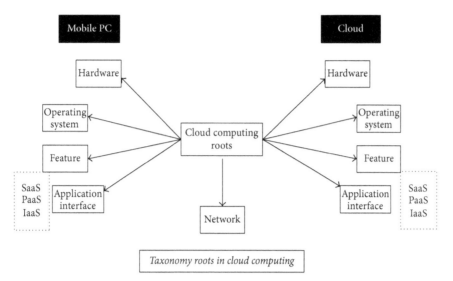

Taxonomy roots in cloud computing

FIGURE 2: Taxonomy levels.

applications may be degraded by errors on virtual resources [1, 2, 4]. This is because of the hierarchical architecture in the cloud computing component. Cloud computing is a part of distributed computing system wherein need to be provided for external customers [14]. For the cloud provider, the service should be achieved and execute large number of tasks for the users regarding the strong infrastructure for the cloud computing. In [9, 10], a new technique called ZXTM was introduced that shares load balancing services and offers a low-cost starting point. Another new technique developed by ZEUS Company has developed software to provide every customer a dedicated application. Thus, many frameworks were provided by ZEUS to enhance and develop new cloud computing methods [15]. According to the proposed frameworks, three-level hierarchical topology are involved to be adopted in the cloud computing. Each node in the cloud computing system can provide full information for the usability and load, which encouraged enhancement of the system performance. Many different methods were used to collect such information of each node [16]. The agent in cloud computing is considered one of these several methods. The agent technology has inherent navigational autonomy and is able to send to some other nodes. In addition, the agent does not need to be installed for each node in the network, but it can be gather the required information through participating in the cloud computing environment, such as CPU utilization and remaining memory. In [8, 17], the authors described a new algorithm called Opportunistic Load Balancing (OLB), which attempts to keep each node busy; hence, the algorithm does not consider the workload for each node. The advantage of the OLB algorithm is to achieve load balancing between nodes; it distributes unexpected tasks to different available nodes regardless of the node workload [18, 19]. In [5], the authors proposed a Minimum Execution Time (MET) algorithm that assigns each task to the node that it is expected to execute in a short time. The MET algorithm dispatches the task without checking the workload for each

node; therefore, the load balancing will not be achieved in this case [20, 21].

3. Taxonomy of Cloud Computing

There are many taxonomies of cloud computing networks and different companies started to offer cloud services according to the perspective of enterprise IT. Cloud computing network has four layers for software applications:

(i) Software-as-a-Service (SaaS).

(ii) Platform-as-a-Service (PaaS).

(iii) Infrastructure-as-a-Service (IaaS) or Hardware-as-a-Service (HaaS) which are considered similar. HaaS is a subset of IaaS and they define a service provision model for hardware that is defined differently in managed services and grid computing contexts. In managed services, HaaS is similar to licensing. In grid computing, HaaS is a pay-as-you-go model.

Briefly, the cloud computing architecture layers are used when needed because they are considered as on-demand services to do or perform a specific job. The users can access the cloud computing services from everywhere around the world, but they need an access point with high performance network and also a permission from the cloud computing to access their accounts as shown in Figure 2.

3.1. Virtualization of Cloud Computing Management. The combination between hardware and software, such as an operating system, is the subject of virtualization management. Cloud computing reduces the cost and enhances the business value in order to improve agility in this regard [22]. The virtualization in cloud computing has many different types, such as server virtualization, storage virtualization, and network virtualization. The main idea of virtualization is to provide an important advantage in sharing resources, manageability, and isolation in the network.

3.2. Cloud Computing Services. Cloud computing networks are the applications and hardware with software. All services are indicated through SaaS. The service provider containing the hardware and software integrated together forms the cloud. Any application requires a model of computation, storage, and communication. Moreover, cloud computing resource allocations and service provision are divided into different layers, as mentioned above. Hereafter, the types of service provisioning can make need-based selections in cloud services. The agility and availability give a great advantage through changing resources in cloud computing quickly, without expenditure. Agility can be measured as a rate of change metric [23]. If cloud computing is considered in terms of agility, then the service provider needs to understand whether the service is elastic and flexible [24]. Here, the pricing for the services between the service provider and users necessitates a service level agreement, which acts as the interface between the data centre and the users. The SLA leads to offer a high quality service to users based on the QoS requirements and ensures resource availability. Security and trust form important factors in cloud computing. Many studies have arisen in developing SW to support the cloud computing system, to identify the security and privacy and then determine a suitable cloud service provider according to the requirements, particularly relating to QoS. The author in [25] proposed the idea of integrated QoS utility to find out the problem of cloud service provider based on multidimensional QoS approach for increasing the user sanctification for the best utilization. The authors in [26] addressed four main issues to solve the service selection problem in the cloud computing within sociability, flexibility, and autometric user support. However, all these parameters such as SLA, QoS, and security are forming important factors in the cloud networks or networks general. When all these factors have been achieved, then the performance of the network will be improved by reducing delay time and increasing the network throughput as shown in the results section. Additionally, the users will start to trust cloud computing service, when they will start to realize that their privacy is secured and protected by the service provider through the SLAs.

4. Proposed Work (Cloud Computing Alarm Techniques)

In this paper, we have proposed a new technique that will lead to notify the node manager about the free and busy node. In addition, the proposed technique will aid in distributing the tasks among all nodes present on the cloud. The Cloud Computing Alarm technique comes to improve service in the cloud computing via providing more information about all nodes under the node manager to distribute the required task requested by the users. Further, this technique requires sending a small packet to the manager node to inform it that it can receive some tasks to execute. Once the free labeled node will receive the task, then the CCA techniques which

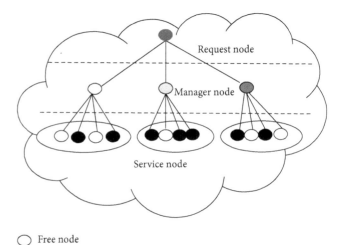

○ Free node
● Busy node

FIGURE 3: Cloud computing networks manager.

are running in all nodes will send a new message to update the information and send it back to the node manager on the cloud computing networks. When the user starts to log in to do some tasks, the node manager will send these tasks to the appropriate node based on the information provided by the CCA.

Whereas, the performance of the CCA technique is considered to minimize the completion time of all tasks. The biggest challenge in CCA technique is to find the free node services, but the enhancements for the CCA technique will be considering the work loading and CPU usage percentage for each node service to assign the task to the best available node. In Figure 3, there are three hierarchical levels for the cloud networks. It shows the first level, which forms the request node manager used to assign the task to a suitable manager node service. For the second level, it contains the service manager used to select and distribute the task to the node service. Figure 4 illustrates the router model when the routing protocol is working in the network. In this figure, we have showed the Open Shortest Path First (OSPF) placement in the route processor. The OSPF allows for the administrated router in each area to hide the other information for all topology, in order to decrease the traffic amount needed to forward or travel between the routers. OSPF is used for any network diameter, such as Router Information Protocol (RIP), due to its advantages in handling large networks performance. In a network, all links have numerical weights; therefore, each router functions as a root and then computes the shortest path tree with itself to destinations in the network. In this figure also, we have showed the placements for the CCA techniques and how to operate with the routing protocol in the router processor to make the performance for the networks better for receiving and transmission data. The Cloud Computing Alarm technique is based on each manager node with its connected service nodes, as shown in Figure 3. After each manager node connected with the service node, then it will start to send small inquiries packets to check which node is available to receive the demand task from

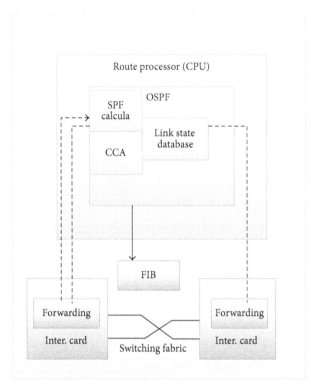

FIGURE 4: Router levels.

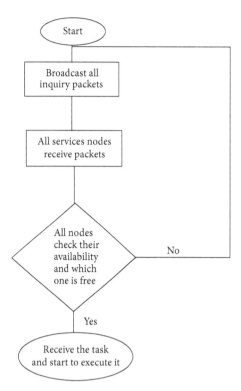

FIGURE 5: CCA flowchart.

the user. Once all service nodes received the packets, then they will reply "yes" or "no" to indicate their availability for taking the task. Figure 5 presents the flowchart for the CCA techniques and how the nodes will act with the messages once they are received. Figure 4 illustrates the router model when a routing protocol such as OSPF is running in its processor. OSPF in the route processor starts to receive Link State Advertisements (LSAs) to precede them to construct the link state database. Through link state database, the OSPF invests the information (which is in the link state database) to perform and compute Shortest Path First (SPF) calculations, which leads to the creation of the Forwarding Information Base (FIB). Through FIB, the line card can determine the next hop used to forward the packets to the outgoing interface. By network operator, each link will assign a weight and the shortest path is computed by using these weights as lengths of link. As we shown in the flowchart, we are making the CCA techniques at the same level in the router layers to cooperate with the routing protocols.

While many proposed solutions intend to make load balancing between nodes using various techniques, the CCA technique has been built to achieve robustness and fast service within a short time by finding the available nodes. The results show that many tasks are distributed randomly without any planning. According to that, CCA technique is trying to find the path for the free node via the inquiry packets between the manager node and its service node. If there are two nodes available, then the first inquiry packets from any of them will be received by the manager node, which will then assign this task to the first replying one, regardless of the location of the node. The main goal of CCA technique

is to reduce delay time for finding the free node to execute and complete the required task. This section illustrates that the core principle of CCA technique is that once the network routers receive notification of the free and available service node, the CCA technique in turn assigns the task via manager node to the best available node.

Additionally, CCA technique approach avoids distribution of other tasks already executed by other service nodes. CCA technique is invoked by the manager node, which can determine after receiving the reply packets from the service node which one can take the task and start to be available for the user. The nodes must regularly update their status once they have completed tasks.

The mechanism of CCA technique has been illustrated in the flowchart as shown in Figure 5 to show the mechanism of selected node. The technique selected the free nodes as the following steps:

(i) Manager node broadcasts the enquiry packets for the services node.

(ii) Services node checks their availability and then sends acknowledged message to the manager node ("yes" or "no").

(iii) Manager node according to the ACK message will decide which node will take the coming task which is required by the users.

(iv) The manager node will keep sending these messages frequently to keep updating node service availability in the network. If there is no positive answer, then the manager node will not accept this task, although, a

Begin{
$S_P \leftarrow \varnothing$
for all s $\in V$
do for all d $\in V$
do if $s = d$
then $q_{sub} \leftarrow \varnothing$ $Q \leftarrow \varnothing$ *Enqueue*$(Q, (q_{sub}, s))$
while $Q = \varnothing$ **and** $P_a(s, d) = \varnothing$
do $(q_{sub}, x) \leftarrow$ *Front*(Q) **for all** $k \in \Gamma(x)$
do $e \leftarrow (x, k)$ **if** $(q_{sub} \cup e) \cap P_r(T_r, s, d) = \varnothing$
then if $P_r(T_r, k, d) \cap P_r(T_r, s, d) = \varnothing$
then $P_a(s, d) \leftarrow q_{sub} \cup e \cup P_r(T_r, k, d) S_P \leftarrow S_P$
}**End**
T_r: The routing table
V: The vertex set of graph $G(V, E)$
$\Gamma(v)$: The set of adjacent vertices to a vertex v $P_r(T_r, s, d)$: The path connecting the vertex s to d as in $T_r P_a(s, d)$:
$P_r(T_r, s, d) \cap P_a(s, d) = \varnothing$
S_P: The set of all generated alternative paths q_{sub}
Q: A queue of couble (paths, vertex)
Enqueue: Insert an element in a queue *Dequeue*: Removes an element from a queue *Front*: The element at the front of a queue

ALGORITHM 1: The CCA technique message inquiry.

huge number of service nodes are still available in the cloud to complete the tasks for the users.

(v) If all answers are negative, the nodes will keep searching until manager node finds the free service node. The codes in Algorithm 1 represent these steps in algorithmic codes.

5. Cloud Modeling and Theoretical Analysis

In cloud computing, the users require to execute some tasks at the same time. The theoretical analysis by using the mathematical method leads to showing how the technique can improve the services even if there are extra inquiry packets that will be sent in the network. In our analysis, we used three equations as follows [20]:

$$\text{Load link metric} = \frac{\text{traffic size}}{(\text{link capacity} * \text{time period})}$$

$$\text{Link Usage\%} = \frac{\text{carried traffic volume} * 100}{\text{link capacity} * \text{interval}}. \tag{1}$$

Hence, if we assume that the CCA inquiry packets will be sent every 30 minutes, then it can be considered a long time. Therefore, we can make some more experiments to send this inquiry packets in less time to find the optimization time number and update the states for all node services to the node manager without making any congestion in the network. Due to change in time for the inquiry packets, this might produce many problems based on the node service numbers. The header packet for inquiry packets includes two fields:

(i) ret: defining the header for the inquiry packets which can contain "0" or "1": "0" known as a negative answer and "1" as a positive answer

(ii) Time interval

The char "ret" is going to be set to "0" if the packet is on its way from the sender to the node which is being inquired, while it is going to be set to "1" on its way back. The double "send time" is a time stamp that is set on the packet when it is sent and which is later used to calculate the round-trip-time. In the following model, we will prove that the inquiry packet will not make any load on each link on the path between source and destination. Assume that there are two nodes A and B; the source will be A and B is the destination; the link capacity is 1 Mb; and the packet size = 1000 kb. We will configure the CCA technique to work on this cloud computing topology and the rate = 500 kb. We will compute the utilization of link with inquiry packet, and we can see the difference between them [17]:

$$\text{Link utilization\%} = \frac{(\text{databits} * 100)}{(\text{bandwidth} * \text{interval})}. \tag{2}$$

Inquiry packets size is 16 bits, and we compute first the inquiry packet with assuming the interval time as 30 min: link utilization% = $(16 * 100)/(1 \text{ Mb} * 1.8e + 6 \text{ ms}) = 1.4e - 8$ [16] As we can see, the inquiry size is negligible even if we make the time interval less than 30 min. In case, the link utilization = 100% that will avoid the inquiry packets to send during that until the utilization is less than 100%. In this case, we decrease the time interval to <30 min; the utilization of link will be also negligible as we showed above.

5.1. Research with Comparative Study of CCA Technique. While CCA technique created inquiry messages to check the nodes service availability and update the node manager about each node service current state, we can compare the cloud computing networks with and without CCA technique of traditional cloud networks. Our study is different compared to other related studies because it is focusing on the full availability for the node services. Also, the inquiries packets that are sent periodically have proved that they do not consume a huge amount of network bandwidth and do not degrade the network performance regarding their small header size as shown in Section 6. Moreover, on some other related works as we mentioned above, some researchers made algorithms to make load balancing and distributed the same job tasks to many node services. It is a good idea but cannot guarantee that the job can executed with less delay or better time. This is because the job task should work with all node services synchronously, and any delay from any node will lead to increasing the delay time and congestion might occurr.

6. Research Environment and Results

A network simulation (NS2) was performed to evaluate the performance of the proposed technique in the cloud computing network. The simulation results of the CAA techniques show the enhancements of distributed the job tasks for the node services. The evidence gathered by the NS2 simulation offered good support for node distribution in cloud computing networks. In the experiments, we make each manager node send or receive a packet to or from its node services to check which nodes are free to receive and start to execute the requirement task. Before evaluating the performance issues of cloud computing network topology with respect to the node manager and how many node services it has, it is important to determine the network's parameters that could affect the QoS of other job tasks. Here, the research focuses on two parameters, which may better reveal the effect of video traffic techniques: Task Deliver Time, the packet duration between sending and receiving data inquiry packets; Average Executed Time, the average time to complete the tasks for each node. In order to evaluate the effect of increasing the node manager or node services, it is necessary to recognize the high number of users that can be joined and looking to complete more tasks.

6.1. Results. Once the CCA technique starts to work in the networks, then the network has improved to receive and execute the job tasks, as shown in Figure 6. The results show that the cloud network with CCA technique executes more tasks. This is because the distribution of the tasks from the node manager to the node service is not random and happens based on the checking list for the manager node and which manager node has a free service node that can start to execute. When the free service node starts to execute the application task for the user and it has no other task, then the response for the task will be faster. Figure 7 shows the results for the cloud computing network with and without CCA technique. It can be seen that the node manager takes less time to distribute the jobs to the node service because the inquiry packets aid the node manager to determine the free node in the node manager DB's information and leads them to distribute all tasks to the node services in less time. On the other hand, Figure 8 shows that broadcasting messages will increase overheads and utilization between nodes in the network. Moreover, the node services are consuming more BW comparing with the node manager because each node

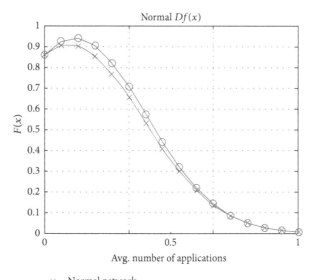

FIGURE 6: User applications are executed.

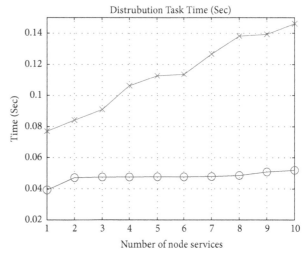

FIGURE 7: Distribution time/sec.

manager will contain a very large number of node services. In this figure, the utilization for the CCA technique is still in a good situation regarding the numbers, as shown in the graph. In this case, we focus on the node manager results because of their responsibilities in task distributions. Figure 10 shows the available nodes after the inquiry packets have been sent to all service nodes. The figure shows the results with different numbers of node managers. As in reality, when the number of node managers is increased then it will take more time to update their information about node services. So the service nodes will be more active and their availability will be increased. Ultimately, the results show a small difference, whereby when the node manager number increases, then the service will be better. If more users join the network and they

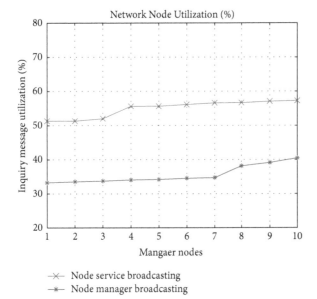

Figure 8: Utilization.

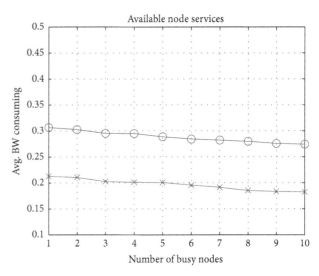

Figure 10: Node manager load.

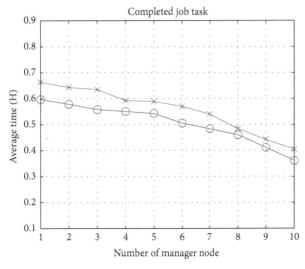

Figure 9: Required time for each job is executed.

as shown in this figure, because the nodes manager directed the task directly to the available nodes without any delay, based on the updates information.

7. Conclusions

This paper introduced a new technique called Cloud Computing Alarm (CCA) mechanism. When the user logs in to do a task through the service offered by cloud computing networks, then this task will be directed to the free node service according to its availability, making the CCA technique work on all manager nodes. The CCA will thus enhance and increase network service performance by reducing searching time for the node manager by updating their information frequently. In addition, the CCA also improves the QoS for sensitive and high priority tasks. Future work for the CCA techniques will try to enhance the mechanism by calculating each task and how much it needs storage and time to be executed and making some sessions for load balancing if the task becomes very large.

Competing Interests

The author declares that there are no competing interests.

References

[1] L. Wang, J. Tao, M. Kunze, A. C. Castellanos, D. Kramer, and W. Karl, "Scientific cloud computing: Early definition and experience," in *10th IEEE International Conference on High Performance Computing and Communications, HPCC 2008*, pp. 825–830, chn, September 2008.

[2] T. Ercan, "Effective use of cloud computing in educational institutions," *Procedia—Social and Behavioral Sciences*, vol. 2, no. 2, pp. 938–942, 2010.

require more job tasks to execute, the cloud computing with more node managers will react with better QoS regardless of the number of inquiry packets already sent.

Based on Figure 9, we compared the completed task with and without CCA technique for the same cloud computing networks. All comparisons used the same environment as that used in the previous results. In CCA, the tasks were completed with small enhancement time when the cloud computing network working was without it. Additionally, CCA performs better with less time when the node managers are increased. A better enhancement for execution and completion of the required tasks from the user was achieved,

[3] K. Q. Yan, S. C. Wang, C. P. Chang, and J. S. Lin, "A hybrid load balancing policy underlying grid computing environment," *Computer Standards & Interfaces*, vol. 29, no. 2, pp. 161–173, 2007.

[4] R. Armstrong, D. Hensgen, and T. Kidd, "The relative performance of various mapping algorithms is independent of sizable variances in run-time predictions," in *Proceedings of the 7th Heterogeneous Computing Workshop (HCW '98)*, pp. 79–87, IEEE, 1998.

[5] M. A. Vouk, "Cloud computing—issues, research and implementations," in *Proceedings of the 30th International Conference on Information Technology Interfaces (ITI '08)*, June 2008.

[6] N. Santos, K. P. Gummadi, and R. Rodrigues, "Towards trusted cloud computing," in *Proceedings of the Conference on Hot Topics in Cloud Computing*, p. 3, San Diego, Calif, USA, 2009.

[7] R. Buyya, R. Ranjan, and R. N. Calheiros, "Intercloud: utility-oriented federation of cloud computing environments for scaling of application services," in *Algorithms and Architectures for Parallel Processing*, pp. 13–31, Springer, Berlin, Germany, 2010.

[8] F. Halsall and D. Links, *Data Communications, Computer Networks and Open Systems*, Addison-Wesley Publishers, 1995.

[9] T. D. Braun, H. J. Siegel, N. Beck et al., "A comparison of eleven static heuristics for mapping a class of independent tasks onto heterogeneous distributed computing systems," *Journal of Parallel and Distributed Computing*, vol. 61, no. 6, pp. 810–837, 2001.

[10] U. Brandes, "A faster algorithm for betweenness centrality," *Journal of Mathematical Sociology*, vol. 25, no. 2, pp. 163–177, 2001.

[11] S. Lor, R. Landa, R. Ali, and M. Rio, "Handling transient link failures using alternate next hop counters," in *Networking 2010: 9th International IFIP TC 6 Networking Conference, Chennai, India, May 11–15, 2010, Proceedings*, vol. 6091 of *Lecture Notes in Computer Science*, p. 186, Springer, New York, NY, USA, 2010.

[12] G. Iannaccone, C.-N. Chuah, R. Mortier, S. Bhattacharyya, and C. Diot, "Analysis of link failures in an IP backbone," in *Proceedings of the 2nd Internet Measurement Workshop (IMW '02)*, pp. 237–242, ACM, Marseille, France, November 2002.

[13] A. Markopoulou, G. Iannaccone, S. Bhattacharyya, C. Chuah, and C. Diot, "Characterization of failures in an IP backbone," in *Proceedings of the 23rd Annual Joint Conference of the IEEE Computer and Communications Societies (INFOCOM '04)*, vol. 4, pp. 2307–2317, IEEE, Hong Kong, 2004.

[14] X. Lin, R. Lu, C. Zhang, H. Zhu, P.-H. Ho, and X. Shen, "Security in vehicular ad hoc networks," *IEEE Communications Magazine*, vol. 46, no. 4, pp. 88–95, 2008.

[15] R. Freund, M. Gherrity, S. Ambrosius et al., "Scheduling resources in multi-user, heterogeneous, computing environments with SmartNet," in *Proceedings of the Seventh Heterogeneous Computing Workshop (HCW '98)*, pp. 184–199, Orlando, FL, USA, March 1998.

[16] L. Garcés-Erice, E. W. Biersack, K. W. Ross, P. A. Felber, and G. Urvoy-Keller, "Hierarchical peer-to-peer systems," *Parallel Processing Letters*, vol. 13, no. 4, pp. 642–657, 2003.

[17] A. Rowstron and P. Druschel, "Pastry: scalable, decentralized object location, and routing for large-scale peer-to-peer systems," in *Middleware 2001*, pp. 329–350, Springer, 2001.

[18] H. Gangwar, H. Date, and R. Ramaswamy, "Understanding determinants of cloud computing adoption using an integrated TAM-TOE model," *Journal of Enterprise Information Management*, vol. 28, no. 1, pp. 107–130, 2015.

[19] M. A. Vouk, "Clouds in higher education," in *Innovative Technologies in Management and Science*, vol. 10 of *Topics in Intelligent Engineering and Informatics*, pp. 17–28, Springer, Berlin, Germany, 2015.

[20] B. Jolliffe, O. Poppe, D. Adaletey, and J. Braa, "Models for online computing in developing countries: issues and deliberations," *Information Technology for Development*, vol. 21, no. 1, pp. 151–161, 2015.

[21] J. A. González-Martínez, M. L. Bote-Lorenzo, E. Gómez-Sánchez, and R. Cano-Parra, "Cloud computing and education: a state-of-the-art survey," *Computers & Education*, vol. 80, pp. 132–151, 2015.

[22] C. A. Ardagna and E. Damiani, "Network and storage latency attacks to online trading protocols in the cloud," in *On the Move to Meaningful Internet Systems: OTM 2014 Workshops*, pp. 192–201, Springer, 2014.

[23] H. Moens and F. De Turck, "Shared resource network-aware impact determination algorithms for service workflow deployment with partial cloud offloading," *Journal of Network and Computer Applications*, vol. 49, pp. 99–111, 2015.

[24] E. N. Alkhanak, S. P. Lee, and S. U. R. Khan, "Cost-aware challenges for workflow scheduling approaches in cloud computing environments: taxonomy and opportunities," *Future Generation Computer Systems*, vol. 50, pp. 3–21, 2015.

[25] M. Whaiduzzaman, M. N. Haque, M. Rejaul Karim Chowdhury, and A. Gani, "A study on strategic provisioning of cloud computing services," *The Scientific World Journal*, vol. 2014, Article ID 894362, 16 pages, 2014.

[26] L. Sun, H. Dong, F. K. Hussain, O. K. Hussain, and E. Chang, "Cloud service selection: state-of-the-art and future research directions," *Journal of Network and Computer Applications*, vol. 45, pp. 134–150, 2014.

21

A Student Information Management System based on Fingerprint Identification and Data Security Transmission

Pengtao Yang, Guiling Sun, Jingfei He, Peiyao Zhou, and Jiangjiang Liu

College of Electronic Information and Optical Engineering, Nankai University, Tianjin 300350, China

Correspondence should be addressed to Guiling Sun; sungl@nankai.edu.cn

Academic Editor: Liangmin Wang

A new type of student information management system is designed to implement student information identification and management based on fingerprint identification. In order to ensure the security of data transmission, this paper proposes a data encryption method based on an improved AES algorithm. A new S-box is cleverly designed, which can significantly reduce the encryption time by improving ByteSub, ShiftRow, and MixColumn in the round transformation of the traditional AES algorithm with the process of look-up table. Experimental results show that the proposed algorithm can significantly improve the encryption time compared with the traditional AES algorithm.

1. Introduction

At present, there are a large number of college students, so the identification and verification of student identity information occur at all times in the campus, as well as the corresponding services given by the students' identification. Therefore, safe and efficient student information management, convenient identification to obtain the required service, and safe and reliable information transmission have become an important task for the student information management [1–3]. Three main features of the proposed system are the following:

(1) This system uses the fingerprint identification terminal to collect the fingerprint information. By means of replacing the campus card with the physiological characteristics of lifelong invariance, uniqueness, and convenience, it has become the basis of student identity authentication. The maturity of the fingerprint identification technology ensures the safety and speed of the process and also eliminates the disadvantages of the campus card which is easy to be stolen and forged and easily lost.

(2) In order to ensure the safety of the students' information, the fingerprint characteristic value is encrypted and transmitted, using the improved AES encryption

algorithm [4], which has the same security guarantee with traditional AES algorithm but reduces the required time for encryption. Therefore, this student management system not only is convenient for students in the college, but also protects the privacy of students.

(3) After the system has been built, because it is easy to maintain and popularize, the modular system design is easier to improve, and it can be widely used in other fields.

2. Description of the Student Information Management System

The system is mainly composed of two parts: terminal and host computer. The terminal is composed of fingerprint identification module and micro controller. The host computer can use personal computers or large servers according to the number of users, and the management of student information database uses SQL Server. The terminal fingerprint sensor uses optical fingerprint recognition module, while the micro-controller uses STM32F4, with 192 KB of SRAM [5]. Each terminal processes and encrypts the collected fingerprint data and then transmits it to the host computer. To ensure the safety of data, the fingerprint data is only stored in the host

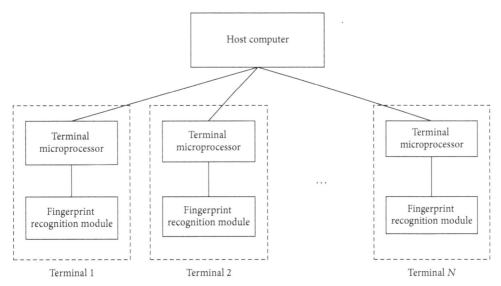

FIGURE 1: System structure diagram.

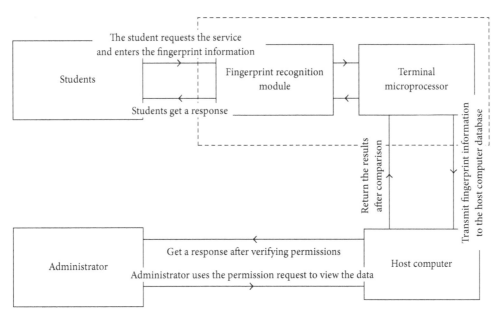

FIGURE 2: System flow diagram.

computer database, and the terminals are only responsible for collection and processing. The system structure is shown in Figure 1.

3. Implementation of the Student Information Management System

The system collects fingerprints through the terminal fingerprint identification sensor. And the microprocessor processes and encrypts the fingerprint information and then transmits it to the server. On the server side, it compares the fingerprint information transmitted from terminal with the fingerprint information stored in the server database. If the identity is consistent, the user is allowed to operate by verification. The overall process is shown in Figure 2.

4. Data Transmission Encryption Method

In order to achieve the campus student consumption, identity registration, and other functions, the student information identification management system based on fingerprint identification and data security transmission needs to transmit student fingerprint information, identity information, and bank card information among the terminal. There is a risk of being intercepted during data transmission. Students' private information has a high commercial value; once intercepted by criminals, the consequences could be disastrous. When using plaintext transmission, security is very low; therefore, the entire data transmission using ciphertext transmission, to achieve a plaintext view and ciphertext transmission effect, greatly improve the security, so that criminals cannot take the opportunity. In order to ensure the security of encrypted transmission and user-friendliness, the encryption process uses the optimized AES algorithm.

AES algorithm is a variable data block length and variable key length iterative block cipher algorithm, and the length of the data block and the key length can be 128, 192, or 256 bits [6]. The most important operation in the AES algorithm is the round transformation operation, where the various operations applied to the process give a high encryption strength. The round transformation operation consists of four steps: ByteSub, ShiftRow, MixColumn, and AddRoundKey, and these steps will be mathematically transformed to eventually construct a new S-box [7, 8].

4.1. Matrix Representation of AES Algorithm Round Transformation. AES algorithm mainly consists of three modules: encryption module, decryption module, and key expansion module. Each round transformation of the encryption module consists of ByteSub, ShiftRow, MixColumn, and AddRoundKey four operations [9]. The decryption module is also composed of four similar operations; the difference is that ByteSub, ShiftRow, and MixColumn are the inverse operation of the encryption module. And the extension key used in AddRoundKey is generated by the key expansion module. The encryption module and the decryption module are the core of the AES algorithm, which are the repetition process of the round transformation, so the simplified round function can improve the operation speed of the AES algorithm [10, 11].

For convenience of description, 128-bit (16 bytes) data is used here and the key is 128 bits.

In the ByteSub transformation, it is assumed that the input is A, $A = [a_{i,j}]$, $(0 \leq i, j \leq 3)$; output is B, $B = [b_{i,j}]$, $(0 \leq i, j \leq 3)$. ByteSub transformation can be expressed as

$$B = (A). \tag{1}$$

And it can also written as

$$b_{i,j} = B(a_{i,j}). \tag{2}$$

In practice, this transformation can be converted to lookup table operation. The table is the AES algorithm byte conversion table, also known as S box.

In the ShiftRow transformation, the schematic diagram is shown in Figure 3. It is assumed that the output is C, $C = [c_{i,j}]$, $(0 \leq i, j \leq 3)$.

Then C can be expressed as a matrix:

$$\begin{bmatrix} c_{0,j} \\ c_{1,j} \\ c_{2,j} \\ c_{3,j} \end{bmatrix} = \begin{bmatrix} b_{0,(j+0)\%4} \\ b_{1,(j+1)\%4} \\ b_{2,(j+2)\%4} \\ b_{3,(j+3)\%4} \end{bmatrix}. \tag{3}$$

In the MixColumn transformation, each column of the state array obtained in ShiftRow is treated as a polynomial on GF(2^8) and modulo $x^4 + 1$ multiplication with a fixed polynomial $03x^3 + 01x^2 + 01x + 02$.

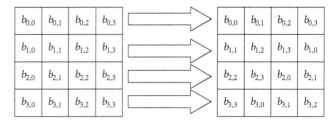

FIGURE 3: ShiftRow transformation schematic diagram.

It is assumed that the output is D, $D = [d_{i,j}]$, $(0 \leq i, j \leq 3)$; then MixColumn can also be written as matrix multiplication [12–14]:

$$\begin{bmatrix} d_{0,j} \\ d_{1,j} \\ d_{2,j} \\ d_{3,j} \end{bmatrix} = \begin{bmatrix} 02 & 03 & 01 & 01 \\ 01 & 02 & 03 & 01 \\ 01 & 01 & 02 & 03 \\ 03 & 01 & 01 & 02 \end{bmatrix} \begin{bmatrix} c_{0,j} \\ c_{1,j} \\ c_{2,j} \\ c_{3,j} \end{bmatrix}. \tag{4}$$

In the AddRoundKey transformation, the expansion round key generated by the key expansion module begins to function. Set the round key to K, $K = [k_{i,j}]$, $(0 \leq i, j \leq 3)$. Set the output to E, $E = [e_{i,j}]$, $(0 \leq i, j \leq 3)$. Then AddRoundKey can be expressed as a matrix:

$$\begin{bmatrix} e_{0,j} \\ e_{1,j} \\ e_{2,j} \\ e_{3,j} \end{bmatrix} = \begin{bmatrix} d_{0,j} \\ d_{1,j} \\ d_{2,j} \\ d_{3,j} \end{bmatrix} \oplus \begin{bmatrix} k_{0,j} \\ k_{1,j} \\ k_{2,j} \\ k_{3,j} \end{bmatrix}. \tag{5}$$

Equations (2), (3), and (4) into (5) can get

$$\begin{bmatrix} e_{0,j} \\ e_{1,j} \\ e_{2,j} \\ e_{3,j} \end{bmatrix} = \begin{bmatrix} 02 \\ 01 \\ 01 \\ 03 \end{bmatrix} S[a_{0,(j+0)\%4}] \oplus \begin{bmatrix} 03 \\ 02 \\ 01 \\ 01 \end{bmatrix} S[a_{1,(j+1)\%4}]$$

$$\oplus \begin{bmatrix} 01 \\ 03 \\ 02 \\ 01 \end{bmatrix} S[a_{2,(j+2)\%4}] \oplus \begin{bmatrix} 01 \\ 01 \\ 03 \\ 02 \end{bmatrix} S[a_{3,(j+3)\%4}] \tag{6}$$

$$\oplus \begin{bmatrix} k_{0,j} \\ k_{1,j} \\ k_{2,j} \\ k_{3,j} \end{bmatrix}.$$

Above we have come to a matrix representation between input A and output E of each round transformation of AES algorithm [15–17].

4.2. Optimized AES Algorithm. In (6), to calculate $\begin{bmatrix} 02 \\ 01 \\ 01 \\ 03 \end{bmatrix} S[a_{0,(j+0)\%4}]$ requires one xtime [4] operation and one exclusive-OR operation. Thus, getting each column vector of a round transformation result E requires four xtime operations and eight exclusive-OR operations (regardless of round key generation). According to the observation we can see in the column vector multiplied by $S[a_{0,(j+0)\%4}]$, $S[a_{1,(j+1)\%4}]$, $S[a_{2,(j+2)\%4}]$, and $S[a_{3,(j+3)\%4}]$, only the three elements: 01, 02, and 03. So we can create a new S box to get directly each element in the $\begin{bmatrix} 02 \\ 01 \\ 01 \\ 03 \end{bmatrix} S[a_{0,(j+0)\%4}]$, $\begin{bmatrix} 03 \\ 02 \\ 01 \\ 01 \end{bmatrix} S[a_{1,(j+1)\%4}]$, $\begin{bmatrix} 01 \\ 03 \\ 02 \\ 01 \end{bmatrix} S[a_{2,(j+2)\%4}]$, and $\begin{bmatrix} 01 \\ 01 \\ 03 \\ 02 \end{bmatrix} S[a_{3,(j+3)\%4}]$ four column vectors by look-up table method, so that we can save four xtime operations and four exclusive-OR operations and get each column vector of a round transformation result E which requires only four exclusive-OR operations (regardless of round key generation). Let data in the original S box operate, respectively, with $01, 02, 03$, and we get a new byte conversion table, as shown in Table 1.

In the use of C language to implement, the table will be set to a two-dimensional array $S_{\text{new}}[256][3]$, so that we can get each element of $\begin{bmatrix} 02 \\ 01 \\ 01 \\ 03 \end{bmatrix} S[a_{0,(j+0)\%4}]$, $\begin{bmatrix} 03 \\ 02 \\ 01 \\ 01 \end{bmatrix} S[a_{1,(j+1)\%4}]$, $\begin{bmatrix} 01 \\ 03 \\ 02 \\ 01 \end{bmatrix} S[a_{2,(j+2)\%4}]$, and $\begin{bmatrix} 01 \\ 01 \\ 03 \\ 02 \end{bmatrix} S[a_{3,(j+3)\%4}]$ four column vectors by look-up table method. For example, in $\begin{bmatrix} 02 \\ 01 \\ 01 \\ 03 \end{bmatrix} S[a_{0,(j+0)\%4}]$, the lower four bits and higher four bits of $a_{0,(j+0)\%4}$ correspond separately to the abscissas and ordinates of the table, so that we get the row coordinates of the two-dimensional array, which is equivalent to determining which grid is in Table 1. The $2, 1, 1, 3$ of the column vector correspond separately to the $1, 0, 0, 2$ in two-dimensional array column coordinates, which is equivalent to determining which element of the grid is in Table 1. The optimized AES encryption algorithm flow chart is shown in Figure 4.

Likewise, a similar new byte conversion table can be created at the time of decryption to achieve decryption optimization.

4.3. Experimental Results and Analysis. In order to test the encryption speed between classical AES algorithm and optimized AES algorithm in this paper, we use C ++ language to implement the two algorithm encryption processes, respectively, the encryption process in Windows 7 operating system, Core i5-3230M 2.60 GHz CPU, and 8 G memory environment. In each experiment we take 100,000 times the encryption time, and we get a total of 10 sets of data in five experiments. The data obtained in the experiments are shown in Table 2.

Through the test results in Table 2 we can see that the encryption speed of optimized AES algorithm has a great improvement compared to the classic AES algorithm. In terms of memory footprint, this optimized AES encryption algorithm requires $256 \times 3 \times 2 = 1536$ B $= 1.5$ KB to store two new byte conversion tables (encryption and decryption). The traditional AES algorithm requires $256 \times 2 = 512$ B $= 0.5$ KB

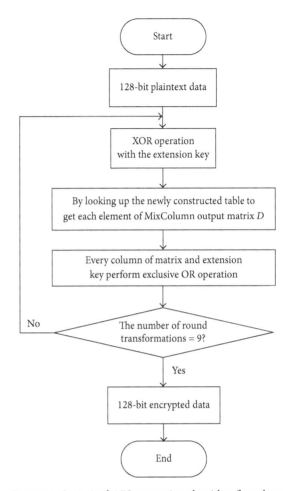

FIGURE 4: Optimized AES encryption algorithm flow chart.

to store two bytes conversion tables, so the optimized AES algorithm does not significantly increase the memory resource occupancy.

5. Conclusion

The system implements the verification of the student identity through the fingerprint, which can make the campus life more convenient. The fingerprint data is only stored in the host computer database after encryption transmission, which makes the convenience greatly improved on the basis of ensuring security. Each terminal connected with the host computer constitutes an integral system to achieve the information sharing among each terminal, and the host computer stores the terminal data and manages the students' information efficiently with less time. The encryption method based on the improved AES optimizes the implementation method of algorithm in the process of simplifying the operation step, and the mathematical structure of the original algorithm is not changed, so that the encryption speed increases rapidly under the condition that the security is not reduced, while the memory occupation does not increase significantly, so it is easy to be achieved in the embedded system. Taking an example of AES with 128-bit plaintext length and key

TABLE 1: The byte conversion table of optimized AES algorithm.

	0	1	2	3	4	5	6	7	8	9	a	b	c	d	e	f
	63	7c	77	7b	f2	6b	6f	5c	30	01	67	2b	fe	d7	ab	76
0	c6	f8	ee	f6	ff	d6	de	91	60	02	ce	56	e7	b5	4d	ec
	a5	84	99	8d	0d	bd	b1	54	90	03	a9	7d	19	62	e6	9a
	ca	82	c9	7d	fa	59	47	f0	ad	d4	a2	af	9c	a4	72	c0
1	8f	1f	89	fa	ef	b2	8e	fb	41	b3	5f	45	23	53	e4	9b
	45	9d	40	87	15	eb	c9	0b	ec	67	fd	ea	bf	f7	96	5b
	b7	fd	93	26	36	3f	f7	cc	34	a5	e5	f1	71	d8	31	15
2	75	e1	3d	4c	6c	7e	f5	83	68	51	d1	f9	e2	ab	62	2a
	c2	1c	ae	6a	5a	41	02	4f	5c	f4	34	08	93	73	53	3f
	04	c7	23	c3	18	96	05	9a	07	12	80	e2	eb	27	b2	75
3	08	95	46	9d	30	37	0a	2f	0e	24	1b	df	cd	4e	7f	ea
	0c	52	65	5e	28	a1	0f	b5	09	36	9b	3d	26	69	cd	9f
	09	83	2c	1a	1b	6e	5a	a0	52	3b	d6	b3	29	e3	2f	84
4	12	1d	58	34	36	dc	b4	5b	a4	76	b7	7d	52	dd	5e	13
	1b	9e	74	2e	2d	b2	ee	fb	f6	d4	61	ce	7b	3e	71	97
	53	d1	00	ed	20	fc	b1	5b	6a	cb	be	39	4a	4c	58	cf
5	a6	b9	02	c1	40	e3	79	b6	d4	8d	67	72	94	98	b0	85
	f5	68	02	2c	60	1f	c8	ed	be	46	d9	4b	de	d4	e8	4a
	d0	ef	aa	fb	43	4d	33	85	45	f9	02	7f	50	3c	9f	a8
6	bb	c5	4f	ed	86	9a	66	11	8a	e9	04	fe	a0	78	25	4b
	6b	2a	e5	16	c5	d7	55	94	cf	10	06	81	f0	44	ba	e3
	51	a3	40	8f	92	9d	38	f5	bc	b6	da	21	10	ff	f3	d2
7	a2	5d	80	05	3f	21	70	f1	63	77	af	24	20	e5	fd	bf
	f3	fe	c0	8a	ad	bc	48	04	df	c1	75	63	30	1a	0e	6d
	cd	0c	13	ec	5f	97	44	17	c4	a7	7e	3d	64	5d	19	73
8	81	18	26	c3	be	35	88	2e	93	55	fc	7a	c8	ba	32	e6
	4c	14	35	2f	e1	a2	cc	39	57	f2	82	47	ac	e7	2b	95
	60	81	4f	dc	22	2a	90	88	46	ee	b8	14	de	5e	0b	db
9	c0	19	9e	a3	44	54	3b	0b	8c	c7	6b	28	a7	bc	16	ad
	a0	98	d1	7f	66	7e	ab	83	ca	29	d3	3c	79	e2	1d	76
	e0	32	3a	0a	49	06	24	5c	c2	d3	ac	62	91	95	e4	79
a	db	64	74	14	92	0c	48	b8	9f	bd	43	c4	39	31	d3	f2
	3b	56	4e	1e	db	0a	6c	e4	5d	6e	ef	a6	a8	a4	37	8b
	e7	c8	37	6d	8d	d5	4e	a9	6c	56	f4	ea	65	7a	ae	08
b	d5	8b	6e	da	01	b1	9c	49	d8	ac	f3	cf	ca	f4	47	10
	32	43	59	b7	8c	64	d2	e0	b4	fa	07	25	af	8e	e9	18
	ba	78	25	2e	1c	a6	b4	c6	e8	dd	74	1f	4b	bd	8b	8a
c	6f	f0	4a	5c	38	57	73	97	cb	a1	e8	3e	96	61	0d	0f
	d5	88	6f	72	24	f1	c7	51	23	7c	9c	21	dd	dc	86	85
	70	3e	b5	66	48	03	f6	0e	61	35	57	b9	86	c1	1d	9e
d	e0	7c	71	cc	90	06	f7	1c	c2	6a	ae	69	17	99	3a	27
	90	42	c4	aa	d8	05	01	12	a3	5f	f9	d0	91	58	27	b9
	e1	f8	98	11	69	d9	8e	94	9b	1e	87	e9	ce	55	28	df
e	d9	eb	2b	22	d2	a9	07	33	2d	3c	15	c9	87	aa	50	a5
	38	13	b3	33	bb	70	89	a7	b6	22	92	20	49	ff	78	7a
	8c	a1	89	0d	bf	e6	42	68	41	99	2d	0f	b0	54	bb	16
f	03	59	09	1a	65	d7	84	d0	42	29	5a	1e	7b	a8	6d	2c
	8f	f8	80	17	da	31	c6	b8	c3	b0	77	11	cb	fc	d6	3a

TABLE 2: Experimental test results.

The algorithm used	Experiment number					The average time of 100,000 times encryption (s)
	1	2	3	4	5	
Traditional AES algorithm	8.472	8.443	8.382	8.427	8.430	8.43
Optimized AES algorithm	1.550	1.471	1.471	1.469	1.533	1.50

length, this paper proposes an optimization scheme based on actual requirement. The scheme can also be extended to the AES with other data lengths, which is suitable for various situations of data encryption, so it has a wide range of applications and strong practicability.

Conflicts of Interest

The authors declare that there are no conflicts of interest regarding the publication of this paper.

Acknowledgments

Special thanks are due to National University Student Innovation Program and Nankai University for the assistance provided to this project.

References

[1] Z. Kai, "Design and implementation of college students' entrepreneurship management system based on B/S structure," *RISTI - Revista Iberica de Sistemas e Tecnologias de Informacao*, vol. 2016, no. 17, pp. 102–113, 2016.

[2] S. R. Bharamagoudar, R. B. Geeta, and S. G. Totad, "Web based student information management system," *International Journal of Advanced Research in Computer and Communication Engineering*, vol. 2, no. 6, 2013.

[3] R. Ahmad and W. Ismail, "Performance comparison of advanced encryption standard-128 algorithms for wimax application with improved power-throughput," *Journal of Engineering Science and Technology*, vol. 11, no. 12, pp. 1678–1694, 2016.

[4] J. Daor, J. Daemen, and V. Rijmen, "Aes proposal: rijndael. Vazirani, efficient and secure pseudo-random number generation," in *Proceedings of the 25th IEEE FOCS*, 1999.

[5] STMicroelectronics, *STM32 Reference Manual*, 10th edition, 2009.

[6] US Department of Commerce and NIST, "Advanced Encryption Standard," in *Proceedings of the National Computer Conference*, pp. 83–87, 2006.

[7] R. Ahmad and W. Ismail, "A survey of high performance cryptography algorithms for WiMAX applications using SDR," *Self-Organization and Green Applications in Cognitive Radio Networks*, pp. 231–246, 2013.

[8] C. Monteiro, Y. Takahashi, and T. Sekine, "Low-power secure S-box circuit using charge-sharing symmetric adiabatic logic for advanced encryption standard hardware design," *IET Circuits, Devices and Systems*, vol. 9, no. 5, pp. 362–369, 2015.

[9] A. M. Youssef and S. E. Tavares, "Affine equivalence in the AES round function," *Discrete Applied Mathematics*, vol. 148, no. 2, pp. 161–170, 2005.

[10] G. Bertoni, L. Breveglieri, I. Koren, P. Maistri, and V. Piuri, "Error analysis and detection procedures for a hardware implementation of the advanced encryption standard," *IEEE Transactions on Computers*, vol. 52, no. 4, pp. 492–505, 2003.

[11] J. Blömer and J. P. Seifert, "Fault Based Cryptanalysis of the Advanced Encryption Standard (AES)," in *Proceedings of the Financial Cryptography, International Conference, FC 2003*, vol. 2742, pp. 162–181, DBLP, Guadeloupe, French West Indies, France, 2003.

[12] J. Daemen and V. Rijmen, *The Design of Rijndael: AES-The Advanced Encryption Standard*, Springer, Berlin, Germany, 2002.

[13] B. Schneier, *Applied Cryptography: Protocols, Algorithms and Source Code in C*, Wiley Publishing, Indianapolis, IN, USA, 2015.

[14] W. Stallings, *Cryptography and Network Security: Principles and Practice*, 1999.

[15] M. McLoone and J. V. McCanny, "Rijndael FPGA implementation utilizing look-up tables," in *Proceedings of the IEEE Workshop on Signal Processing Systems-Design and Implementation-(SIPS) 2001*, pp. 349–360, October 2001.

[16] J. Gong, W. Liu, and H. Zhang, "Multiple lookup table-based aes encryption algorithm implementation," *Physics Procedia*, vol. 25, pp. 842–847, 2012.

[17] J.-F. Wang, S.-W. Chang, and P.-C. Lin, "A novel round function architecture for AES encryption/decryption utilizing look-up table," in *Proceedings of the 37th Annual 2003 International Carnahan Conference on Security Technology*, pp. 132–136, October 2003.

Permissions

List of Contributors

Fragkiskos Sardis
Department of Informatics, King's College London, LondonWC2R 2LS, UK

Glenford Mapp, Jonathan Loo and Mahdi Aiash
School of Science and Technology, Middlesex University, London NW44BT, UK

Alexey Vinel
Halmstad University, 301 18 Halmstad, Sweden

Jingjie Zhang, Qingtao Wu, Ruijuan Zheng, Junlong Zhu, Mingchuan Zhang and Ruoshui Liu
Information Engineering College, Henan University of Science and Technology, Luoyang 471023, China

Mumu Aktar, Md. Al Mamun and Md. Ali Hossain
Computer Science & Engineering Department, Rajshahi University of Engineering & Technology, Rajshahi 6204, Bangladesh

Zhicheng Lu and Zhizheng Liang
School of Computer Science and Technology, China University of Mining and Technology, Xuzhou 221116, China

Aggeliki Vlachostergiou, Georgios Stratogiannis and George Siolas
Intelligent Systems Content and Interaction Laboratory, National Technical University of Athens, Iroon Polytexneiou 9, 15780 Zografou, Greece

George Caridakis
Intelligent Systems Content and Interaction Laboratory, National Technical University of Athens, Iroon Polytexneiou 9, 15780 Zografou, Greece
Department of Cultural Technology and Communication, University of the Aegean, Mytilene, Lesvos, Greece

Phivos Mylonas
Intelligent Systems Content and Interaction Laboratory, National Technical University of Athens, Iroon Polytexneiou 9, 15780 Zografou, Greece
Department of Informatics, Ionian University, Corfu, Greece

Xuefeng Fan and Fei Liu
Key Laboratory of Advanced Process Control for Light Industry, Jiangnan University, Wuxi 214122, China

Jianzheng Liu, Chunlin Fang and Chao Wu
College of Computer Science and Information Engineering, Tianjin University of Science & Technology, No. 1038, DaGu Road, HeXi District, Tianjin 300222, China

Jingpei Wang and Jie Liu
Information Security Research Center, China CEPREI Laboratory, Guangzhou 510610, China

Yun Zhang
School of Mechanical and Electrical Engineering, Nanjing Forestry University, Nanjing 210037, China

Chao Ni
School of Mechanical and Electrical Engineering, Nanjing Forestry University, Nanjing 210037, China
Bio-Imaging and Machine Vision Lab, Fischell Department of Bioengineering, University of Maryland, College Park 20740, USA

Dongyi Wang
Bio-Imaging and Machine Vision Lab, Fischell Department of Bioengineering, University of Maryland, College Park 20740, USA

Qing Zhao and Congcong Xiong
Tianjin University of Science and Technology, Tianjin 300222, China

Peng Wang
Tianjin House Fund Management Center, Tianjin 300222, China

Shupeng Wang and Kai Huang
Department of Information Science and Electronic Engineering, Zhejiang University, Hangzhou 310027, China

Tianyi Xie and Xiaolang Yan
Institute of VLSI Design, Zhejiang University, Hangzhou 310027, China

Kewen Xia
School of Electronics and Information Engineering, Hebei University of Technology, Tianjin 300401, China

Xiaoqing Jiang
School of Electronics and Information Engineering, Hebei University of Technology, Tianjin 300401, China
School of Information Science and Engineering, University of Jinan, Shandong, Jinan 250022, China

Yongliang Lin
School of Electronics and Information Engineering, Hebei University of Technology, Tianjin 300401, China
Information Construction and Management Center, Tianjin Chengjian University, Tianjin 300384, China

Lingyin Wang
School of Information Science and Engineering, University of Jinan, Shandong, Jinan 250022, China

Jianhua Cao, Yancui Shi, Dan Wang and Xiankun Zhang
College of Computer Science and Information Engineering, Tianjin University of Science and Technology, Tianjin, China

Lei Lei and She Kun
Laboratory of Cyberspace, School of Information and Software Engineering, University of Electronic Science and Technology of China, Chengdu 610054, China

Urko Zurutuza and Roberto Uribeetxeberria
Electronics and Computing Department, Mondragon University, 20500 Mondragon, Spain

Oscar Somarriba
Electronics and Computing Department, Mondragon University, 20500 Mondragon, Spain
National University of Engineering (UNI), Managua, Nicaragua

Laurent Delosières
ExoClick SL, 08005 Barcelona, Spain

Simin Nadjm-Tehrani
Department of Computer and Information Science, Linköping University, 581 83 Linköping, Sweden

Shanxiong Chen, Hailing Xiong and Xianping Yu
College of Computer and Information Science, Southwest University, Chongqing 400715, China

Maoling Peng
Chongqing City Management Vocational College, Chongqing 400055, China

Xinchen Guo and Fugeng Zeng
College of Ocean Information Engineering, Hainan Tropical Ocean University, Sanya, China

Xiuling Fan
Henan Xuehang Education and Information Service Co., Zhengzhou, China

Xiantian Xi
Shanghai Renyi Technology Co., Ltd., Shanghai, China

Lixia Xie and Chong Wang
School of Computer Science and Technology, Civil Aviation University of China, No. 2898, Jinbei Road, Tianjin 300300, China

Jian Jiao, Qiyuan Liu and Hongsheng Cao
Beijing Key Laboratory of Internet Culture and Digital Dissemination Research, Beijing Information Science and Technology University, Beijing, China
School of Computer Science, Beijing Information Science and Technology University, Beijing, China

Xin Chen
School of Computer Science, Beijing Information Science and Technology University, Beijing, China

Radwan S. Abujassar and Moneef Jazzar
Information Technology and Computing, Arab Open University, Kuwait Branch, Al-Ardiya, Kuwait

Pengtao Yang, Guiling Sun, Jingfei He, Peiyao Zhou and Jiangjiang Liu
College of Electronic Information and Optical Engineering, Nankai University, Tianjin 300350, China

Index